Antique Furniture
of Québec

In fond memory of my maternal grandmother, Zélie Tardif, who was born in Saint-Joseph de Beauce in 1872. She died in 1976 at the venerable age of one hundred and four. A clear-minded woman, who had given birth to twenty children, she had a passionate love for books. We often used to read together.

Graphic design and computer layout: Josée Amyotte
Image processing: Mélanie Sabourin
Layout co-ordination: Martine Lavoie
Editor: Linda Nantel

Photograph of central armoire on cover page: Michel Létourneau

Copyright ©2002 by Michel Lessard

First published in French by Les Éditions de l'Homme, ©2001, a division of the Sogides Group

All rights reserved. The use of any part of this publication reproduced, transmitted in any form or by any means, electronic, mechanical, photocopying, recording, or otherwise, or stored in a retrieval system, without the prior written consent of the publisher – or, in case of photocopying or other reprographic copying, a licence from the Canadian Copyright Licensing Agency – is an infringement of the copyright law.

National Library of Canada Cataloguing in Publication Data

Lessard, Michel, 1942-
Antique furniture of Quebec : four centuries of furniture making

Translation of: Meubles anciens du Québec.
Includes bibliographical references and index.
ISBN 0-7710-4670-7

1. Furniture—Quebec (Province)—History. 2. Furniture design—Quebec (Province)—History. 3. Furniture, Early Canadian—Quebec (Province)—History. 4. Furniture—Quebec (Province)—Pictorial works. I. Title.

NK2442.Q8L4713 2002   749.211'4   C2001-903030-4

We acknowledge the financial support of the Government of Canada through the Book Publishing Industry Development Program for our publishing activities. We further acknowledge the support of the Canada Council for the Arts and the Ontario Arts Council for our publishing program.

Typeset by Les Éditions de l'Homme, Montréal
Printed and bound in Canada

McClelland & Stewart Ltd.
The Canadian Publishers
481 University Avenue
Toronto, Ontario
M5G 2E9
www.mcclelland.com

1 2 3 4 5   06 05 04 03 02

MICHEL LESSARD

FOUR CENTURIES OF FURNITURE MAKING

Antique Furniture of Québec

Translated by Jane Macaulay and Alison McGain
assisted by Benjamin Waterhouse

The Cupboard

It is a wide carved cupboard; the dark oak,

Very old, has taken on the pleasant quality of old people;

The cupboard is open, and gives off in its shadow

Delightful odors like a draught of old wine;

Crammed full, it is a jumble of strange old things,

Of sweet-smelling yellow linens, bits of clothing

Of women and children, of faded laces,

Of grandmothers' kerchiefs embroidered with griffins;

— There you would find medallions, locks

Of white or blond hair, portraits, dried flowers

Whose smell mingles with the smell of fruit.

Oh cupboard of old time, you know many stories

And you would like to tell your stories, and you murmur

When your big black doors slowly open.

Rimbaud, October 1870

[Translation of "Le Buffet" in Wallace Fowlie, *Arthur Rimbaud, Complete Works*]

1
Two-tiered buffet with two drawers and four doors decorated with lozenges. Period hardware, stripped pine, Québec City region, first half of the 18th century.

To the Reader

To prevent ambiguity, and for greater convenience, I have ascribed specific meanings to certain words in this book.

The word *"canadien,"* in italics, is used essentially in its historical sense to indicate a link with the French settlement of North America; in other words, I use it with the meaning it held from its appearance in the 16th century until it was replaced by *"québécois,"* the term used in the 20th century to designate roughly the same human reality. A piece of furniture, a book or a house labelled as *canadien* belongs to this specific expanse of space and time.

The word "Canadian" indicates a link with the Anglo-Saxon community in Canada. Furniture, books, glass and ceramics labelled as Canadian form part of the production of the Anglo-Saxon community that began to take shape in the 19th century.

The word "Canada," in quotation marks, refers to the territory under French control until its transfer to the British conquerors in 1760 and the official confirmation of this transfer in the Treaty of Paris in 1763.

The word "Canada," without quotation marks, refers to a mainly English-speaking geopolitical entity requiring a constitutional and geographic redefinition of its associated States.

The word "Québec" refers to a North American geopolitical entity, having a territory and a common language, French, requiring a constitutional redefinition based on an optimal degree of sovereignty within a framework of associated States. Québec is the homeland and the mother country of Quebeckers. The use of the word "province" — a crushing, reductionist term with colonial connotations — to refer to the national territory should be abandoned. Since the time of Premier Jean Lesage, the term "Québec state" has been in use.

The word "national," as used in this book, applies to the Québec people, regardless of the origin of individual members, provided they have demonstrated their attachment to French culture. National textiles, national archives, national culture and national museums, the national flag, national holiday, national assembly, national capital and national pride – all essentially refer to entities found or experienced mainly on Québec territory, but do not exclude our fellow citizens of French America. I refuse the sociologically improper use of the word on the part of Canadian politicians at present.

To describe the corpus of old artifacts from the so-called *canadien* era in Québec, in other words up to the early 20th century (I have set the cut-off point at 1910), I have used the term *canadiensia*. Old books, old furniture and old houses – in fact, all the objects produced in this country before the cut-off date – form part of *canadiensia*. I unhesitatingly reject the word *canadiana*, which flouts both the basic construction of Latin-based words and the elementary rules of that language.

To designate the corpus of objects belonging to the *québécois* period of our history, in other words from the early 20th century (let us say from 1911) on, I have used the term *quebecensia*. A Royal wood stove made by Bélanger in Montmagny, the book *Chez nous* by Adjutor Rivard, a papier-mâché toy horse made by Albert Sheinks in Lévis, and the fumed oak sideboards made by the Megantic Manufacturing Company Limited are all part of *quebecensia*.

I have referred to the citizens of the United States as U.S. citizens, since I consider that Brazilians, Mexicans and Quebeckers are just as entitled to be called Americans.

To facilitate the identification of individual illustrations among the hundreds appearing in this book, and to accurately ascribe credits to owners and photographers, I have numbered them consecutively. At the end of the book, two alphabetical lists, one of collections, the other of photographers, provide direct references to owners and photographers. The references for those who preferred to remain anonymous are listed under "Private Collection."

By the Same Author

Québec, City of Light. In collaboration with photographer Claudel Huot. Montréal: Les Éditions de l'Homme, 2001. 256 p.

L'île d'Orléans. Aux sources du peuple québécois et de l'Amérique française. Montréal: Les Éditions de l'Homme, 1998. 415 p.

Montréal au XXᵉ siècle. Regards de photographes. Edited by Michel Lessard. Montréal: Les Éditions de l'Homme, 1995. 336 p.

Antiquités du Québec. Objets anciens. Vie sociale et culturelle. Montréal: Les Éditions de l'Homme, 1995. 300 p.

Objets anciens du Québec. La vie domestique. Montréal: Les Éditions de l'Homme, 1992. 304 p.

Montréal, métropole du Québec. Images oubliées de la vie quotidienne 1852-1910. Montréal: Les Éditions de l'Homme, 1992. 304 p.

Québec, ville du Patrimoine mondial. Images oubliées de la vie quotidienne 1858-1914. Montréal: Les Éditions de l'Homme, 1992. 256 p.

L'Hôtel-Dieu de Lévis 1892-1991. Une belle histoire…. Lévis: Hôtel-Dieu de Lévis, 1992. 128 p.

Histoire de la photographie au Québec. Montréal: Département d'Histoire de l'art, Université du Québec à Montréal, 1990. (A collection of articles by the author in various periodicals, intended for his students. Limited print run. Roughly 350 p.)

Magie et puissance de l'image. 150 ans de photographie. Québec City: Éditions Carni Ltée, 1989. 96 p. (Special commemorative issue of *Photo Sélection*.)

Les Livernois photographes. Québec City: Musée du Québec, 1987. 338 p. (English version published by the Musée du Québec in 1987 under the title *The Livernois Photographers*.)

La photo s'expose. 150 ans de photographies à Québec. Québec City: Musée du Québec, Musée du Séminaire de Québec et al., 1987. 136 p.

L'art traditionnel au Québec. Trois siècles d'ornements populaires. Drawings by Huguette Marquis. Montréal: Les Éditions de l'Homme, 1975. 464 p.

La maison traditionnelle au Québec. In collaboration with architect Gilles Vilandré. Montréal: Les Éditions de L'Homme, 1974. 494 p.

Encyclopédie de la maison québécoise. Drawings by Huguette Marquis and Gilles Vilandré. Montréal: Les Éditions de l'Homme, 1972. 728 p.

Encyclopédie des antiquités du Québec. Drawings by Huguette Marquis. Montréal: Les Éditions de l'Homme, 1971. 526 p. (English version published in 1974 by Hart Publishing Inc., New York, under the title *Complete Guide to French Canadian Antiques*, 255 p.)

The Need to Publish

An understanding of material and artistic culture is one of the fundamental components of a collective identity. However, globalization and standardization threaten to blur distinctions between all the nations on earth and make them uniform, even in the depths of their souls. If a range of identities is to be maintained, if freedom is to be allowed to flourish, then the historical values and original forms of expression of all peoples must be upheld and their differences respected. An interest in "heritage," in its broadest sense, appears to be the most dynamic and effective way to understand a people's origins, inclinations and talents. Quebeckers form a unique people, a nation forged by its environment, by the meeting of four integrated cultures and by over four centuries of history as a French-speaking land.

More than ever before, at the dawn of a new millennium, we must present our history carefully and methodically, using all available means, and never let our identity be defined by others. Every nation must take responsibility for recording its history. In a society with a colonial past marked by a relationship between oppressed and oppressors, too many subjects have been, and are still, subject to biased interpretations long overdue for revision.

History is a mirror that must be polished afresh by each new generation, a task that must be performed by universities and researchers working for national organizations. Business leaders and corporations must help promote the same objective by funding projects to reaffirm national identity and preserve culture. The state must support the process by establishing a clear heritage policy under the responsibility of a competent, motivated and efficient leadership. To meet these expectations, official bodies, such as a national heritage institute and a heritage trust, should be established.

Research cannot be conducted in a vacuum: research findings must be made widely known and new interpretations must be disseminated using all possible channels. In the era of the Internet and instantaneous planetary communication, it is clearly the responsibility of Quebeckers to disclose the source and meaning of their collective undertaking, to describe the suffering, effort and success that they have met with along the way, and to explain their choices and demands as a modern society. Québec's virtual image must remain under its own enlightened command. Québec's national television network, Télé-Québec, must seize responsibility for transmitting Québec history, because only a state-controlled specialized television channel can give an adequate, realistic representation of the state's society. The curators of art and history museums are the editorialists of our time. Every exhibition presented in Québec's national institutions — the Musée de la civilisation, the Musée du Québec, the Montreal Museum of Fine Arts and the regional museums — should generate permanent records in print, on tape or in electronic form. Too many costly, meaning-filled projects fail to have a lasting effect; in many cases, this waste of energy could be averted simply by publishing a brochure, booklet or reference work.

Books are the most effective means of transmitting knowledge. It is important to continue to publish meaningful studies, to broaden the range of subjects considered, to produce low-priced books that make culture more accessible and to work with publishers to design well-structured thematic series. All the above approaches could lead to a much-needed reinforcement of our historical roots and the propagation of our shared cultural riches. It is also important to publish the best of these books in English, to give our fellow citizens in English-speaking North America an opportunity to enjoy an unprejudiced, accurate and in-depth view of our past and our centuries-old concerns. In addition, such translations would correct the inaccurate versions of Québec's history and concerns, at present commissioned from a distance and supported by media that are directed by spiritual mercenaries. Québec's exchanges with the peoples of Latin America and the rest of the earth should also be fostered through the dissemination of an image that better reflects Quebeckers' deepest values.

Québec's memory belongs to Quebeckers alone. The motto, "Je me souviens," directs Quebeckers to cultivate their memory and deploy an on-going effort to present a stimulating, accurate image. Quebeckers are a generous people, historically in contact with the world around them, more than willing to hold the dual nationality they have always been refused. It is important to make effective use of all the tools available to promote these social realities and to advance, together, along the broad avenues of the future, ever mindful of planetary diversity.

MICHEL LESSARD
February 11, 1999

Table of Contents

THE NEED TO PUBLISH	9
Medieval Traditions and Classicism in Québec	13
Neoclassical Trends	21
Vernacular Revivalism in Québec	29
Pre-Modern Movements in the Belle Époque	37
Modern Tastes	45
PREFACE	53

CHAPTER 1
By Way of Introduction…
Québec Furniture and the Ever-Changing Story of Stylistic Movements 59

1640-1790
THE NEW FRANCE STYLE

CHAPTER 2
Provincial Traditions of the Ancien Régime and Classicism
Furniture in the French Manner 143

1790-1840
THE CONSTITUTIONAL STYLE

CHAPTER 3
The Merging and Melding of Cultural Influences
Neoclassical Furniture in the St. Lawrence Valley 235

CHAPTER 4
Traditional Craftsmanship Meets the Industrial Revolution
Revival-Era Furniture in Québec 323

1840-1890
THE CONFEDERATIVE STYLE

CHAPTER 5
Between Historicism and Industrial Functionalism
Pre-Modern Furniture in Québec 401

1890-1920
PRE-MODERN STYLES

CHAPTER 6
Mass Production and Studio Design
Modern Furniture in Québec 483

1920-1960
MODERN STYLES

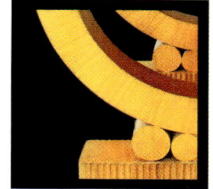

CONCLUSION
Post-Modernity at the Turn of the Century and the Millennium
Québec Furniture at the Threshold of a New Era 521

1960-2000

Glossary 534

Bibliography 538

Index 540

Credits 542

The Influence of France

Medieval Traditions and Classicism in Québec

1534-1790

With the first landing of Jacques Cartier, in 1534, and the founding of Québec City by Samuel de Champlain in 1608, France established itself in North America, claiming a territory far too large to be administered systematically and efficiently. This territory was named New France, and part of it, along the St. Lawrence River, was known from the outset as Canada. In cultural terms, this French province across the seas represented an amalgam of the enduring heritage of the Middle Ages, maintained by the peasantry, and the mannered classicism then in fashion among the elite. The 17th and 18th centuries, corresponding to the reigns of Louis XIII, Louis XIV and Louis XV, saw the arrival in New France of tens of thousands of settlers who, at the time of the defeat by the British forces in 1759, formed a population of over 70 000. These pioneering men and women, who quickly defined a stratified society complete with civil servants and administrative buildings, brought with them the tastes and customs of the regions from which they had originally set sail, along with the current artistic and cultural values of both the provinces and the capital. This characteristically French spirit was to survive well after the loss of the colony – at least until the end of the 18th century and even later in certain seigneuries.

2
Monsieur and Madame Eustache Ignace Trottier *dit* Desrivières in 1793. Oil painting on canvas by François Malepart de Beaucourt (1740-1794). The portraits depict, in affluent surroundings, two members of the generation that lived during the New France period and also experienced the 1759 defeat at the hands of the British. The artist has captured the likenesses of this couple from the Montréal bourgeoisie in all their elegant prosperity. The husband, in a fine velvet jacket with large shiny buttons, wears an embroidered waistcoat and a lace jabot and holds a hand of cards to represent his favorite pastime. His wife, née Marguerite Alexis Mailhot, is about to pour tea from a substantial silver samovar, for the daily ritual – even at this early date ! – of English life. The old Québec furniture presented in this book reflects the life of all classes of society, from settlers to city gentry.

FURNITURE IN THE
FRENCH MANNER

The New France Style

3
Aubert de Gaspé manor at Saint-Jean-Port-Joli, ca. 1880. Unknown photographer.
New France was like an overseas province of France. The architecture of the St. Lawrence Valley was inspired by that of provincial France. This fine manor, built soon after an older building had been destroyed by the invading British army, displays all the characteristics of French domestic architecture. These characteristics include the way the building sits low to the ground, the steep 45° to 53° pitch of the roof, the façade turned to the south for sunlight and warmth, casement windows with 20 to 24 small panes and a lack of eaves trim or overhang. Additions made to the manor in the course of the 19th century gave it some Neoclassical features as well. It was the long-time home of Philippe Aubert de Gaspé, the author of *Anciens Canadiens*, and inspired some of the scenes of social life described in the novel. The building was destroyed by fire in 1906.

4
Superior Council Room at Louisbourg, ca 1740.
Louisbourg was a strategically important nerve centre in New France and had its own colonial government. This reconstruction of an imposing meeting room in the fortress gives a good idea of how rooms were furnished and laid out in the palaces of intendants and governors in the different governments of "Canada" — Québec, Montréal and Trois-Rivières — in the 17th and 18th centuries. All of this heritage, so deeply linked to the identity of the French in North America, has been lost or obliterated.

5
Os de mouton armchair. Yellow birch, Québec City, ca. 1740.
This elegant, graceful Régence armchair displays the curves and roundness that characterized the Louis XV style. The chair has been recently reupholstered with an Aubusson tapestry called "Flemish verdure"; traces of this same material were discovered under the seat tacks.

6
Chest in the Louis XIII manner with V-shaped moulding. Original hinges and color, mid-18th century.
Popular for over two centuries, the Québec chest with V-shaped moulding contrasts with its French counterpart, whose V points upward.

7
Two-tiered buffet with incomplete diamond points and a broken pediment. Original color, pine, Montréal, first half of the 18th century.

8
Tall-post bed with a tester and turned, carved posts. Yellow birch, Québec City, late 17th century.
The Augustinian Hospitaller order arrived in New France in 1639 and built the Hôpital Général in Québec City. Their hospital still holds this bed, which belonged to Jean-Baptiste de la Croix de Chevrières de Saint-Vallier (1653-1727), the second bishop of Québec City.

9
Two-doored armoire with shaped panels in the Louis XIII manner, with Louis XIV and Régence touches. Québec City region, mid-18th century.
The elegant curving motifs on the upper doors are reminiscent of the cartouche that held the Sun King's coat of arms. This piece is exceptional from an ethnohistorical point of view. The photograph shows it as it was found, without any cleaning, waxing or restoration work. Inside the right-hand door, the name Mari-Claire is incised, while the missing "e" for "Marie" is carved into the left-hand door. The latches were obviously added later.

In the Wake of the British Conquest

Neoclassical Trends

1790~1840

BEGINNING IN THE LAST QUARTER OF THE 18TH CENTURY, the victorious British, having taken control of French America by force, gradually introduced and promoted the Georgian and Regency fashions initiated by the Adam brothers and other great English designers. Québec began to adapt to certain Neoclassical values. In England especially, this new style drew inspiration from ancient Greece and Rome, as well as from Renaissance artists such as Andrea Palladio. At the same time, France, which remained a cultural and artistic reference for Québec, was following a similar historical and stylistic path, setting out the canons of the Empire style. In the United States, the foundations were laid for what would later become known as the Federal style. In Québec, the British newcomers — garrisoned soldiers, administrators, prosperous businessmen, craftsmen and settlers — made their presence felt throughout the country, seizing control of trade and supervising the first industries. A wave of Loyalists, those unwilling to live in the new independent republic declared by the Revolutionaries in 1775, fled the United States and soon swelled the ranks of the British settlers. The new colonial power found it opportune to enlist the support of a first contingent of French bourgeoisie, enthralled by the conqueror's glamor. Between 1790 and 1840, during a period of economic prosperity created by advantageous customs duties, the architecture, interior design, furnishings, and general culture of Lower Canada — roughly corresponding to present-day Québec — all began to reflect prevailing Western values. In the St. Lawrence Valley, a genuine artistic revival found original ways to express these many influences. As elsewhere among Western peoples, the pressures of the amalgamated society that was taking shape on the North American continent lent renewed vigor to Neoclassical taste, as clearly demonstrated in religious and domestic architecture and household furnishings.

10
Pierre Amable de Bonne (1758-1816) and his wife, née Louise Elizabeth Marcoux. Oil paintings on canvas by William Berczy (1744-1813), 1808. The spirit of Neoclassicism is very much in evidence in this portrait of one of the leading scholars of the period, aged 58, and his young, 23-year-old wife. A militia officer, lawyer, politician and judge, De Bonne was a member of the liberal bourgeoisie of his time. Posing with a copy of Montesquieu's *De l'esprit des lois*, he is comfortably installed in an upholstered armchair with a curved back and armrests ending in carved scrolls. His wife, dressed in the Empire style and displaying the latest fashion in hairdressing, is wearing a diadem in the manner of the Empress Josephine. A bird, probably a canary, has alighted on her forefinger, ready to fly away to freedom.

NEOCLASSICAL FURNITURE

The Constitutional Style

11
Louis-Bertrand house at L'Isle-Verte, ca. 1890.
This elegant residence was built by Louis Bertrand in 1853 on the site of an older dwelling that had recently been destroyed by fire. A totally new kind of house developed in Québec during the Neoclassical era. It was particularly well adapted to the extremes of summer and winter weather and was characterized by the way it stood high off the ground, by its bell-cast roof overhanging the front and back walls, by its symmetrically distributed openings and chimneys, and by its portals and moulding based on classical orders. (For the history and description of this exceptional house, see Chapter 4.)

12
Drawing room in the house of Joseph Elzéar Cyril Pelletier, public notary, at Beaumont in Bellechasse county, built in around 1840.
Some houses seem to be unmarked by the passage of time. In this room, furnished with mid-19th-century pieces and accessories, the woodwork has never been painted. The cast-iron stove comes from the William Stratton foundry in Dundee, Scotland, and was imported in about 1845. The room as a whole provides a very good idea of the atmosphere in Neoclassical interiors, as well as displaying the skill with which contemporary craftsmen could bring out the beauty of wood.

13
Card table with bracket feet in the Neoclassical style. Mahogany veneer over pine, Québec City, ca. 1840.

14
Chest of drawers with ring-turned corner columns, five drawers and a shaped skirt. Imitation mahogany-grain finish, Rivière-du-Loup area, ca. 1830.

15
Writing cabinet. Mahogany veneer, over secondary pine, Québec City, ca. 1830.
This piece in the Late Georgian manner was no doubt made in Québec City. The starkness of the cabinet's façade is offset by the turned corner columns, with their rope-carved and lattice patterns, ending in lion's-paw feet and topped with capitals. This piece belonged to the Morewood family of Québec City.

16
Traditional armoire in the Neoclassical style. Stripped pine, early 19th century.
The decorative elements that characterized the Neoclassical style are found in abundance on this armoire. It displays the grooves, fluting, dentils, chevrons, rope carving, fans and festoons favored by the Adam brothers and has block-carved recessed panels. This piece demonstrates how Québec furniture makers, trained in the traditional French manner, were able to integrate new trends into their heritage.

17
Empire sofa attributed to cabinetmaker Thomas Nesbett (1776-1850) of St. John, New Brunswick, ca. 1830.
The old furniture found throughout Québec includes many pieces originating from neighboring parts of Canada and the United States. Furniture makers in the St. Lawrence Valley exported some of their production, while many people imported items from Europe and the rest of North America. This model of sofa with curved armrests was very popular during the Neoclassical period and a number of furniture makers in Québec City and Montréal produced their own versions of it. The one shown here is adorned with lion's-paw feet, dolphins on its armrests and rope carving along its skirt.

The Fusion of Three Cultures

Vernacular Revivalism in Québec

1840-1890

THE 19TH CENTURY WAS STRONGLY INFLUENCED by the universal curiosity aroused by the exploration of time and the continents. The Industrial Revolution, the impetus provided by the emergence of a liberal society, and the technological innovations that triumphantly vanquished nature were all factors that contributed to a pride in the current century that was unmatched in history. In every field of learning, scholars worked to discover original sources, to shed new light on knowledge and human relations. The work of Charles Darwin on the origin of the species offers a striking example. The encyclopedic approach engulfed everything in its path. Architecture and the decorative arts were marked by references to historic periods, giving rise to "revivals," as they became known. The triumphs of the machine age made it possible to recreate the very best that mankind had produced. Classical antiquity, the Middle Ages, the Renaissance, and French classicism, whether Baroque or influenced by Rococo elements, were some of the many different styles that inspired furniture design. Sometimes borrowings from various geographical areas, such as the Far East, introduced even greater variety into a movement with an endless appetite for diversity. Universal fairs, beginning with the Great Exhibition in London in 1851, and the wide distribution of attractive catalogues stimulated the spread of Western trends to various cultures. This international movement based on historical references has been labelled "Revivalism." In the St. Lawrence Valley, influences from France and the United States colored a fashion that swept the northeastern seaboard of North America in a creative maelstrom that had never before been experienced on the continent. In Québec, standing at the crossroads of three cultures, the Revival movement unlocked a store of inventiveness and an astonishing display of skill.

18
Madame Cyrice Têtu, née Caroline Dionne, and her son Amable, and Cyrice Têtu (1818-1890) and his daughter Caroline. Oil paintings on canvas by Théophile Hamel (1817-1870), Québec City, 1852.
These fine portraits from the Revival era show the attractive family of a prosperous merchant in the capital. Cyrice Têtu came from an influential, wealthy family from the south shore of the St. Lawrence River. His brothers included a priest, a notary, a physician, five merchants and four farmers. The clothes and settings in the portraits announce a new, elaborate approach to the decorative arts, in direct contrast to that of the preceding period.

REVIVAL
FURNITURE

The Confederative Style

19
The Jean-Baptiste-Pâquet house in Lévis, ca. 1915.
Pâquet was a member of the judiciary. The house he built on Guénette Street in Lévis in around 1885 was designed in the Second Empire style, as interpreted by U.S. house model catalogues. The building, with its mansard roof and Renaissance Revival tower, also shows touches of French classicism. It is made of red brick, highlighted with buff-colored Scottish brick quoins at the corners and around openings. The dramatic flourishes of this romantic, history-inspired architecture are displayed here in the openwork fence and gate, the profusion of decorative elements and the elaborate woodwork of the long verandah.

20
Revival-era drawing room in the Louis-Bertrand house at L'Isle-Verte, as decorated in around 1870.
The atmosphere of another period survives intact in some old houses. The Bertrand family was once at the centre of cultural life in L'Isle-Verte, a small village east of Rivière-du-Loup. The Bertrands, who were also involved in politics and business, were fairly well-off, as can be seen in this comfortable drawing room. Everything in the room — the piano, the furniture, the curtains, the carpets, the lights and the pictures on the wall — is as it was in the Revival period. Architecturally, the house belongs to the Neoclassical era, but the rooms inside are mainly decorated in the Victorian style.

21
Rococo Revival card table. Walnut, Québec City, ca. 1865.
One of the trends in Victorian Revivalism favored curves and countercurves. This piece shows the influence of the Louis XV style in its top, apron, legs and X-stretcher. The Québec City craftsman who made this graceful table embellished it with decorative carving.

22
Renaissance Revival chest of drawers with mirror. Walnut, marble and glass, Montréal, ca. 1875.
This piece, like much Revival furniture, is decorated with carving combined with veneer work and geometrical appliqués. The hardware is quite typical of the period.

23
Renaissance Revival bed. Walnut with figured walnut veneers, Montréal, ca. 1875.
After 1865-1870, Renaissance Revival furniture was often abundantly decorated with geometric medallions and glued moulding.

24
Renaissance Revival sideboard. Walnut, Québec City, ca. 1875.
In the last quarter of the 19th century, immense sideboards dominated the dining rooms of large bourgeois homes. Most of these sideboards were adorned with carved still lifes, braces of game fowl, bunches of fruit or flowers and garlands of all types.

25
Part of a Rococo Revival drawing room suite made by Philippe Vallière (1832-1919), a Québec City furniture maker, for Mme Jean-Charles Chapais (1830-1888), née Georgina Dionne, of Saint-Denis, Kamouraska. Walnut and horsehair, 1866. (Includes ladies' chair, card table and gentlemen's easy chair.)
In 1866, businessman Jean-Charles Chapais (1811-1885) had repairs done on his house in Saint-Denis. His wife went to Québec City and bought various pieces of furniture at Vallière's store. Letters and bills from the period give details about her purchases. Mme Chapais preferred Vallière's, she wrote, because " At Drum's, it's impossible to buy the slightest thing, it's so expensive. " [Translation]

*The Effects of North American
Mass Production*

Pre-Modern Movements in the Belle Époque

1890–1920

THE LAST QUARTER OF THE 19th CENTURY and the first quarter of the 20th century mark a time of transition between two approaches to design, production and distribution. Against a backdrop of widespread population movements and strong growth in immigration and urbanization, the furniture industry set its sights resolutely on the new mass markets. Catalogues issued by manufacturers, wholesalers and retailers disseminated new trends in North American taste across the continent. The advent of the marketing age brought an end to craft-based production, which survived only to serve the elite. Two long-lasting trends began to emerge in furniture design. The first drew on history-inspired Revivals, which were now simplified to satisfy the constraints of machining and mass production. The second trend was innovative, breaking away from the mimetism and over-elaborateness of the preceding period, and emphasized functionality, sobriety and increasingly streamlined shapes. Some of the underlying tenets of Art Nouveau were based on gracious effect, and several movements launched by daring creative artists such as Morris, Eastlake and Stickley reflect an aesthetic vision that shied away from gratuitous decorative clutter. Bentwood, wicker and metals such as iron, copper and brass were some of the materials and techniques used to support the innovative formal momentum of the period. The United States, in particular through the influence of the furniture industry centred in Chicago, played a determining role in the evolution of taste in North America. Once again, Québec's willingness to embrace all markets and all trends led to the development of an original form of Pre-Modernism.

26
Wedding portrait of Georges Bouchard (1888-1956), Member of Parliament for Kamouraska from 1922 to 1940, and Cresence Pouliot, daughter of Justice Joseph-Camille Pouliot, the future owner of the Mauvide-Genest manor in Saint-Jean, Île d'Orléans. The marriage was celebrated on August 24, 1915. This photograph is attributed to Samuel Belle of Rivière-du-Loup. Signs of the Pre-Modern era include the Arts & Crafts chair, supplied by the photographer, and the bride's dress, which even reveals her ankles. The use of photography to mark rites of passage is another sign of changing times.

27
Gil'Mont, the summer residence of Sir Rodolphe Forget (1861-1919) at Saint-Irénée-des-Bains in the Charlevoix region. Photograph by Quéry Frères of Montréal, 1906.
"Lady Forget, you make me think of Queen Victoria in her Vatican," exclaimed one visitor, overwhelmed by the opulence of the house where the Forgets lived in summer when away from their Montréal home. The photographers William and Adélard Quéry prepared an album — now kept in Montréal's central library — presenting 54 pictures of this sumptuous villa in the Pre-Modern style known as Arts & Crafts. Sir Forget was an immensely successful politician and businessman, but was eventually ruined.

28
Dining room with Pre-Modern oak furniture in Adophe Lambert's home in Québec City, as decorated in around 1910.
The Pre-Modern period was a time of transition, shared by the reassuring styles of the past and the aesthetic reforms proposed by people like Morris, Eastlake, Godwin and Stickley. This dining room reflects the less adventuresome of the two trends. The style of the chairs shows a conservative attachment to the past that was not entirely absent from the principles espoused by Morris and Eastlake. The classically styled glazed china cabinet, with its vertical lines, was practically a showcase for crystal and silver. It was a recently introduced piece of furniture in this period of oak and imitation grain finishes.

29
Ladies' slant-top desk. Oak, Lévis, 1900.
The curves and sinuous lines of this functional but elegant little piece are a reflection of the influence of Art Nouveau on industrial production.

30
Side chair with steam-embossed decoration. Yellow birch with golden oak finish, Lévis, ca. 1905.
After 1880, the furniture industry offered a limitless variety of chairs, some of which were embossed in steam chambers. This one bears a medallion with the effigy of Sir Wilfred Laurier, the Prime Minister of Canada. The chair was part of a set with a matching armchair and rocker.

31
Morris chair. Golden oak, Québec City, ca. 1900.
This chair, whose shape is borrowed from the Roman curule seat, has armrest boxes for storing smoking accessories. It might well be termed a "smoker's chair."

32
Cupboard with drawers in the Eastlake manner. Québec City, ca. 1895.
In the Belle Époque, several factories and workshops offered highly simplified furniture with almost flat surfaces, lightly decorated with grooving and stylized floral motifs. These pieces were marked by their geometrical lines, angularity and discreet festooning. The style was named after an English architect named Eastlake, who promoted the notion that machine-made furniture could be in "good taste."

33
Combination china cabinet and sideboard with mirrors and stained-glass panels. Oak, Lac-Saint-Jean, ca. 1900.
After 1875-1880, oak furniture became dominant in the products offered by the market, which now could reach every corner of the continent through sales catalogues. Industrial furniture was made in large series for a range of socio-economic classes but always reflected the major artistic trends and aesthetic values of the Belle Époque.

*20th-Century Mimetism
and Functionality*

Modern Tastes

1920-1960

Québec has always been receptive to outside influences. Beginning in the 17th century, with virtually no time lag, all the main Western trends in the decorative arts reached the shores of the St. Lawrence, either through imported goods or through the original productions they inspired. The 20th century was no exception. In the interwar period, furniture continued to show close links with the past, since the early colonial styles still had their admirers, but at the same time a whole segment of the woodworking industry and craft-based or industrial design adopted new aesthetic values. The new trends were often introduced and promoted by specific workshops or groups, which were mainly European and gave a decisive impetus to the Art Deco and International styles. Québec's arts and trades schools, and particularly the École du meuble de Montréal founded by Jean-Marie Gauvreau, displayed all the paradoxes of a period torn between the shapes of the past and modernity. The furniture school was split between two approaches: a reformulated traditionalism and the new spirit of the avant-garde creators and movements. Talented designer-craftsmen energetically explored the latter path, showing much inventiveness. Québec industry also made original contributions to the conventions of Modernism, as reflected in the fashion for chromed-tube furniture.

MODERN FURNITURE

34
Émilien Poulin and Jeannette Blain on returning from their honeymoon. Hand-colored silver gelatine print, Studio Desjardins, Sorel, May 1943.
Modernity influenced all strata of society. Fashion, modes of representation and architecture are some of the areas affected by the new trends.

35
Bourdon house on Saint-Louis Road in Québec City, built according the plans made by architect-decorator Robert Blatter, 1934.
During the 1920s and 1930s, Québec, like the rest of North America, was caught up in the Art Deco style, popularized by the Exposition internationale des Arts décoratifs et industriels modernes held in Paris in 1925. The exhibition marked the true arrival of Modern art. Architect-designers like Robert Blatter in Québec City and Marcel Parizeau in Montréal became standard bearers for the new aesthetic as it applied to buildings and interior decoration. Furniture in this style was promoted by Jean-Marie Gauvreau, who founded Montréal's furniture school, the École du meuble, in 1935. The architectural landscape received forms and textures that had never been used before. The designers insisted that no aspect of a building was unrelated to their work. Having a hand in both furniture design and room layout, these people created the notion of the architect-interior decorator.

36
Dining room furniture designed by Alphonse Saint-Jacques, a teacher at the École du meuble in Montréal, and built by his students. Maple and yellow birch veneer, 1936.
The École du meuble was known for its support of Modern design. In 1936, Henri Kieffer, the head of Québec's Forestry Protection Service, ordered this furniture from Jean-Marie Gauvreau as a wedding present for his daughter, Simone. The suite, now part of Québec's national collection, consists of a table, eight chairs, two sideboards and a long-case clock. The rug was designed by Robert Blatter.

37
Low table designed by Robert Blatter. Polychrome wood and glass, ca. 1930.
This piece is part of an exceptional set of furnishings designed to give unity to the interior decoration of a house belonging to the surveyor Henri Bélanger of Québec City. Architect-decorator Robert Blatter began to work on the house plans in 1927 and completed the project in 1929 and 1930.

38
Art Deco dressing table. Bird's-eye maple with basswood as secondary wood, Montréal, ca. 1930.

39
Sideboard. Wood, aluminum, glass and vinyl, ca. 1950.
In the period when chrome tubing dining room suites were popular, several manufacturers offered matching sideboards. This one, with flowing lines, is covered with padded vinyl secured with decoratively arranged studs.

40
Side chair designed by Alphonse Saint-Jacques, a teacher at the École du meuble de Montréal. Yellow birch and leather, 1936.
This chair is part of Henri Keiffer's Art Deco dining room suite, presented on the preceding page.

41
Art Deco dressing table. Québec City, ca. 1930.
This piece comes from the Taschereau family of Québec City. It belongs to a bedroom suite said to have been made in this city by A.-E. Rousseau according to a design by Robert Blatter.

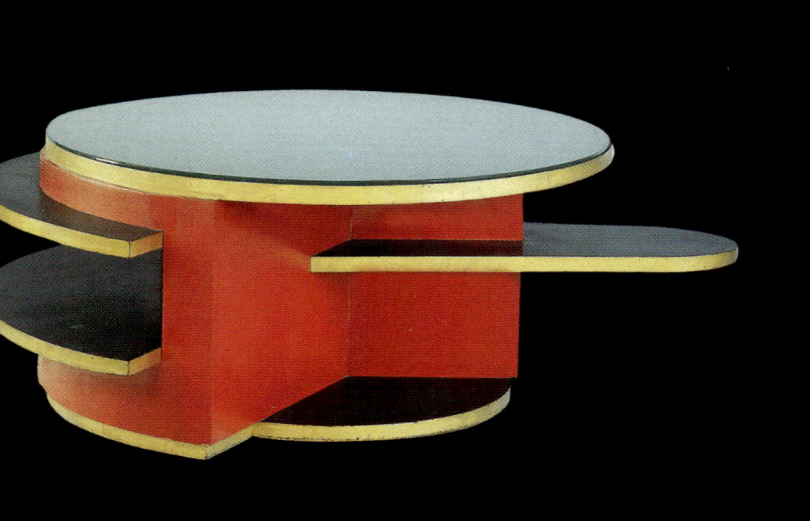

42
Overstuffed easy chair. Wood, metal and damask velvet, ca. 1930.
The history of Québec furniture touches on all kinds of styles and social
levels. As of the mid-19th century, a large part of this furniture was
manufactured in Québec factories. The piece shown here, photographed
in a house at L'Isle-Verte, embodies certain Art Deco tastes.

Preface

It is difficult, if not impossible, to compress the history of the old furniture of Québec into a few hundred pages, so rich and varied is the subject matter. For four centuries, Québec, thanks to its geographical location and the spirit of its people, has been a genuine cultural melting pot, open to many outside influences. Québec City and Montréal, respectively the capital and the largest city of this French land within North America, are among the continent's deepest inland ports; their ability to receive the ocean-going ships that ply the St. Lawrence has had a major impact on the economic development and cultural dynamics of the Québec people. Since the establishment of the French colonial regime in the 17th century, Québec has seen the arrival of a wide range of objects and fashions from many different sources, representing many different trends, and the results are clearly visible in the architecture and material culture of the land. Anybody who takes the trouble to tour our towns and villages, to explore the hallways and rooms of centuries-old institutions, to visit rectories, manor houses and country and town houses belonging to people from all social classes and from all the groups that have over time forged modern Québec, will be able to testify to the wealth and diversity of the objects found. The dominant influences have come, at various times, from France, Great Britain and the United States.

This book completes a trilogy begun in 1994 on the subject of Québec's material culture. The first two books in the series, *Objets anciens du Québec. La vie domestique* and *Antiquités du Québec. Objets anciens. Vie sociale et culturelle* examined various ethnohistorical groups of artifacts other than furniture as such. A dictionary of old artifacts will eventually complete this series of general surveys.

Once again, in order to produce a clear, accessible overview of the subject, I have organized the sometimes overwhelming history of furniture production into periods corresponding to the actual evolution of the decorative arts in Québec. I have also attempted to bring the objects to life by placing them against the background of the time period, social stratum or group to which they belong, an approach comparable to the scientific approach of art historians and ethnohistorians. As usual, photographs, whether old or taken recently by collaborating photographers, play a key role in the process of raising awareness and providing a popular, eye-catching introduction to the identity and history of a people.

The first chapter provides a general introduction to the field, summarizing the relationships between furniture, interior design and architecture. This chapter also examines the sociological dimension of furniture through the ages from a synchronic perspective and deals with the technical aspects of craft production — timber species, joining methods, paint, varnishes, color, hardware — and the various types of decoration. This opening chapter also surveys the documents, manuscripts, printed materials and pictorial evidence connected with the subject. It underlines the wealth of objects discovered in the field during explorations of private, institutional and public collections. I also considered it important to establish, from the outset, the stylistic dynamics that underlie my analysis. This is also where I address the question of settlement furniture which, because it remains outside established canons and rules, cannot easily be considered within the stylistic periods defined and examined in the main chapters.

The history of Québec furniture can be divided into five main periods, as indicated in the Table of Contents, corresponding to five cultural or socio-economic movements that also influenced other artistic and creative fields. I intend to make this division definitive, to rationalize it and to use it in all future historical surveys. The periods are presented in chronological order.

French control of New France for 150 years meant that Québec furniture was influenced by both medieval styles and a Baroque-inspired form of provincial classicism over the course of the 17th and 18th centuries. Until 1790, France was the mother country for the majority of Quebeckers and remained the main reference point, providing a sense of continuity. After the defeat of 1759, England gradually began to introduce Neoclassical values into the conquered colony, and between 1790 and 1840 English taste, in its purest form, was quickly amalgamated with a French influence coming from the south, where the United States had fallen under the spell of French design. The results, both in architecture and in furniture design, were highly original. Toward the middle of the 19th century, more specifically between 1840 and 1890, Western Revival styles began to appear along the shores of the St. Lawrence as a result of French, English and U.S. influences, and this led to the development of an original school of woodworking. The "Québec Victorian" style, a label that I have deleted from my vocabulary and replaced with the term Revivalism, attained a degree of artistic and technical refinement and of originality that is relatively well demonstrated by John Porter in *Living in Style: Fine Furniture in Victorian Québec*. Next, during the Belle Époque — a period which in my classification runs from the appointment of Honoré Mercier as Premier in 1887 until the Great War of 1914-1918 — Québec, like the rest of the Western world, underwent a period of major realignment in many different cultural spheres. The decorative arts and furniture design were affected by movements that started elsewhere in the West, when a number of designers challenged the cluttered eclecticism and stuffy mimetism of the preceding decades, proposing a new aesthetic approach based on sobriety and simplicity. I have used the term Pre-Modernism to designate the period from 1890 to 1920, which was characterized by an avant-garde approach that, in fact, prefigured the main principles and mass production techniques of the following period. Last, once peace had been re-established after the Great War, the feverish pace of the so-called Roaring Twenties, guided by the crucial changes that had taken place in the preceding decades, swept over into the arts. Québec, with its furniture school (École du meuble), its designers and its production capacity, quickly and unhesitatingly adopted the modern values espoused by the decorative arts under the influence of Art Deco and the International style. This era, from 1920 to 1960, corresponds to the last period in my analysis, which I have called the Modern period. In the conclusion, I examine Post-Modernity as it has emerged at the close of the century and the millennium.

Each chapter in the book presents a summary of a particular period that could, in itself, constitute the subject matter of a separate book. While saluting the pioneering work of Jean Palardy in his *Les meubles anciens du Canada français*, I venture to suggest that the whole question of French-influenced furniture requires a thorough re-examination. The author of this catalogue of old "French Canadian" objects discussed vernacular furniture without making the necessary distinctions between French, English and U.S. influences; such furniture must be reconsidered within the specific context of each period. In every period, an astonishing combination of formal and decorative borrowings or references offers fascinating insights into the dynamics of the decorative arts and the inexhaustible inventiveness and imagination of all classes of society. Apart from the specialized research of Donald Blake Webster of the Royal Ontario Museum, there has been little serious attention given to either Québec Neoclassical furniture, with its links to Georgian and Regency design, or the profoundly vernacular furniture inspired by the same convergence of underlying forces in this great stylistic movement that strongly influenced the domestic architecture of the St. Lawrence Valley. To complement John Porter's survey of the production of the elite classes during the Revival period, it would also be useful to re-examine the Revival furniture of the bourgeoisie and middle classes in the time of Papineau and La Fontaine. Lastly, Pre-Modernism and the true Modern period have received practically no attention at all. The many different workshops, manufacturers and schools dating from these periods represent worthy topics for scientific study and publications.

The investigations in which I have been involved provide clear confirmation of the fact that Québec furniture design is not limited, as some researchers have been content to state, to furniture produced in the French tradition. During the various periods in which Québec increasingly sought to reaffirm its French origin and to define the characteristics of a distinct society, it was only natural that everything that provided a link to such roots — in particular architecture and material culture — should be glorified. However, insofar as it was able, Québec was actually just as active in subsequent periods of the history of the decorative arts; its craftsmen and manufacturers disseminated the whole range of tastes and fashions that arose in Europe and, especially, North America. The integrative capacity of a society at the crossroads of three cultures, together with a creative spirit fed by three sources of inspiration and regenerated from within, produced a continuous flow of original designs.

How did this book come about? First, I should point out that it is the end result of 30 years of fieldwork involving numerous trips to museums and museum reserves, venerable religious institutions, historic sites and private collections within Québec and beyond its borders, especially in Ontario and the United States. This work has been on-going since the late 1960s; I first reported on it in the *Complete Guide to French Canadian Antiques* (1974), and since then it has been constantly enriched as I have examined various periodicals and made discoveries of many sorts. The process picked up speed after 1990, when I decided to write a series of studies about material culture. I would like to take this opportunity to salute the work of private collectors who pursue their interest by purchasing and restoring old furniture. All the collectors I managed to locate, amounting to several dozen fellow citizens, welcomed me warmly as they shared their discoveries. I would particularly like to acknowledge the generous contribution of my friend Ronald Chabot, of Lévis, for making available many hundreds of catalogues issued by manufacturers, wholesalers and retailers inside and outside Québec, providing exceptional insights into the commercially produced furniture used by our forebears over a period of 125 years. At my suggestion, and in order to do his part for science, businessman Ronald Chabot has steadfastly built up this unique body of documentation on Québec's material culture and the fashions it has followed. I also consulted most of the studies written on this subject over the last 30 years, whether in France, England or the United States, visited many decorative arts museums in those countries, especially their furniture divisions. I passed entire days in the major U.S. institutions, such as those in Winterthur and Williamsburg, and the great museums in New York, Washington and Boston, as well as many different historical villages. I also visited the Victoria and Albert Museum in London, the Musée des Arts décoratifs in Paris and numerous other such institutions, observing, taking notes and comparing. I combed through the holdings of the library of the former École du meuble in Montréal, a collection now preserved at the Cégep du Vieux-Montréal. The books I found, mainly in the rare books section, were a gold mine of information, as was the Ramsay Traquair collection at the Blackader-Lauterman Library of Architecture and Art at McGill University. I did research in the Musée du Québec and the Musée de la civilisation in Québec City, the Montreal Museum of Fine Arts and several other intermediate and regional museums and also benefited greatly from visits to the collections of many religious communities, such as the Séminaire de Québec and its Château Bellevue at Cap-Tourmente, the Augustinian Hospitallers, the Grey Nuns in Montréal, the Sisters of Charity of Québec City, and the Hospitallers of St. Joseph at the Hôtel-Dieu in Montréal, to name but a few. I also selected illustrations from collections of early photographs, wherever possible. The book's design involved considerable effort, and simply setting up the pieces of furniture for the photographs required thousands of hours of work in often difficult conditions.

No single person can claim to have an in-depth knowledge of all the periods and all the aspects of furniture in Québec, since the field is too vast and complex. To compensate for this, I have consulted experts, well-recognized collectors and people who have inherited family property, using the information they provided in interviews to summarize their impressive experience and knowledge. Each chapter includes excerpts from these inquiries.

Ideally, of course, I would have been able to base my research on a broad sampling of well-conserved objects in their original state for each period, designer and region, and to consult data on manufacturers and users. Furniture with documentary support provides precious information that sheds light on the era to which it belongs. However, in general, documentation is only available for workshop-produced furniture from the 20th century. Except in a few extremely rare cases, all other furniture is undocumented. Old Québec furniture is almost always unsigned, and all traces of a piece's history have often been lost in the web of commerce and succeeding generations.

Many of the pieces of furniture that have come down to us have been altered in terms of their original finish and others have undergone physical alterations. Between 1920 and 1970, old furniture was systematically stripped down to bare wood. In *Secrets et ressources des bois du Québec*, a book by Jean-Marie Gauvreau published in 1943, the focus was on stripping and recipes were given for bleaching processes to reveal wood grain and surfaces. The fashion was for stripped, waxed furniture, which, it was believed, brought to light the skills of the craftsman, revealed the materials, and cleansed surfaces of all distasteful signs of past use. Two or three generations of collectors and museum curators were quite willing to sacrifice original colors and patinas. Today, varnished furniture produced on an industrial scale is being subjected to the same reductionist treatment.

The active market of the past 50 years has also led to the questionable transformation of a number of pieces of furniture, ranging from an artificial rejuvenation of colors and varnishes to a reshaping that borders on forgery. Original doors are fitted to a frame from a different source to produce a new armoire, with a skilful use of final coloring to unify the whole. A few remnants of a table with turned legs form the basis for a surprisingly convincing reconstruction using carefully disguised old timber. In many cases, high prices are asked for furniture that has been outrageously camouflaged, even in the details of its moulding and hardware. Furniture is also imported from France or Haiti because it bears a striking resemblance to old furniture from Québec.

The corpus of old Québec furniture, especially from before 1840, is limited. This is partly because much of our heritage has disappeared in smoke as towns and cities were plagued with recurrent fires. The book *Statistiques rouges*, containing data compiled and edited by Eugène Leclerc in 1932, shows how much of our heritage has been reduced to ashes since the 17th century. The journal of Captain John Knox, who acted as secretary to James Wolfe, describes how thousands of houses were destroyed along with their contents when the British army invaded New France in 1759. During the industrial era, another large segment of the stock of old furniture fell victim to fashion, thrown onto the junk pile or used as firewood, with a few more fortunate items dispatched to the shed or sugar shack, where they would be discovered many years later.

Many of the items — often the most attractive — that were spared or rescued from changes in fashion have left Québec territory. For many years old Québec furniture has been held in great esteem in Ontario and the United States. Some antique dealers from Québec City still do good business in Toronto's antique fairs. The extensive collections of the Royal Ontario Museum provide clear evidence of the interest of our "Canadian" neighbors in Québec furniture. This trend goes back a long way. In the July 1925 issue of *La Revue Populaire*, a Montréal monthly, when an interest in this facet of Québec's heritage was beginning to emerge, Jules Jolicoeur expressed his concerns over the exodus in an article entitled "Nos vieux meubles" (Our Old Furniture):

"Whatever its origin, old furniture is of inestimable value to furniture enthusiasts. And, at the moment, it is in the United States that wealthy collectors are most numerous. Some of them collect everything, regardless of the period, the place of origin or the style. Others, in contrast, are interested only in one period or concentrate on a single passing fashion.

"For the last year or so, the furniture the most in demand among these people has been that from New England and Québec. In all areas of the countryside, from Maine and Vermont (where there was always an active cabinetmaking industry) in the north, to Kentucky and Virginia in the south, and in even the remotest villages in Québec, one can find furniture over a century old and, in many cases, the owners are unaware of its real value. This furniture is precious because of its age, the quality of its fine solid wood, and its style. It was produced by the hands of skilled, conscientious craftsmen. It does not, like Modern furniture, possess the banality of the mass-produced objects that equip our houses. And its most precious quality, in the eyes of connoisseurs, lies in its authenticity, of which there can be no doubt. Whereas the age of the furniture sold by antique dealers is generally suspect, since certain cabinetmakers in Canada and the United States, and also in Europe, specialize in copies of early models, furniture found in the countryside is genuinely from the period indicated by its style and age. Some pieces have not been moved for generations, and seem to be almost rooted to the ground. Until now they have attracted little interest, but since certain collectors have made them fashionable, they are in great demand, and they are fetching high prices in antique stores and auctions. Antique dealers are busy combing through the oldest regions of Québec to divest our houses of this precious booty whose owners, as I have stated, are unaware of its value.

"We do not advise that it should be sold at a high price, now that we recognize its value, but rather that this fine old furniture, which should represent some of the dearest memories in every family, should be kept." [Translation]

In 1931, in an article published in the November issue of *Technique*, Jean-Marie Gauvreau also dealt with this cultural "vampirism" and reported on its negative effects.

Outside Québec, interest in traditional furniture, especially that made of pine, was followed by a fashion for Neoclassical furniture in mahogany and various hardwoods, and then for richly carved Revival furniture. Interest abroad is now focused on Arts & Crafts and Mission furniture from the late 19th and early 20th centuries. This latest fashion provides interesting insights into the mechanism underlying the export market and cultural despoilment.

Since the 1980s, our neighbors to the south have renewed their interest in the movement launched by William Morris and his disciples, as well as in its U.S. version, known as "Mission" furniture. The production of the period that ushered in the Modern age, with its great cultural significance in the United States, has been highlighted by university research, museum exhibitions, popular and scholarly publications and reprinted commercial catalogues from major Belle Époque (or Edwardian) manufacturers. In the Soho district of New York, antique stores offer room after room full of items from this period. In Québec, no researcher has as yet focused on this material, which arouses passionate interest in English-speaking North America. However, the pickers who comb the countryside to supply the market are aware of this furniture's popularity in the United States and the resulting demand for it. They also know that the style was especially popular in summer-home areas. During my fieldwork, I located at least 30 models of Morris armchairs linked to the movement. Dealers buy them for a song and sell them at high prices in weekly auctions held in central Québec that draw many buyers from south of the border. Given the strength of the U.S. dollar, these people are easily able to beat local bids and generally leave with well-filled trucks. On several occasions, I have examined this sector of activity and condemned the practice on television, identifying the purchasers and their places of origin. Because of the relatively small amounts of money involved, no federal law prevents this cultural draining of the heritage of a fragile society.

Québec is often one generation behind the rest of the Western world, or at least the United States, in establishing a society-wide consensus and this has had an adverse affect on the identification and appreciation of certain aspects of material culture. Small countries often lag behind larger countries in terms of major trends and movements, and the fact that we border on the most powerful nation on earth is not always an advantage. Québec's heritage has been largely dilapidated and its museum collections have suffered as a result, at least as far as research and development are concerned. The problem is not new, as shown by the quotations from Jolicoeur and Gauvreau above, and touches many different types of old objects, from ceramics to scientific instruments. The situation has affected Québec's search for a collective identity and our ability to defend our image.

Ideally, furniture should be examined from a technical and formal viewpoint and also considered in terms of "comparative stylistics" — the domain of art historians — in order to place it in the context of a specific movement, era or workshop. As well, taking the ethnological dimension into account makes it possible to relate furniture to social conditions and socio-economic levels, utilizations and needs, and construction processes that combined aesthetic concerns with conditions and methods of production. Despite the succinct nature of my study, throughout the book, and in particular when analyzing specific items, I have taken these three aspects into consideration and linked them together in order to shed as much light as possible on the subject. Furniture, if I may be allowed this comparison, is an open book containing a multitude of stories.

It is surprising to note that, despite considerable public expectations and a highly active market, research in this major cultural field has progressed very little since the late 1960s, almost as though the book by Palardy had brought all discussion to a close. The development of museum collections has suffered and will continue to suffer from the dearth of serious research. The way furniture is held to relate to the question of Québec's collective identity, although based on accurate perceptions, does not do full justice to the reality of the situation, and the loss of cultural goods to places with better documentary background and a greater awareness of the stylistic trends of former times has diminished a weakened heritage even further.

Québec is a land of wood. Our predecessors gave voice to the wood as they used it for various purposes, including furniture, and their originality shines through their artistic endeavors. In compliance with certain trends, they did not hesitate to import exotic species. Craftsmen, workers and designers boldly drew on all the major trends in the Western decorative arts, never failing to display their inventiveness and mastery of technique and an undeniable aesthetic flair. Old Québec furniture bears witness to the cultural wealth of this land, its power to absorb fashions and values from elsewhere, and the vigor of Québec's creative minds.

MICHEL LESSARD
July 20, 1999

43
Trucker posing with a load of rocking chairs. Victoriaville, ca. 1940.
Early photographs help to illustrate various facets of the furniture market.

44 a, b, c, d
The story of changing movements and styles can be read in furniture details and decoration: a lozenge-carved panel in the Louis XIII manner; the base of a Rococo Revival arm stump; a volute on a Georgian sofa; and a box on the writing-arm of a Morris chair. All of these pieces were made or used in Québec.

Chapter 1

By Way of Introduction…

Québec Furniture and the Ever-Changing Story of Stylistic Movements

I CAN IMAGINE that the curious reader is already beginning to wish to know what sorts of trees grow in these great forests, and whether they are the same everywhere. What are they good for? can any use be made of them? are they large? are they tall? is their wood sound?

* * * * *

There is another kind of tree called maple, which grows very large and high; its wood is very fine, but is used only for fuel and for making handles for tools; for which purpose it is very well adapted, being both smooth and strong.

* * * * *

The tree called cherry birch grows big and high, and very straight. Its wood is used for making household furniture and the stocks of firearms. It is red inside, and makes the most beautiful wood of any in these parts. It has been named cherry birch because its bark resembles that of the wild cherry tree in France.

Two sorts of oak are found here, the wood of one of which is of a more open grain than that of the other, and is therefore more fit for the making of household furniture and for joiner's and carpenter's work. These trees grow tall and large and straight, particularly in the neighbourhood of Montreal.

PIERRE BOUCHER in *Histoire véritable et naturelle des productions du pays de la Nouvelle-France vulgairement dite Canada*, 1664 [Translation by Edward Louis Montizambert, *Canada in the Seventeenth Century*, 1883]

WE FIND IN THE PROVINCE a considerable amount of furniture made in the eighteenth century, some indeed as early as the late seventeenth. Much of this furniture was undoubtly made in French Canada, but furniture was also brought out from France, and it is not always possible to distinguish between the importations and the Canadian product. Enough remains, however, to show that there were competent furniture makers from very early times.

In the refectory of the Hôpital Général at Quebec are six fine tables of late seventeenth century type.

RAMSAY TRAQUAIR
McGill University, 1947
From an unpublished chapter written for *The Old Architecture of Quebec*

Québec Furniture and the Ever-Changing Story of Stylistic Movements

If one were asked to find a single term that would describe Québec furniture from a historic viewpoint, the most obvious choice would be "variety." From its beginnings as a colonial crossroads to its development into a modern state, Québec has always looked outward and been open to the wide world. The present contours of this young society were shaped in particular by three great cultural influences originating in France, Great Britain and the United States. These influences succeeded one another in time but eventually intermingled. The people of Québec developed their own way of expressing major trends in the decorative arts. In doing so, they invented ingenious and truly original technical and stylistic combinations that demonstrated a remarkable talent for integrating the values of others (Québec has been called the Japan of North America) and making the most of the rich complexity of their social fabric. The dynamic results of this openness and willingness to integrate new ideas are marked by inventiveness and go well beyond simple mimicking.

Knowledge of the history of furniture in Québec remains fragmentary. In studying this material culture, each example may be thought of as a document providing valuable information for both ethnology and the history of architecture. The study of furniture calls for a minute examination of quite diverse aspects: the types of wood used, whether local or imported; the production methods and procedures adopted; and, of course, the one thousand and one details related to colors, varnishes, fabrics and hardware.

A good part of old Québec furniture resists standard stylistic labelling. An example is the type of article termed "primitive," or "settlement" furniture, characterized by a stark concern for sturdiness and practicality. Over the years, this furniture's visual charm and pure lines have won the hearts of many heritage enthusiasts, who see reflected in it the mind-set of a deeply humble, unpretentious people and a simple, economical way of working that was revived each time new land was opened for settlement in a vast expanse of territory.

Given this resistance to standard labels, an investigation of how trends and styles succeeded one

45
The small Turkish drawing room at Gil'mont, the summer home of Rodolphe Forget at Saint-Irénée-des-Bains, in Charlevoix county. Photograph by Quéry Frères, 1906.
A study of the history of furniture in Québec reveals a great openness to the world and to other cultures, often interpreted with imagination.

61

another is the best way to establish a diachronic nomenclature that expresses Québec's historic realities.

All furniture comprises structural, utilitarian and aesthetic elements. In short, every piece of furniture is characterized essentially by three aspects: construction, which underlies the object's solidity; function, which determines how it will be used; and aesthetic presentation, constituted by form, lines and ornamentation. In the following examination of the trends and styles that have shaped this field of the decorative arts in Québec, the above three constituent parameters are considered for each item and each period. A piece of furniture may be seen as a historic document, since it testifies to a certain period in the past through the technical nature of its construction, through its sociological and ethnological import, and through the aesthetic expressed by these elements. Style, as presented in the following paragraphs, above all represents the manner of a period.

The concept of style presented here takes as its starting point the great stylistic movements that influenced Europe and North America, such as Neoclassicism (which enjoyed enormous popularity in the West from about 1780 to 1840), Revivals and the Modernist movement. This concept of style may also use reference points such as the reign of a monarch, like Louis XV in 18th-century France, or a particular political administration, like the U.S. Federal style of the late 18th and early 19th centuries. As well, style may be defined by an individual designer or school of furniture that marked a whole area of production. For example, André Charles Boulle (1642-1732), Louis XIV's favorite cabinetmaker, gave his name to a special cabinetmaking technique, while Louis Majorelle (1859-1926) marked Art Nouveau with his audacious flights of fancy. Similarly, the École du meuble de Montréal, the school founded by Jean-Marie Gauvreau (1935-1970), produced a type of furniture that reflected Québec's identity. The terms *Boulle* style, *Majorelle* style and *École du meuble* style are now well established and are seen to some degree as signatures. In another vein, styles may be named after a form or motif. For example, medieval and Gothic Revival furniture is said to be in the *ogival* style, late-Louis XV furniture is in the *rocaille* style, and an episode in North American design between 1930 and 1960 is designated as the *streamline* style. Sometimes the national or regional character of a piece is emphasized; the terms *Scottish*, *Norman*, *Breton* and *New England* are applied to styles that are observed in a corpus showing formal affinities related to geographical origins. Finally, an extravagant style may earn an irreverent epithet; for example, the somewhat affected bronze crockets that decorated certain Second Empire desks and chests of drawers inspired the name *moustachu* style, since they were reminiscent of the moustache worn by Napoleon III.

Beneath the formal façade of a style there always lie deep societal values corresponding to the ideological climate of the time. A style may be short-lived, but it expresses the innermost soul of a people or a period. An eloquent example of this is the stylistic revival known as *Gothic Revival* in 19th-century England. The predilection for medieval styles, which eventually gave impetus to the *Arts & Craft* school of William Morris (1834-1896), embodied the admiration of certain prominent intellectual and philosophical leaders for this long-ago period. Augustus Pugin (1812-1852) and John Ruskin (1819-1900) are prime examples of the type of thinker who was moved by the medieval world — by its inventiveness, original purity and straightforward relationship with the material and the sacred. This powerful style, invented in Albion itself at a time of national pride, when Queen Victoria's empire dominated the world — when "Britannia ruled the waves" — seems to express the ethnic character of England better than the classical styles that came from abroad, or even the Palladian style of Greco-Roman inspiration, despite the English fondness for it.

A piece of furniture may also be categorized by its method of manufacture. It is said to be homemade when made by a person for his or her individual needs. When hand or mechanical tools are used to produce pieces one by one, following so-called traditional methods of design and construction, handed down from one generation to the next, the result is referred to as handcrafted furniture. Finally, when an article is designed for machine-tool manufacture and mass production, it belongs to the category of industrial furniture, which began to be common after 1870. Regardless of the method of manufacture, the quality of the product varies widely in every case. However, it is evident that mass-produced furniture is far more likely to present examples of poorly made articles, sometimes to quite a remarkable degree.

Although industrial production became the norm in the second half of the 19th century, it is still possible today to find handmade furniture produced by an individual or a skilled cabinetmaker who uses time-proven methods of crafting, often with fine veneers of imported wood. When a "Sunday carpenter" or worker of some sort flouts conventions by adding a touch of whimsy to such work, the result is called folk art. Certain collectors surround themselves with folk art furniture that is astonishing from many points of view.

Furniture may also be classified according to levels of society or the sociological relation it has to a model that dominates fashion at a given time. In the absence of major studies dealing with the entire historical development of furniture production and use from a sociological viewpoint, it has been necessary in this book to create classification terminology and invent new categories. This has proved to be far from an empty exercise, since it has led to a better understanding of the whole field.

I have chosen the term *settlement furniture* to cover the essentially utilitarian homemade or handcrafted production that developed almost entirely outside major canons and regional trends. Whether the settlers in question had just landed on Île d'Orléans in the 17th century, or were establishing farms in the Eastern Townships in the mid-19th century, or were clearing new lots in the Abitibi or the Gaspésian hinterland in the interwar era, these people started off with simple, solid, basic furniture, which was often replaced after they were better established. This furniture sometimes ended up as firewood, or perhaps in some shed, such as a sugar shack. The architecture of homes and religious buildings constructed in Québec in times of settlement reflects the same spirit.

The term *vernacular furniture* encompasses all the types of furniture used by the majority of people in a given period, both in the pre-industrial period and throughout the various phases of the industrial era. In Québec's earliest days, vernacular furniture was inspired by that of the French provinces from which settlers came in the 17th and 18th centuries, and it became traditional in the St. Lawrence Valley. The notion of vernacular furniture also covers the handcrafted or proto-industrial production later inspired by the British *Late Georgian* and *Regency* styles as well as the French *Directoire*, *Empire* and *Restoration* styles. Examples of this category include articles made of local wood, such as chests of drawers with scrolled corner columns (popular until the last quarter of the 19th century) and arrow-back chairs with curved backs and legs. Vernacular furniture also includes industrial items in a diluted Revival style or showing tinges of Modernism, as well as the plethora of catalogue furniture available after 1870, made of golden or fumed oak in pseudo-historic styles. The term vernacular may also be applied to the bentwood furniture made by the Thonet brothers in Austria and marketed throughout the Western world from 1842 onward, the chrome and Formica dining suites of the 1930s and 1940s, and the production of Québec industries such as J.W. Kilgour & Brothers, Mégantic Furniture and Victoriaville Furniture (named after the towns in which they were located), to name but three of the dozens of businesses that flourished in the first half of the 20th century, offering products intended for a very general clientele.

Another category, *period furniture*, encompasses types of furniture that have developed according to well-defined conventions, or canons, and are distinguished by a set of recognized characteristics — for example, certain lines and motifs — dictated by a given fashion. Period furniture sets the tone for the more widely produced vernacular furniture and is eminently suited to providing formal points of reference for categorizing pieces diachronically or synchronically. The era in which such furniture was built and the canon it represents may be indicated by the name of a monarch, a political period, a school or cabinetmaker. Thus, a piece of *Louis XV* furniture was made in this monarch's reign (from 1715 to 1774), while a *Victorian* item was made during the reign of Queen Victoria (from 1837 to 1901). Furniture that was not produced within these two periods or that does not strictly follow the respective canons of these styles should be seen as a further development and referred to as being in the *Louis XV style* or the *Victorian style*. Other furniture may display a more or less distant relation to an original concept or style. Common sense dictates that such furniture should be recognized at the very most as being derived from a style. It may thus be said that a

46
Interior of the house belonging to the photographer, J.-B. Martel, Artillerie Sreet, Québec City, April 19, 1931. Photograph by J.-B. Martel.
Furnishings take on their true sense when they are viewed as part of a period interior. A rich discourse is revealed by the interior decoration of various social classes, particularly when furnishings are studied from a synchronic perspective, that is, according to social class, and from a diachronic viewpoint, or with respect to a sequence of periods and movements.

47
Chairs
If there is any one piece of furniture that reflects every movement, every style and every social level, it must be the chair. These examples, belonging to Québec's national collection, represent the following styles: French Louis XIII (yellow birch) and Louis XV (yellow birch); British Neoclassicism, in the form of a Windsor chair (yellow birch and pine); Victorian Revivals (black cherry); and the Pre-Modernism of the Reform movement, in the form of a small Thonet bentwood chair (yellow birch).

PERSONAL ACCOUNT

The Antique Dealer

I have been working as an antique dealer and cabinetmaker in the country for over 40 years now. When I began, back in 1953, I was only 19 years old. Old furniture and old objects from every period and in every style have passed through my hands. I'll tell you a secret: every single purchase I have made from the very beginning, and every sale as well, has been marked down in a register. It records thousands of pieces of furniture. Everything is there.

I was born into carpentry, into the woodworking crafts, and grew up among old things. The Du Saults arrived at Écureuils, not very far from here, in 1640. It was my maternal grandfather, Alfred Petit, who introduced me to the art. I was the only boy in the family. At the age of about four or five, even before I went to school, I would go on walks with him and he taught me to understand and love wood. He was an inventive man. He often told me, "If someone is able to make something, I can do it too." He constructed houses, made furniture and built vehicles. The town of Grand-Mère has a large woodworking shop that he opened with his father-in-law at the beginning of the century. Together, they did the finishing work on Saint-Paul's Church in this town and it's a real monument. He had a fine workshop. I have kept all his equipment and hand tools of all sorts, including a jack plane, a smoothing plane and an adjustable rebate plane. My workbench belonged to my grandfather's grandfather. It has followed me everywhere — it's precious. In my family, the carpenter tradition goes back five generations. My grandfather also followed farm auctions. I remember him buying a richly carved black walnut table. "You can't imagine how beautiful this piece will be once it's restored," he whispered in my ear.

I never really decided to be an antique dealer. In 1953, our old parish priest, who had lived in Deschambault for 40 years, left the village. I began to feel concerned about what would happen to certain cultural goods and works of art in the care of the churchwardens. I had Gérard Morisset come to find out how much I should expect these articles to be worth. It was then that I met Émilie Leclerc, an experienced antique dealer from Québec City. I myself was a cabinetmaker. I practised my trade by finishing houses. After the war, everyone wanted kitchen cabinets and a bathroom. Madame Leclerc, knowing that I lived in an old village and being aware of my interest in history and heritage, asked me to keep my eyes open and pick up any items that seemed interesting to me. Word got out. Shortly afterwards, I was asked the same thing by the Montréal antique dealers, Baron, Breitman and Cogan, some of whom had been in business since the Great Depression. In 1954, I was able to buy the old presbytery and I restored it meticulously to make it into my workshop and warehouse. I continued my cabinetmaking work in homes, but at the same time I was buying and restoring old furniture. More and more professionals and furniture lovers came to visit me. Demand was strong. Eventually, in 1966, I gave up finishing houses and opened my own antique shop on the main street of the village. To start I acquired the collection of a reputable Neuville antique dealer, Hélène Gagné, who was like a second mother to me. I then extended my collecting territory to Québec City.

There's some good and some bad in everything, whether it's painting, sculpture or music. The same thing applies to furniture. In the 18th century, people had beautiful furniture. The colony remained under the influence of the Louis XIII style. The Louis XIV and Louis XV styles did not have much success on the shores of the St. Lawrence. In the course of my career, I have not seen very many pieces belonging to these styles. In the countryside, it was the simple geometric shapes of Louis XIII that continued to appear in well-made furniture that was nicely balanced but perhaps a little heavy. Having examined and compared them, I can say that Québec furniture from this period was better crafted and made more carefully than the furniture found in the French countryside at the same period and even later.

In the 18th century, pine and butternut were the sorts of wood used the most. Jean Palardy, whom I knew well, said that the oldest country furniture was in maple and yellow birch, which are hardwoods. After the Conquest, furnishings became more refined. The British liked comfort. Storage furniture had to have tight closures. The British introduced dustboards between the drawers in commodes and used panelled backs instead of tongued and grooved planks, which shrink as they dry and allow dust to get inside. In this period, the pegged mortise-and-tenon joint was still used, but the technique became more refined, as did the dovetail technique. Moulding also improved, offering more orderly curves. Louis XIII furniture is sometimes lacking in balance and symmetry.

I believe that the meeting of the two cultures was a source of enrichment for us, with respect to both house construction and furniture. The lovely *Québécois* house, so refined and comfortable, appeared after the Conquest. The single-room dwelling disappeared. With the arrival of the British, an orderliness of some sort was established. Interiors began to be divided so that people could have rooms to themselves with a certain intimacy. The British are individualists. We imitated them.

I've had Chippendale furniture, some of it in the Chinese version. I've found Hepplewhite and Sheraton furniture as well, for in the first half of the 19th century the Georgian and Empire styles were favored. This period produced true masterpieces of mahogany veneering. Craftsmen knew how to put crotch grain, heartwood and the fancy figures of burls to good use. The "ostrich feather" figure — known as flame in Europe — is a good example of the way this skill was mastered.

In the country, people produced quite special versions of furniture in the British spirit, using pine and butternut. Grondines, the village neighboring mine, must have had excellent cabinetmakers, judging by the amazing pieces I've found there. The houses are also lovely, with their finishing details. I have found five or six chests of drawers in the classical manner, dating from the 1830-1840 period, inlaid with flower-bouquet and bird motifs in maple, yellow birch and black walnut. In every Québec village, and to an even greater degree, in every town, there were plenty of cabinetmakers and craftsmen who expressed their talent in pieces of furniture that corresponded admirably to the fashions of each period.

There was also a country version of the Victorian style in Québec. Such furniture was distinct from the sophisticated pieces made by manufacturers like Vallières, in Québec City, whose production was intended more for prestigious homes and presbyteries. The village craftsmen who made articles in this style used ordinary wood and imbued their work with a certain humility. Before 1965, antique furniture from this period was not much in demand. Such items didn't sell. An armchair carved with swags of roses might go for 50 or 60 dollars. Since this type of furniture was scarcely 100 years old and collectors had their choice of older goods, there was a preference for traditional handcrafted furniture, which had more meaning in the ideological values of the time. Today, people are looking for objects from the 1920s and 1930s. Collectors have trouble finding anything older. At one time, if someone found an old pine armoire with only its doors in good condition, the person would often buy just the doors. Sometimes I have bought an armoire without doors, realizing that I had bought them separately many years before with no idea of where they came from.

Here in the country, there was very little in the way of furniture in the Arts & Crafts, or Mission, style. However, Eastlake was popular. It was a very architectural style adapted to industry and favoring furniture that was integrated with interior design. In the 1920s, Arthur Perron, who would be almost 100 today, made furniture in this style, drawing his inspiration from the catalogues sent out by P.-T. Legaré. He was the one who told me all this.

Québec City has beautiful furniture and is probably richer than Montréal in this respect. I have come across exceptional pieces there. The capital city was for a long time occupied by a garrison. British soldiers travelled throughout the world when they were posted to the Empire's colonies. Québec City was open to all the continents. I have found several pieces of English furniture there, as well as articles made in China.

My trade has given me the chance to mount a vast collection of tools and hand-forged articles. When I meet an old cabinetmaker, I try to follow him all his life. And when he leaves this world for the next, I attempt to obtain his finest tools, so that they will not be lost.

Today it has become difficult to find beautiful pieces of any type. More than ever, Americans come here in search of them. For a while, I followed auctions on the south shore, in central Québec. Every valuable piece, without exception, left for the United States.

Yes, indeed, a lot of furniture has passed through my hands in the course of my career. If I had listened to Barney Kaine, an old Québec City antique dealer who invited me at the end of the 1950s to buy objects and even borrow money at six or eight percent to stock up on goods, I would be a millionaire today, just like the big Montréal antique dealers…

Jean-Marie Du Sault, antique dealer and cabinetmaker
Deschambault, June 1998

Québec or French provincial armoire is in the *Louis XIII manner* or in the *Louis XV manner* because of certain formal or decorative details that recall these styles. Similarly, the fine maple chests of drawers inspired by English Neoclassicism and patterned on the work of George Hepplewhite (died 1786) or Thomas Sheraton (1751-1806) may be said to be in the *Late Georgian manner*.

Finally, I have chosen the term "simplified" — as in *simplified Queen Anne, simplified Louis XV* or *simplified Jacobean* — for furniture that shows only a rough approximation of the defining features of a certain style. For example, in the industrial era, mass-produced suites for dining rooms, living rooms and bedrooms were systematically given a historic flavor through the techniques made possible with machine-tools. Such furniture borrowed freely from the stylistic heritage of the French and British decorative arts (and, through the commercial promotion of catalogues, was identified as belonging to revivals of all sorts).

Before concluding this brief theoretical overview, it should be pointed out that each style went through a period of transition, during which certain features of the older fashion and the new one could be melded in the same work. Examples of this melding are referred to as "transition furniture."

Dealing with these many facets in an organized way is by no means simple. A researcher must not only impose some order on the many movements and styles that have succeeded one another in Québec but also integrate the different modes of production and varying quality of construction. The material to be studied ranges from handcrafted pieces veneered in exotic wood to slip-shod mass-produced articles, from the brass bed to the chromed kitchen suite, with its vinyl chair seats in once-modish colors that match the Formica tabletop. Certain challenges are presented by an ethnohistorical analysis that takes into account both the synchronic dimension — or factor of social levels — and the diachronic dimension — or chronological sequence.

New ways of looking at and classifying the material must be developed, since such aspects have so far been neglected by art historians, who have tended to focus exclusively on the aesthetic dimension. Meeting these challenges is imperative if justice is to be done to the story of furniture.

As has already been stated, the soul of the Québec nation is a complex one. A community that grows at the crossroads of three great cultures must surely (unless it is crushed by them) benefit from such a historical context. If today Quebeckers feel equally at ease in Paris, Mortagne and Brussels, or London and Edinburgh, or New York, Boston and San Francisco, it is no doubt because their "cultural

48

Chinese cupboard. Lacquered wood and bronze, ca. 1830.
Québec's national collection contains several dozen pieces of Chinese furniture acquired by the Jesuit community and conserved in a fascinating museum based on their religious mission in China. Fieldwork and visits to homes and institutions make it clear that the old furniture of Québec includes items from every corner of the world.

THE EVER-CHANGING STORY OF STYLE 67

genetic" program contains the "chromosomes" and "genes" that favor this feeling of ease. The story of Québec's furniture, like that of its art, reflects a progression towards otherness, towards an eclecticism that welds together the best outside influences with the tastes, manners and technological capacities found at home.

To do justice to the interaction of the many forces that have forged the Québec nation and to account for the way styles combined in different eras, this book organizes the production of furniture into five major movements that echo developments in the history of art and the decorative arts in the West and eventually throughout the world. These categories are: furniture in the classical French manner, Neoclassical furniture, Revival furniture, Pre-Modern furniture and Modern furniture. The Post-Modern style that has characterized the turn of the millennium will be dealt with briefly in the conclusion of the book.

Within each of these great movements, furniture may be read in a number of ways. It may be categorized according to how it was made: by hand at home, by a craftsman in a shop, or mass-produced in a factory. Association with a certain social level may classify it as settlement furniture, vernacular furniture or period furniture. The period-furniture category, based on the specific canon associated with a given reign, government, school or designer, may engender two other categories: furniture in the manner of a given period, inspired largely by the rules of that style, and simplified furniture, retaining only the general lines of a period style. As often occurs when different cultures and countries are studied, this book uses terms that have been specially coined to mark "the architecture of the times" in Québec before the Modern era.

French classicism

During the period of Québec history corresponding to the French Regime, that is from the colony's beginnings to its loss to the British in 1760, the styles that held sway in monarchist France were Louis XIII, from 1610 to 1643, Louis XIV, from 1643 to 1715, Régence, from 1715 to 1723, and Louis XV, from 1723 to 1744. It was Louis XV who, preferring West Indies cane sugar to maple sugar, signed the Treaty of Paris at Versailles in 1763 and, in doing so, signified the abandonment of New France. Canada, as the valley of the St. Lawrence was known then, was part of the vast territory covered by New France. It had a population of over 70 000 settlers and administrators. Its composition and heritage at the time must have made it very much like a French province, situated overseas. As in all the divisions of France during the Ancien Régime, provincial furniture tended to imitate the styles favored by the wealthy. The furniture of the poorer classes was inspired by bourgeois tastes but executed with less attention to principles and rules. It is therefore quite natural that Québec furniture from this period includes pieces that belong to one or other of the categories mentioned above. On the one hand, period furniture decorated the interiors of the colony's prestigious buildings: the convents, schools and hospitals of the religious authorities and the headquarters of public administration, such as the palaces of the governor and the intendant. On the other hand, ordinary people used humble vernacular furniture, very much like that of the French peasants and working classes in Rouen, La Rochelle, Saint-Malo or Mortagne. The furniture produced in New France, clearly belonging to the great movements of French classicism and Baroque, was strongly influenced by the geometric character of the Louis XIII style and the lyricism of Louis XV, with its penchant for volutes, scrolls, curves and serpentine shapes. Defeat at the hands of the British cut the colony off from the mother country to a significant degree, yet the fashion for these two styles, adapted in a regional manner, continued to be followed traditionally until around 1790 and even later in some parts of Québec.

Considering the very diverse origins of the settlers, it is not surprising that the furniture surviving from this time displays the forms and decoration that were popular in various parts of France, especially Normandy, Perche and Brittany.

This colonial production should not be compared with the sumptuous formal pieces made in the homeland's great styles — relentlessly presented in certain French furniture studies taking such an elitist approach that they concentrate only on the type of antique found in the Louvre des antiquaires in Paris. The socio-economic situation of the colony is better taken into account by an approach that includes humbler practices, such as those treated admirably in the two volumes of *Le Meuble populaire*, by Guillaume Janneau and Jacques Fréal, published in 1977.

In France, provincial furniture was usually made of hardwood. Québec furniture in the French manner, strongly marked by regional styles and inspired by French fashions, was generally made of pine and butternut, materials that were light and easily worked. The work of Québec cabinetmakers sometimes combined the influences of several French provinces in a single item. The furniture from this period now found throughout Québec is fairly representative of what was being produced in the administrative divisions of the Ancien Régime, especially in the Paris region and in the north-west of France. Since these various provincial canons followed their own evolution in New France, it is appropriate to use the label *New France* style for the furniture produced from the colony's founding, in 1603, to 1790.

BRITISH AND QUÉBEC NEOCLASSICISM

The second period studied, covering the years 1790 to 1840, corresponds to what is generally accepted as the Neoclassical period. To place this stylistic movement in a Québec context, I have labelled it *Constitutional*, since the Constitutional Act of 1791, which created the first parliament in the Americas, instituted a political framework that was maintained until the Act of Union, in 1841. The dates for this period thus very closely match those delimiting the beginning and end of the Neoclassical movement in North America. Almost everywhere in the Western world, from the last quarter of the 18th century to the middle of the 19th century, there was a fascination with the values of classical antiquity and the stylistic orthodoxy nourished by contemporary archaeological discoveries was taken very seriously. In France, the movement commenced under Louis XVI (1774-1793), continued during the post-Revolutionary Directoire period (1793-1797) and encompassed the Empire style under Napoleon Bonaparte (1800-1814) and the Restoration style under the Bourbons (1815-1830), that is, during the rule of Louis XVI's two brothers, Louis XVIII, from 1814 to 1824, and Charles X, from 1825 to 1830. In Great Britain, the Late Georgian style (1760-1800) was dominated by furniture makers who also drew inspiration from ancient Greece and Rome. The Neoclassical taste and manner were made better known through treatises published by designers such as Robert Adam (1728-1792), George Hepplewhite (died in 1786), Thomas Sheraton (1751-1806) and Thomas Chippendale (1718-1770), who was deeply influenced by Chinese styles. English Neoclassicism continued on in the Regency style, which lasted from 1800 to 1820, corresponding more or less to the rule of the Prince of Wales, the future George IV, who replaced his father, George III, in 1811 when the older king had become too ill to exercise power. George IV was succeeded by his brother, William IV, who reigned until 1837, when Victoria came to the throne. During this period, British Neoclassicism dictated the precepts of good taste in the Western world by brilliantly adapting the French repertoire. At the same time, Great Britain identified its neighbor on the other side of the English Channel with the spirit of Revolution and saw it as an enemy to be vanquished.

In the United States, the fashion was for a mixture of French and British styles. The Federal style, born during the Thirteen Colonies' momentous struggle for sovereignty and independence, combined the aesthetics of George Adam, the English cabinetmaker, with those of the French Louis XVI style. Admiration for France, which had supported the Colonies in their struggle for freedom from the British yoke, found expression in the *Directoire-Sheraton* style, also known as *Early American*.

There were also changes in the furniture of Québec during this turbulent period in both Europe and North America. Furniture makers continued to find inspiration in the old French sources. Although politically orphaned after the defeat of 1759, Québec still had cultural attachments with France. Father Jérôme Demers (1774-1853) and François Baillairgé (1759-1830), two key figures in the decorative arts, were representative of those who expressed their enthusiasm for the values of French Neoclassicism through their work, while integrating aspects of the British style. After 1790, the flow of British immigrants became increasingly stronger. The newcomers rapidly took control of business and trade. Trying their luck in the colonies, they liked to surround themselves with goods that were similar in style and make to those in the country they had left. Many of them brought furniture with them, while others had such articles made by craftsmen who had themselves arrived only recently.

One of the repercussions of the American Revolution was the flight of the Loyalists. These people, who had remained loyal to the monarchy and refused to accept the Thirteen Colonies' new republican sovereignty, fled north to resettle in British North America, whose territory now included Québec, still under the control of a garrisoned army. Many of these quite conservative newcomers chose to settle in the St. Lawrence Valley.

Québec furniture of the time reflected this intermixing and developed cross-cultural adaptations in a Neoclassical vein. Composite period furniture combining features of the three dominant cultures began to be made in the St. Lawrence Valley. Vernacular furniture continued to show the influence of the previous period but borrowed the Neoclassical values of elegance and restraint, expressed in a certain lightness, balanced design and symmetry. An article's proportions and decorative references might derive from any one of the three major cultures. The originality of Neoclassical Québec furniture lies in an unpretentious ability to blend these distinct sources of inspiration elegantly, reflecting the position in which the people of Québec found themselves — at the crossroads of three cultures. Interpreting these cultures with creativity and inventiveness, they produced a new type of furniture, both vernacular (in pine or

49 to 52
Four stylistic values expressed in architecture
Domestic architecture clearly mirrors the sequence of movements and styles. The Sifroy-Roy house (Beaumont, ca. 1730) represents the rural French provincial tradition in the style of New France. The residence belonging to the notary, Amable Morin (1793-1877), (Saint-Roch-des-Aulnaies, ca. 1840) is a magnificent example of the Neoclassical vernacular Québec house in the Constitutional style. The country house built for a Mr. Gurd (Montréal, ca. 1885) in a Confederative style expresses the romantic values of the Revival era. Finally, the sumptuous residence of W. R. Miller (Montréal, ca. 1890) displays the integration of Pre-Modernist principles and the ideas of the British Reformers at the end of the 19th century. Every style had architectural impact in a broad range of social levels.

53 to 56
Four Stylistic Values in Furnishings
Furniture design is influenced by major movements in the decorative arts. Bedroom in the New France style showing French influence, Charleville manor, Boischâtel, Côte-de-Beaupré: tester bed and *arbalète*-fronted commode, 18th century; Neoclassical furnishings in the Constitutional style, sleigh bed and chest of drawers with column-shaped corner posts, Chapais house, Saint-Denis, Kamouraska, ca. 1850; Revival-era bedroom furniture in the Confederative style, Sir George-Étienne Cartier house, Montréal, ca. 1870; foot of bed with scroll decoration and chest of drawers with fumed oak finish in the Pre-Modern style, Garneau house, Québec City, ca. 1900.

butternut) and period-style (in mahogany and hardwood). In the United States and Québec, the values of Neoclassicism remained important in the following period and continued to show up until 1880 in the form of revivals inspired by ancient Greece and Rome or influenced by the Empire style.

Revivals

The Revival era is the label chosen to identify the third period in the story of movements and styles in the furniture arts of Québec. For the purposes of the present study, this period is considered to extend from 1840 to 1890. Since Québec's links with this important movement in Western art germinated and matured in the period during which the two nations that made up Canada entered a confederation, it is proposed that the Revival era in Québec be referred to as Confederative. The term emphasizes the fact that the two communities forming Québec in the second half of the 19th century shared a taste for such styles, at a time when the country's furniture makers were showing great mastery of their art.

Revivalism was born of a philosophical and spiritual movement led by a man called Victor Cousin (1782-1867). This theorist espoused the idea that excellence could be attained by taking what was best from every system of thought or creativity. New production techniques encouraged a fashion for pastiche and imitation, which was also influenced by people's expanding curiosity and desire to bring the reassuring values of ancient times to the thinking and art of living of their own times. In the decorative arts, the dominant features of every era and every civilization were promoted, and each nation was drawn to the periods and symbols with which it most identified. The rapidly growing bourgeoisie lived in what might be termed decorative theatre; the interiors of their houses were like exhibition halls, displaying a combination of styles from different chapters in the history of art. It was an age of historic romanticism.

In France, the Revival movement started during the reign of Louis-Philippe (1830-1848), but came into full bloom under Napoleon III (1848-1871), continuing on for a few decades after the fall of the Second Empire and the episode of the revolutionary Commune. The movement borrowed elements from the nation's history, favoring the styles of the Renaissance, Louis XV and Louis XVI, which was also known as Louis XVI-Impératrice, because of the admiration expressed by the Empress Eugénie, Napoleon III's wife, for Marie-Antoinette. Another source of inspiration was England, which had maintained royal traditions and still supported and aided the European aristocracy in difficult times.

The influence of Japanese, Chinese and Arab styles are discernible throughout this period, with its penchant for natural themes. Ornamentation on beds and sideboards combined bamboo motifs with carved roses and birds. At the same time, still lifes with fish and game were in vogue. In Britain, this period corresponded with Queen Victoria's reign, which lasted from 1837 to 1901 and which was remarkable for being not only one of the longest in the history of the monarchy but also one of the most prosperous for the country. British styles at this time also looked backward, seeking inspiration in a medieval past that people identified with readily. As in the 17th and 18th centuries, the Gothic style returned to the fore. The Jacobean, William and Mary, and Queen Anne styles were revived. Queen Victoria, who wished to restore relations with France, reciprocated French interest in England by favoring the Napoleon III style and its references to the past.

The United States, now a fast-growing nation, was influenced by both Second Empire and Victorian styles but added a personal touch often inspired by the French furniture makers who had established businesses in the country's large urban centres and were well acquainted with Parisian fashions. Workshops and factories indulged a great enthusiasm for Naturalism and the Renaissance. There was an overwhelming demand for furniture with spiral, ball and spindle turnings in the Renaissance Revival style, which was already popular in Louis-Philippe's France and Victorian England. This fashion soon spread to the St. Lawrence Valley. All these romantic, history-themed aesthetic trends were shown to the public in world's fairs, which drew increasing numbers of visitors after the resounding success of the first one held in London's Hyde Park in 1851. Goods began to be marketed through catalogues sent out by manufacturers, wholesalers and retailers, and this

printed promotional material grew increasingly elaborate. As a general rule, each era sees the introduction of furniture that fulfils new functional roles in the interior of a house, and the Revival period was no exception.

Pre-modernism

The term Pre-Modernism is used in this book to designate the period between 1890 and 1920, corresponding essentially to what is often referred to as the Belle Époque (1870-1914) or Edwardian period. The reigns of monarchs and political forces began to lose their aptness as labels for chronological stages in the development of the arts. Instead, movements developed around avant-garde aesthetic notions that were initiated and promoted by certain artists and theorists. Their imaginative ways of thinking won public favor and produced stylistic periods that spread throughout the entire Western world. At this time, the furniture world was influenced by two tendencies. The first one, which was innovative in every respect, was driven by designers who often worked together in groups to develop, produce and market furniture that was crafted individually or in limited series. Much of this well thought-out furniture was made to order for the upper middle class. These designers had remarkable visibility in moneyed and cultivated circles, and they profited from the influence they enjoyed there; they rapidly became well known through generous press coverage, attractive publications and their presence in popular exhibitions and fairs, which were always attended by the design critics of the day.

A number of figureheads dominated this innovative trend. A Belgian, Victor Horta (1961-1947), is considered to have initiated the *Art Nouveau* style (1900-1930) with the villa he built in Brussels in 1893; the Frenchman Hector Guimard (1867-1942) is best known for his penchant for plant-like ornamentation, especially on the cast-iron archways and railings decorating the entrances of Paris metro stations; another Belgian, Henry Van de Velde (1863-1957), designed furniture that was free of any superfluous adornment. Émile Gallé (1846-1904) and Louis Majorelle (1859-1926) were two French furniture makers who loved shapes inspired by nature. All of these men were famous as members of the Art Nouveau school; the principles they espoused spread through Europe and influenced both handcrafted and industrial production in North America. In this new style, ornamentation was often created by the form of the furniture itself. Many elements were borrowed from the civilizations of the East and Far East (Northern Africa, Turkey and Japan). Nature, and especially plant life, inspired inventive and imaginative decorative motifs in the shape of vines, tendrils, blossoms and seaweed, but furniture was also graced with the forms of lithe female figures with long flowing hair. Curves and double curves in the Baroque and Rococo manner were reinvented with unprecedented elegance.

Parallel to this rather lyrical style, there developed another, more geometric one. It had begun somewhat earlier but already showed clear signs of the simplified lines and theoretical rationalism of the Modern period that would follow. This movement sprang from the ground-breaking work of Englishman William Morris (1834-1896) and his group of designer-craftsmen. Inspired by the Gothic Revival style advocated by John Ruskin, Morris soon became the champion of a return to medieval craftsmanship and the functional simplicity of the furniture associated with it. The trend he started in the late 19th century to promote manual work and the use of local materials became the *Arts & Crafts* movement (1880-1910). Despite its basis in an idealization of the past, this movement actually heralded the simple lines of modern Minimalist Functionalism. Morris also intended that his art should belong to the people and be made by and for them. This Western movement, with its somewhat static forms, was adopted by a Scotsman, Charles Rennie Mackintosh (1868-1928), as well as by U.S. designers Frank Lloyd Wright (1867-1959), Charles Greene (1868-1957) and his brother Henry Greene (1870-1954).

The avant-garde designers' influence was felt to some degree in all the decorative arts but especially in the furniture industry both in Europe and the United States. It was an era of efficient marketing, directed at an urban population that was undergoing rapid demographic growth on either side of the Atlantic, and this favored the mass production and distribution of furniture that the general public could afford. Such furniture no doubt is of more interest to an ethnologist concerned with the synchronic aspect of design and interior decoration — that is, an analysis based on levels of society — than it is to the art historian who prefers to deal only with movements suited to works written for an elite readership.

The Arts & Craft style was taken up in the United States and given a radically simplified form by Gustav Stickley (1857-1942), as well as by imitators and competitors who followed in his wake. These people eventually turned the style into an industrialized one, which spread rapidly under the name of the Mission style. An example of such furniture was the Morris Chair, an oak armchair with an adjustable reclining back. It came in an infinite variety of models manufactured either in small series — in which case, they were relatively well made — or mass-produced for the purpose of flooding the market. Interest in archaic British furniture was also kindled by a book entitled *Hints on Household Taste*, a best-seller promoting a return to basics in interior decorating, published in 1868. The author, Charles Locke Eastlake (1836-1906), was to give his name to a movement that would sweep through all of North America. The Eastlake style called for simplified industrial goods, adapted to the limitations of machine tools. The result was somewhat plain furniture with straight lines and minimal decoration consisting of fine grooving, fluting or appliqués moulded out of aggregate. The fashion spread through North America like wildfire and Québec, too, was caught up in it. The furniture proposed by this movement, in stark contrast to the cumbersome Revival styles of the previous period, was ideally suited to mass production. William Godwin (1833-1886), another British citizen concerned with furniture reform, started the *Art Furniture Movement*, which favored sturdiness, simple design and tasteful machine-produced goods. Along with others, he took part in the *Aesthetic Movement*, whose members advocated educating the public to appreciate a lighter style, restrained decoration and a certain Japanese-influenced approach to furniture.

The increasingly close interaction between Art Nouveau and the unfettered merchandising of the era is reflected in the story of Michael Thonet (1796-1871) of Austria. He became well known as a furniture maker in 1842 and soon found himself at the head of a large and lucrative business. His innovation was to take wood, steam-bend it into parts for furniture, especially chairs, and ship the product out for assembly near sales outlets. Thonet set up factories in a number of places, some of them in North America. The models produced in this manner enjoyed great popularity. The bistro chair — light, solid and economical, with a cane seat and elegant, clean lines — is still much appreciated today. Thonet inspired numerous imitators.

The Art Nouveau style of the time gave prominence to avant-garde artistic conventions that made clever use of curves and countercurves. This type of decoration was perfectly suited to iron furniture, including chairs but especially beds, adorned in some cases with brass or cast-iron elements. The delicate openwork of the headboards and footboards, with their slender, flowing lines, gave the effect of lace. The same innovative stylistic precepts governed the design of brass beds (actually brass-plated), which became the rage in the northeast of the continent. The lyrical, Baroque-influenced lines of these various items were nourished by the same stylistic spirit, arising from the then-fashionable aesthetic and social philosophy which held that everyone, regardless of social class, should be able to enjoy beautiful furniture. This era also saw the birth of the concept of producing goods that could be afforded by ordinary people, who were now offered the Kodak camera, the stereoscope, the kerosene lamp and the sewing machine.

In this time of transition and of bold innovation on the part of a few reformers, the relationship between Art Nouveau and industry encouraged the fashion for wicker and woven plant-fibre furniture, which became popular among all classes of society. This exotic style soon became established and proved long-lived. It continued into the following period, first in verandah furniture and then in drawing room furniture both in town and country houses, and its producers regularly adapted its lines to trends in interior decoration.

After 1880, industrial Revival-style oak furniture became common. The town of Grand Rapids, in Michigan, had large reserves of oak trees, which were native to the Midwest, and used this natural advantage by specializing in the production of furniture suites. The regional industry supplied goods to Chicago, which had just been rebuilt after the terrible fire of 1871. The Chicago companies Sears Roebuck and Montgomery Ward influenced taste by distributing large, attractive catalogues. Sent to every home, the mail-order catalogue became the second most popular book after the Bible. The entire continent, even in the most remote corners, was solicited by these merchants who had mastered the latest techniques for marketing consumer goods. The promoters of Grand Rapids were soon imitated in other states by a number of industrialists hoping for their share of the profits generated by catalogue sales.

The production of oak furniture was dominated by three stylistic tendencies. The first was the Art Nouveau manner, embodied in suites of furniture or individual items such as tables, chairs, sofas and writing desks with sinuous lines and elegant curlicues. The second was the Mission style, a simplified U.S. version of Arts & Crafts that thus owed something to the spirit of William Morris and his love of medieval forms. The third tendency was characterized by a somewhat diluted Revivalism, inspired by both the U.S. Colonial style and the great European traditions, ranging from the Renaissance to the 18th century. North of the border, Québec and particularly Ontario were quick to fall in step and eagerly adopted these North American models, which could be adapted to different markets depending on the quality of the goods manufactured. In both places, there sprang up businesses specialized in furniture either in the Arts & Crafts—Mission manner or the geometrical Eastlake manner, combining mechanical-gouge decoration with turned or moulded ornamentation strongly influenced by the Aesthetic Revival style of William Godwin. Some furniture businesses drew inspiration from the other aesthetic trends of the 19th century. In Québec, links with France made it inevitable that the canons of Art Nouveau would color a whole segment of our industrial production in this prolific period. Québec also experienced the rage for wicker and brass furniture and several of its businesses catered to this vogue. Over the past two decades, the somewhat uneven products of this period have begun to be marketed as cultural goods and antique objects. The period is a prelude to the Modern era and its production gives a preview of the stylistic, aesthetic, functional and commercial trends introduced by the 20th century.

57
The interior of a 20th-century collector's home
Since the interwar era, people who are aware of furniture's heritage value have been collecting and meticulously restoring articles from various periods in the history of the decorative arts in Québec. These enthusiasts provide museums with donations of all sorts for the benefit of future generations.

Modern furniture

The Modern style grew naturally out of the Pre-Modern period just described and developed certain of its characteristics even further. Both styles encompassed numerous new aesthetic trends that gave rise to various innovations in product types and modes of production, which in turn opened the way to the use of novel materials. The idea that production should be adapted to a wide range of tastes and budgets fostered an unprecedented rapidity in the rate at which changing fashions followed one another and thus generated profits for the industry. For the purposes of this book, the Modern period in the history of Québec art is considered to have lasted from 1920 to 1960. The period has received detailed analysis in a monograph entitled *L'avènement de la modernité culturelle au Québec*, written by Esther Trépanier and Yvan Lamonde (Institut québécois de la recherche sur la culture, 1986).

This period was marked by an increasing number of furniture trends that became ever more international with respect to both the production and distribution of goods. The search for comfort and a concern for ergonomics took on an importance unequalled since the Renaissance. Experimentation with new materials made possible unusual forms that grew out of attempts to adapt furniture to the human body; this was part of a quest for increased functional efficiency within a new art of living that was marked by industrial design, based on the aesthetic and functional values that ruled mass production. Although its first stirrings could be detected in the Pre-Modern period, the Modern movement truly came into its own with two trends that influenced the dynamics of furniture design.

The first of these trends, like so many before it, drew inspiration from all sorts of periods in the history of the decorative arts in Europe and the United States. A historical air was given to suites of furniture for the living room, dining room and bedroom, including occasional tables, various types of chairs, writing desks and solid bureau bookcases, often with veneers and inlay. Such items were not all of the same quality. Some were well finished, sturdy and attractive, while others show the signs of assembly-line mass production. The United States and Canada enthusiastically adopted this return to a more or less reinvented past and a somewhat diluted Revivalism. The printed material distributed by Canadian and Québec manufacturers and retailers between 1920 and 1950 give an excellent idea of the type of merchandise offered to the general public, with more luxurious versions intended for the upper middle class. Anyone working their way through the voluminous general catalogues published by Canada Manufacturers Limited during this period will find ample evidence of how important history-inspired furniture was to Ontario, which had begun to export goods to the St. Lawrence Valley. The catalogues put out by P.-T. Legaré demonstrate that Québec retailers were also attracted by these styles. Another source of information on this tendency in marketing is a directory entitled *American Manufactured Furniture. A Complete Guide to Furniture Produced in the 1920s*, published in the Schiffer Books for Collectors series in 1996. With the Great Depression, starting in 1929, many of the North American factories catering to the vogue for history-inspired furniture were forced to shut down, but the style nevertheless became fashionable once again after World War II.

A similar popularity was enjoyed by Colonial furniture in the northeast of the continent. The fashion started in the interwar period and at first involved authentic pieces, which were much sought-after by collectors, but went on to include reproductions made by small- and medium-sized industries. The Colonial style enjoyed a revival in the 1950s and is still with us. It is easy to understand how people had a strong interest in their material past in the 1920-1930 period, when the unbridled nationalism that had taken hold in all the world's communities came to a head, with each group seeking to emphasize the purity of its ethnic and cultural origins. From the beginning of the 20th century onwards, museums in the United States presented a number of exhibitions on Colonial furniture. In 1915, Wallace Nutting began to publish a series of books which became particularly popular between 1928 and 1933, with the release of his *Furniture Treasury*, illustrated with some five thousand drawings.

In Québec, this period was when the search for traditional Québécois furniture began in earnest. Departments in technical schools specializing in furniture and cabinetmaking, as well as a large sector of the École du meuble de Montréal, turned for inspiration to this magnificent heritage. During the 1960s and 1970s, when Québec was in the throes of the Quiet Revolution, the attraction of traditional modes was further heightened by the publication of Jean Palardy's *Les meubles anciens du Canada français* in 1963. A host of craftsmen were inspired to create articles made according to the rules of the art as set down in this book. A glance through issues of the Québec magazine *Decormag* shows clearly how important this imitative movement was.

At the same time that this somewhat commercial trend, with its Revivalist or historic tones, dominated Western culture, a second, truly innovative trend developed. It took two different forms. In one form, it favored traditional cabinetmaking techniques such as inlay, lacquer, veneering with rare or precious wood and the use of fine materials, including leather, natural fibres and metals like iron and brass. This approach produced elegant forms, whose symmetry, curves, circles and decorative elements recall past styles; storage furniture, in particular, evoked

Louis XV and Louis XVI styles, while chairs owed something to Directoire and French Restoration styles. Such furniture offered rather classic shapes and indulged in a certain opulence, with a preference for parallelepiped volumes and for sharp, rounded or cut-off corners. Other geometrical shapes were also favored, with the circle and octagonal showing up in mirrors and tabletops. France was the first to develop this modern language of interior decorating and championed it boldly in the age of jazz and Cubism. In 1925, Paris held a world's fair called the Exposition Internationale des Arts Décoratifs et Industriels Modernes, which showcased a new aesthetic discourse that became known as Art Deco, because of the fair. The movement spread to numerous countries, where it was adopted in original ways. In this period, many craftsmen, concerned by the way their art was diffused, agreed to work for large stores. At the same time, the notion of furnishing a home had become inextricable from the whole idea of interior decorating, and certain artists began to work as interior designers and decorators. In Québec, this approach was taken by several architects and decorators, most of whom worked in the Montréal area. The architect Robert Blatter is an example. In France, people like Maurice Dufresne (1876-1955), Paul Follot (1877-1941), Jacques Émile Ruhlman (1870-1956), Louis Süe (1875-1968) and André Mare (1885-1932) led this movement, which was promoted by schools as prestigious as the venerable École Boulle in Paris. It was there that the cabinetmaker Jean-Marie Gauvreau, the founder of Montréal's École du meuble, did his apprenticeship between 1926 and 1930, when the movement was at its peak. He shared his enthusiasm for the new trend in the decorative arts in his 1929 book, *Nos intérieurs de demain*, in which he emphasized the movement's Parisian roots and, in passing, praised the talents of his teachers. Supported by other talented designers who were captivated by the avant-garde, Gauvreau became a standard bearer for the new style and its adoption in Québec. Here, as elsewhere, the general furniture industry was strongly affected by the movement.

The second form taken by the innovative trend of this period brought a sociological perspective to the decorative arts and furniture, as well as a totally new aesthetic. The proponents of this young movement considered that the Art Deco "traditionalists" profiled above were mistaken in their attachment to artisanal production methods that limited their services strictly to an elite class. They maintained that furniture design should stop resisting the machine and integrate mass-production methods, an argument that had already been made by the followers of the British Art Furniture Movement and the Aesthetic Movement in the 19th century. For these designers, who sought to reach a broader clientele, the most important objectives became simplicity, sturdiness and efficiency, as well as elegance, achieved through an attention to form, proportion and color. A few of those leading this new reforming trend went so far as to claim that "form follows function" and "ornament is squandered work," although such categorical declarations later became more nuanced. The age of industrial design had dawned. It engendered the Functionalist or International style, whose simple geometric lines rapidly gained popularity. Furniture designed in this style retained remarkable aesthetic qualities but was adapted to mass-production techniques. A total rethinking of furniture was expressed in pure forms stripped of any ornamentation, structures of chromed tubing, boldly curved plywood, lacquer, frosted glass and eventually plastic and polyester. Every country experienced its own version of this revolution and there sprang up dynamic schools of thought and schools of design that took the market quite by storm in the late 1930s and especially after World War II. Several designers created true classics, still copied for the market today. A few names stand out in this revolution in the design arts: the Bauhaus school in Germany, with Walter Gropius (1883-1969); Hungarian Marcel L. Breuer (1902-1981), who trained at the Bauhaus and became the creator of the celebrated Wassily chair in leather and chromed-steel tubing; Ludwig Mies Van der Rohe (1886-1969); the Swiss, Pierre Jeanneret, known as Le Corbusier (1885-1965), who with another designer, Charlotte Perriand, created numerous chrome-tubing chairs, including the well-known continuously adjustable chaise longue; the German, Peter Behrens (1868-1940); Alvar Aalto (1898-1976), a Finnish master craftsman who introduced the rest of the world to Scandinavian design through furniture that exploited the flexibility of white birch; Scotsman Charles Rennie Mackintosh (1868-1928), a forerunner of the avant-garde; and Gerrit Thomas Rietveld (1868-1940) of the Netherlands, with his famous red and blue chair. Several of these designers went to work in the United States, with the result that the entire industry in North America was deeply influenced by the thinking of these innovative artists in the Modern movement. In Québec, the new movement was represented brilliantly by those graduating from the effervescent École du meuble during the 1950s and 1960s, as well as by other craftsmen, who had trained abroad. The country's industrialists, some of whom converted to the chrome-tubing furniture widely distributed between 1950 and 1970, took part in the movement by adapting its concepts to the production of cheap imitations of sometimes doubtful quality.

From 1960 to the present, in the period referred to as post-Modern, the movement has been advanced by a cohort of industrial designers and craftsmen whose work has been guided by a concern for comfort, ergonomic standards and an increasingly demanding clientele's need for functional furniture. In Québec, these designers and craftsmen work both locally and on the international scene, exploring audacious forms and, at times, new materials. While Québec is more open than ever to the world's production, it has also set out to conquer new markets, particularly in North America.

58
The integrated collection
Some people express a love of history and heritage, as well as closeness with their ancestors and pride in their roots, by embarking on a long-term project. They buy an old house, restore it according to the rules of the art and then furnish it with articles in keeping the building's period and, as much as possible, the original occupants' social class. Annie Bonhomme and architect Pierre Cantin, of Boischâtel in the Côte-de-Beaupré area, have undertaken the restoration and furnishing of the Charleville manor, a house in the French-influenced style of New France, built in the first half of the 18th century. A great part of their free time is spent searching out and acquiring old objects that correspond to their vision of how the house evolved through time. Decorating an ancestral home means combining historic veracity with respect for contemporary needs and thus reaching satisfactory compromises. The interior of this house reflects the way heritage homes and furnishings are envisioned in Québec today.

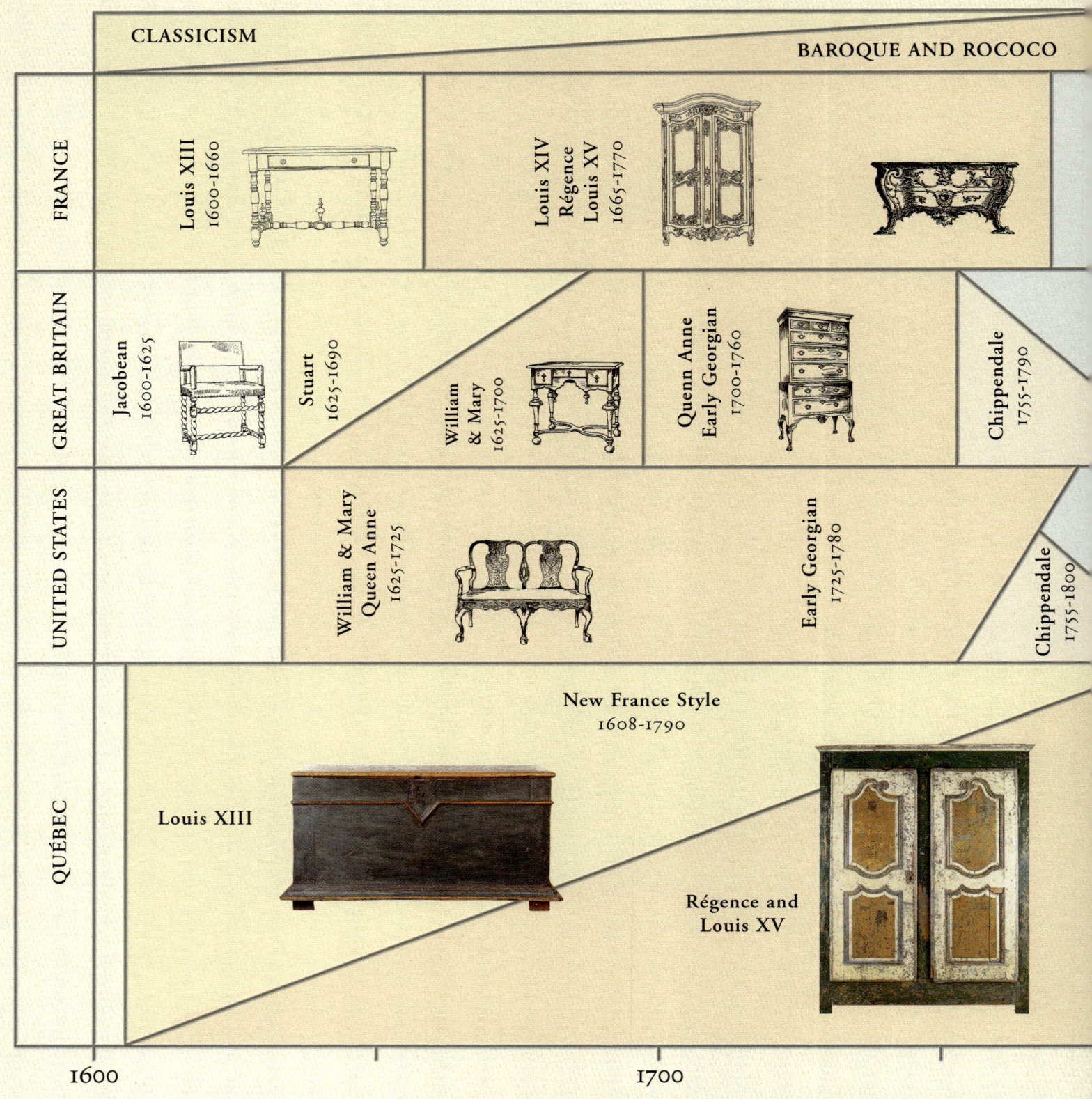

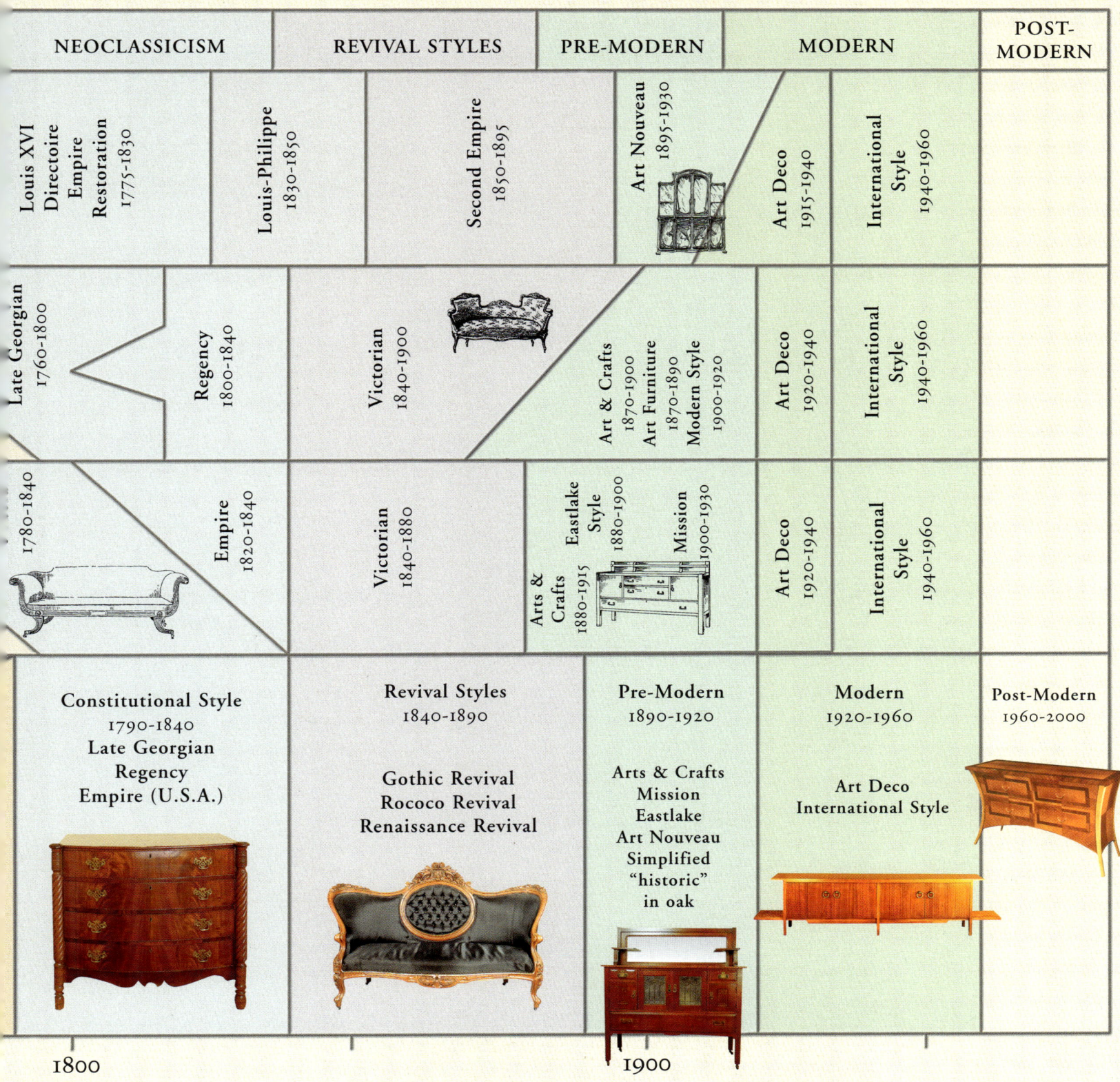

Sources

The history of furniture can be traced through numerous documentary sources: notarized deeds; printed material of all sorts, including newspapers and sales catalogues; iconographic documents of every kind — paintings, engravings, drawings and photographs — and, of course field studies. Oral tradition can sometimes give life to a piece of furniture that has survived the passage of time, placing it both in an era and a setting. These various sources, whose usefulness to science is well summed up in Suzanne Tardieu's scholarly work, *Le Mobilier rural traditionnel français*, can provide researchers with a good picture of the many facets of furniture history.

59
Paintings and drawings are useful iconographic sources for the history of furniture. This scene, *L'atelier du menuisier*, was painted by Firmin Girard (Somme, ca. 1910); although the painting is French, it gives a good idea of a craftsman's workshop at the end of the 19th century.

60
A watercolor by R. S. M. Bouchette, a Québec hero incarcerated by the British authorities. The scene, painted in his Montréal prison in 1838, shows chairs and a table reflecting the Neoclassical values of the 19th century.

Iconographic Sources

Time has spared thousands of diverse documents illustrating various aspects of the history of furniture, such as manufacturing in workshops or factories, distribution and use among different social classes, and the many ways in which the trade was taught.

Among visual documentary sources, paintings and drawings are of prime importance. Artists like Cornelius Krieghoff, Clarence Gagnon and Edmond J. Massicotte are among the many who used their palettes and easels or their burins to produce remarkable works that show us what interiors looked like and, consequently, how they were furnished. The oldest such painting was done in Québec City in 1809 by William Berczy (1744-1813) and represents the Woolseys, a bourgeois family living in the capital; eight family members are depicted, with some of them sitting on Sheraton chairs around a Neoclassical drop-leaf table. The mirror, mantel, floor covering and clothing all belong to the Neoclassical style.

By the middle of the 19th century, the genre painting practised by English landscape painters, who were fond of evoking both city life and the rustic ways of the Québec countryside, enjoyed a certain popularity with Cornelius Krieghoff (1815-1872), a German painter who visited the country. Some of his drawings, which are often of a humorous nature, show rural interiors. The wood stove dominates these rooms, which are generally furnished with a primitive table and crude chairs, surrounded by people having a good time together. Other artists chose to depict the bourgeois interiors of the Belle Époque. The more traditional styles of the country were especially well captured by Edmond J. Massicotte (1875-1929), who was provided with material by his brother Édouard Zotique, an archivist with the City of Montréal. Édouard Zotique Massicotte worked with Marius Barbeau, collecting information on Québec's heritage to make it better known. The artist Edmond J. Massicotte set himself the task of minutely recording the activities, actions and customs that survived in rural areas, as well as the traditional material culture still to be found there. The artist's serious approach and the

meticulously ethnographic character of his documentation are reflected by the hundreds of pencil sketches conserved by the Musée du Québec in copious notebooks. He used this pioneering ethnological work to plan large compositions, which he simplified for effectiveness, as well as to determine the sociological values to be emphasized in his illustration of "ancestral" life. Several of his paintings, such as *La prière en famille* (1924), *La fête des rois* (1926) and *La «grand' demande»* (1921), depict an activity taking place inside a home furnished and decorated in rural tastes. Charles Huot (1855-1930), who painted works like *Le Sanctus à la maison* (1897), worked in the same vein. In the interwar period, a number of artists chose to exploit the folkloric roots of Québec's identity. At the same time that Marius Barbeau was conducting his scholarly research, these artists depicted country life, often concentrating on home activities. The painter André Biéler (1896-1989) was attracted to Île d'Orléans, while Edwin H. Holgate (1892-1977) and

61 to 64

In this painting by William Berczy (1744-1813), presenting the Woolsey family of Québec City in 1808-1809, it is possible to identify a Sheraton armchair, a Late Georgian drop-leaf table and a mantle in the Adam manner. These furnishings were typical of certain Québec homes at the beginning of the 19th century. Such specimens of material culture representing an era or social class are today kept in private and public collections.

THE EVER-CHANGING STORY OF STYLE

65
There is much to be learned about rural furnishings from drawings by Edmond J. Massicotte (1875-1929) such as this one, *La prière en famille*. Even though his compositions were deliberately simplified to make interiors serve as effective backdrops for the ideological message of religious authority at the time, the decors he depicted are not very far from the truth, as is demonstrated by his field drawings, kept in large sketchbooks at the Musée du Québec and in private collections.

66
Watercolor over pencil, by Katherine Jane Ellice (died in 1864), done in 1838. It shows the drawing room in the Beauharnois manor and captures the Neoclassical style of a comfortable bourgeois interior at the time.

67 to 69
Old photographs provide much information about the history of furniture. The upper photograph, by J. G. Parks, shows the dining room in the Louis-Joseph Papineau manor at Montebello in about 1880. The Renaissance Revival dresser, columned sideboard with Neoclassical lines, Hepplewhite armchairs and Eastlake sideboard create a truly eclectic interior. The other photograph is of a Belle Époque drawing room in Québec City. Page 88 shows a photograph of a floor in Zéphirin Paquet's department store in around 1900. Oak and wicker were in style at the time, while sideboards and light chairs with steam-embossed backs were extremely popular items.

Alexander Y. Jackson (1882-1974) were drawn to the Charlesvoix region. Clarence Gagnon is one of the best known of the many artists who specialized in "ethnographic" painting, turning to traditional life for material. After World War II, there were dozens of other artists, including the Bolduc sisters of Baie-Saint-Paul, who gave artistic expression to themes inspired by their own memories, producing art that was much sought-after by collectors.

All of this rich production provides information for the history of furniture and design. In addition to the visual universe of the painter, there are engravings in 19th-century newspapers and magazines from here and abroad, as well as almanac illustrations, which occasionally showed scenes of daily life, and especially country life. Another eloquent example is provided by the fine drawings of traditional life in the Charlesvoix and Kamouraska regions, published in a major article in *Franck Leslie's Illustrated Newspaper* of New York in the spring of 1884.

Photographs are of course one of the best sources of information. The oldest photograph of the interior of a house was taken in the 1860s by the Notman studio in Montreal. It shows two young women working in the main room of a rural home, very likely on Île d'Orléans or at least in the Québec City region. Light from the open window falls on a low buffet with raised panels and on three little rustic chairs with babiche seats. This photograph was followed by a profusion of others, taken by both professionals and amateurs, either to put in family albums or to illustrate

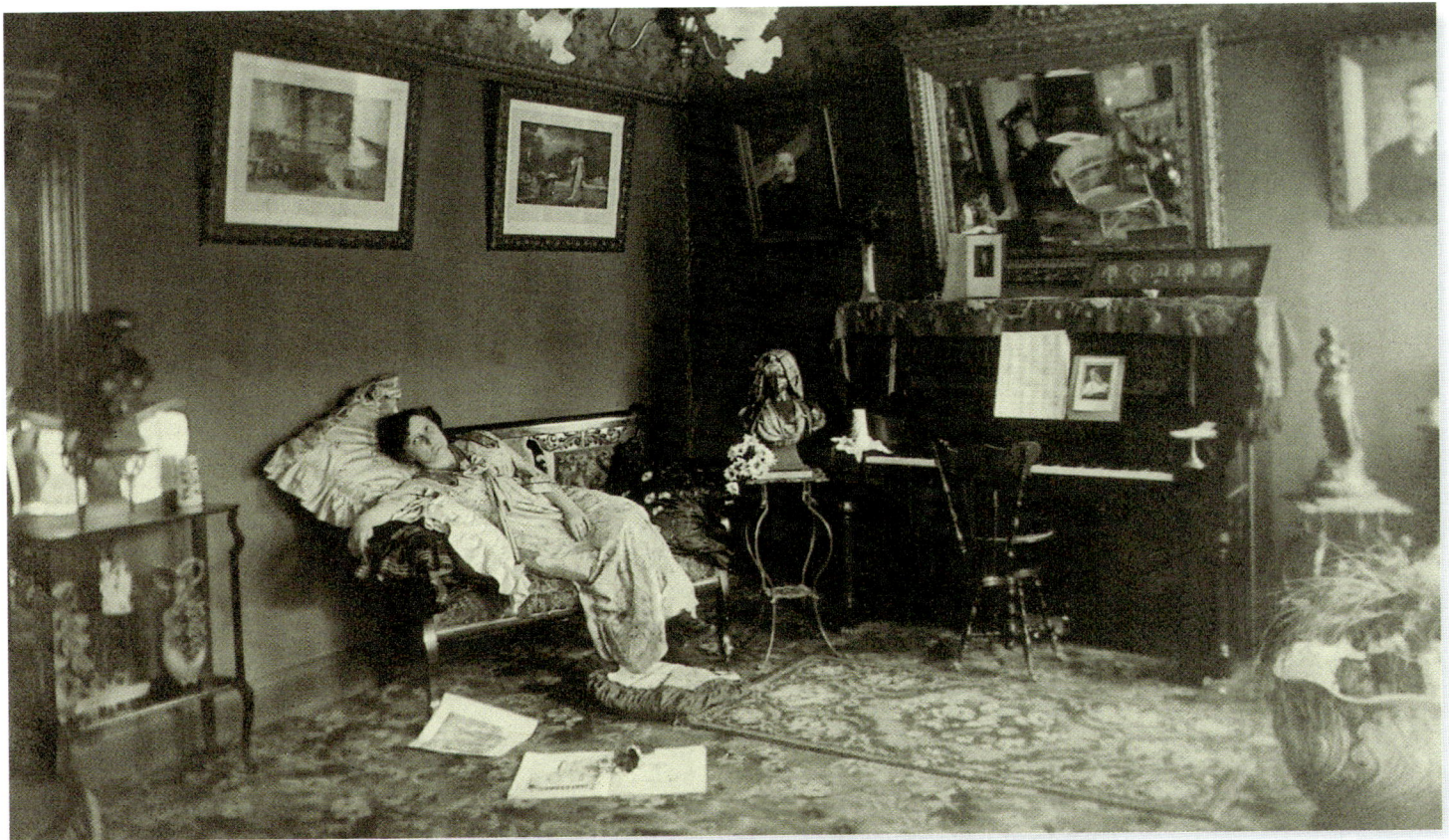

THE EVER-CHANGING STORY OF STYLE

70
Photograph of a rustic interior, possibly on Île d'Orléans, by the Notman Studio of Montréal in around 1860 and probably the oldest picture of interior furnishings taken in Québec. The style is clearly that of New France.

and document the interior decoration of houses and various institutions. For example, in 1906, the Quéry brothers were engaged to record the Gil'Mont estate, owned by Sir Rodolphe Forget, in a photograph album. Copies of this voluminous album are kept in the Salle Gagnon in Montréal's central municipal library and in the National Archives in Québec City. This methodical photographic report shows the exterior and interior of an opulent villa designed in the Arts & Crafts and Mission manner, as well as the estate's numerous outbuildings. The formal rooms are richly furnished in the same styles. The interiors of other bourgeois homes and institutional buildings in both of Québec's major cities were captured in the many photographs produced by the Notman studio in Montréal and the Livernois and Vallée studios in Québec City. This body of work speaks eloquently of the furnishings of the time and several of the photographs are used to illustrate the present book. Further sources of photographic illustrations for this book include the work of the architects Ramsay Traquair and Sylvio Brassard, and the records of other researchers who over the past few decades have conducted ethnohistorical and art history studies on the heritage of Québec furniture and houses. The history of the École du meuble has received considerable attention in this respect. The history of furniture in the Modern era is enriched by the visual contribution made by magazines such as *Decormag* and *Décoration chez soi*, as well as other publications in both French and English from the first half of the 20th century. Snapshots, some of them treasured in family albums, constitute a rich source of documentation that is far from exhausted.

Manuscript Sources

Many notarial records, containing precious information on the articles used to furnish and decorate houses, are safeguarded in Québec's National Archives. In accordance with a practice taken from the *Coutume de Paris*, an inventory of a dead person's belongings was made soon after death so that their value could be divided among the legal heirs. The notary would go to the deceased's house and draw up an exhaustive list of items to be inherited, each one written down on a separate line, with its condition and market value. Preparing these probate inventories was a normal legal procedure from the colony's beginnings to the middle of the 19th century. Since the scrivener generally worked in an orderly and methodical fashion, going from one room to another, it is not too difficult for a researcher to establish where a given object stood in the layout of a house. These documents are also informative with respect to the date at which a type of furniture appeared and how common it became. Certain notaries went so far as to take down details about the item's size, technical features and color.

A similar source of written information is the donation *inter vivos*, which tells us considerably more about domestic life. When homeowners were advanced in years and wished to bequeath their belongings while still alive, they would have a detailed contract drawn up by a notary. Every item to be bequeathed was identified and evaluated, while the heirs' obligations were clearly stated, so that the legators would not be bereft of their belongings or prevented from using them before death. There was a minute description of the beneficiary's duties with respect to providing shelter, clothes, food and transportation for his father and mother, as well as their dependent children if any. Furniture and immovables received the same attention as they did in probate inventories. These sources have been very profitably explored by an entire school of ethnohistorical researchers, working under the guidance of Robert-Lionel Seguin of the Université du Québec à Trois-Rivières. Another researcher, Bernard Audet, has also turned such sources to good account in his remarkable study of material culture in the 18th century, *Avoir feu et lieu dans l'île d'Orléans*.

Notaries' records also contain apprenticeship contracts between master joiners and the young men they trained; this type of traditional training agreement would cover several years. The records very occasionally reveal a contract for making a piece of furniture, specifying the type of wood to be used and the item's form, decoration and color. Much can be learned from probate inventories made after a craftsman's death or the lists drawn up when a workshop went bankrupt; these are full of information on cabinetmakers' tools and equipment, as well as the wood kept in their shops for future use.

Details about interior design and furniture can sometimes be gleaned from passages in diaries or certain letters, such as those of Julie and Louis-Joseph Papineau. Another source is represented by old invoices with personalized headings and commercial postcards related to furniture manufacturing. People who collect these bits of yellowed paper know that they provide very explicit information about orders and deliveries involving producers both here and abroad, making it possible to follow marketing trends in furniture. The full administrative records of a 19th- or 20th-century Québec craftsman or furniture factory would no doubt be extremely informative, but unfortunately the only such documents that could be consulted for this book were the exceptional records of Pierre Drouin and Honoré Roy's Québec City workshop, which were studied by a team led by John Porter. This collection of documents had been in a family's safekeeping and was acquired by Parks Canada in Québec City.

71
Old invoices are interesting for the commercial labels of furniture makers and merchants; they also provide information about distribution networks, the value of articles and numerous other details related to the history of furniture. For some collectors, such documents are a real passion.

72

The sales catalogues published by manufacturers, distributors and large stores constitute a source of precious information about furniture from the last quarter of the 19th century and the 20th century. This is a page from the 1917-1918 issue of P.-T. Legaré's general catalogue, published annually and running to nearly 500 pages. The merchant also published special furniture catalogues from time to time.

Printed Material

Printed material represents another important source of information. Newspapers and, later, various business publications such as yearbooks and trade directories, listed and advertised workshops and factories. Certain of these documents — for example, the periodical *Le mouvement ouvrier* — sometimes related the history of a business. In combination with official decennial census records, they furnish a multitude of facts about Québec production and imports in the 19th and 20th centuries. The liberally illustrated advertisements in these documents make it possible to follow trends in fashion. Establishing a list of these abundant and diverse sources has been the goal of painstaking, patient labor on the part of a number of researchers, including myself, over the past few decades.

Printed catalogues became common in the 1875-1880 period and provide much of our knowledge about furniture from that time. In this early stage of the merchandising era, industries, wholesalers and retailers used catalogues to complement their normal market. The illustrations in the oldest catalogues are done with line work, while by the end of the 19th century half tones started to be used. Color began to appear in the early 1920s, and suites of furniture were shown in interiors, sometimes enlivened with human figures in inviting scenes. The Québec market was widely solicited in this manner, at first by the United States, through Chicago catalogue businesses like Sears Roebuck and Montgomery Ward, and then by Ontario, through Toronto establishments such as Eaton's and Simpson's. In 1871, a fire destroyed Chicago, then the major centre of furniture production. The void left by "The Windy City" was filled by Grand Rapids, in Michigan, catalogue promotion attained new heights as businesses there took full advantage of rail transport, which now made it possible to reach many more customers in every corner of the continent.

Printed material of this type, sometimes found in Québec's secondhand stores and flea markets, provides very useful documentation for researchers interested in modern material culture. In 1910, P.-T. Legaré, a Québec City merchant with outlets in cities and large villages, decided to add furniture to the horse-drawn vehicles and farm equipment he had been offering. His catalogues, both general and specialized in furniture, were distributed for about 50 years, and the some one hundred numbered issues provide a good idea of the industrial production that was in fashion in both urban and rural areas. Like a number of other merchants in this period, P.-T. Legaré obtained his stock from Ontario manufacturers, who had been exporting massively to the St. Lawrence Valley and the Eastern Townships for a long time. This topic is dealt with more thoroughly in an article of mine entitled "De l'utilité des catalogues commerciaux en ethnohistoire du Québec," which appeared in the 1994 issue of the *Cahier des dix*.

I have consulted several hundred of these commercial publications that once circulated in Québec. The wealth of information they contain may be conveyed by the example of the iron and brass bed that was in vogue during the Belle Époque: to evaluate this one piece of furniture, I went through three catalogues put out by Québec industries, each of which presented close to one hundred models. The printed advertisements distributed by a big Québec City department store like Compagnie Paquet Ltée also provide information. Those I consulted from the year 1904, for example, indicate the precise moment in the early 20th century when industrial furniture in the Arts & Crafts, Mission and Art Nouveau styles appeared in Québec.

Censuses taken in the past provide information on the number of businesses established in each municipality, how many workers they employed and the size of each workshop or factory. Trade directories for Québec City and Montréal, as well as for the various regions, were published sporadically at first but eventually came out annually. They enable researchers to establish a list of furniture makers with their business addresses and, to some degree, to follow the evolution of their establishments from year to year. This source is particularly helpful from the beginning of the Revival era on. A number of researchers have used the material contained in censuses to draw up lists of manufacturers and their business addresses. Paul-Louis Martin took this approach in his study of the Québec rocking chair; his book lists manufacturers who were active between 1790 and 1890

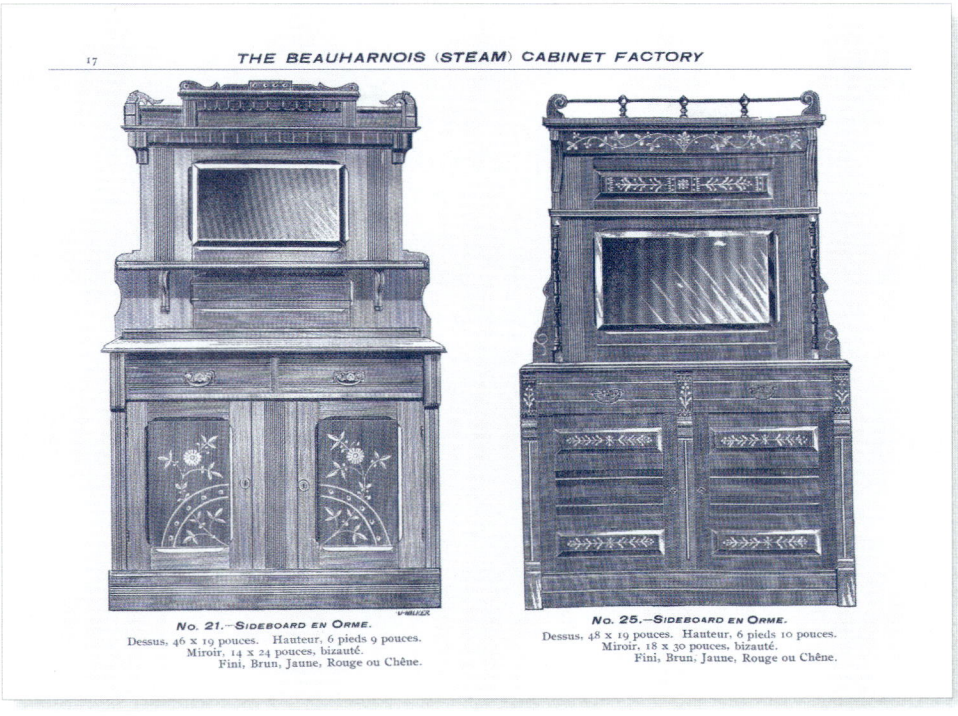

throughout Québec, categorizing them as chair makers, cabinetmakers, turners, furniture makers and upholsterers. As part of a Parks Canada project, Luce Vermette turned her attention to Montréal and Québec City workshops between 1850 and 1870. Daniel Drouin investigated the participation of designers in provincial, international and world's fairs between 1850 and 1900 for his master's thesis at Université Laval. Elisabeth Collard documented the furniture makers of Montréal from 1800 to 1850 in a long, in-depth article published in the May 1974 issue of *Antiques*. Other researchers have made similar use of printed material to advance our knowledge of regions such as Ontario and the Maritimes, both of which exported a quantities of furniture to Québec. Each of these studies makes its own contribution. One of the facts they reveal is that furniture makers formed tightly knit families in which tools and workshops were handed down from one generation to the next. The young men apprenticed to masters came from the same lineage, and often marriages were contracted between the members of furniture-making families.

73-74
A page from the Kilgour brother's Beauharnois Furniture catalogue, ca. 1885. The pictures of Eastlake-style sideboards were engraved by a Montréal artist, John Henry Walker. A page of the 1901 Eaton catalogue showing rocking chairs and various models of the Morris armchair.

P.-T. LEGARÉ

The Furniture King

Pierre-Théophile Legaré was born in 1851 in Charlesbourg, one of oldest centres of settlement in Québec. He was born into a long line of farming families and, working on his father's farm, young Legaré was introduced to hard physical outdoor labor. His father also sold agricultural machinery and consequently the young man learned about business as well as farming. He studied at the Séminaire de Québec and the Collège Sainte-Anne in Sainte-Anne-de-La-Pocatière and then undertook further training in the United States. He married his first wife in 1876 and they eventually adopted 15 children. Two other children were born of a second marriage, contracted in 1903. Throughout his life, this venturous businessman felt close to those who worked the land, and he maintained a model farm at Lake Legaré in the county of Témiscouata. In 1877, at the age of 26, he left his father's farm and business for good and became a representative for Cossitt Brothers of Brockville, Ontario, a firm specialized in the manufacture of ploughing implements.

PIERRE-THÉOPHILE LEGARÉ
(1851-1927)

75
A page from P.-T. Legaré's 1917-1918 general catalogue. Oak furniture was very much in fashion at the time. Advertisements made liberal use of sexual stereotypes, with each figure in a given role.

Legaré enjoyed rapid success at a time when the market was soaring and he was thus able to acquire large Montréal and Ontario firms in the farm-machinery and horse-drawn vehicle sectors, including Dominion Carriage in Montréal. The businessman also chose an opportune moment to become involved in automobile sales, a rapidly expanding sector.

By 1921, at the age of 70, Pierre-Théophile Legaré had become a great philanthropist — as a fervent and generous Catholic, he had been made a Commander in the Pontifical Order of St. Gregory the Great in 1919 — and ruled over what was truly a commercial empire in Québec. He offered an amazing array of merchandise, including everything needed to run a modern farm (at a time when Québec was largely a rural society), everything needed to furnish a farmhouse or a middle-class home in town, every model of horse-drawn carriage and wagon both on wheels and on runners, and makes of cars that were among the most popular on the continent. All these goods were available in 4 main stores, 25 branch stores and 16 warehouses. No fewer than 1 325 local sales representatives worked for Legaré. The firm's headquarters were located in Québec City. Linked by dynamic printed promotional material, its vast network included Montréal, Sherbrooke, Victoriaville, Rimouski, Chicoutimi, Beauceville, Joliette, Lac-Mégantic, Montmagny, Plessisville, Rivière-du-Loup, Saint-Georges in the Beauce and Trois-Rivières, to name but the main towns. The super-retailer was supplied by a great number of businesses in Québec, Ontario and the United States.

THE CATALOGUE AS STORE WINDOW

To stimulate his business, Legaré began to make use of printed advertisements and mail-order sales in the first years of the 20th century. For the next 40 years, he published over 100 catalogues. Some of them have nearly 500 pages and present all the merchandise available; others, less voluminous but equally attractive with their line drawings and photographs, concentrate on horse-drawn vehicles, wood stoves, household accessories, furniture, phonographic equipment and musical instruments. The historical value of the sales catalogues published by P.-T. Legaré, as well as those of other merchants using the same promotional and retailing method in the St. Lawrence Valley, cannot be overstated. They constitute a major source of information about the material culture of Québec from the end of the 19th century on. For the people of that period, catalogues were a way of staying in

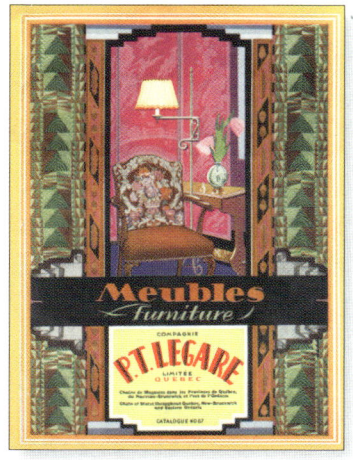

touch with contemporary styles, and this contact had a marked influence on several generations with respect to taste and the art of living. For example, it is possible to follow developments in the Pre-Modern fashion for oak furniture in the "U.S." style simply by studying the furnishings catalogues published by Legaré. The catalogues also reflect the evolution of the Arts & Craft, Mission and Art Deco styles, which were enthusiastically adopted by Québec between 1880 and 1940. The catalogues' presentation of iron beds and wicker articles is equally enlightening.

The scope of Legaré's mail-order service can be conveyed by a few figures. According to a promotional text prefacing a catalogue at the beginning of the 1920s, the Québec City headquarters received or sent out 6 500 to 9 000 letters and orders every day. While the catalogues provide precious information concerning the kind of merchandise offered over several decades and about production and marketing networks — for Legaré signed exclusive agreements with a number of North American manufacturers — they also mirror changes in the art of advertisement and in marketing strategies aimed specifically at people in the country. Attractive color plates very often present the catalogue goods in settings that show how they would look in and around the house, thus showing or suggesting a style of living or a way of decorating. Quite frequently, ethnographers working in the field still find traces of this influence in old homes that were furnished or renovated in these periods. From time to time, Legaré would provide his customers with eloquent photo stories on factory manufacturing techniques, and these are another mine of information for the ethnohistorian.

Pierre-Théophile Legaré died in 1927, at the age of 75, with his business at its zenith. He did not live to see the skies darken above the general store he had nurtured with boundless passion and energy. Powerful Toronto merchants who had been active for several decades in the St. Lawrence Valley, operating almost entirely by mail order, now established themselves in Montréal, setting up true emporiums in opulent, palatial buildings. In the same year that P.-T. Legaré died, Eaton's, whose Montréal store had just opened, launched a vast distribution of its attractive catalogue in French. The Dupuis Frères store then revamped its sales tactics by adopting the same approach and published numerous catalogues filled with temptingly displayed goods. But by then, the Great Depression was at the door.

76 to 79
P.-T. Legaré's Québec City business put out both general catalogues and special furniture catalogues. They make it possible to trace the story of industrial vernacular furniture and how tastes in interior decorating evolved in Québec during the first half of the 20th century. Kitchen, drawing room and bedroom suites were often shown in home settings. These are examples of the catalogues published between 1920 and 1930.

80-81
Catalogues from the 1930s show how Art Deco values were integrated into industrial furniture produced for the general market. Top: page from the 1939 P.-T. Legaré catalogue illustrating drawing room furniture made with chrome tubing, a novelty at the time. Above: illustration of a bedroom suite in the new style, taken from the 1936 catalogue put out by Simons of Montréal. Catalogues were aimed at every social class and promoted furniture intended for every categoriy of household.

Another useful source of information concerning old Québec furniture is represented by advertisements published in trade directories, newspapers and magazines. On the shores of the St. Lawrence, advertising is as old as the press itself. As early as June 28, 1764, the year in which the *Gazette de Québec* was launched, the English merchant Henry Taylor announced that he had just received all sorts of goods from London, including "Lampblack, […] red and yellow Ochre, Litharge, white and red Lead, with different Kinds of Paint." It is more than likely that these various colors were used to paint furniture. Two years later, on June 12, 1766, William Abbott, a Lower Town merchant, used the same newspaper to announce that he had just received a shipment from England and offered "a good Choice of Cabinet Ware, consisting of Mahogany Chairs, Tables, Desks, Commodes, Fire Screens, Looking Glasses, Bed-steads and Furniture, Tea-boards, Waiters and other Articles in the Cabinet and Upholstery Way; and a quantity of Fine Porter in Bottles and Barrels." This was the beginning of 'Britishization,' a process of cultural colonization which affected furniture as much as it did everything else.

Promotional material for furniture became increasingly common throughout the 19th century, as the marketing era came into being and competition among manufacturers and merchants grew. The "distinguished customers" appealed to in both English and French were informed that such-and-such a business or craftsman offered a large assortment of articles in the most fashionable London and Paris styles and at the lowest prices. Advertisements always declared that the workshop was prepared to fill the orders of the most demanding customers for a great variety of items and that their furniture was all manufactured with the greatest care and possessed the most elegant lines; they boasted that their workmen were the most skilled in town; and that they used only dry wood, with the types of wood available sometimes listed. And if a business had won a prize in a local, national or international fair, the advertising insert would be sure to vaunt it, sometimes showing images of the medal or trophy. In many cases, line drawings gave some idea of the style being promoted — whether Rococo Revival, Renaissance Revival, Eastlake, Arts & Crafts or Mission — and reflected new production methods using bentwood, wicker or cast iron. The abundance of long-winded promotional material represents a productive source of information on the history of Québec furniture over the past few centuries. These many sources have been thoroughly exploited in researching the present book.

Studies and Reports

Two 19th-century sociological studies, which were avant-garde for their time, recorded fundamental information about rural life in this period and provide details about the way farmhouses were laid out and furnished. These studies are *Paysan de Saint-Irénée d'après les renseignements recueillis sur les lieux en 1861 et 1862*, by Charles-Henri-Philippe Gauldrée-Boileau, and *L'Habitant de Saint-Justin*, presenting the results of research undertaken in 1887. Both works, read before the Royal Society of Canada on June 25, 1897, offer a full description of material culture and constitute the foundation of any scientific documentation of the history of Québec furniture.

Interest in old Québec furniture dates back to the first quarter of the 20th century. The previous decades had seen the advent of an industrial society that operated at ever-growing speed and was about to toll the death knell for the age-old rhythms of traditional production. Like others in the Western world, Quebeckers felt the need to protect the vestiges of their material culture. After the First World War, a new interest in history began to arise from a sense of national aware-

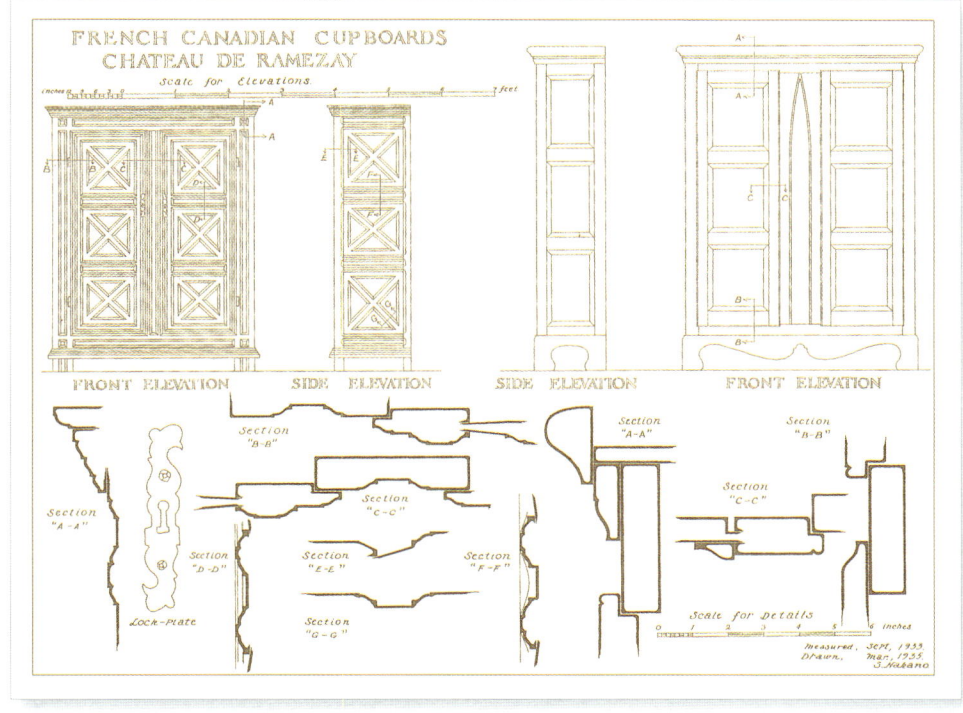

ness that had been growing since the mid-19th century. The St. Lawrence Valley was not immune to the self-regarding, backward-looking attitude adopted by many societies throughout the world at the time.

A people's heritage always embodies a search for identity to some degree. At first, in Québec, academics and well-informed amateurs concentrated on religious architecture and sacred art — for the country's artists had for three centuries primarily celebrated the majesty of God — but general interest soon grew for seigneurial manors and, somewhat later, old houses. In 1887, a young lawyer named Arthur Aimé Bruneau, who would become a member of the House of Commons from 1892 to 1907 and then a judge on the Québec Supreme Court from 1907 to 1928, wrote an article in a local paper, *Le Patriote*,

82-83
Between 1925 and 1935, Ramsay Traquair, a professor at McGill University, in Montréal, had his students make a number of scale drawings of old Québec furniture. His project on the history of Québec architecture was originally supposed to contain a chapter on furnishings. Today these drawings are a valuable documentary source of information on the evolution of the decorative arts in the St. Lawrence Valley.

vigorously opposing the demolition of the old windmill in Sorel. He extended this argument to Québec as a whole, invoking the French preservation movement led by Prosper Mérimée in the 19th century and supported by celebrities like Victor Hugo and François René de Chateaubriand. Bruneau loudly and clearly demanded a law on historic monuments to prevent the loss of property that was intimately linked with Québec's identity.

A preservation movement, backed up by studies and inventories, was then organized by both English- and French-speaking Quebeckers. The movement included Percy Nobbs, Cecil Burgess and Ramsay Traquair of McGill University. Charles Marius Barbeau began his field studies and joined the group of militants working to safeguard Québec's heritage. In 1921, the granddaughter of the historian François-Xavier Garneau sounded the alarm in cultural circles, warning that there were plans to auction off Louis-Joseph Papineau's seigneurial manor at Montebello. She wrote to Prime Minister Taschereau and published her letter in the daily *La Presse*. The great patriot's descendant asked the Québec government to protect this highly significant monument so that future generations might know about "our taste, our survival and our patriotism." The manor's perfectly intact furnishings, reverently preserved by the Papineau family, were of true artistic and ethnohistorical interest. The cry of alarm given by Garneau's granddaughter did not go unheeded. The following year, in 1922, the Québec government passed the Historic Monuments Act. Gradually, people's interest spread to material culture and furniture. *Le Bulletin de recherches historiques*, published since 1895 by Pierre-Georges Roy, dealt with such topics occasionally. In 1935 the Société des Dix was founded by pioneers in the field — Victor Morin, Aegédius Fauteux, Olivier Maurault, E. Z. Massicotte, Gérard Malchelosse, Boucher de la Bruyère and Pierre-Georges Roy — and its famous *Cahier des dix* was launched as the group's annual publication. The engineer William Coverdale was familiar with preservation efforts in the United States, having worked in New York for a long time and been in the Rockefellers' circle when they were involved in the restoration of Williamsburg, the first capital of the Thirteen Colonies. Coverdale, who ran Canada Steamship Lines, set out to revitalize an old hotel owned by the company in Tadoussac by refurbishing it with traditional Québec furniture. Aided by May Coles, he launched a veritable treasure hunt for old objects in Québec. While this project advanced, interest grew on the part of academics, such as architects Lorenzo Auger and Sylvio Brassard, art historian Gérard Morisset, and Paul Gouin, president of the Commission des biens historiques du Québec. The ever-growing demand for objects from the past fostered an antique business which was initially developed by antique dealers from Jewish communities in Québec City and Montréal. All this occurred in the interwar period.

When the Second World War came to an end, interest in heritage took off once again. The movement was given impetus by a number of factors: at Université Laval, folklore archives were set up and a centre was founded to promote teaching and research in heritage studies; articles on these topics were published in several magazines and reviews; and national pride began to develop among French and English Quebeckers at the dawn of the Quiet Revolution. These various factors spurred the quest for historic property that established Québec's collective identity, with houses and furnishings being the most sought-after items. People wanted to surround themselves with goods that recalled their roots.

Jean Palardy was a painter for members of the wealthy middle class who went to the Charlesvoix region in summer; he was well aware of the interests of people like Coverdale and a handful of collectors, several of whom were English-speaking. In 1963, he published *Les Meubles anciens du Canada français*, which was a truly a revelation. The impact it had is reflected in the annotated bibliography in *Objets anciens du Québec. La vie domestique*, the first volume of my series on Québec's material culture; the entry for Palardy's book gives a critical evaluation of it and lists the principal works it inspired. In 1967, for example, Robert-Lionel Seguin ventured beyond the iconographic catalogue and published *La Civilisation traditionnelle de l'«habitant» aux 17e et 18e siècles*, which was the fruit of a colossal labor of research in the notaries' deeds mentioned earlier.

Ethnographic monographs began to appear. In 1960, Nora Dawson published her study of Saint-Pierre on Île d'Orléans, giving special attention to the furniture and furnishings that characterized this small rural community. A number of students in the folk arts and traditions program at Université Laval chose to pursue graduate work on an aspect of material culture. One of them, Paul-Louis Martin, who was later president of the Commission des biens culturels, published *La Berçante québécoise* in 1973. This ethnographic study focuses on the rocking chair, which was extremely popular in the St. Lawrence Valley. My book, *Encyclopédie des antiquités du Québec*, came out in 1971; this work is intentionally addressed to the general public and devotes an entire chapter to furniture. All of these publications suffered from the same shortcoming: they concentrated almost exclusively on traditional furniture in the French manner, totally neglecting other styles and periods. This tendency was maintained in a large body of specialized literature published in French and English art reviews, decoration magazines and antiques journals in both Québec and Ontario. Researchers and collectors were interested solely in handcrafted work and in very specific types of old furniture, such as the chest, the armoire, the buffet and the commode.

Donald Webster of Ontario was the first to turn away from the traditional French vein and take an interest in the Anglo-Québec Neoclassical and Victorian styles, the latter term being used to refer to 19th-century furniture in Revival fashions. This period really received full attention only when a team of 15

84 to 88

When painter Jean Palardy's study, *Les Meubles anciens du Canada français*, was published in 1963, it opened Quebeckers' eyes to a little-known facet of the history of their decorative arts. Many people were inspired to become collectors after reading this illustrated catalogue. The work, appearing in the middle of the Quiet Revolution, invited Québeckers to "touch" their history. The illustrations of furniture stripped to the bare wood encouraged a fashion for systematic paint removal, which sacrificed the colors and painted decoration that had characterized most of these cultural goods throughout their existence.

THE EVER-CHANGING STORY OF STYLE 97

89 to 92
Scientific research and furnishings
Scientific research carried out by various professionals advances our knowledge of old furniture. Raynald Bilodeau, of Parks Canada's Québec City branch, is a specialist of colors used historically in the decorative arts; his meticulously documented models are eloquent interpretations of the way farmhouse interiors were furnished in the 19th century.

In 1993 and 1994, the Montreal Museum of Fine Arts and Québec City's Musée de la civilisation presented an important exhibition on Revival-era furniture and published an impressive companion catalogue with scholarly texts by some fifteen researchers. These are photographs of some of the rooms in this highly popular exhibition.

researchers, art historians for the most part, undertook an organized scientific study under professor John Porter of Université Laval. The project, named MOBIVIQ for "Mobilier victorien québécois," led to the publication of a remarkable work, *Living in Style: Fine Furniture in Victorian Quebec*. This admirable book places the furniture of an era and a certain social class in a number of contexts, showing how it related to history, society, technology and the corridors of cultural influence. An exhibition worthy of both the project and its subject was presented in 1993 at the Montreal Museum of Fine Arts and at the Musée de la civilisation in Québec City. In the wake of the book and the exhibition, a number of articles were brought out by those who had contributed to the project. In short, the project's impact on interest in furniture was comparable to that of Palardy's book in 1963.

John Porter had previously led a more specialized study on the furniture makers Pierre Drouin and Honoré Roy and thus had already dealt with an aspect of the furniture industry in Québec City during the Victorian era. The study was based on an exceptional documentation that had survived intact through the years, providing researchers with unprecedented sources and insights into the way furniture workshops were run. In 1982, Esther Poisson, an M.A. student at Université Laval produced a thesis that studied the vocabulary of household furniture in the Bois-Francs region. In 1992, as mentioned earlier, Daniel Drouin wrote a master's thesis that brilliantly evaluates the participation of Québec furniture makers at national, international and world's fairs between 1850 and 1900.

A number of specialists in various disciplines have worked on reconstructing old interiors. The documentation centres of the Ministère de la Culture and Parks Canada in Québec City contain unpublished studies that were carried out for these institutions. In 1981, Jean Provencher and Marcel Moussettte made a very detailed study on the half-timbered Lamontagne house in Rimouski and produced a 174-page document entitled *Le Mobilier et la mode de vie des habitants de la maison Lamontagne à la fin du XVIIIe siècle*. Several municipal buildings in Québec City's Place Royale were the object of similar research. In the same vein,

THE EVER-CHANGING STORY OF STYLE

house, built by his master locksmith ancestor at the turn of the 18th century. In it, entire bedrooms are kept exactly as they were over a century ago. Even the religious images hanging on the walls and the accessories laid out on the chests of drawers have remained in their places. Climbing to the attic, one sees several well-built storage chests lined up along the roof's stringpiece.

For every period in the history of the decorative arts, field interviews are one of the most rewarding approaches to furniture research, whether in great religious institutions, episcopal palaces, manors and presbyteries or the houses of ordinary people from every social class. It is not unusual to meet a family member who is only too happy to talk about the pieces of furniture he or she has inherited and now treasures.

96 to 98
The first person to do fieldwork on material culture, including furniture, was Charles Marius Barbeau, an anthropologist at the Canadian Museum of Man, in Ottawa. At the end of the 1910s, he began to collect information in notebooks, capturing living heritage with a cylinder phonograph and numerous photographs. Here we see Mademoiselle Gagnon of Grandes-Bergeronnes, posing beside homemade rocking chairs (1946). The next photograph shows an Île d'Orléans farmer holding two posts that had been cut from a tall-post bed belonging to the family and then stored in the attic (1926). The lower photograph is of two children, also on Île d'Orléans, standing beside the family's old pine cradles, which had been brought out for the researcher to see. The Barbeau collection contains hundreds of snapshots like these.

99 to 101
Throughout Québec, fieldwork frequently leads to the discovery of houses that have preserved countless pieces of furniture, sometimes in completely intact period interiors. Old attics can be full of antique objects and furnishings. In the attic belonging to the Letourneau family of Saint-Roch-des-Aulnaies, the fruits of the earth — bushels of peas, beans, onions and tomatoes — are stored away for winter, while chests and an old cradle are lined up along the stringpiece. The next two photographs are of the attic in the Château Bellevue at Cap-Tourmente, a 200-year-old summer residence belonging to the Séminaire de Québec — a true treasure chest.

The social character of furniture

Like architecture, furniture reflects the different social levels of production and use that can be identified within the same style and same period of sequential changes. In a stratified society, the tone is almost inevitably set by the upper classes. At the top of the pyramid of power and culture, church authorities and members of the upper middle class who manage private and public institutions have always sought to fill the spaces in which they work and live with furniture in keeping with their status. From the impressive armoires standing in the Montréal, Trois-Rivières or Québec City palaces of the governors or intendants of New France to the Mazarin-style writing desk used by a bishop in his episcopal palace in the capital and the Louis XIII turned yellow birch chairs — now identified as originally belonging to Madame D'Ailleboust — lined up symmetrically in the parlor of the Augustinians' Québec City convent, such furniture displays the finest craftsmanship and possesses an aura of prestige. These items, which served notables both in their work and in the maintenance of their standing in good society, have little in common with the humble goods found during the same period in the farmhouses of the Côte-de-Beaupré area, Île d'Orléans and the Richelieu Valley. Sometimes the furniture belonging to the upper classes possesses dimensions, careful finishing and decoration in a certain style or canon that make it possible to identify a piece with the name of a prestigious designer. Chairs are particularly revealing in this respect.

In around 1830, for example, an elegant house in Québec City, Kingston or Halifax would be furnished with side chairs in the Sheraton or Hepplewhite style, reflecting British Neoclassical tastes. In more ordinary houses one would find chairs that echoed this style only in their general shape, with curved backs and rear legs, while working class homes might contain chairs that borrowed a few weak references to the characteristic style of the times.

The industrial age was marked by a profusion of various furniture suites; often imported from the United States or Ontario, they were generally of good quality, although some similarly styled but less well-finished items intended for mass consumption were also marketed. People who were skilful with their hands sometimes found their own solution when they were captivated by a catalogue illustration but lacked the means to obtain the latest style: they would make a bedroom suite, récamier, sofa, chair or rocking chair for themselves or to order for others.

Experience in examining and recognizing a piece of furniture, or any other object related to domestic life, when combined with the right questions put to those who have used it, leads to a better notion of its history and the social level it belongs to.

102 to 106

As various movements shaped the history of furniture, each social class found a way of adopting the style of the times. The drawing room in the Papineau manor in Montebello, a Revival-era bourgeois home, expresses the period's eclectic spirit as fully and opulently as possible.

Furniture from every era reflects the stratification of society. The facing page shows a variety of buffets, or cupboards, from the time of New France: one from a settler's dwelling, one from a well-established *habitant*'s home, another from a dining room in a city residence and finally a sumptuous two-tiered buffet inspired by upper-class French furniture. All served the same purpose in about the same period but were given very different treatments depending on the socio-economic situation of their owners.

THE EVER-CHANGING STORY OF STYLE 107

JOINERY AND CABINETMAKING

From Craft to Industry

An old piece of furniture — and for present purposes, the term can apply to even the most recent productions — may have been made by a craftsman, an ordinary person possessing a certain amount of skill or a manufacturer using industrial production methods. Pieces of furniture built by ordinary people are often extremely simple and sometimes almost primitive, although others can be quite astonishingly ornate, with shapes, colors and decorations cleverly arranged to express the wildest flights of fancy in folk art.

Furniture making has always been well served by two main categories of professional craftsmen — joiners and cabinetmakers. From the very early days of the French colony, such craftsmen in Québec City could belong to the "Confrérie des Menuisiers de Madame Sainte-Anne," the woodworkers' guild that took St. Anne as its patron saint.

Throughout the history of Québec, towns and villages have always had at least one general woodworking shop, where joiners, depending on their ability, filled orders for doors and windows, bodies for horse-drawn vehicles, pieces of furniture or the finishing work in the room of a house. Oral tradition identifies several such workers who were active as long as 100 years ago and to whom various well-conserved articles can be attributed. The pieces of furniture produced in the joiners' workshops were solidly built, assembled according the rules of the art, and are generally of undeniably good quality. Designed with a certain attention to balance and harmony, they are decorated with moulding and carving that reflect the fashionable tastes of the time. Finishing was often left to the customer.

Cabinetmakers, the other group of craftsmen who produced furniture, were more specialized. As may be inferred from the word "cabinet," these skilled workers were trained in making somewhat complex articles, often involving the use of precious or exotic wood. In Québec, any piece of furniture that is even slightly complicated — regardless of whether its wood is hard or soft, local or imported, veneered or not — can be identified as the work of a cabinetmaker. From the beginning of the history of furniture in Québec to the present, our cabinetmakers have adapted their production to the artistic trends that have marked our collective evolution.

Occasionally, a treasure hunter has the good fortune to come across one of the boxes used by joiners or cabinetmakers to keep the vast array of tools used in their trade. These well-made, functionally designed toolboxes are decorated in a tasteful and sometimes quite imaginative manner.

After 1850, furniture was influenced by industrial methods of production. Numerous articles on factories were published in this period and, along with various types of advertisements, they convey something of the hothouse atmosphere in which a host of specialized machinery was invented; often such machinery is listed, to the delight of anyone researching the topic. The introduction and growing use of the new machinery had a impact that is well exemplified in the October 9, 1880, issue of *Scientific American*, a magazine that circulated in the St. Lawrence Valley, as evidenced by the collections of certain institutional libraries. This issue devotes a whole page to the equipment that was revolutionizing the North American furniture industry.

Many types of documents make it possible to trace the way finished goods were transported, from freight trains and trucks to the overloaded wagon of the local itinerant chair maker, who used to go about in spring and summer selling the handicraft he had produced over the winter.

To better understand types of wood and the history of their use in furniture making, as well as to grasp three centuries of joining methods, colors and varnishes, and the hardware appropriate for various styles, I turned to restoration experts — people who for the past 10, 20 or 40 years have worked in the field and never lost their passion for it. Since such information is not taught, most of these people learned their skills on the job. Their knowledge and expertise are based in great part on critical observation of furniture. They accorded me extremely informative interviews about the highly specialized fields that they work in and which I have limited knowledge of. These experts are: Jean-Marc Belzile, of Lachute, who has been a tireless collector for the past 40 years; Jeannot Bélanger and Raynald Bilodeau, respectively a restorer-cabinetmaker and a finishing restorer with Parks Canada in Québec City; Donald Dion, a specialist of old hardware; and Patrick Albert, a restorer with the Centre de Conservation du Québec, one of the best-known restoration centres in the world.

107
Toolbox belonging to the cabinetmaker David Bell. Pine, mahogany and ebony, ca. 1860.

JOINING METHODS

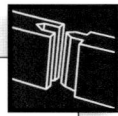

To solidify the components of a piece of furniture, craftsmen may use a number of joining methods. The French tradition favored pegged mortise-and-tenon joints. Dovetail joints characterize Québec furniture made by British cabinetmakers. In the second half of the 19th century, the North American furniture industry mainly used doweled joints. The way a piece was put together is thus an indication of the period or cultural trend to which it belongs.

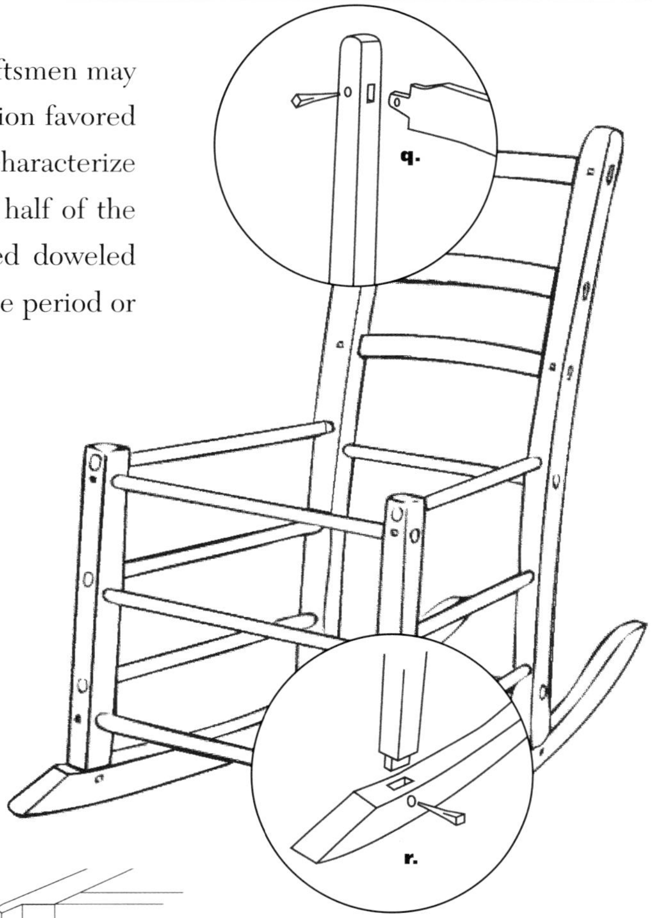

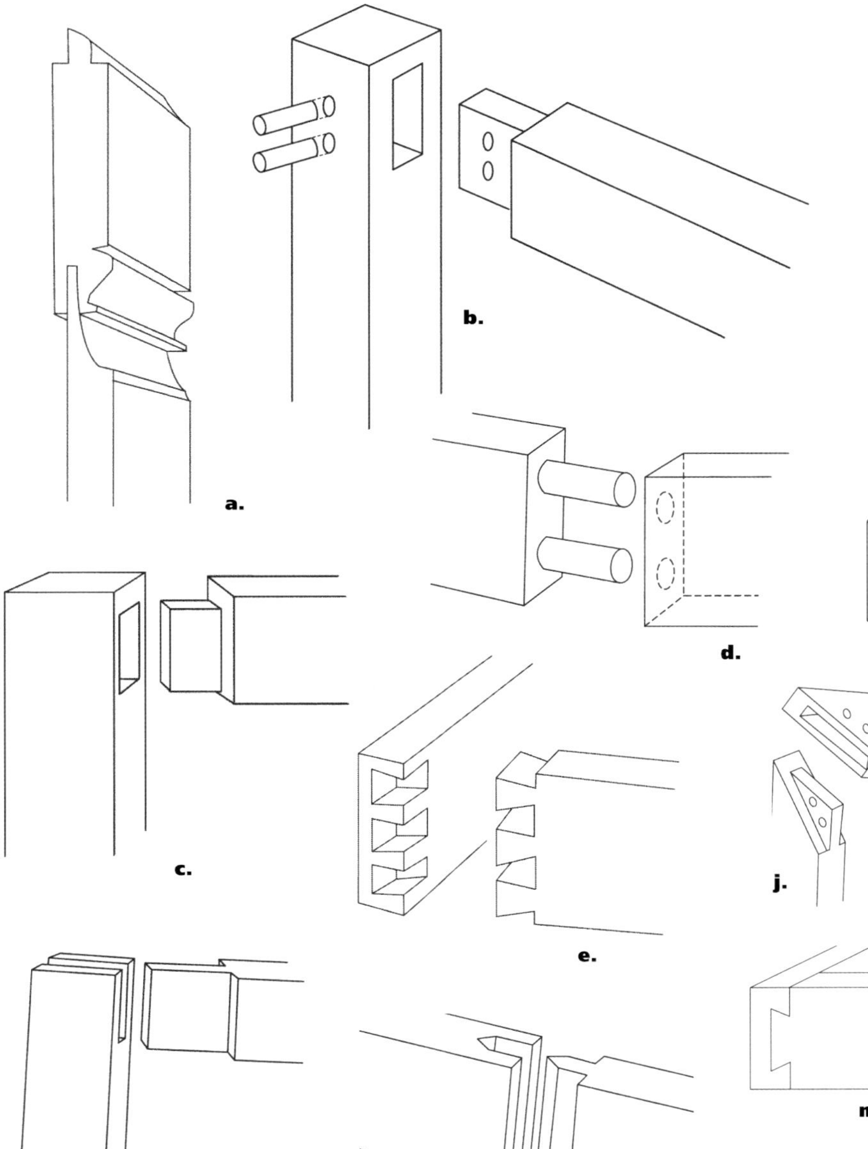

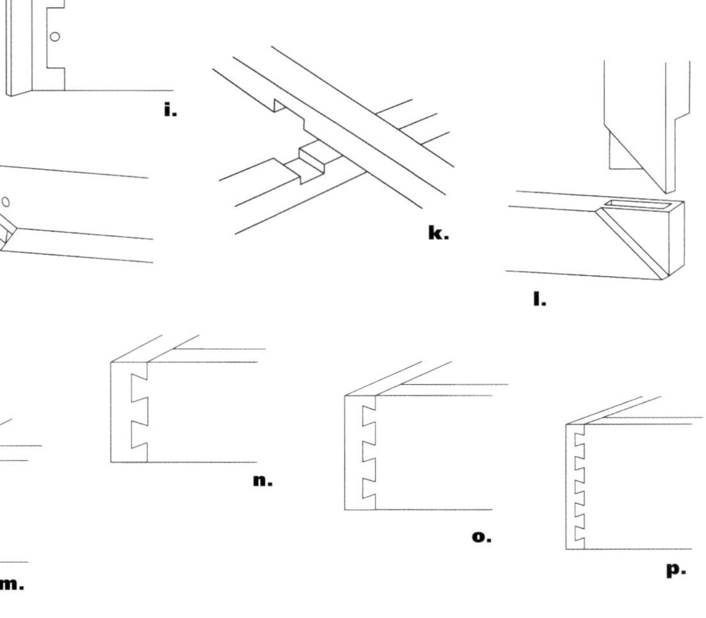

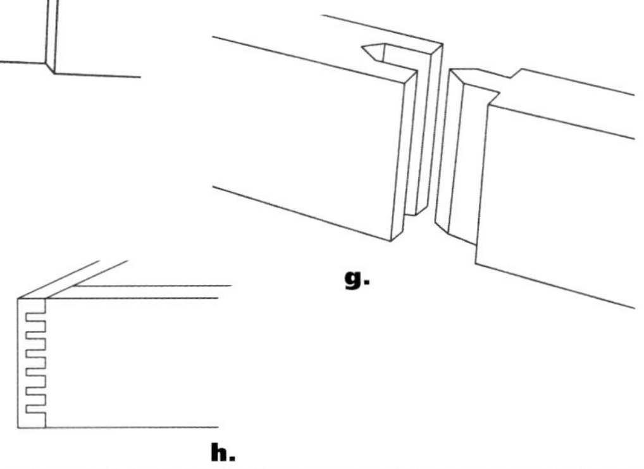

a. rabetted (in panels). **b.** and **c.** mortise-and-tenon with and without pegs. **d.** doweled. **e.** lapped dovetails. **f.** slip-mortise. **g.** tongue-and-groove. **h.** multiple small dovetails (after 1875). **i.** nailed open mortise. **j.** tongue-and-groove miter. **k.** cross-lapped. **l.** haunched end-lap miter (rare). **m.** single lapped dovetail (17th and early 18th century). **n.** two lapped dovetails (18th century). **o.** three lapped dovetails (first three quarters of 19th century). **p.** multiple lapped dovetails (1820-1875). **q.-r.** pegged mortise-and-tenon joints in a rustic chair.

THE EVER-CHANGING STORY OF STYLE

THE CRAFTSMAN

The Life of a Restorer

I have always loved Québec wood. My entire career has revolved around this field. Everything and anything that can be created out of wood touches me deeply. This is how I became friends with the sculptor Jean-Julien Bourgault of Saint-Jean-Port-Joli, an artist who truly knew how to bring out the beauty of wood.

I first became interested in old objects in 1960, when I married Danielle. She and I began with little things. We read a great deal, mostly in English, to gather information. When Palardy's work came out in 1963, it was truly a revelation. With its beautiful photographs, the book admirably presented a whole field of craftsmanship and the use to which one of the country's great resources may be put. As a history enthusiast and lover of wood, I was delighted. The book was followed by others, like those of Lessard and Marquis. All books are important. Each one contributes something to culture; each one makes advances in knowledge. Over the last 40 years, I have lost nothing of my fascination with old furniture. I've restored a great deal of it, for myself and for others. If you take the time to read every detail, you eventually develop expertise concerning the ancient art of joiners and cabinetmakers, the models produced in different regions, and the aesthetic values and techniques represented by a given piece. Our passion is shared by our children, and especially our daughter Annick, who has become a restoration specialist. In our home, a piece of old furniture can be the object of heated discussion, particularly when we have to decide how it should be restored. Old furniture is part of our national heritage. It's important not to err in restoring old pieces. They are too precious.

Wood types

With the amount of furniture I have seen and restored, I can make a few general remarks about the sorts of wood that were used for articles made before the machine age. Until 1850, ash, which is not considered a noble wood, was hardly ever employed. However, in the second half of the 19th century it gained popularity and eventually became the most common wood used in furniture industry of the 20th century. From the country's beginnings to the end of the 19th century, honey-colored pine was the wood most favored by craftsmen because it does not crack, is light, strong and easy to work and provides good wide planks. It was chosen not for its grain — for it was always painted — but rather for these qualities.

Butternut was also frequently used and is generally considered the second most popular wood. It is as easy to work as pine, has an attractive grain and does not darken with time. Unfortunately, it does not have a very interesting patina. In the 19th century especially, poplar began to be used extensively, particularly as secondary wood. In 90 percent of cases, this extremely soft and crack-resistant wood was chosen over basswood, or whitewood. I have seen very old pieces, dating back more than two centuries, made of our native hardwoods, maple and yellow birch. Finally, in the Neoclassical era in the first half of the 19th century, Québec's furniture makers became interested in period furniture and were attracted to exotic imported wood, such as mahogany, as well as native hardwoods like maple.

The pioneers and *habitants* did not have the tools needed to work hardwood. At the time, the beauty of the wood grain was not an important criterion. The priorities were sturdiness and, to some degree, the ease with which something could be built. Pine and basswood were usually chosen because of their resilience and softness, but these qualities lent themselves to utilitarian articles rather than to elegant furniture. However, the cabinetmaker's middle-class customers were of course more demanding.

Since elm warps easily, it was not favored until about 150 years after the arrival of Europeans. Elm is a magnificent wood with a lovely grain and is more solid than oak. With improvements in drying procedures in the 20th century, it became attractive for the furniture industry. It was used extensively by Thibault, a large manufacturer. Elm had to be dried for three or four months.

In reality, each region used local species of wood. In this respect, Québec is not a homogenous territory. For example, the Rimouski region has no oak. Yellow birch abounds from Montmagny to Matane. To appraise a piece of furniture properly, one has to be able to "read" the wood it is made of. At the end of the 19th century and the beginning of the 20th, in the era of oak furniture, a number of manufacturers were quick to realize that Ontario ash had a grain that was almost identical to that of oak, even to expert eyes. About 80 percent of the "oak" production of this time is actually ash, a wood with a fine, smooth grain.

Joinery

Québec furniture in the French tradition tends to have been built with pegged mortise-and-tenon joints and rabetted panels. Dovetail joints are more likely to correspond to British construction methods. When a piece of furniture is made entirely with dovetail joints, it is of British influence. Other common features of British furniture are elaborate moulding and tongue-and-groove joints. In my opinion, British production was most refined in the 18th century and first half of the 19th century.

Color

My observations have led me to conclude that during the French Regime vernacular furniture was for the most part not given any coating or color. The raw wood was left exposed and with time would develop a patina. Contrary to the claims of certain researchers, the pigments listed in some stores' inventories very early on were not used for such furniture but rather were intended for the interiors and furniture of bourgeois homes, or sold to artists and architects working for the Church and the wealthy classes. At this period, color for furniture was obtained with the same recipes that our great-grandmothers used for dying cloth in the country: beets were used for burgundy red, spinach for medium green, walnut stain for dark brown, hemlock bark for golden yellow and blueberries for dark or light blue, depending on the concentration; highbush cranberry was used as it had been by Amerindians, to obtain a light red. Paint at this time was made with various natural binders and vehicles, such as water, linseed oil, turpentine and casein, a protein obtained from dried whey and mixed with a liquid and a natural color or pigment. Vegetable or mineral colors diluted in casein produce a fairly heavy coating. In around 1940, in Saint-Clément, near Rivière-du-Loup, I personally saw Arsène Tremblay, the father of one of my uncles, prepare a coating with ox blood, which served as a binder and a pigment. He obtained a thick, rich, burgundy-colored paint. Throughout my life, I have seen barely a dozen pieces of furniture with this special finish, applied in several layers. Of course, people use the word "oxblood" to refer to a certain color, just as they say "sky blue." But real ox blood was used to paint furniture. The blood of hogs was too dry for this purpose and was used for blood pudding instead. I saw the finished article, a small

108
Side panel of a cupboard decorated with an overpainted grape-vine motif. Pine, Trappist monastery, Oka, ca. 1860.

serving table, after my uncle's father had painted it. Ox blood finish should not be confused with red ochre, which was extremely popular as a base or finishing coat on numerous items.

It would be very worthwhile if the whole issue of furniture color was studied by a group of scientific researchers, including chemists. By carrying out analyses of the coatings used, such a group could elucidate points that remain obscure, answer unresolved questions and verify the hypotheses and approximate assessments made about color, pigments and binders. This process would ideally take into account the ethnological and sociological aspects of color.

With the arrival of the British, commercial pigments began to be more common. At the end of the 18th century, economic prosperity and expanding markets meant that paint became much easier to buy and thus grew increasingly popular.

The Art of Rejuvenating Color

Removing paint from an old piece of furniture is an art and requires a methodical approach. Certain pieces have over 60 coats, some of which can be as thick as one-eighth of an inch. My mother painted our rocking chairs every year. On our country road, it was common for people to repaint the interior of their houses every one or two years, not only for the sake of cleanliness but also to give homes a fresh new look. Changing one's decoration was a sign of intelligence. And when the interior was painted, everything else was too. Paint removal is a question of technique, and the technique is the method used to obtain what is being sought. The quest for the original coat, the very first one, should not become an obsession. It is important to make probes, take samples, study the situation and discover the article's history through its layers of successive finishes. For example, between 1825 and 1875, there was a fashion for painting cupboards with motifs of plants and animals, especially birds. Imitation wood grain was abundantly used in the Neoclassical era. A piece may have been painted in one main color with a second and even a third hue used for accents. All of this is lost if one concentrates exclusively on the original coat, allowing the article's history to be erased.

In Québec, there have been a number of approaches to restoring furniture. Until about 1965-1970, the preferred method was to strip the paint down to the bare wood, which was then waxed to obtain a fine patina. Despite all the controversy around this approach now, the results were fairly authentic in the case of many old pieces, which were often left as they were for quite a long time before receiving their first coat of color. Later methods favored trying to find the original color. Many people continue to defend this philosophy. However, to reach this coat they must remove all the later ones, which are nonetheless equally significant. This approach attempts to freeze time and denies history. It is often difficult to attain the first coat without going through it in places, since the grain of the wood is so close. If a piece is then touched up to obtain an even surface, the result is artificial — the piece will essentially have been repainted. My technique treats history with more respect. To restore an armoire and get it to the state I want can take 100 to 200 hours of work. It should be accepted in the market place that an item worth several thousand dollars deserves such attention, even though this is relatively costly. A piece of furniture should never be recolored, as there is an unfortunate tendency to do.

When someone removes the paint from a piece of furniture, over a dozen coats may be taken off at the same time. When I come across a solid old layer, whether it is the third, the fifth, the seventh or the last, I stop there. And for the cornice and perimeters of the panels, I keep accents in another solid color that harmonizes with the first one, as was often done long ago. All the colors chosen are part of the item's history and reveal different stages in its existence. It is possible to combine more than one period. I generally prefer to stop at the third or fourth color, which is still attractive and not too far removed from the item's early life.

Perhaps in a few years' time, furniture will be kept just as it is found and simply cleaned. Philosophies and approaches are always changing.

All beautiful furniture interests me. But I am particularly fond of work inspired by the Louis XIII and Louis IV styles. It is my heritage. I am a man of the country and our old vernacular furniture, which was made in these styles, affect me deeply, probably because of its intrinsic qualities. This by no means implies that Québec-produced furniture in the Victorian Rococo or Louis XV Revival styles is without interest. However, such pieces are too ornate for my tastes. I would not be able to live in rooms decorated with Sheraton or Hepplewhite furniture in the British Neoclassical style. While I appreciate this furniture, which is part of our history, it does not suit me. I am more strongly drawn to the warmth, clean lines and straightforwardness of Louis XIII structures and decoration. Such furniture is constructed generously out of solid wood, and I love wood. I am sometimes profoundly moved by certain armoires with their harmonious proportions, inspired by a respect for balance and symmetry. For me, these works are of undeniable artistry. The simple geometry of furniture in the Louis XIII spirit did not require those who made it to be skilled sculptors. The great popularity of this style over such a long period in the provinces of France and in the St. Lawrence Valley can be explained by the furniture's solidity and its relation to the clarity of classicism. This country manner is indeed to my taste and suits us as society.

Jean-Marc Belzile, Lachute, 1999

PERSONAL ACCOUNT

The Cabinetmaker-Restorer

My fascination with making wooden furniture and sculpting wood began to develop when I was about 15 years old. I received basic training at the École du meuble in Victoriaville between 1969 and 1972. As soon as my studies were completed, I was hired at the conservation and furniture reproduction workshop of Parks Canada.

Twenty-six years have now passed and I still practise my profession in this institution, or, more specifically, in its Québec City laboratories. Throughout my life, I have taken several specialization courses, notably at the Smithsonian Institute in Washington D.C. and at Williamsburg, the former capital of the United States. I even took part in an intensive, three-month training session in Paris, at my own expense, in order to study with Jean-Pierre Lecouvéour, one of the five remaining great masters of French cabinetmaking. Through him I was able to learn old skills now forgotten by my contemporaries. This contact was very fruitful and enabled me to develop my art much further than before.

A person who is interested in old cabinetmaking has no choice but to learn on the job. For a long time now, I have read everything that has been published on the subject in Québec, France, Great Britain and the United States. I find old treatises on cabinetmaking by far the most fascinating works in all this material. I have also visited Gilles Bourgault's workshop in Saint-Jean-Port-Joli. I love to have discussions with other enthusiasts in the field, but unfortunately they are not very numerous.

The most audacious project in which I have been involved as part of my work is incontestably the George-Étienne-Cartier house in Montréal. I was responsible for both restoring the original furniture and reproducing period pieces.

For this ambitious project, I happily and respectfully adopted the approach taken by craftsmen in Québec City, Montréal and other towns 150 years ago. I took the time to let my hands learn to follow those of the old masters, especially when it came to making a parlor table in mahogany. I had an original in front of me and referred to it constantly for measurements as I worked out my plans and drawings. I feel that one thing has been undeniably missing in my work and that is critical discussion with colleagues to resolve certain problems. Formerly, people in workshops did not have this problem. I like to imagine that there must have even been a kind of healthy competition among cabinetmaker-sculptors — that they must have taken risks attempting to outdo each other in the quest for excellence and for the satisfaction to be gained from finishing a piece of work with unparalleled mastery. However that might be, the period's legacy belongs to the realm of great art. For the initiated, certain achievements of that time are astonishing, and even disarming. The Québec Victorian style inspired what are surely works of art, marked by great originality. The exquisite artistry with which mahogany and black walnut is used in the Rococo Revival style inevitably causes modern-day cabinetmakers to ask themselves: How can I equal these craftsmen? To work with such mastery? The cabinetmakers of the period developed their own techniques. Going from workshop to workshop, they garnered precious knowledge that was passed on from one generation to the next. They shared unusual solutions and the secrets of their fraternal society. Woodworking and traditional techniques were seen cohesively in a way that encouraged creative freedom and great daring.

I always tell my students that all furniture can be restored. I make them check the truth of my words by asking them to bring a piece of furniture in more or less good condition, whether belonging to their family or bought from an antique dealer, and show it to the class. Looking at these pieces, we discuss how they might be restored. No challenge is unachievable for skilled hands and an inventive mind. Starting with a table leg and a segment of an apron, it is possible to rebuild the whole piece. The thing that moves me the most in my work is to see a piece suddenly emerge, a little like a revelation. Inspired by my predecessors, I try to exceed myself with each piece. I always think about the people who are going to live with these beautiful objects, and this idea guides my gestures. When I examine an old piece of furniture, I also imagine the person who made it — the challenges met and the questions asked. I share the craftsman's feeling of success and am filled with wonder. I also sense the happiness of those who lived with the piece throughout their lives. As my mind wanders through time, I find inspiration, discover the right manner, and feel respect, while my cabinetmaker-restorer hands work to return the piece to its former splendor.

Jeannot Bélanger, cabinetmaker and restorer, Québec City, June 1998

FURNITURE OF TASTE... THE CABINETMAKER'S ART

Making a Rococo Revival table in mahogany takes knowledge, skill and a sense of artistry. The tradition has been lost. Drawing inspiration from an original work by a Québec City cabinetmaker named Honoré Roy *dit* Belleau (1821-1892), Jeannot Bélanger, a modern-day cabinetmaker in the same city, rediscovers the traditional sequence of work and the gestures of 19th-century craftsmen.

Once the parts of the table have been shaped and trimmed, motifs are pencil-drawn on the wood to guide the sculptor.

Cabinetmaker Jeannot Bélanger sculpting the apron of a Louis XV Revival mahogany table in Parks Canada's restoration and reproduction workshop in Québec City.

The motif is then carved and the background given a stippled texture. This illustration shows a scallop shell and rose motif.

After taking careful measurements of the components of the original table used as a model, the cabinetmaker cuts his wood — Honduras mahogany — to match the forms and outlines of his plan and then assembles the pegged components, using animal glue.

Various parts of the table gradually take shape. This is the fruit bowl forming the finial on the plinth in the centre of the X-stretcher.

Next, each cabriole leg is carved and joined to the apron. The serpentine stretchers receive the same treatment. Because of its weak joints, made with pegs in thin layers of wood, and its daring balance, such furniture is always extremely fragile. Furniture of this type found today is often very shaky or may have fallen apart.

The table is then sanded, sealed and stained (with walnut stain and umber), and finally finished with lacquer varnish, as most furniture was in the period. Reynald Bilodeau, a finishing specialist, assisted in the project by carrying out this part of the restoration.

COLOR

In its lifetime, a piece of furniture may have received as many as 50 coats of paint and, in some cases, even more. Some pieces were given several coats of varnish, which eventually darkens. At one point, it was the fashion among furniture collectors in Québec to have these finishes stripped off and rub the exposed wood with beeswax to obtain a patina. By the 1970s, increased public awareness, resulting in large part from the efforts of ethnohistorians, led to the search for the original color, which was touched up and repainted when the other coats had been removed. Today, there is another approach to conservation: a number of old layers are allowed to show as accent colors, all of which played a role in the evolution of the piece. Color reflects the history of taste.

Panel in the Régence manner, with old paint left as accent colors. Some collectors remove layers of paint to rediscover a certain period in the life of a painted object.

Louis XV panel with painted wood-grain decoration. Between 1820 and 1860, the grain of certain wood was preferred to others. Consequently, less "interesting" wood was often painted to look like the grain of a certain tree or like the figures obtained from a particular part of a tree, such as crotches and burls. These finishes can have an exaggerated effect. In the 20th century, demand for the procedure showed no signs of abating.

Restoration specialist at work.

Small armoire in the Louis XV manner with dovetail joints. Pine, Cap-Saint-Ignace, second half of the 18th century. Paint may be removed until the original coat is reached, to show how the piece looked when first used.

Armoire in the Louis XV manner. New color, pine, late 18th century. Photographs taken in the 1950s show this armoire, belonging to the museum of the École du meuble in Montréal, stripped down to the bare wood. In around 1960, certain parts of the piece were remade and the blue color applied. Among collectors and ethnologists, such an approach is now condemned.

Carpenter's chest. Pine, Saint-Roch-des-Aulnaies, ca. 1850.
Removing paint can reveal an entire decorative universe. This chest displays a profusion of swallows and fleur-de-lis, a crown of maple leaves and stylized initials. The chest represents everything in the woodworker's country and life.

Below the cornice, a grooved recessed panel with block-carved moulding has been stripped to an old blue layer. It was decided to stop removing paint on the moulding when a light green layer was reached. A craftsman seeking an article's former colors may stop when an even coat is found and when the colors harmonize.

Two-doored armoire decorated with 12 raised panels. Early colors and accents, pine, ca. 1825.
As is often the case, this piece was covered with numerous coats of paint when it was discovered. Its previous colors were simply brought to light, without any retouching or over-painting. From the rat-tail hinges and the forged nails in back to the armoire's frame, nothing has been changed.

This detail of the cornice shows the main colors that were kept in the stripping process: cream, red, burgundy, blue and pale green. The armoire was originally blue. Note the dentil moulding at the base of the cornice and the pegs with which the doors were joined.

The raised panel is slightly thicker than the door's stiles and rails. The panel's central surface has been left cream-colored, the perimeter blue and the carved moulding pale green. Instead of creating such accents, the restorer could have also stripped the paint down to a single layer from one of the stages in the article's history.

Detail of the shaped base showing the narrow panel on the centre post with its block-carved moulding. The panel is decorated with a gentle relief torus.

Stencil decoration on an arrow-back chair. Original state, pine, ca. 1820.
Pieces of furniture were often decorated with overpainted motifs; this practice was especially popular in the first half of the 19th century. It is possible to find old articles of this type with the original colors still intact.

THE PRESENT STATE OF KNOWLEDGE

Colors and Varnishes

There is a story to be read in the layers between a piece of furniture's underlying material and its last coat of color. These layers relate its entire life and the roles it played in the house or houses where it was used, depending on its function. Before the 1960-1970 period, the preferred way of reviving a piece of "old French Canadian furniture," as it was called then, was to strip it down to the wood and then simply wax and polish the surface. The systematic stripping procedures used at the time were so severe that they literally killed the surface of the wood and its grain, leaving it wan and inert.

In the 1960-1970 period, ethnohistorians' arguments gained ground, and consumers began to appreciate the search for the original color. Since the first layer applied adheres to its support, it is difficult to reveal this paint evenly, and the surface of furniture receiving such treatment will have patches of wood showing through the color.

Throughout the same period and beyond, the search for the original color led some to accept the idea that exposed patches of wood might be touched up, that is covered with a color to match the original, to obtain a relatively homogenous surface. The color is thus "redone." The extent of such touching up can vary.

An old piece of furniture may have been repainted 40, 50 or 60 times, and sometimes even more. It is impossible for even expert paint-removers to work coat by coat. They instead work according to various thickness, perhaps a layer that is more solid than the others or a sequence of layers that stick together. Whether the work is done with scrapers alone, with heat or with controlled-release chemicals, the results are very similar. The restoration craftsman may decide to reveal the color from one period and thus chooses a single "outfit" from among the vast assortment worn by the piece in the past. And, if in this period, the perimeters of the panels or the cornice were another color, or if the article had a painted design, all these elements will be revealed as well, since they belong to the same chronological layer. It corresponds to "the period defined by restoration," which may be earlier or later, depending on the customer's tastes. To obtain this layer, many other coats, or "outfits" must be sacrificed and many others must be left hidden underneath.

Another approach to restoring an old piece of furniture and giving it a colored finish consists in going through the layers and stopping at a certain point, as far as possible from the last layer and as close as possible to the first one, when the different colors from various stages in the item's history produce an interesting effect. The flat surface of an article's panels might be left in one color corresponding to a given period, the recessed areas left a second color from another period, the frame left a third color and certain moulding or decorative details left a fourth. A restoration craftsman following this option chooses where to stop on the basis of several guidelines — the colors should harmonize, the surfaces should be solid and even, and the layers to be removed should come off smoothly. But such guidelines are very subjective. From an ethnohistorical viewpoint, a piece of furniture never wore such colors together at any one time in its past. Nevertheless, this approach can produce very aesthetically pleasing results and is highly instructive from a didactic perspective, since several aspects of an article's "wardrobe" are displayed. However, once again, many layers belonging to the chromatic evolution of the object must be sacrificed, while others are left concealed.

Still another approach consists in conserving a piece of furniture as it was found. Ideally, of course, such an article has received only one coat and thus kept its original color or was not repainted for a very long time, as sometimes occurs; in this case, it deserves to be given a place where it can reign in all its splendor. An increasing number of furniture lovers and museums now accept that a piece of furniture can be left with the most recent finish in its history after a simple clean-up. Some even believe that it is all right to cut tiny windows into the paint in an inconspicuous area, so that distinctive periods in item's chromatic history are revealed.

A furniture lover thus has several options. Continuing debate and future ideas will no doubt clarify choices and probably suggest new approaches. However, one thing is certain: it is quite wrong to strip an article down to the bare wood or give it an irreversible coat of modern paint. Much of the finest pine furniture, stripped of all paint a few decades ago, is being revived today. Ingenious craftsmen are being asked to give these pieces an antique-looking color and a realistic patina in order to increase their market value. And the shrewdest of such craftsmen sell this furniture in markets outside Québec, taking advantage of the strong demand for such goods. Buying a very costly piece of old furniture calls for a specialist's knowledge and in Québec there are professionals who are experienced in this domain.

The color of a piece of furniture is not without significance. Old beds were often painted red, as were dough boxes. Specific colors were characteristic of certain periods, styles and regions. There is an enormous amount of research to be done in this field, with respect not only to techniques and ethnohistory, but also semiology.

With the Neoclassical period, varnished furniture became the norm among the middle classes. There was an appreciation of wood grains, the color of different types of wood and patterns of burls, gnarls and crotch graining, as well as the curly, bird's-eye and tiger-striped figures of exotic wood. This interest was reflected in highly decorative inlay and veneering. Such finishes were so popular that a fashion arose for imitation grain produced with special instruments and techniques. Between 1820 and 1860, a considerable quantity of furniture was finished in this way, so that wood with an uninteresting grain was given the appearance of fancier material.

109
Panel decorated with linenfold motifs. Original color, pine, 18th century.
Many restorers seek the object's first, and perhaps most significant, color.

It is quite difficult to restore a piece of furniture that has been painted over its original varnish. Whether veneered or not, a varnished article should never be stripped down to the bare wood and then refinished. To do so is a heresy and it is a shame that industrial furniture from the end of the 19th century and first half of the 20th century is subjected to such treatment almost systematically. This approach is no doubt commercially profitable, especially given the difficulty of rejuvenating 20th-century synthetic varnishes, but it is just as harmful as the wholesale stripping of pine furniture in the 1940-1960 period. An article loses its aesthetic value and historic interest when its varnish is removed.

Original varnishes should be conserved. An expert in the field can always remove subsequent layers, often of poor-quality lacquer, which over time have cracked, darkened, and become gummy with dirt that hides the wood grain. Once the object is cleaned this way, the original varnish can be rejuvenated. Using appropriate substances and well-tested methods, and applying a minimum of new lacquer, the restorer seeks to respect the original effect of the piece. Such work requires patience and experience. Like a piece of painted furniture, a varnished article can be kept as found after a simple cleaning that leaves its patina intact and allows the various stages in its life to show. Synthetic varnishes require a light touch, and every case should be assessed on its own.

In conclusion, a painted or varnished item should never be stripped down to the bare wood; color or varnish should never be reapplied to a surface. Conservation calls for a middle path, which is constantly evolving. The extent of restoration may vary but the object's history must be respected.

Michel Lessard

SCIENTIFIC ANALYSIS

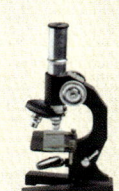

Identifying Ox Blood in a Paint Sample

At the request of historian Michel Lessard, I carried out an analysis of a paint sample taken from a table which, according to the owner, had been painted with ox blood.

Appearance of the Sample

To the naked eye, the sample resembled a shiny coating of a very deep burgundy color; it was soft, elastic and sticky to the touch. When ox blood dries, it usually takes on a much more brownish color and has a dry, brittle texture with a matte surface. However, this difference in color was not incompatible with the information given by the owner, since a soluble colorant and/or pigments could have been added to the blood, which would have acted as a binder and partial colorant. Blood is proteinic in nature, as are egg albumen and milk casein, both of which have been used as binders in paint.

Microchemical Analysis

BENZIDINE TEST

I carried out a benzidine test, which is intended to detect the presence of haemoglobin, an element that is specific to blood. A parallel test was carried out on a blood sample as a control.
RESULT: the control sample tested positive, while the sample to be analysed tested negative.

BIURET TEST

This test using copper sulfate is intended to identify the presence of proteins. Since blood is proteinic in nature, this second test was considered advisable. A parallel test was carried out on a blood sample as a control.
RESULT: the control sample tested positive, while the sample being analysed tested negative.

SOLUBILITY TEST

When alcohol and chloroform were applied to the sample, it dissolved into a reddish orange liquid. This suggests that its color was produced by a dye. The dissolved portion was taken up with blotting paper and examined under ultraviolet light. A yellow fluorescence, characteristic of linseed oil, was visible.

When dilute hydrochloric acid was applied to the sample, the red color turned yellow. When sodium hydroxide was applied, the sample partially dissolved and turned brown.

PYROLYSIS

Pyrolysis was also carried out on the sample. The latter liquefied completely, becoming transparent brown. The pH of the fumes was slightly acidic (pH 4). The presence of a little sulfur was detected and a somewhat acrid smell was given off.

PLUMTESMO

This test was carried out to determine whether lead had been used as a drier, extender or pigment with the oily binder. The Plumtesmo indicator paper contains a reagent that is extremely sensitive to the presence of lead. It produced negative results with the sample to be analysed.

Microscopic Analysis

MICROSCOPIC EXAMINATION OF A THIN SECTION AND CROSS SECTION

In order to examine a cross section under a microscope, a sample of the paint was mounted in a polyester resin. Using reflected light, this technique makes it possible to detect successive layers. A microscopic slide of a thin section was also prepared so that it could be examined with transmitted light and the pigments, if any, identified.

The thin section revealed the abundant presence of an extender, appearing as large, transparent crystals that were anisotropic under cross polarisers. Also visible were large isotropic glassy blue crystals — probably smalt — and a smaller quantity of isotropic red-colored gel formations representing the dye.

Viewed as a cross section, the sample displayed two successive layers: the first, very dark and opaque, the second, very bright light red and unpigmented. No pigment was visible, even at maximum magnification (X400). This suggests that the red color was produced by dye.

Conclusion

The sample does not contain blood. The binder is not proteinic but rather lipidic. Given the pH of the pyrolysis fumes and the fluorescence, it is likely that linseed oil was used as a binder. The paint contains a mineral charge that has not yet been identified but is probably calcium sulfate. The coating has two successive layers: one is almost black and appears to contain smalt while the other is a bright transparent red produced by a dye which is very likely toluidine. The use of ox blood in paint remains a plausible hypothesis, but the presence of this material was not detected in the sample submitted. The nature of the paints used on furniture has never been the object of serious scientific study. Such a study would have to be complemented by research in the field so that the recipes for producing paint might be made known to researchers. I have found references in the literature mentioning a recipe based on ox blood, tartar and oil of vitriol (sulphuric acid) used to produce the pigment Prussian blue. After such treatment, ox blood would probably not be detected by the methods described above; at the most, Prussian blue pigments would be found.

France Rémillard,
chemist and curator-restorer, CCQ
August 21, 1999

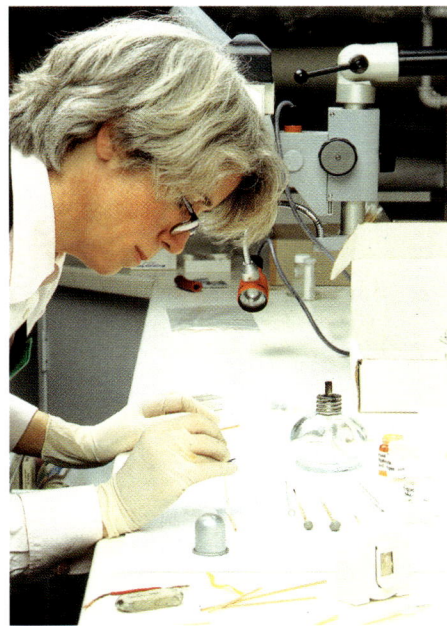

110
France Rémillard, preparing a microtest in the laboratories of the Centre de conservation du Québec (CCQ).

THE ART OF THE RESTORER

All furniture bears the marks of time. Each piece therefore requires basic restoration work. An article can continue to have a long and happy life if the right steps are taken — varnish may be rejuvenated, a seat recaned or rewoven, a moulding or worn-out foot repaired and a broken piece of hardware replaced. Québec is endowed with a group of well-schooled restorers who carry out essential restoration work, with respect for the object and in accordance with the rules of the art.

Harmonium belonging to the Musée de la Côte-Nord in Sept-Îles, before and after treatment. Certain composite pieces of furniture require the participation of various specialists. The pedals, keys and the case are all made of different materials calling for specific skills.

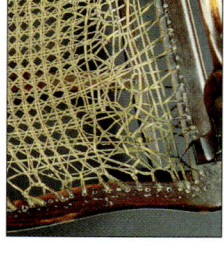

Caned Regency armchair before and after restoration by a professional specialist in the private sector. The Centre de conservation du Québec occasionally calls upon the services of external experts for certain types of work.

Corner cupboard with concave-cornered panels, found in the Valcourt region, before and after paint removal. Pine, first half of the 19th century. Approaches to discovering an old piece of furniture's colors can vary. There is debate among experts, who are influenced by different and relatively subjective theories, as to whether the original color or simply early colors should be sought.

The furniture restoration workshop at the Centre de conservation du Québec (CCQ). Québec's government-run restoration laboratories are among the most outstanding in the world. They receive trainees from countries around the globe and serve national and regional museums.

Armoire with raised panels, in as-found condition. Pine, early 19th century. Old furniture is often covered by dozens of coats of paint or numerous layers of varnish. With long use, hardware tends to wear out and elements such as bases may break. In this case, the armoire has lost its cornice. Basic restoration work would involve replacing it.

Whatnot before and after treatment at the CCQ. Black walnut, ca. 1875. Old varnishes can be restored by simply cleaning the surface, softening and smoothing out the original coat of lacquer and then giving it a polish.

FURNITURE HARDWARE

hile hardware is a functional element of furniture and is adapted to the object's use, it also adds an aesthetic touch, always influenced by major trends in the decorative arts. When the original locks, hinges and handles remain on a piece of furniture, they help to date it.

Hand-forged hardware in the French tradition, 18th century

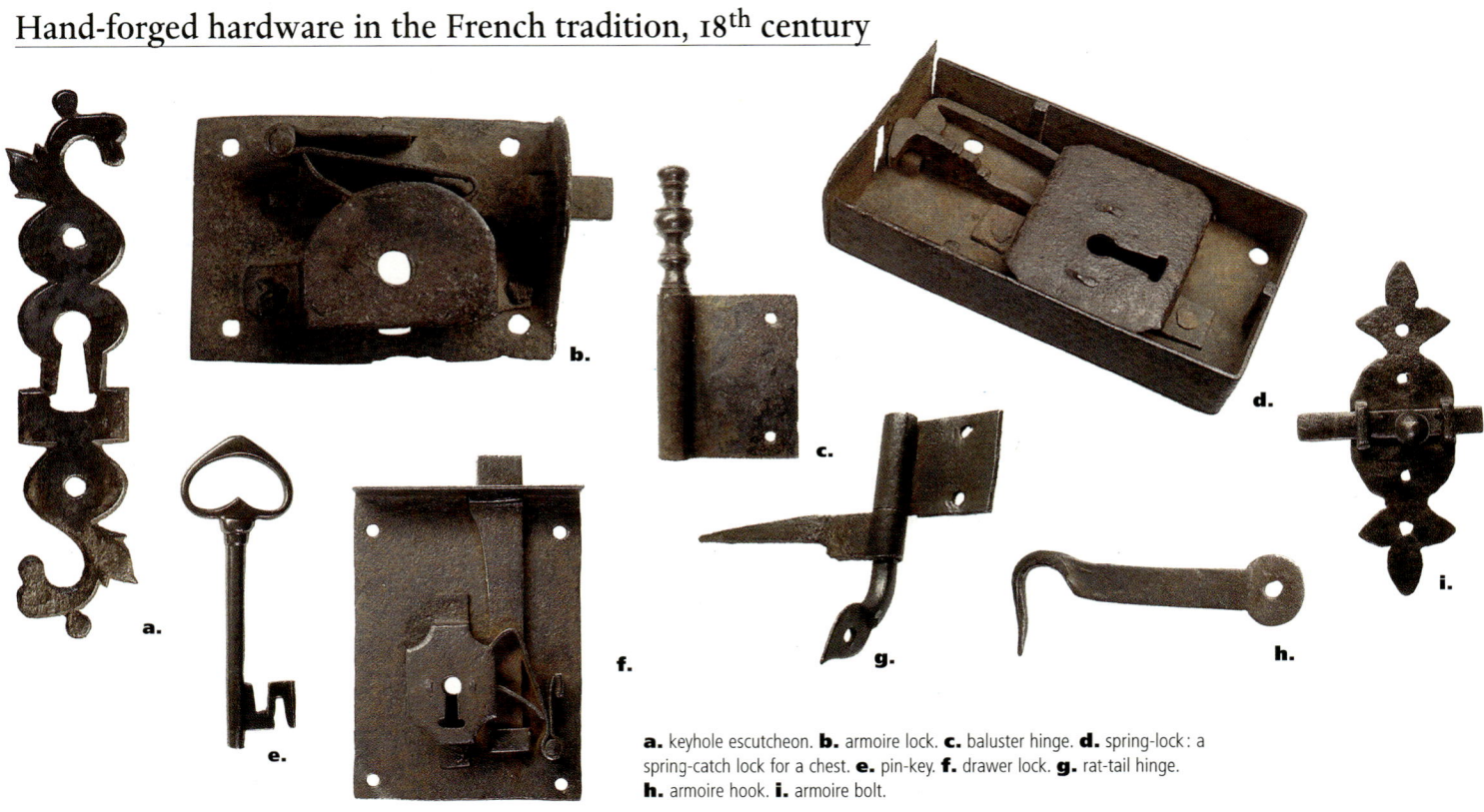

a. keyhole escutcheon. **b.** armoire lock. **c.** baluster hinge. **d.** spring-lock: a spring-catch lock for a chest. **e.** pin-key. **f.** drawer lock. **g.** rat-tail hinge. **h.** armoire hook. **i.** armoire bolt.

Proto-industrial manufactured goods in the British tradition, first half of the 19th century

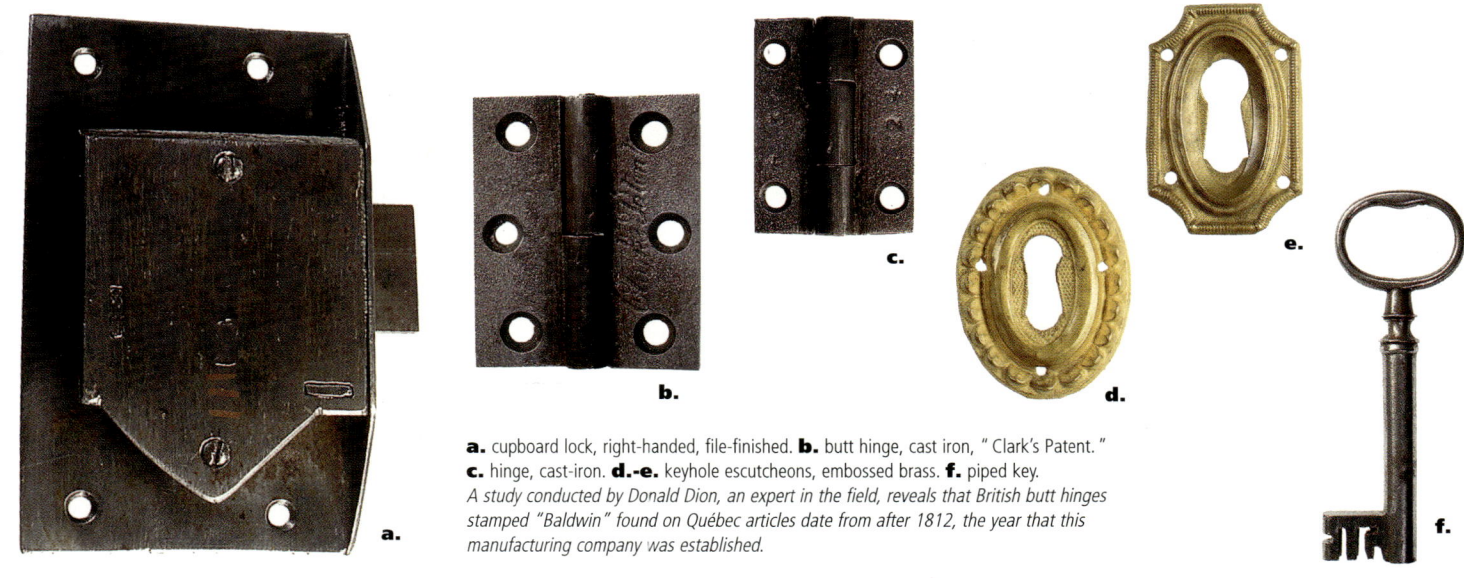

a. cupboard lock, right-handed, file-finished. **b.** butt hinge, cast iron, "Clark's Patent." **c.** hinge, cast-iron. **d.-e.** keyhole escutcheons, embossed brass. **f.** piped key.
A study conducted by Donald Dion, an expert in the field, reveals that British butt hinges stamped "Baldwin" found on Québec articles date from after 1812, the year that this manufacturing company was established.

Industrial manufactured goods in the North American tradition, 2nd half of the 19th century

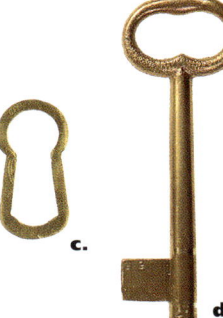

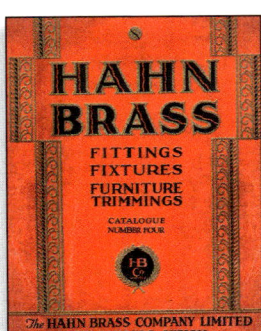

a.-e. cupboard catches, cast-iron. **b.-c.** keyhole escutcheons, cast in brass. **d.** pin-key. **f.** butt hinge, riveted laminated iron. **g.** reversible cupboard lock (right- or left-handed), stamped laminated iron. **h.** reversible cupboard lock, cast-iron, U.S.A.

Anyone who wants to understand the history of furniture hardware and recognize classics in every style and from every period will find an invaluable tool in the catalogue put out by the Hahn Brass Company Limited of New Hamburg, Ontario; it was the largest manufacturer of such goods from the end of the 19th century to World War II.

An Expert in Old Hardware

My curiosity about old hardware began in the 1970s, when there was a real rebirth of interest in this field in Old Québec. Before that, restoration projects never reused door and window hardware that represented all the ironmongery of early periods and particularly the 19th century. It was treated as worthless and old-fashioned, even when it was still in good condition. Almost all of these architectural elements came from Great Britain or the United States. Over the years, my interest grew into a veritable passion. I eventually collected thousands of pieces, all of which were used in Québec prior to 1920 and many of which have been scientifically documented. This collection has proved extremely useful for understanding and restoring old buildings.

It is difficult to have such a passion for architectural hardware and not also be attracted to the hardware used on furniture.

The hardware found on old furniture in Québec, in contrast to what may be observed in France and England, for example, has less to do with ornamentation and aesthetics than with function; the primary purpose of such hardware was to hang a door or efficiently close and lock a door, a drawer or shutter.

Hardware may be classified not only according to the piece of furniture to which it was attached — chest, chest of commodes, armoire or sideboard — but also on the basis of its cultural origins. Until the beginning of the 19th century, hinges, locks, handles and bolts were hand-forged here in Québec by the members of the "Confrérie de Saint-Éloi," a guild-like association under St. Eloi, the patron of metalwork. From 1790 onward, as is shown by archival documents and various articles on furnishings, Lower Canada (what is now Québec) was inundated with hardware from Great Britain, corresponding to British tastes and manners. These inexpensive goods were made first with mass-production methods and eventually with the assembly-line techniques that soon monopolized the manufacturing sector. As a result, the weak local production, which was never hallmarked, gradually dwindled and eventually disappeared.

The Locksmith's Art in New France

Furniture in the French manner, essentially pieces from the 17th and 18th centuries such as chests, armoires and commodes, were made with locks and hinges imported from France. This iron hardware, some of which was struck with the craftsman's hallmark, was always hand-forged. At Saint-Roch-des-Aulnaies, Roland Létourneau lives in his family's old home, built at the turn of the 18th century. It once housed the workshop belonging to his ancestors, master locksmiths who had moved from Québec City to Saint-Roch, where they continued to practise their trade. In this heritage home, the workshop has been kept much as it would have been long ago, according to a 1767 French treatise on locksmithing,

(continued on page 123)

FURNITURE HARDWARE

Furniture hardware always harmonizes with the stylistic trends of an era. Keys, handles and knobs reflect the taste of the times.

a. keyhole escutcheon, Louis XV manner, cast brass, France, mid-19th century. **b.** handle with keyhole escutcheon, cast brass, Ontario, ca. 1925. **c.** keyhole escutcheon, cast brass, Ontario, ca. 1925. **d.** piped key, patented terminal design, U. S. A., 1859. **e.** piped key, bronze, U. S. A., ca. 1880. **f.** piped key, bronze and iron, U. S. A., Belle Époque, 1900. **g.** piped key with folding terminal, France, ca. 1920. **h.** double-bit key, U.S.A., early 20th century. **i.** keyhole escutcheon for roll-top desk, U. S. A., late 19th century. **j.** keyhole escutcheon for roll-top desk, punched brass, U. S. A., early 20th century.

a. drop handle, wood and brass, last quarter of the 19th century. **b., c., d., g.** glass knobs, 20th century. **e.** brown ceramic knob, late 19th century. **f.** brass mushroom knob, first half of the 19th century. **h.** turned wood knob, first half of the 19th century. **i.** cupboard turn, porcelain and brass, England, ca. 1860.

L'Art du serrurier, by Duhamel du Monceau containing engraved plates dating from the very early 18th century.

British Production

In the 19th century, the age of Neoclassicism, furniture hardware was no longer made of wrought iron but rather of cast and laminated metal. The resulting articles were not only more polished and lustrous but also generally better finished. Hinges were almost always made of cast iron or brass.

The furniture hardware used in the St. Lawrence Valley until 1860 was of British production. As of 1780, all trade was controlled by the nation that had won the Seven Years' War. Commercial connections were maintained exclusively with Britain, and furniture hardware reflects this change, as well as the effects of the industrial revolution and a new market dynamic.

North American Hardware

In the mid-19th century, hardware produced in the United States began to compete with British goods and soon supplanted them. In a number of fields, Québec maintained a close trading relation with its neighbor to the south, where mass production was expanding rapidly. In Québec City's long-closed locksmiths' shops and hardware stores dating from this period, I have found big catalogues of over 700 pages, published by Yale & Town or Eagle Lock, two Connecticut manufacturers that supplied our furniture retailers and industries, which were also expanding rapidly. Ontario marketed similar products as of 1880.

Keys with decorative terminals are among the most attractive items of furniture hardware offered in this vast market. Since they were very visible in a lock, they were fashioned artistically. Most were made of brass and some were even plated with gold or silver.

All kinds of materials were used to manufacture furniture handles. The second half of the 19th century saw numerous inventions. The market offered decorative handles in carved wood or moulded wood pulp, for use on chests of drawers and other bedroom furniture. Turned wood knobs, in various sizes, appeared very early on. The simplest and most rustic of all hardware is the wooden or metal latch for closing doors. In the Belle Époque, before the introduction of plastic, knobs were made of different colored glass, porcelain and ceramic. The hardware of each style and period was adapted to the major artistic movements of the time. In the Art Deco period, fashionable hardware was designed with fluid lines and was made out of aluminum, chrome and plastic.

For me, having a curious mind and restoring hardware is more important than collecting. People come and ask me to open an old lock, or repair it or find its key. Although some of these locks have held their secrets for a long time, none of them has kept it from me forever. I believe that, in its way, the story of furniture hardware recounts the development of old furniture in Québec. Hardware, in combination with other elements, enables us to improve our knowledge and scientific interpretation of this aspect of Québec's material culture and decorative arts.

Donald Dion, May 1998, Québec City

a., d., e., g., h. drawer handles, brass (**g.** England, ca. 1800), (**d.-e.** Ontario, ca. 1900), (**a.-h.** U. S. A., ca. 1875). **k., m., o.** drawer handles of carved wood and (**m.**) of wood pulp. (**k.-o.**) U. S. A., ca. 1875. **b., c., f., i., j., l.** drawer handles, cast iron, North America, Belle Époque in Pre-Modern manner. **n.-p.** Art Deco handles, plastic, alloys, enamelled and plated steel, North America, ca. 1930. **q., r., s.** International-style handles and knobs, plastic, chrome- and brass-plated steel, North America, ca. 1950.

SETTLEMENT AND UTILITARIAN FURNITURE

The study of furniture production over three centuries reveals certain pieces whose design defies classification on the basis of the styles and great movements that influenced the Western world and therefore affected Québec. Such pieces show a more or less marked lack of reference to styles or tastes, whether from France, Great Britain or our neighbors to the south. These articles are known collectively as settlement furniture, although terms like "survival" or development-era furniture have also been used. Distinguished by its elementary forms, this furniture is found wherever people lived. It seems to have been made by hand out of necessity, simply to provide people with basic furniture for sleeping, storing goods and preparing and eating food.

111
Bucket bench. Pine, Saint-François, Île d'Orléans, late 18th century.
Buckets of water taken from outside wells were traditionally kept on benches like this one or on small, fairly open-face cupboards near the front door of rural houses. The yoke hanging from the wall made it easier to carry two buckets at a time.

112
Line drawing of a family room in a farmer's home, by an illustrator-reporter for *Harper's New Monthly Magazine* (New York, August 1883). Two women work around a chair-table.
A considerable amount of rural furniture in Québec does not belong to any specific stylistic movement. Many articles were intended above all to be functional.

This unpretentious furniture, possessing almost no stylistic references, was designed above all to be sturdy and functional. It was made with resources found in the immediate vicinity, and the most durable and easily worked wood was generally used. Québec pioneers usually chose pine and butternut — with yellow birch for seats — when they wanted to construct a table, sideboard, bed, chair or armchair, which are the principle items belonging to this category.

This household furniture generally belongs to a rural past, dating from the earliest period in which people settled the land in different regions. Such articles, whether moveable or built-in, were made and used in the primitive temporary shelters that settlers erected when they first arrived — dwellings that they usually enlarged or rebuilt later as permanent houses. In his book entitled *À la façon du temps présent. Trois siècles d'architecture populaire au Québec* (1999), Paul-Louis Martin offers insights into the phenomenon through a study of the rural home in the Trois-Rivières region, the geographical heart of the country. Furniture often paralleled the manner in which settlers occupied the land, evolving as they became better established. Once people were well settled in, they made or ordered new furniture that was better suited to their improved surroundings and condition. These new articles were made in fashionable styles or reflected the influence of such trends. The earlier furniture was relegated to the summer kitchen, the attic, a shed or the maple sugar shack. It was also sometimes used for storage in the space under sloping garret roofs. I have often seen functional articles belonging to this category in attics; simple chests and wardrobes for storing old clothes and extra household linens were often made to order to fit into these spaces.

Settlement furniture comes from every period in which land was settled. In the 1930s, when land was opened in the Abitibi, the Gaspé Peninsula and the hinterland of the lower St. Lawrence, the first people to clear the land also made such goods. This furniture was put together with wire nails instead of the cut or forged nails that were used before the end of the 19th century. The form, function and dimensions of such furniture were shaped by a certain concern for the aesthetics of the time and for certain loosely defined stylistic trends.

The enduring attraction of settlement furniture resides in its functional simplicity, clean lines and straightforward solidity, as well as a certain elegance that shows how closely the language of the hands is related to that of the heart and true taste. These basic values were taken up by 20th-century Functionalists, whose furniture developed out of the Industrial Design movement.

113
Pie safe. Original color, pine, Bellechasse, late 19th century.
This piece of furniture was mainly used to keep meat pies, pastries and other provisions for winter feasts. It was placed in the summer kitchen, which became a cold storage room when temperatures fell.

THE EVER-CHANGING STORY OF STYLE

114 to 119
Chairs

114
Three similar chairs with four slats and seats of woven elm splints. Ash and yellow birch, Trois-Rivières region, last quarter of the 19th century.

115
Graceful Chambly-type chair with turned back posts, delicate slats and elm splint seat, showing U.S. influence. Original color, yellow birch, last quarter of the 19th century.

116
Chair with four shaped slats and rush seat. Original color, maple, Montréal region, last quarter of the 19th century.

117
Rush-seat chair of a type known as *à la capucine*, with shaped slats. Ash and yellow birch, Montréal region, late 19th century.

118
Exceptional chair with a shaped crest rail and a woven babiche seat. Original color. Québec City, ca. 1880.

119
Bellechasse-type chairs attributed to a certain Salomon Denault *dit* Luneau, with openwork crest rails joined with double tenons. Original colors, ash and yellow birch, ca. 1890.
The middle chair is a rocker.

THE EVER-CHANGING STORY OF STYLE

120 to 122
Highchairs
Children's highchairs. Ash and yellow birch, late 19th century.
Handcrafted or homemade children's highchairs are among the most touching types of chairs. Although such items were already being produced industrially in the last quarter of the 19th century, the arrival of a first child was often a perfect opportunity for many new fathers to express their happiness by constructing a highchair with materials on hand or to stop by the village carpenter's shop to order one. Time has spared a great number of these meaningful rustic articles, which were no doubt much in demand, given the high birthrate known as the "revenge of the cradle."

123 to 131
Rustic armchairs with backs made with shaped or openwork slats or turned spindles, and plank or babiche seats. Original or reapplied color, ash, yellow birch and pine; unknown origins, between 1850 and 1890.
There are boundless variations on the country-made Québec chair. Each chair maker gave his work a personal touch, although it is always possible to detect certain links with the major stylistic trends of the day or with specific types of chairs.

THE EVER-CHANGING STORY OF STYLE 129

132 to 148
Rocking chairs

Rustic rocking chairs, like country-made chairs and armchairs, are found in an endless variety. There is a tendency to consider such articles as being much older than they really are. When a chair is 100 years old, it is very, very old. Atttributing an age of 150 years or more to such an item is not very realistic. Some of these rocking chairs were constructed according to a U.S. technique: the pine seat was formed first and the rest was structured around it. Others are made in the French manner: the front and back stiles gave the basic form of the finished product. The seats on French-style rocking chairs may be of elm splints, babiche, rush, cord or ash wicker. Certain Québec rockers can be associated with a specific region, while others are related to models found in the United States. Along with pine for seats, the chief types of wood used to build rocking chairs were yellow birch, white birch, ash and maple. Not very long ago, it was quite common for rocking chairs to be made by hand and given a very personal touch. Paul-Louis Martin's study, listed in the bibliography, is highly informative on this subject. Rocking chairs were usually single-seated, but double ones for sweethearts are also found, especially in the Rivière-du-Loup region. The chairs may have plain or shaped slat backs, and the crest rail may be decorated with openwork motifs. Others have backs formed with spindles or splats that may be solid or ornamented with openwork designs. A rocking chair found today may have been painted only once, left with its most recent color, or stripped down to a coat that represents a given stage in the object's history. There are any number of techniques for joining the rockers to the chair. All of these rocking chairs, found in the antique market, date from between 1850 and 1930.

THE EVER-CHANGING STORY OF STYLE 131

149 to 151 a, b
Benches
There is an endless variety of simple rustic benches — from table benches, porch benches and settles to settle-beds, coffer-benches and rocker benches.

149
Table bench, in as-found condition. Pine, ca. 1850.

150
Porch bench, in as-found condition. Yellow birch, 19th century.

151 a, b
Rustic settle-bed (shown open and closed). Pine, 19th century.

THE EVER-CHANGING STORY OF STYLE 133

152 to 155
Primitive beds and cradles

152
Homemade child's potty chair. Pine, ca. 1860.

153
Rustic hooded cradle with shaped edging and scrolled rockers. Pine, Lacolle region, late 18th century.

154
Hooded cradle with corner posts. Pine, yellow birch and ash, Sorel, ca. 1850.

155
Rustic bed with turned posts. Yellow birch, ca. 1840.

156
Rustic open-face dresser assembled with both forged and cut nails. Original red, turquoise and salmon colors, pine, Eastern Townships, ca. 1850.

157 to 162
Service furniture
A traditional home contained several pieces of furniture used for bread making, holding water buckets or storing food. Such articles were often brightly painted. Each one has its own personality.

157
Panelled dough box. Original color as found, pine, Québec City region, early 19th century.

158
Rustic dough box. Original color as found, pine, Québec City region, 19th century.

159
Bucket bench. Original color, pine, Québec City region, late 19th century.

160
Bucket bench with backboard crest in moose-antler design. Pine, Bellechasse, ca. 1880.

161
Larder with panels decorated with block-carved lattices. Bare pine, late 18th century.

162
Pantry. Original color, pine, 18th century.

THE EVER-CHANGING STORY OF STYLE 137

FOLK ART AND FURNITURE

Throughout the history of furniture making in Québec, there have always been people who give their imagination free rein and invent all kinds of unusual forms with astonishing painted or carved decorations. Such folk artists are generally not furniture craftsmen. Their work is spontaneous, nourished by a world view that is quite divorced from the universe of stylistic canons and fashions. Avid collectors of folk art are entranced by the wild, often surrealistic, whimsicality of these pieces.

163
Small cupboard of Amerindian origin, decorated with painted diamond on door and asymmetrical geometric pattern on frame and assembled with forged nails. Original colors, pine, belonging to the Bastien family of Lorette, early 19th century.

164
Neoclassical cupboard with 12 raised panels, fitted with two doors and two drawers. Original color with whimsical plant-inspired motifs, pine, Côte-de-Beaupré, first quarter of the 19th century.
An exceptional piece.

165
Niched sideboard, decorated with inlay. Wood, glass and porcelain, Saint-Georges-de-Beauce, ca. 1890.
A whimsical take on Revival and Pre-Modern fashions. The maker, a certain Dubé, drew inspiration from Renaissance Revival sideboards and the Eastlake decorative style of the late 19th century to create a dining room sideboard enlivened with geometric inlay, generally in the shape of diamonds, squares and rectangles. The piece is crowned with turned finials and hoops with crosier-shaped scrolls that radiate like the rays of the sun as it marks the passage of time.
Twelve niches in basket-handle arches with banding reminiscent of the medieval Romanesque style each present a scene with figures. The lower row shows people enjoying pastimes — playing checkers, arm-wrestling, playing cards, drinking wine and reading. The upper row displays two black men in discussion, people exchanging snuff, two Amerindians, a lumber jack and a worker leaving home and a hobo's visit. This piece of folk-art furniture definitely offers material for lively conversation among guests around the table.

THE EVER-CHANGING STORY OF STYLE

CONCLUSION TO THE FIRST CHAPTER

The period from the colonization of New France and the founding of Québec City to the present spans four centuries marked by incredible developments in the history of the decorative arts and of furniture. Over time and throughout various movements, from the French manner of the rural late Middle Ages to the age of international modernity, the St. Lawrence Valley has displayed great openness in integrating and adapting cultural values from other places, from French classicism to Neoclassicism and from the Revival style to the proposals of the Pre-Modernist reformers. Although Québec never entirely abandoned handcrafted production, industry took over furniture making from the middle of the 19th century, meeting somewhat uneven success in its interpretation of the new ideas put forward by various thinkers, designers and architects whose achievements dynamically changed the evolution of interior decorating. Modern manufacturing technology and new materials made it possible to produce shapes that were quite without precedent and sometimes simply astonishing. Modern furniture design was governed by rationalism, functionalism and a search for comfort, with increasingly well-considered respect for the science of ergonomics. Finishes also followed this trend, resulting in very unusual effects.

As a producer, Québec has secured its share of the market by doing its best to integrate the principles of all the great movements that have swept through the West, and eventually through the world, over the past four centuries. But at the same time, Québec has welcomed goods produced by the inventive spirit and dexterity of foreign craftsmen. A study of the market in the last half of the 20th century makes it clear that furniture imported from France, England, the United States, Italy and the Scandinavian countries has found a place in the living and working spaces of Québec.

Throughout our land, a vast array of quite well-documented furniture has stood the test of time. Through this heritage it is possible to trace the sociocultural history of furniture as it developed at the crossroads of the three major cultures that forged modern Québec — the cultures of France, Great Britain and the United States. Numerous manuscripts, along with printed and iconographic material, provide a source of information that can guide field interviews and help to identify and examine articles that have survived the passage of time. Furniture that has been carefully conserved by religious communities, heritage-conscious families and private collectors, as well as national and regional museums, constitutes a true gold mine for research.

The history of furniture is intimately linked with developments in the decorative arts, interior decorating and architecture. It goes almost without saying that the most dedicated effort to safeguard precious old items comes from ordinary citizens whose awareness and love of furniture has led them to recognize the value of these treasures of our national identity and jealously preserve them. Many individual people have devoted themselves to acquiring, documenting, restoring and practically "living for" old furniture; these collectors bring great enthusiasm to their ventures and often pass the torch on from one generation to the next. Because of these people, certain pieces of furniture made several decades ago are still intact. It is such heritage enthusiasts, often trained on the job, who taught me the most about hardware, colors, conservation philosophies, trends, styles and fashions. Having met many of these enlightened thinkers and enjoyed long discussions with them — and having often had the opportunity to verify this opinion in the course of my research — I can say without the slightest hesitation that people in the private sector offer the most advanced, scholarly and avant-garde reflections on this area of material culture. This family of furniture devotees has always helped museums to flourish and acquire a wealth of material.

The next chapters will shed light on Québec's participation in the great movements affecting the decorative arts and material culture, and consequently the furniture industry. They will follow this development from the country's infancy to the present and cover domestic, handcrafted and industrial modes of production. This exercise would necessarily be incomplete without a synchronic view that takes into account each and every social class. A study like this one is inevitably subjective, since it is limited to the present state of knowledge about the field. The history of furniture represents a cultural area of such scope and density that it should logically occupy a whole contingent of researchers and mobilize the energy of an entire working team. Due to circumstances no doubt familiar to furniture enthusiasts, such an ideal situation is yet to be attained.

The book's divisions have been determined by questions of style. The types of articles that are not encompassed by the canons of a given era, or that seem fairly remote from the manner of known styles, have been dealt with in the sections on settlement furniture and folk art furniture in this chapter. Finally, furniture may be said to be very much like sculpture — you have to walk around a work to judge its real worth. I have therefore chosen an approach that allows pictures to speak for themselves.

166
Interior of a rural house, Calixa-Lavallée (reconstruction)
All these pieces of furniture — the armoire with recessed panels, Chambly-type chairs, washstand, gate-leg table and built-in armoire with raised panels — have been arranged to look as they would have in the living area of a 19th-century country home.

167 to 170
Details of New France-style furniture dating from the 18th century. Table leg ending in a scroll-carved foot; armoire panel in the Louis XV manner with ornamental details highlighted in contrasting color; shaped skirt and scroll foot of a commode; chair leg with baluster turnings mixed with rectangular sections.

Chapter 2

Provincial Traditions of the Ancien Régime and Classicism

Furniture in the French Manner

1640-1790
THE NEW FRANCE STYLE

THE INTERIOR OF THE HOUSES IS WELL FURNISHED: different sorts of tapestries, as we have, a commode with many drawers placed between two windows, a large mirror with a gilded frame hanging above the commode; various likenesses on the walls, among which a good number of priests and monks; similarly many images or paintings of saints, as well as fairly numerous depictions of Our Savior on the cross or of the Virgin Mary holding Our Savior in her arms. There are usually near the beds some of those curtains which are no longer fashionable in our homes in Sweden; a bed which differs from ours in that the canopy of the bed rests on an iron support and there are no posts at the foot. In truth, I have also seen beds with four posts, like our old Swedish beds.

Voyage de Pehr Kalm au Canada en 1749
[Translation based on John A. Fleming, *The Painted Furniture of French Canada 1700-1840*]

THE MATERIAL WEALTH OF THE *HABITANT* was reflected mainly in his furniture, which was considered the most beautiful in North America. The predominant style was Louis XIII, with doors decorated with diamond points, lozenges or square-shaped motifs in the manner of pieces from Normandy. Armoires and buffets were generally Louis XIII in spirit, while commodes were in the Louis XV style. Furniture in the Régence manner was very rare.

Canadian furniture was usually made of pine, although other types of wood were also employed.... Yellow birch, the next most commonly used type, served to make tables, chairs, chests, armoires, buffets, pedestal tables, and especially tall-post beds with canopies, or testers. In June 1673, Jeanne Mance already had a number of yellow birch tables, one of which was fitted with a drawer.

[Translation]
Robert-Lionel Séguin
La Civilisation traditionnelle de l'«habitant» aux 17ᵉ et 18ᵉ siècles

Long-case clock, first half of the 18th century.

Furniture in the French Manner

Furniture in the classical French manner includes built-in and movable furniture that was produced throughout the French Regime in the St. Lawrence Valley. This area, known as "Canada"[1] at the time, formed one of the administrative regions of New France, a vast territory that belonged to the French crown. The colony also encompassed French Acadia, Labrador, the King's Posts (from Sept-Îles to Les Éboulements, or the entire Lake Saint-Jean basin), the hinterland (the Great Lakes region, starting at Lachine), the West (from the Great Lakes to Saskatchewan) and Louisiana (the entire Mississippi River basin).

Most of the people who settled in this new French-speaking colony lived in three political subdivisions of "Canada." These subdivisions, known as governments, were defined by the geographical boundaries of Québec, Trois-Rivières and Montréal. The Government of Québec was the largest of the three, extending from Les Éboulements to Grondines on the north shore of the St. Lawrence River and from Rimouski to Deschaillons (including the Beauce region) to the south. This government also exercised more socio-political responsibilities than the other two subdivisions, in addition to having a larger population; it was inhabited by 40 000 people in 1760, the year the French were defeated by the British. Québec City was the capital not only of the Government of Québec but also of "Canada" and New France. The Government of Trois-Rivières stretched from Sainte-Anne-de-la-Pérade to Maskinongé on the north shore of the river and from Saint-Pierre-les-Becquets to Yamaska on the south shore. It had a population of around 6 000 when the colony was lost to the British. As for the Government of Montréal, it extended west from Maskinongé and Yamaska to Fort Saint-Jean, Châteauguay and Vaudreuil, which were located on the western limits of "Canada." Nearly 15 000 people lived in this subdivision.

Between 1608 and 1760, some 10 000 French men and women left their native land and its restrictive feudal system to make a dangerous trans-Atlantic voyage in search of freedom, property and a more promising future. Marcel Trudel, a historian who has studied this period in depth, has

171
Furniture in the Louis XIII manner at the Hôpital Général de Québec. Photograph by Ramsay Traquair, 1926.

172 a, b
(Pages 146-147)
Construction analysis and plans at a scale of 1:5 of a Louis XIII armchair by H. M. Magne, published in *Le mobilier français* (Paris, 1920). Walnut, 17th century, Musée de Cluny collection.
Fine example of an upholstered armchair with a trapezoidal plan, an H-stretcher, curved armrests and a raked, or inclined, back.

173 c
(Page 147)
Louis XIII armchair. Butternut, Québec City, early 18th century. Furniture of French derivation in the colony sometimes looked exactly like furniture found in France in the 17th and 18th centuries.

1. See "To the Reader," page 8.

THE NEW FRANCE STYLE
1608-1790

LOUIS XIII
1601-1643

LOUIS XV
1710-1774

SOURCES: French **LOUIS XIII**, Louis XIV, Régence and **LOUIS XV** styles.
The full repertoire of decorative elements, from classical geometric designs to the lyrical motifs of the Baroque and Rococo.

WOOD AND MATERIALS: pine, butternut, poplar, basswood, yellow birch and maple; black walnut and mahogany at the end of the period.

Louis XIII table, Québec City, 18th century.

COLLECTIONS: Musée de la civilisation in Québec City, museums of religious communities in Montréal and Québec City, Musée d'art de Saint-Laurent, Montreal Museum of Fine Arts, Royal Ontario Museum in Toronto, and Louisbourg in Atlantic Canada.

determined the origin of these immigrants quite accurately. Most were from Normandy, Île-de-France and Paris, Brittany and Poitou, Aunis, Île de Ré and Île d'Oléron, Guyenne, Saintonge, Languedoc and Perche.

When the colony fell into the hands of the British in 1760 during the Seven Years' War – a loss ratified by the Treaty of Paris, signed three years later – "Canada" had a population of 70 000 souls scattered throughout slightly over 200 seigneuries located along the main route into the colony: the St. Lawrence River and its tributaries.

A seigneury was a large piece of land that the King granted to a privilege-holder, or seigneur, who, in return, had to divide it into concessions and settle it with colonists or tenant farmers (*censitaires*). The seigneur was also obliged to build a grist mill and a manor where he would live (*tenir feu et lieu*). Colonists who obtained land under this system had to make a statement of vassalage (*foi et hommage*) to their seigneur, in compliance with a symbolic ritual of respect and authority. They also had to pay annual rent (*cens et rentes*) in cash or in kind by remitting part of their produce to him, and pledge to fulfil certain collective and community work duties. Despite these obligations and responsibilities, "Canadian" *habitants* had far more freedom than peasants under the Ancien Régime in France.

A well-organized society rapidly took shape in the colony. By the early 18th century, "Canada" was like a French province situated overseas, endowed with a political structure and system of laws and subject to the religious authority of the Catholic Church. As the guardian of public morality, the Church was determined to evangelize Aboriginal people and convert pagan souls for the love of God. The colony had a fairly complex administration, with civil servants, governors, intendants and controllers in charge of various sectors of activity. This is not to mention the many military officers and soldiers posted at strategic locations for the purpose of pacifying Native people and keeping an eye on the British. The troops concentrated their operations in the vicinity of "Canada's" borders, which were not very well defined or defended at the time. The colony also boasted a large number of social institutions, owned by the secular and regular clergy. Consisting of seminaries, schools, convents, hospitals, almshouses and orphanages, their architecture dominated the urban landscape. Several religious communi-

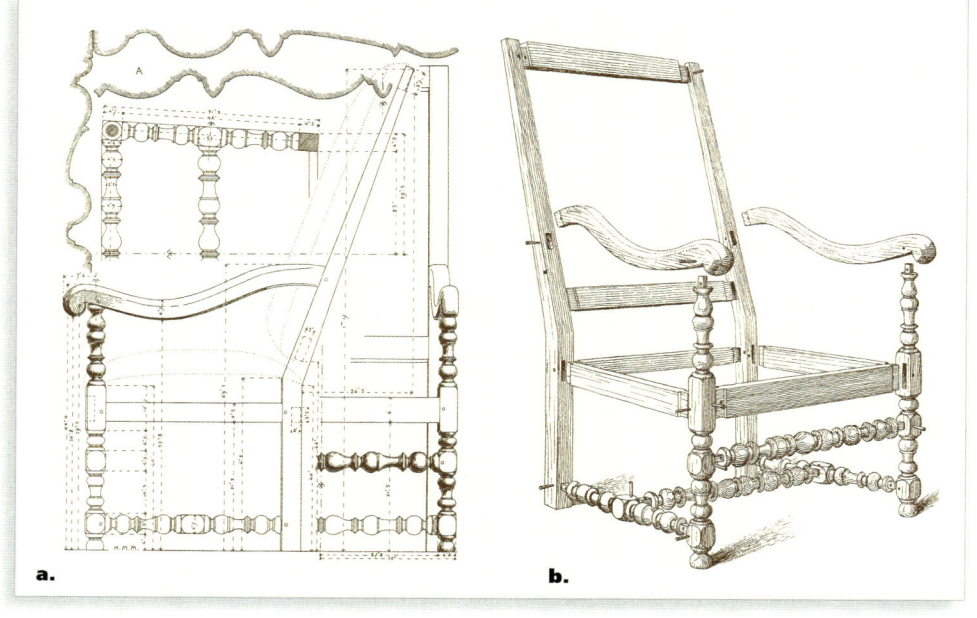

a.   b.

ties provided social services in their establishments, all of which housed a steepled chapel evoking the presence of the Church of Rome. "Canada's" religious communities included the Recollets and the Jesuits, who arrived in the colony in 1615 and 1625 respectively; the Ursulines, a teaching order of nuns, and the Augustinian Hospitallers, both of which came to Québec City in 1639; and the Grey Nuns and the Hospitallers of St. Joseph in Montréal, two congregations that were founded here in the 17th century. The colony was divided into parishes, each devoted to a saint and furnished with a church whose monumental architecture testified to the presence and supremacy of the sacred world. The church, its consecrated enclosure and its presbytery were the centre of community life in each parish. Every Sunday and on each of the 37 holidays of obligation observed during the liturgical year prior to 1744, the faithful assembled in their house of worship, adorned with statues and paintings, to implore the protection of a benevolent pantheon.

The colony also had its share of businessmen and businesswomen (often widows), who were active for the most part in the fur, timber and grain trades, shipbuilding or the importation of goods for the retail market. This bourgeoisie established enterprises in urban areas, mainly Québec City, which was the business centre of the day.

The vast majority of the population was confined to the bottom of the social scale and consisted of *habitants*, craftsmen plying various traditional trades, and soldiers. *Habitants* earned their livelihood from farming and often operated a fishery on the banks of the St. Lawrence. Knowledge, techniques, land and tools were handed down from father to son, as each extended family preserved the material heritage and skills of a tightly knit occupational network. People associated with and married individuals who were involved in the same trade.

Under these circumstances, the culture that colonists brought with them from their native French provinces remained relatively unchanged on the shores of the St. Lawrence. Their collective memory and the knowledge they had acquired in the country they left behind shaped not only their language, accent, customs and relation to the sacred world, but also the architectural landscape of the colony's rural and urban areas, the tools and accessories used for domestic or artisanal purposes, and the interior decoration and furniture of settlers' houses. The colonists thus recreated their mother country in their new homeland.

Since immigrants from different French provinces were concentrated in the St. Lawrence Valley, this area witnessed the blending of secular cultural experiences with the traditions associated with the parts of France where these colonists were born. Furniture and domestic architecture became veritable melting pots of the medieval and classical provincial tastes and styles imported from these regions.

During the 17th and 18th centuries, Québec furniture essentially reproduced regional French models from Normandy, Brittany and Île-de-France, which were very different from those used by the French nobility. Québec did not resemble Versailles, but rather Mortagne,

THE NEW FRANCE STYLE 147

THE SPIRIT OF FRANCE 1600-1790

The French colonial period lasted until the signing of the Treaty of Paris in 1763. For over 150 years, "Canada" was like a French province situated overseas. During that time, the material culture of the St. Lawrence Valley was influenced by the stylistic values in vogue in the mother country. The Louis XIII and Louis XV styles shaped the spirit of objects in their relation to classicism and the Baroque.

French faience, 18th century.

Pewter plate with shaped rim in the Louis XV manner, 18th century.

Votive painting of Madame Riverin and her children, Québec City, 1703.

Coat of arms of the King of France, carved by Noël Levasseur in Québec City around 1727.

Ivory crucifix, France, 18th century.

Dispensary table of Louis XIII inspiration, Montréal, 18th century.

Michel Sarrazin (1659-1734), surgeon, physician and "Canadian" naturalist, by Pierre Mignard.

Men's embroidered vest, once owned by Chartier de Lotbinière, Québec City, ca. 1765.

Charest house, Saint-Pierre Street, Québec City, 1757.

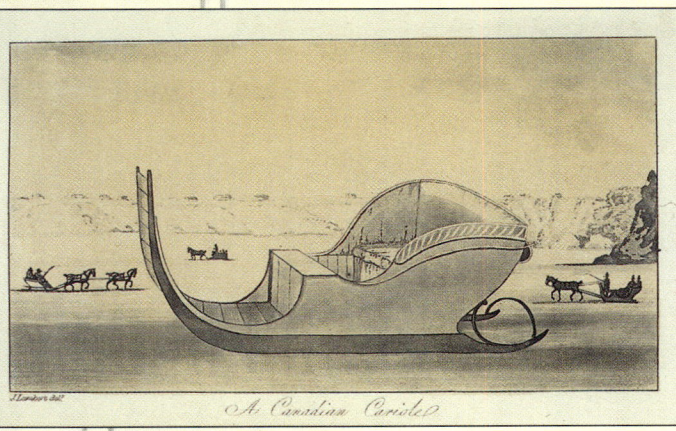
"Canadian" sleigh by John Lambert, ca. 1810.

Betty lamp (rustic lighting device), iron, 17th century.

Diamond-point armoire in the Louis XIII manner, ca. 1775.

Cast-iron stove from the Forges du Saint-Maurice, Trois-Rivières, ca. 1760.

Ecclesiastical robe chest, or vestry commode, of Louis XV derivation, ca. 1750.

THE CABINETMAKER

A Master Cabinetmaker in the Capital of New France
Germain Villiard (1693-1749)

Germain Villiard was born in Germany in 1693 to André Villiard and Anne-Magdeleine Culliers, who once lived in the Twelve Apostles Parish in the city of Cologne. It is not known why Germain Villiard came to Québec City, although it may have been for a military service engagement. This is suggested by the fact that Sieur Damariton, the captain of a company of the French navy, acted as his father on his wedding day. The captain described himself as Villiard's "protector in this land." Villiard married Françoise Guillot in Notre-Dame Church in Québec City on November 4, 1721. She was the daughter of one of the King's master carpenters, Jean Guillot, who was already well established in the city. The signature of joiner Villiard, written with a sure, clear hand, appears at the bottom of the marriage contract signed in the house of his protector on Saint-Famille Street on the eve of his wedding.[1]

Like many other craftsmen of the time, Germain Villiard built up a business network through advantageous family alliances and carefully maintained professional relations. The guarantors or witnesses who accompanied him when he made contractual commitments, had his children baptized or gave them away in marriage consisted of joiners, carpenters and masons, an upholsterer by the name of Henri Arnault, a merchant named Philippe Biraud de La Ferté, a ship's captain by the name of Abel Olivier and, on several occasions of course, Sieur Damariton, his protector.

Germain Villiard lived in Québec City's Upper Town, first in a house on Saint-Flavien Street and then on Saint-Joseph, now known as Garneau Street. He kept the house on Saint-Flavien, but rented it out, as shown by the land registers of the Séminaire de Québec, to which the rent was paid.[2] The inventory of community property drawn up after the death of his first wife reveals that he was already fairly wealthy by that time. He married again in 1743, taking as his new wife a widow by the name of Marie-Angélique Renaud, who had 15 children. She brought her three youngest ones with her when she came to live with Villiard and his two sons from his first marriage.[3] When Villiard died in 1749, his real estate holdings, the property he left to his heirs (furniture, silverware, pewter, cash, outstanding debts) and his daughters' dowries reflected the good fortune that had smiled on this joiner from Germany.

Various archival documents mention that Villiard took part in the finishing work on the church in Saint-Augustin-de-Desmaures in 1723 and helped to repair the bishop's palace the following year.

Villiard's workshop contained not only a large amount of wood of different types and sizes, but also dressing and joining tools, drawing pens, measuring instruments, arithmetic books and all the accessories needed to design and draw the objects he planned to make. Villiard had such a good reputation as a designer and master joiner that Étienne Cugnet, who was in charge of the Forges du Saint-Maurice, commissioned his services in 1737.[4] Perhaps Villiard helped to decorate some of the buildings at the ironworks, including the *Grande Maison* (ironmaster's house), or to design some of the wooden models used to make moulds for casting objects such as stoves. Although it is impossible to confirm these hypotheses, Villiard's relations with the directors of the ironworks seem to have continued throughout the 1740s, given that his tools were still there when he died in 1749.

The probate inventory drawn up on August 29, 1750 after Villiard's death is highly informative not only with regard to the type of articles he made but also as far as his work methods and sources of inspiration are concerned.

For example, it lists the different accessories he used to design his products:

"a small shagreen case containing a copper compass, a pen holder with two drawing pens, and a compass point; a very small wooden box containing two razors in poor condition and a piece of leather; fifty new prints or engraved plans used in the occupation of the deceased; three small books of drawing paper with seven detached pieces used in the occupation of the deceased, all old or damaged." [Translation]

It also mentions a number of unfinished pieces of furniture:

"wood for three commodes, the said wood being *bois des Isles* [mahogany]; another similar bundle, yellow birch for making three more commodes; another bundle of unsawn yellow birch for making three commodes; five cornices with rollers and four without rollers; a new wooden sofa frame, ready for assembly; a new yellow birch armchair frame mounted with its webbing." [Translation]

The inventory also lists numerous pieces of wood, including exotic types, such as mahogany and black walnut; dozens of beams and planks of yellow birch, pine and spruce; pieces of maple in poor condition; piles of walnut of different sizes; a pile of maple planks, wavy-grained at one end; smoothed and squared planks of pine; another small pile of walnut from the Niagara area (black walnut); three pieces of mahogany; a pile of pieces of logs and quartered logs of maple; and lastly, a large quantity of planks, joists and beams of pine, maple and yellow birch, set out to dry in the attic of Villiard's house or stored in his backyard.

The tools and equipment still located in the joiner's workshop after his death appear in the inventory as well. Besides two yellow birch workbenches (nine and seven feet long respectively), one of which was equipped with a vice, the shop contained trying planes, mandrels for making screws, dozens of moulding planes, including several curved ones, plough planes, rebate planes, smoothing planes, beading planes, squares, a cooper's adze, straight and angled rasps, paring chisels, an adze, mortise chisels and gouges, hand saws, a brace with bits, files, wooden and iron clamps, rip saws, a large three-foot-long dog, a hammer, two marking gauges, a folding ruler, a compass, a small bow saw with a frame, a large German saw with a frame, an old brass pot with three legs and an iron handle for making glue, a hinged iron candleholder for lighting the shop, a set of seven whetstones for sharpening tools, fifteen pounds of strong glue for use in the shop, and so forth.

Germain Villiard was no doubt one of the highly skilled craftsmen who helped to decorate or furnish some of the most prestigious buildings and residences in New France. Given that he arrived here around 1715, he had the good fortune to live during what was not only the most peaceful period of the French Regime but also the most prosperous, owing to the activities of the royal shipyards, the establishment of the King's ironworks, and triangular trade with the West Indies. This joiner, who obtained supplies from the Caribbean (mahogany), the Great Lakes region (black walnut from around Niagara) and of course Québec City, drew his inspiration from European masters and made fine furniture for a wealthy clientele. His work thus differs from that of most other joiners in New France, since it was produced during a kind of golden age on the shores of the St. Lawrence.

We have tried to trace some of the furniture made by Villiard that is described in the inventory of his belongings after his death and that remained in his widow's possession in accordance with the terms of their marriage contract. These pieces consist of a "yellow birch commode measuring around four feet long by three and a half feet wide with two large drawers, two small ones, hardware and pulls, the whole locking with a key" [Translation]; "six dark-colored spindle-back chairs with turned legs, made of yellow birch" [Translation] and a "medium-small mirror with its old gilded frame measuring twelve inches high by eight inches wide." [Translation] These items reappear in 1764 in the probate inventory of Villiard's oldest daughter, Françoise Germaine, wife of merchant Joseph Voyer.[5] We have not found any trace of them, however, after that date.

More extensive research would surely reveal the names of other extremely gifted artisans who, like Germain Villiard, worked wood so beautifully.

Paul-Louis Martin
Historian and ethnologist
Professor at UQTR

---

1. ANQQ, Me Dubreuil, November 3, 1721, Nº. 1754. Marriage contract between Germain Villiard and Françoise Guillot. Folio 19v contains the registration of the contract in the register of civil status of Notre-Dame de Québec Parish on November 4.
2. Archives du Séminaire de Québec, Terriers S-208, p. 44 and S-209, p. 7.
3. 1744 census, RAPQ, 1940, p. 67.
4. According to the company accounts submitted to the Intendant, Germain Villiard received the sum of five livres between 1737 and 1739. Public Archives of Canada. MG1, C11A, Vol. 111-2, September 6, 1742. A note to the inventory of Villiard's belongings after his death indicates that, since the joiner had died at the ironworks in August 1749, the notary Barolet requested that the tools of the deceased be sent to him. (ANQQ, Greffe Barolet, August 29, 1750, Nº. 2327. Inventory of the community property of the late Germain Villiard and Marie-Angélique Renaud.)
5. ANNQ, Greffe Saillant, April 10, 1764, Nº. 1492. Inventory of the late Françoise Germaine Villiard, widow of Joseph Routier and Joseph Voyer.

PERSONAL ACCOUNT

A Passion for Old Furniture

I began to take an interest in Québec's material culture in the early 1960s. Harvey Rivard, a photographer and the father of a friend of mine, was an experienced collector of old furniture of French derivation, mainly armchairs, chairs, tables, commodes and other pieces in the Louis XIII and Louis XV manners. When I saw this furniture in the home of Mr. Rivard and his wife, it was love at first sight. I was struck by the workmanship, patina and charm of the objects they had collected since 1934, the year my hometown, Trois-Rivières, celebrated its 300th anniversary. My future wife Marie and I decided, long before we were married, to furnish our own home with traditional Québec furniture.

In the 1960s, people were keenly interested in their origins and in objects from the past. During an impromptu conversation with one of my professors, Luc Lacoursière, when I was taking an arts degree at Université Laval, he suggested, after noticing my interest in old objects, that I do research on Québec rocking chairs. I had originally planned to study the chest, an object that fascinated me since it was fraught with so much significance and endowed with a certain mysterious quality. The chest not only was the forerunner of all furniture, including the buffet, the commode and several types of case furniture, but had an extremely long history, as shown by the discovery of some very old specimens in Egypt. Nevertheless, I soon learned that Luc Lacoursière had made an excellent suggestion given that the rocking chair seems to have an even richer history than the chest.

My wife and I gradually built up a collection of sorts. Even though we have replaced some objects with more interesting ones over the years, we have always kept our first purchase: a small red table dating from the 1820s, which looks beautiful in our home. When I started doing research for my master's thesis on rocking chairs, I discovered that I knew very little about joinery, chair making, cabinetmaking and upholstering techniques. Since the university had no specific reference material on the subject, I decided to learn the techniques firsthand by working with Jean-Marie Dussault, an antique dealer and cabinetmaker in Deschambault, who had preserved the rich tradition of woodworking. I followed a kind of on-the-job-training program with him, similar to programs offered today, and learned a great deal about different kinds of wood, joining techniques, construction methods and so forth. I will never forget the many months I spent studying furniture and domestic objects, interviewing older people, and touring the countryside with "pickers" in search of old treasures, happily immersed in the very real world of antique dealing. The contact I had with objects during that time has always stood me in good stead.

For me, Québec furniture from the 18th and 19th centuries is very eloquent. To begin with, the materials used to make it are extremely beautiful. I have always been fascinated with its wide pine planks, thick members and well-chosen, knot-free wood. Behind such choices was the craftsman, who obviously studied his materials carefully. Anyone who has ever stripped an old piece of furniture has no doubt felt to some extent as if he or she were retracing the steps of the person who made it — a feeling exactly like that experienced by the restorer of an old house as he or she removes traces of modern renovations and repairs, explores every inch of the structure and gradually discovers how it was built.

Contact with an object brings us closer not only to the person who made it but to the person who used it. For example, when one restores an old rocking chair, one can feel the marks left by the elderly woman who counted her strands of wool on it or by the old man who struck his matches beneath the seat when he lit his pipe. One can see signs of damage in spots and determine how they occurred, or even detect in the wood the position in which a person usually sat there. On one occasion, as I was looking inside an old armoire, I discovered carved dates and engraved lines, marking perhaps the number of days a person had spent waiting for a loved one... In other words, by looking beyond the superficial appearance of a piece of furniture, it is possible to make contact with the people who made and used it. We can thus forge ties with our forefathers, gain insight into their tastes and customs and uncover endearing reminders of how daily life leaves its mark on the things around us. These statements reflect a very romantic attitude no doubt, but doesn't our short time on this earth make us all part of this process? I always find it interesting once I know the provenance of a particular piece to imagine all sorts of links with our predecessors. Objects move me because they have a history and bear tangible traces of the past.

The everyday furniture of each country has its own special character. Although our craftsmen may not have invented new furniture forms, given that joiners in towns and cities usually perpetuated French traditions, they drew considerable inspiration from the new world around them, as shown by the animal and plant motifs found on beautiful armoires like those of the Rivière-Ouelle type. In addition, our ancestors learned how to take advantage of the qualities of each of the types of wood at their disposal. Pierre Boucher's description of the colony in the 17th century shows how they strove, from the very start, to identify the specific characteristics of each species in order to put it to the best possible use. The materials they chose and their knowledge of the qualities of each type of wood are precisely what reflect the true genius of our ancestors. Moreover, they mastered all the necessary techniques while demonstrating a keen sense of beauty and craftsmanship as well as a certain originality.

Paul-Louis Martin
Historian and ethnologist
Saint-André de Kamouraska
June 1999

174
Sifroy-Guéret-*dit*-Dumont house, Saint-André de Kamouraska, 1840.
Office of the merchant Sifroy-Guéret *dit* Dumont. This house, which was built in 1840, still has its original interior design and finishing. Note the integrated two-tiered buffet-armoire and its doors with recessed panels, the baseboard with its grain-painted finish in imitation of oak, the board and batten ceiling and rich moulding. This room, which is finished entirely in pine and has never been painted, has acquired a lovely patina over the years. The chest, with its imitation elm burl finish and trompe l'œil inlay, is also made of pine and comes from Côte-de-Beaupré (ca. 1840). This photograph captures the spirit of a rural bourgeois interior in the Neoclassical style.

the capital of Perche, from which some two hundred colonists originated, or Rouen or La Rochelle. The people emigrating from these places brought their traditional furniture forms with them when they settled in the colony. Such transfers explain the marked similarly between *habitant* and peasant furniture on both sides of the Atlantic. The furniture of Québec merchants, civil servants and religious communities was very much like that of their counterparts in the various French provinces, not only in terms of its form, finishing, ornamentation and color, but also with regard to its function, given that it was designed to meet the same needs. However, it was less influenced by the stylistic rules that governed the production of the period pieces in vogue among the upper classes. The homes of the elite, namely, the Governor, the Intendant and the Bishop, and those of the bourgeoisie in Place Royale in Québec City and in the walled part of Montréal, were furnished like French mansions, while seminaries and convents were fitted out like the motherhouses of their respective religious communities in France. While Québec architecture is undeniably linked to French models, with some inevitable adaptation to the North American climate, the few pieces of old Québec furniture that have survived, usually as religious community property, bear a striking similarity to pieces produced on the other side of the Atlantic.

It should be noted that much of our current knowledge about Québec's material culture comes from our religious communities which, bound by their vows of poverty and enclosure, have preserved a number of domestic objects that now provide insight into daily life during the early years of the colony. In certain cases, these objects correspond to personal property inherited over the years from private sources. Nuns, for example, sometimes inherited luxurious items on the death of important people whom they had taken into their hospitals and hospices – items that furnished the rooms of these people at the end of their days. These objects, which are now exhibited in museums run by these communities, shed light on Québec's early ethnohistory.

A scientific study of the pieces preserved by religious communities and various individuals, as well as of pieces that are now part of our national heritage collections, has made it possible to draw certain conclusions about Québec furniture during the 1640-1790 period.

First, two styles, namely, Louis XIII and Louis XV, dominated the French Regime, with the Régence and Louis XIV styles exerting a minor influence. The Louis XIII style, which was heavily informed by the classical lines of the Renaissance, was relatively simple, favoring geometrical shapes and baluster or ball turnings. In contrast, the Louis XV style was very lyrical. Developed in the wake of the Baroque, it was embellished with serpentine lines and shaping, and drew its inspiration from the vast repertoire of animal and plant forms. Such forms can be seen, for example, in the cabriole legs, scroll feet, *rocaille* motifs and shell carvings found on Louis XV furniture, and in the shaped panels and sometimes elaborate phytomorphic ornamentation that decorated armoire doors in this style.

Both the Louis XIII and Louis XV styles were modified to some extent in "Canada." Although numerous archival documents reveal that certain items such as chairs, armchairs, chests, armoires and commodes were imported, especially early on, almost all furniture was made in the colony. A variety of local woods were used for this purpose, particularly pine and butternut, since these species were easy to work with hand tools. However, as in traditional French furniture making, hardwoods, such as yellow birch, walnut and oak, were also employed to a certain extent. In fact, judging from a perusal of early notarial records, it seems that the colonists took advantage of all species at hand. Sometimes with the help of models, experienced joiners with a thorough grounding in traditional French techniques skilfully used saws, planes, gouges, compasses and squares to build solid, functional, expertly assembled pieces of furniture, which they painted, stained or, less frequently, varnished. According to the many probate inventories drawn up by notaries – which provide considerable information on the furnishings of rural and urban homes in the last quarter of the 17th century – domestic interiors were already surprisingly well organized in the early days of the colony, being equipped with chests, armoires, buffets and tester beds. The rich interior decor and range of furniture found in homes at the time is well documented by the works of Robert-Lionel Séguin, which cover all aspects of colonial life during the French Regime, and in a study by Bernard Audet on the material culture of Île d'Orléans in the 17th century.

Although the various furniture makers, the area where they made and sold their products, and their genealogy and family ties can be established through historical records and while these yellowed archives occasionally provide detailed descriptions of the tools and type of wood found in the workshops of these artisans when they died, almost nothing is known about the pieces each craftsman produced, since no signatures appear on any of the furniture that has survived. Even though a few families have preserved objects dating from the 18th century, which were fortunately handed down from one generation to another, these rare legacies provide no clues as to the identity of the joiners and cabinetmakers who built them or to the sociological and ethnological characteristics of the milieu in which they plied their trade.

Furniture in the French provincial manner is fascinating. Its solidity, almost always harmonious proportions, color and decoration all evoke the presence of France in America and our ties as Quebeckers with a country and a source culture that contributed so much to the development of the colony in its early years and of the continent as a whole when it was first explored. The patina of each piece reflects its history, while its form testifies to the sense of beauty and design that emerged during a period marked by the spirit of the first settlers from France. By skilfully adapting their knowledge and experience to the realities of their new homeland, they truly helped to carve out this nation.

An awareness of the importance of our historical ties with France emerged during the period between the two world wars and in the 1960s and 1970s. And it was through the reading of old furniture that Quebeckers, who were in search of their identity at the time, gained the most insight into their origins. The demand for antiques rose sharply, leading to the creation of institution-based collections. Unfortunately, conservators and collectors neglected and even ignored periods other than the French Regime, even though these periods were just as interesting with regard to the history of furniture. Demand for pieces of French derivation grew to such an extent that prices soared and the market was almost depleted. Once all the intact, original pieces had been spoken for, there began to appear remodelled specimens made from components taken from several different articles. The alterations involved in producing these "reconstructed" items are often so well camouflaged that it is sometimes difficult, even after careful examination, to tell such objects apart from genuine antiques.

The production of classical French provincial furniture did not cease with the British conquest in 1760. Since the styles and models associated with this type of furniture were the only ones that craftsmen knew and had mastered before England severed the colony's ties with France, they persisted in traditional furniture forms until the end of the 18th century, and even much later in certain rural areas.

Over time, however, designs became lighter in response to the new stylistic and technical trends that emerged at the end of the 18th century. For example, heavy pine armoires that had doors and panels framed with block-carved moulding in the Louis XIII or Louis XV manner and were fitted with forged-iron hardware gave way to armoires with simple panels surrounded by nailed strips of moulding, fluted or reeded stiles in the Neoclassical style, dentil cornices and industrially cast hinges and locks. All of these characteristics were soon integral to the British and U.S. versions of the new furniture fashion that were becoming extremely popular in the St. Lawrence Valley.

What remains of the furniture made during the early part of Québec's history? Despite the laudable conservation efforts of the various religious communities, especially those made up of women — where the veneration of individuals who played a founding or pioneering role in the development of their congregations has always been very important — much early Québec furniture was destroyed by the numerous fires that ravaged the colony's cities and towns. This is not to mention the disastrous effect of armed conflicts such as the Seven Years' War, which resulted in the loss of the French colony to England. During this war, the invading army did not hesitate to burn thousands of houses along the St. Lawrence Estuary and ruthlessly bombard the capital and its major institutions, reducing much of the colony to ruin. Other factors have also had a destructive, if not devastating, effect at all levels of society on the preservation of the furniture that constitutes such an important part of our heritage. These include a chronic, general lack of appreciation of historical values, the massive arrival of new styles marked by British and U.S. influences in urban and rural areas, and the emergence of a merchandising economy which, from the outset, encouraged the full-scale revamping of interior design. In addition, there was the never officially declared determination of the British elite to erase a period of tremendous significance for the identity of Quebeckers in order to assimilate them more effectively and eliminate almost everything from this chapter in their history except for a few remnants of their material culture and urban architecture. In an article published in the journal *Technique* (Vol. VI, No. 9, pp. 1-4) in November 1931, Jean-Marie Gauvreau, a cabinetmaking teacher, made the following grim observations, echoing comments made by many of his contemporaries since the beginning of the 20th century:

"Over one hundred years ago we had very beautiful old furniture in the Province of Québec. What has happened to these naively carved, white pine objects, these masterpieces of rustic art? Tourists bought some of them for absurdly low prices before antique dealers began to take an interest in such items. Then trains filled with early furniture left annually for the United States, where it sold for astronomical prices. Although a number of concerned citizens, including Alphonse Désilets of Québec City and his friends from the Société des Arts, Sciences et Lettres, tried to put a stop to this sorry spectacle by saving a few pieces, most people merely replaced this furniture. Instead of being alarmed at the loss of these objects, whose character made them part of our national heritage, they simply bought new ones that were cheap, mass-produced and utterly devoid of charm." [Translation]

In the 1960s, a number of religious communities that could trace their history back to the beginning of the colony sold many pieces of furniture of considerable significance at the insistence of family and friends. Owing to the gradual erosion of this part our heritage, furniture from the 17th and 18th centuries, a period so closely linked to the identity of Quebeckers, is now very rare. Nevertheless, the few pieces that have survived should be the object of more effective enhancement measures on the part of Québec institutions.

FRENCH PROVINCIAL FURNITURE

*Q*uébec furniture of the 17th and 18th centuries borrowed forms and decorative motifs from the French provinces that sent colonists to New France. The lines and workmanship of certain old pieces are the same as those of French provincial models, reflecting the close cultural ties that existed between France and New France during the early days of the colony. The following drawings by historian Jacques Fréal were done in some of the native provinces of the first immigrants.

f.

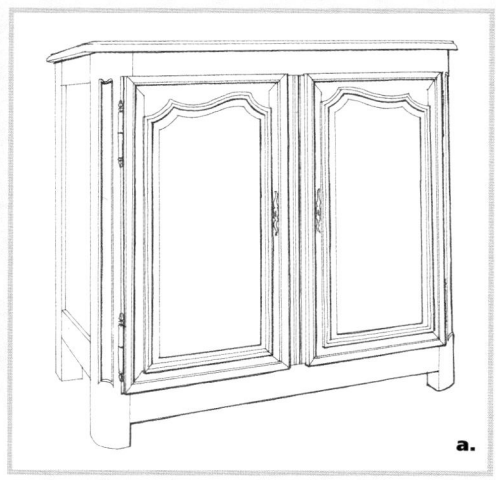
a.

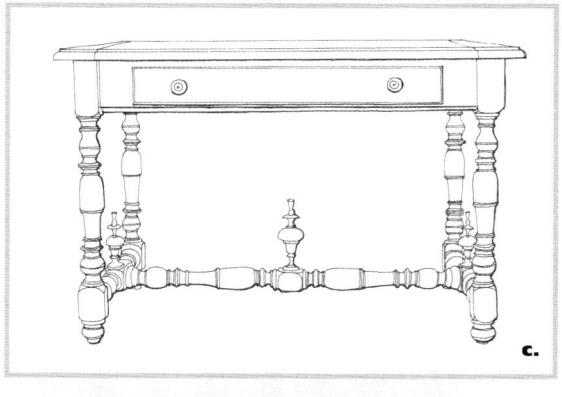
c.

g.

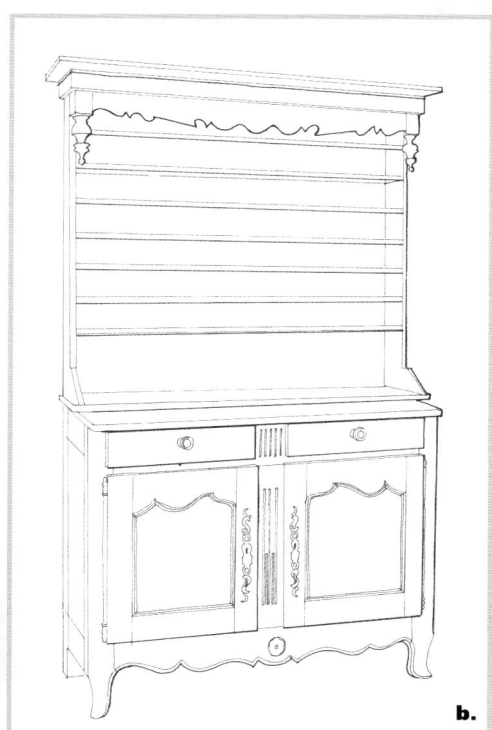
b.

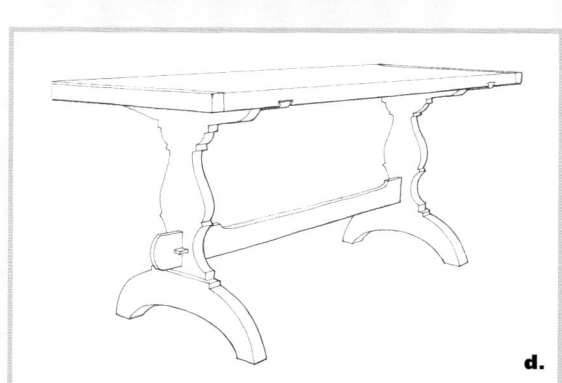
d.

h.

e.

i.

j.

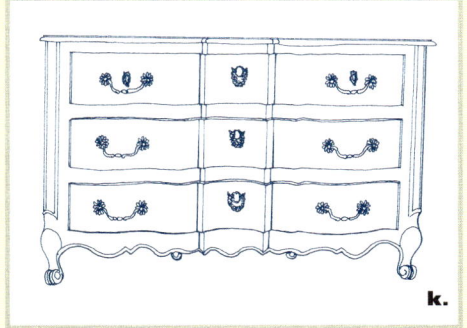

k.

m.

l.

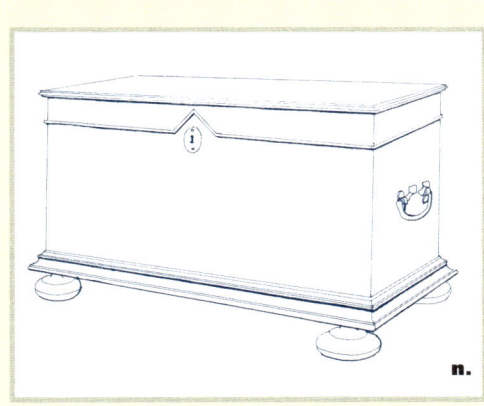

n.

o.

a. Low buffet with shaped panels (Normandy). **b.** Buffet-dresser with shaped panels (Lorraine). **c.** Table with turned legs and an H-stretcher (Lorraine). **d.** Kitchen table with cut-out baluster-shaped legs (Lorraine). **e.** Table with turned legs (Vendée). **f.** Stool turned in the Louis XIII manner (Lorraine). **g.** Chair with turned legs, a box stretcher and an open back (Franche-Comté). **h.** *Bonne femme* (rush-seated) chair with shaped back slats and turned legs (Lorraine). **i.** *Bonne femme* armchair (Lorraine). **j.** Small table with curved legs (Anjou). **k.** Crossbow or *arbalète*-fronted commode with three drawers (Bourgogne). **l.** Two-tiered buffet with shaped panels (Provence). **m.** Tall-post bed with spiral-turned posts and a tester (Normandy). **n.** Chest with gable-shaped moulding (Franche-Comté). **o.** Louis XIII armoire (Auvergne).

CHAIRS

Religious communities in Québec City, Trois-Rivières and Montréal have preserved a number of 17th- and 18th-century chairs, objects that were often venerated because they belonged to a founder of one of the congregations established in the St. Lawrence Valley or to an early colonist. Four stylistic trends can be observed in the time-tested pieces preserved by these communities. Numerous specimens, all well built, are in the Louis XIII style and often have baluster-turned legs and H-stretchers. Others reflect the tastes of the Louis XIV, Régence and Louis XV periods and have features typical of the Baroque styles in vogue at that time. Some were made in France and imported into the colony.

175 a, b
Construction analysis and plan at a scale of 1:5 of a Louis XV chair by H. M. Magne, published in *Le Mobilier français* (Paris, 1920). Carved and waxed walnut, French national furniture collection. This model has a rectangular back, a trapezoidal plan and curved legs joined by a serpentine X-stretcher. Small Louis XV chair with shaped back slats. Walnut, Québec City, ca. 1750.

176
Screened parlor of the Augustinian Hospitallers of the Hôtel-Dieu hospital in Québec City. Photograph by Jules Livernois, ca. 1935. This room, where people from the outside world came into contact with these Augustinians who had taken a vow of enclosure, is furnished in the Louis XIII style. The table and chairs made of varnished yellow birch probably belonged to Madame D'Ailleboust, widow of the third governor of New France. She left these furnishings to the nuns when she passed away at the Hôtel-Dieu in 1685.

177
Louis XIV chair. Walnut, Québec City, 18th century.
This piece, which has a caned seat and back, carved skirt and legs and a serpentine X-stretcher, has been stripped.

178 to 182
18th- and 19th-century chairs in the Louis XIII manner. Québec City area.

178
Chair of the Île d'Orléans type with a curved back, combining features from two different periods and styles. Yellow birch and pine, Québec City, mid-19th century.

179
Île d'Orléans chairs (one with a turned understructure and back). Original color, yellow birch and pine, 19th century.

180
Île d'Orléans chair with turned legs and stretchers. Yellow birch and pine, 19th century.

181
Île d'Orléans chairs with H-stretchers, chamfering and moulding. Original color, yellow birch and pine, 18th century.

182
Chair with baluster turnings. Walnut and pine, Québec City, 18th century.

183
Reconstruction of an 18th-century urban interior in Québec City. Note the beautifully set table and other furnishings in the Louis XIII manner. Probate inventories providing detailed descriptions of an owner's possessions at the time of his or her death are valuable sources of ethnohistorical information and may thus be used to reconstruct historic interiors. The buffet is made of pine and the chairs of yellow birch and pine.

184 to 191
Chairs in the Louis XIII manner, wool-winder and stools. Yellow birch, maple and pine, 18th and 19th centuries.
Some of these objects (wool-winder and stool immediately below) still have their original color, while others are in their as-found condition, with their most recent finish. As shown by these pieces, including the three Île d'Orléans chairs, early furnishings were often painted bright colors.

192
Table and chairs of the Île d'Orléans type with H-stretchers. Early or original color, yellow birch, maple and pine, 19th century.

193
Rustic interior reconstructed in the 1960s by the owners and restorers of the old Imbault house in Saint-François, Île d'Orléans.

FURNITURE IN THE FRENCH MANNER

THE NEW FRANCE STYLE 161

ARMCHAIRS

Religious communities in major Québec cities have preserved an excellent sample of armchairs in 18th-century French styles, particularly Louis XIII, Régence and Louis XV. Most of these pieces were left to the communities when individuals died. Judging from the objects that have survived and those described in the records kept by these institutions, all types of armchair – whether straight-backed (*à la reine*) or round-back (*en cabriolet*), with very simple or very elaborate forms and decoration – were used during the New France period and for many years afterward. An analysis of their wood often reveals that they were made in the colony.

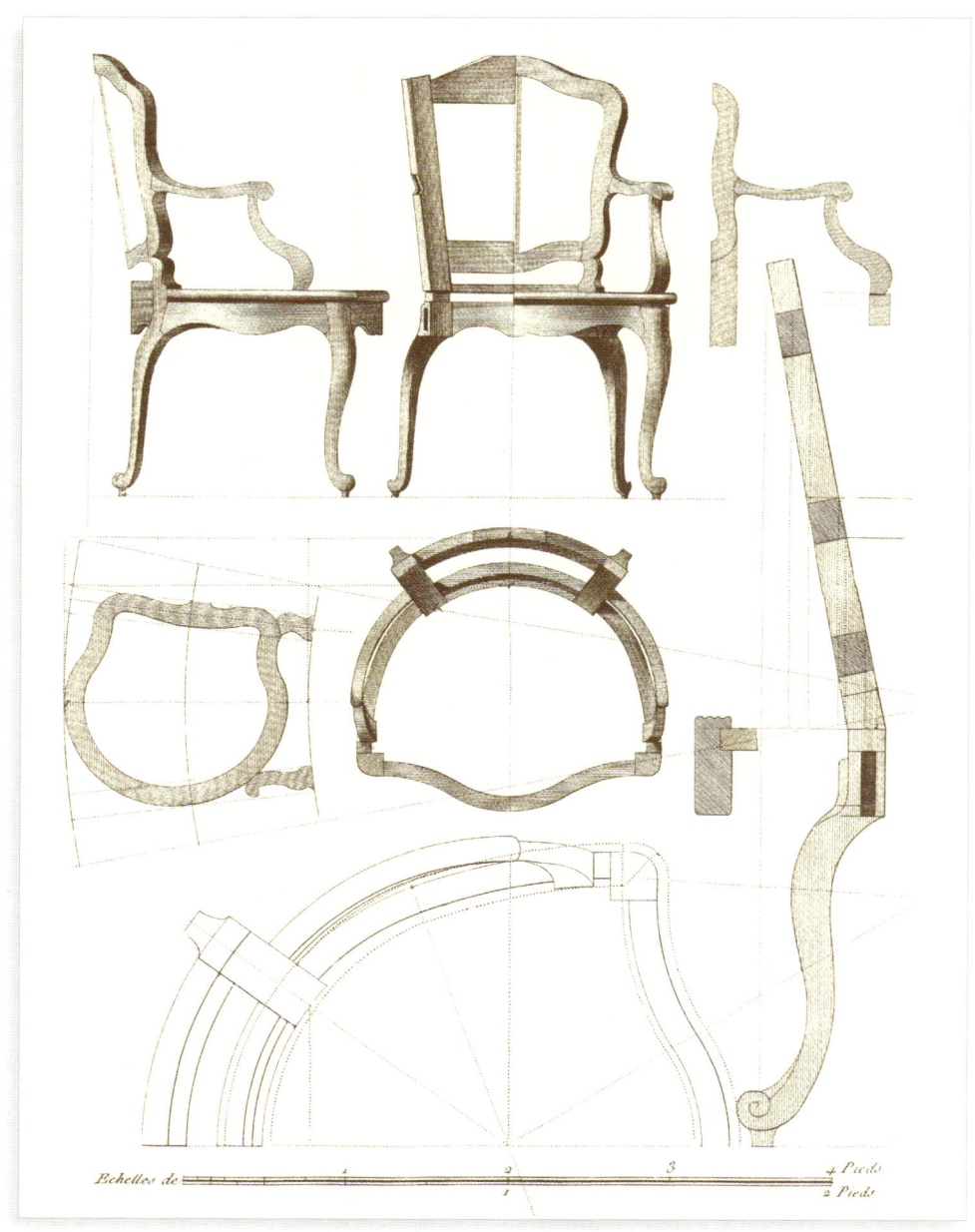

194
(Pages 162-163)
Engineer's dining room, Fortress of Louisbourg, ca. 1750.
The reconstruction shown here, based on inventories of old buildings on this strategic site in New France, recaptures the atmosphere of colonial bourgeois interiors during the Régence period and at the beginning of Louis XV's reign. It provides an excellent idea of upper-class life in the colony's capital and major cities on the eve of the defeat of 1760.

195 a, b
Louis XIII-style armchair in which Molière was sitting when he was afflicted with the illness that led to his death on February 17, 1673. Comédie-française collections, Paris.
This leather-covered hardwood chair with turned legs and an H-stretcher ressembles chairs found in New France during the French Regime. A few other similar pieces have survived to this day.
Scale drawing of a round-back armchair from A.-J. Roubo, *L'Art du menuisier en meuble*, 1772.

196
Armchair in the Louis XIII manner with turned legs and stretchers and a panelled back embellished with delicately carved balusters. Walnut, yellow birch and pine, Québec City, late 17th century.
Exceptional piece of furniture.

FURNITURE IN THE FRENCH MANNER

197
Armchair *à la capucine* with three shaped back slats and a structure profusely adorned with baluster turnings. Maple and yellow birch, 18th century.
This very graceful New France-style chair is covered in *point de Hongrie* (a material using several different color combinations always in a dart pattern).

198-199
Armchairs of Louis XIII inspiration with straight backs, turned understructures, H-stretchers and full upholstery. Yellow birch, Québec City, 18th century.

200
Os de mouton armchair. Yellow birch, ca. 1720.
This type of armchair in the Louis XIV manner derives its name from the shape of its legs and stretcher, which resemble sheep bones. It has recessed armrests, a serpentine crest rail and a pleasingly shaped skirt.

201
(Pages 168-169)
This detailed reconstruction of the engineer's salon at the Fortress of Louisbourg in 1740-1750 reflects the spirit of the Louis XIV and Régence styles in the colony. The sofa and armchair are of the *os de mouton* type, while the commode, with its scroll-carved feet, reflects the Baroque tastes of the time. Another interesting reproduction of a colonial bourgeois interior during the New France period.

THE NEW FRANCE STYLE

202 to 210

Straight-backed armchairs derived from the Louis XIV, Régence and Louis XV styles with upholstered or caned seats, carved cabriole legs with scroll feet, and shaped and relief-carved skirts and backs. Yellow birch, 18th century.

During the New France period, all of the styles in vogue in the mother country were adapted to colonial tastes. Baroque furniture remained popular well into the 19th century. Certain armchairs in public or private collections or on Québec's antique market have a date range of over 150 years, and it is not easy to determine exactly when they were made without doing scientific wood and color analyses. Some have been stripped, while others have undergone extensive, well-camouflaged restoration.

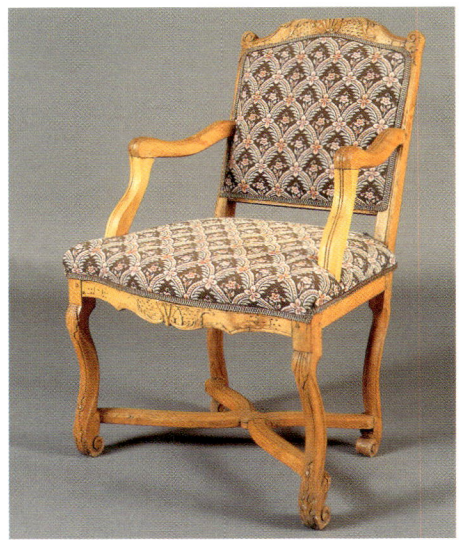

THE NEW FRANCE STYLE

BEDS

Since a number of probate inventories contain references to enclosed beds (*lits clos*, *lits-cabanes*), it can be affirmed that this type of bed was used in Québec.

Another model frequently encountered during the New France period was the French bed with tall chamfered or turned posts, a tester, or canopy, and curtains or hangings affording protection from the cold and a certain measure of privacy. Simple beds with four low posts, a plank headboard often assembled with slip-mortise joints, and a straw mattress were also common.

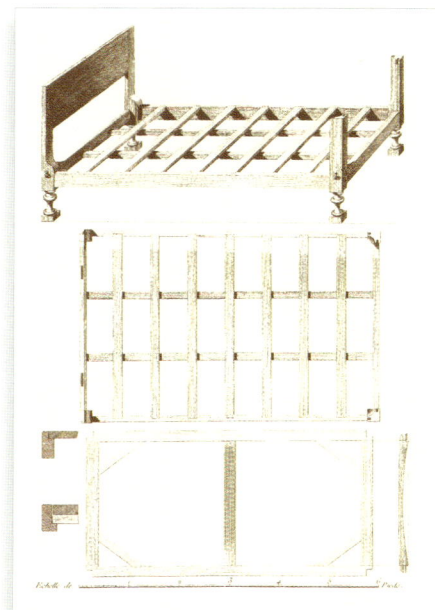

211
Simple bedstead, from A.-J. Roubo, *L'Art du menuisier en meuble*, 1772.
This type of bed was widely used in the St. Lawrence Valley during the 17th and 18th centuries.

212
Tall-post bed in the Papineau manor in Montebello. Yellow birch, late 18th century.
Photograph by Edgar Gariépy, ca. 1940.
The heavy forms and baluster turnings of this piece associate it with Québec's New France and Constitutional styles.

213
Tall-post bed with spiral-turned posts in the Louis XIII manner. Yellow birch, Québec City, 17th century.
This bed with masterfully executed turnings, dating from the early days of the colony, belongs to the Augustinian Hospitallers of the Hôtel-Dieu hospital in Québec City.

214
(Pages 174-175)
Bedroom of the Engineer's House in Louisbourg, ca. 1740.
This reconstruction provides an excellent idea of what a bedroom looked like in an 18th-century bourgeois home in New France. The room is dominated by the bed with its tester and curtains and the large Louis XV armoire with rounded corners, shaped panels, scrolled bottom rail and curved feet terminating in scrolls.

215
Lit à la duchesse in the Governor's bedroom at the Fortress of Louisbourg. This reconstruction, based on Duquesnel's inventory of 1744, evokes the atmosphere of bedrooms of important colonial figures at the time.

216
French tall-post bed with a tester and turned and carved posts. Yellow birch, Québec City, late 17th century.
This exceptional piece of furniture preserved by the Augustinian Hospitallers of the Hôpital Général de Québec belonged to the second bishop of Québec, Monseigneur de Saint-Vallier (1653-1727). He probably died in this bed.

CRADLES

The cradle is one of the most endearing pieces of furniture. In the 1920s and 1930s, a time of nationalist fervor, many poets celebrated the cradle, as if their verses, inspired by pride in the proverbial birthrate of Quebeckers, could ensure the continued growth so essential to the survival of this French-speaking population in North America.

In the past, all households had cradles for new-born babies. Most were made of pine and had corner posts with baluster turnings. All were fitted with heavy, shaped rockers. Some were very rustic models suspended from a frame, while others had a hood to protect the baby's head.

217
Cradle with corner posts of French derivation. Pine, Québec City, late 18th century.
This photograph was taken by architect Sylvio Brassard around 1935 on the porch of the old Villeneuve house in Charlesbourg. The old family cradle was brought down from the attic for the occasion.

218
Cradle of French derivation with baluster-turned corner posts, rollers and shaped rockers. Pine and yellow birch, Québec City area, end of the 18th century.

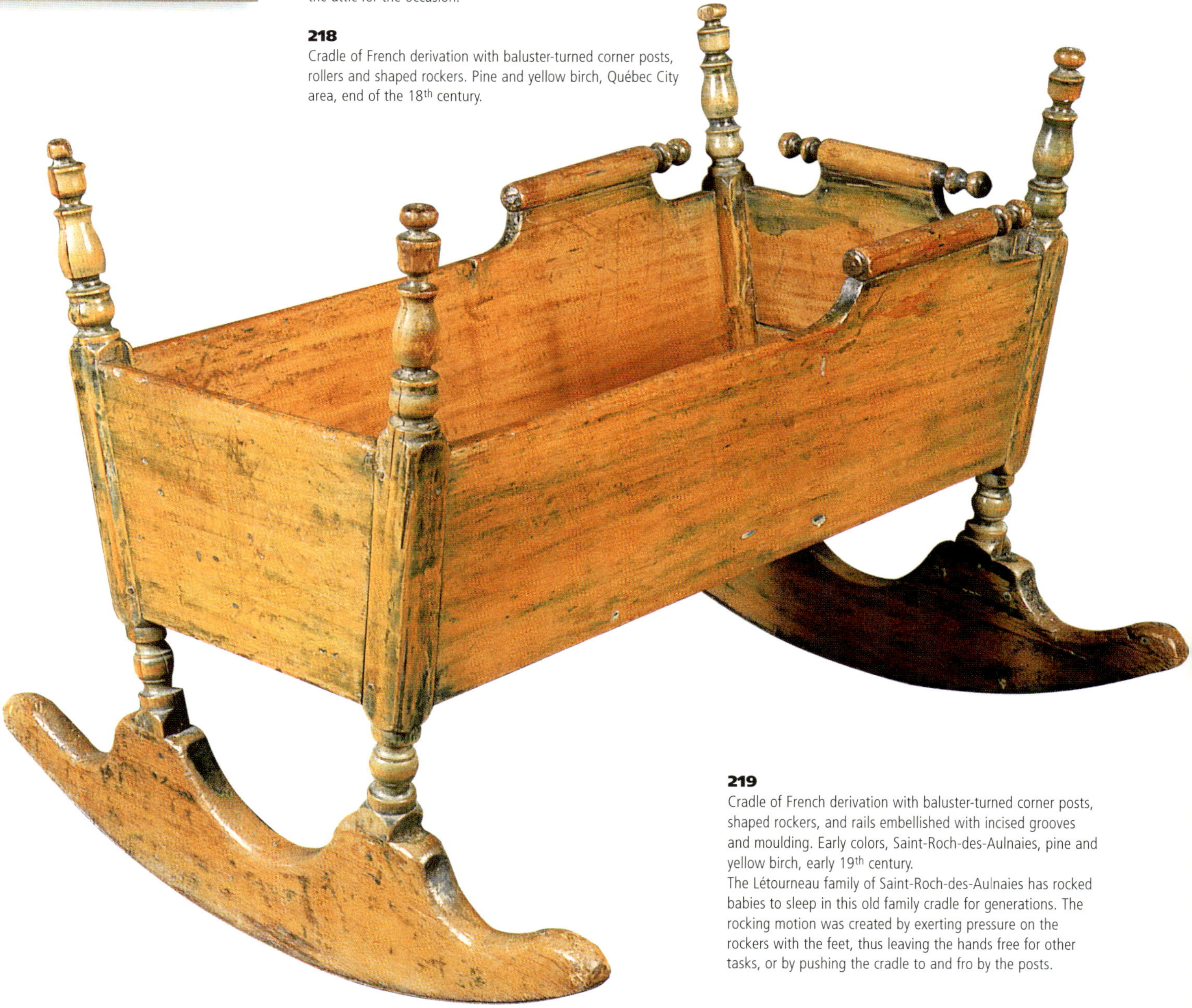

219
Cradle of French derivation with baluster-turned corner posts, shaped rockers, and rails embellished with incised grooves and moulding. Early colors, Saint-Roch-des-Aulnaies, pine and yellow birch, early 19th century.
The Létourneau family of Saint-Roch-des-Aulnaies has rocked babies to sleep in this old family cradle for generations. The rocking motion was created by exerting pressure on the rockers with the feet, thus leaving the hands free for other tasks, or by pushing the cradle to and fro by the posts.

178 FURNITURE IN THE FRENCH MANNER

CHESTS

The chest was the most common type of case furniture in traditional Québec society. According to probate inventories, each house contained several of these objects. When a bride went to her new home, she generally brought a chest along filled with her trousseau, or the linens and clothing she would need to begin married life.

Chests were usually made of pine and had hardwood corner posts. Many were equipped with a tray as well as a drawer beneath the tray for storing papers, jewellery and clothing accessories. The repetition of stereotyped models points to the existence of stylistic "standards" as well as artisans who specialized in making these touching pieces of Québec furniture. The chest was the forerunner of most other traditional case furniture forms.

220 a, b
(**b** on page 181)
Chest with V-shaped moulding, and detail of its keyhole escutcheon. Original color, pine and yellow birch, 18th century.
This outstanding piece of furniture, which is fitted with straight legs, still has its original color and hardware. While traditional Québec households usually kept several storage chests in their bedrooms and attic, many also owned small boxes of all shapes and sizes, ornamented with a wide array of motifs.

221
19th-century pine chests with V-shaped moulding, aligned in the attic of the Villeneuve house in Charlesbourg, built in the 18th century.
Photograph by Sylvio Brassard, architect, ca. 1935-1940.

222
Panelled chest. Pine and yellow birch, original color, Québec City area, ca. 1830.

223 a, b
Detail of the scroll-carved feet on a *sabot*, or hoof, belonging to the chests on the next page. These decorative components, made of yellow birch, are extensions of the corner posts. This type of foot is Louis XV in spirit.

224
Chest deriving from the Louis XIII style with straight legs, V-shaped moulding, and dentil moulding around the base. Original color and hardware, pine and yellow birch, Saint-Augustin-de-Desmaures, end of the 18th century.

225
Chests in the manner of Louis XV with scroll feet and rounded corners. Early bright colors, pine and yellow birch, Île aux Coudres, ca. 1840.

THE NEW FRANCE STYLE 183

226 to 231
Early chests of French derivation with square or turned feet or scroll feet on a hoof, original hardware and more or less elaborate base moulding. Pine and yellow birch; first half of the 19th century, except the dome-topped chest, which is earlier.
Some of these pieces still have their original color, while others have been stripped. In certain cases, the turnings on the feet combine British and U.S. influences with the French tradition.

232 to 234
Chest of French derivation with original hardware and color. Pine and yellow birch, 18th century.
The upper photographs provide an excellent view of the tray and drawer inside this case piece and of the hand-forged strap hinge ending in the shape of a fish tail.

THE NEW FRANCE STYLE 185

COMMODES

Commodes were found only in bourgeois homes during the French Regime and were thus limited in number. Pieces in the New France style that have survived to this day reflect classical or Baroque traditions. They have straight, serpentine, crossbow or *arbalète*, breakfront or reverse-*arbalète*, or broken fronts, all of which are illustrated in Palardy's catalogue. The reverse-*arbalète*-front commode sometimes has a concave central projection. Usually made of butternut, pine and yellow birch, and sometimes maple, the commodes produced in the St. Lawrence Valley show British and U.S. influences.

235
Detail of a cartouche with relief-carved *rocaille* motifs located on the piece on the next page. The skirts on early commodes often had bas-relief ornamentation, consisting mainly of naive or stylized shells reflecting Régence or Louis XV tastes.

236
Plan, cross-section and elevation of a serpentine-fronted commode showing two different types of drawer front, from A.-J. Roubo, *L'Art du menuisier en meuble*, 1772.

237
Ecclesiastical robe chest with a serpentine front in the Louis XV manner fitted with doors rather than drawers, scroll feet and a shaped and carved skirt adorned with a Baroque cartouche. Both doors have trompe l'oeil drawer fronts and one has a false centre post. Butternut, Montréal, second half of the 18th century.
The false drawers have lost their original handles and the turned knobs are later additions. Outstanding piece of furniture, whose lines and ornamentation derive from late Baroque religious sculpture at the end of the 18th century.

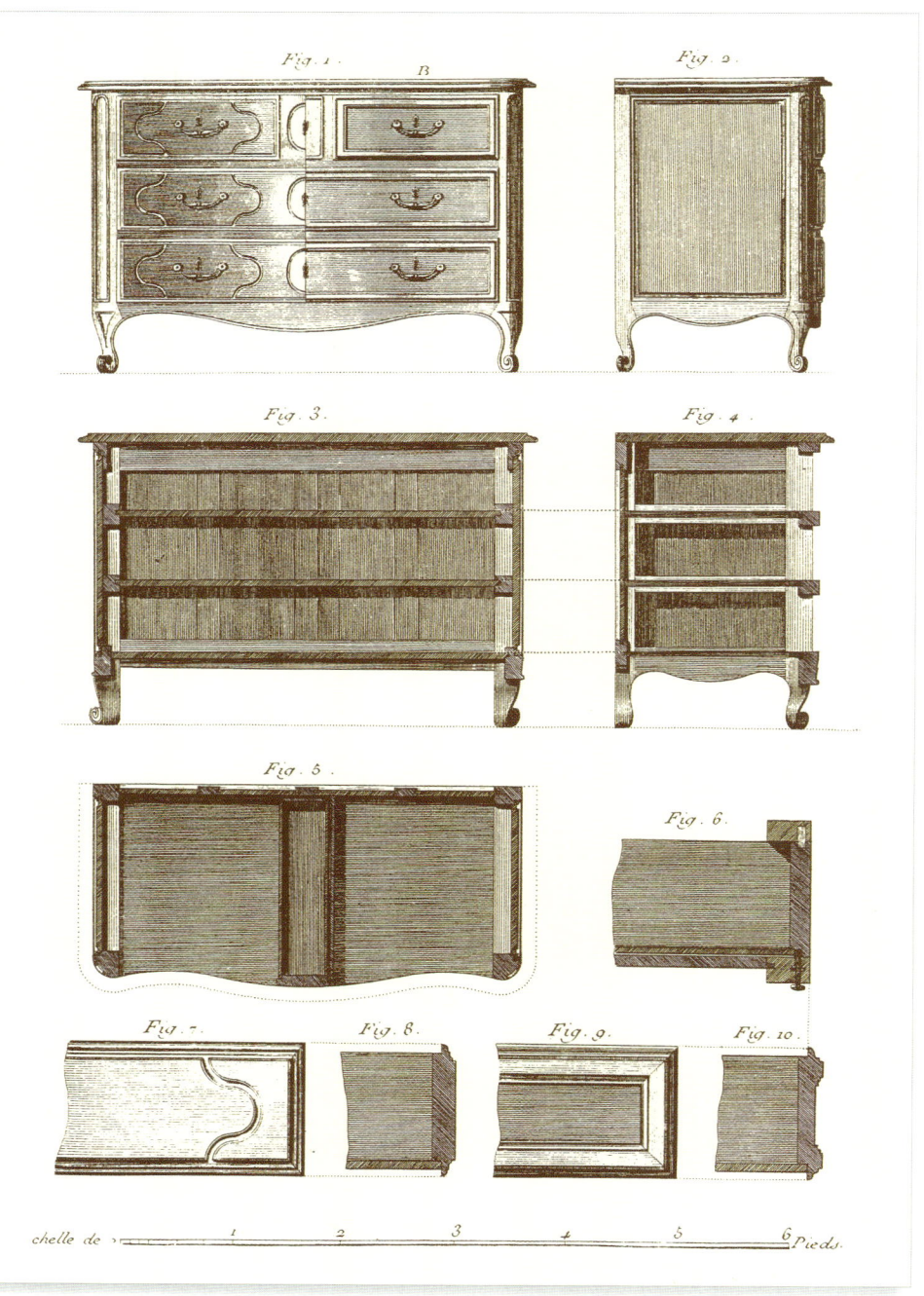

238 to 248

Commodes with different profiles and feet, and straight or shaped skirts (one embellished with openwork). All (except for the commode at the bottom right) are in the Baroque manner. Pine, walnut, yellow birch, maple, second half of the 18th century and first quarter of the 19th century. The older piece at the bottom right – which belonged to Madame D'Ailleboust, the wife of the third governor of New France – dates from the 17th century and derives from the Louis XIII style, as shown by its baluster-turned H-stretcher. Commodes with ball-and-claw feet are marked by Chippendale influences. Originally, all of these pieces were either varnished or painted.

249
Bombée commode, i.e. with swelled front and sides, and Louis XV armchair with padded armrests, Louisbourg, ca. 1840. This reconstruction of part of the Governor's apartment at the Fortress of Louisbourg provides an excellent idea of what the living quarters of important people in New France looked like during the 18th century. Owing to the use of imported furnishings, the interior decoration of colonial homes resembled that of houses in the mother country. During the French Regime, opulent decors like the one shown here were encountered in the sumptuous residences of Québec City, the capital of France's North American empire.

250
Reconstruction of part of an 18th-century bourgeois home in Québec City. Estèbe house, Place Royale.

" This graceful and elegant Régence-style armchair, whose curves and rounded forms already foreshadow the Louis XV style, probably dates from the middle of the 18th century and comes from the Québec City area. The artisan borrowed the arched silhouette of the back and the *os de mouton* shape of the legs and stretcher from the Louis XIV style. He also borrowed from the Régence vocabulary of forms when he designed the crossbow or *arbalète*-shaped skirt and the downcurved armrests, set back from the front legs. Recently reupholstered with a replica of its original covering of Aubusson " Flemish verdure " tapestry – small strips of which were still in place beneath the original tacks – this chair testifies to the quality of urban interiors during the French Regime.

" The large armoire, probably from Verchères, may well have been located initially in the sacristy of a church or in a large residence. It is unusually tall and wide. Its three shelves, which may have been used for storing fine linens and clothing, were readily accessible on account of the false centre post.

" The basic design and the lozenge-carved and diamond-point panels of this piece, which is made entirely of pine and was probably painted at first, are borrowings from the Louis XIII style. The shape of the mouldings near the top of the two doors is derived from a style in vogue during the latter part of Louis XIV's reign and already foreshadows the Régence style. As for the high relief of the moulding around the doors and drawer at the bottom, it creates a fascinating play of light and shadow. This very attractive piece of furniture was probably made at a workshop in the Québec City area.

" The Estèbe house – one of whose rooms is shown here – was built in 1752 by Guillaume Estèbe, a prosperous merchant and large landholder. His residence on Saint-Pierre Street had 21 rooms and 8 fireplaces. One of these fireplaces is still equipped with a cast-iron fireback dated 1752 from the Forges du Saint-Maurice. When the house was refitted in the late 18th century, panelling in the Régence/Louis XV style was installed in certain rooms. The Musée de la civilisation has preserved certain parts of this rich decor, which constitutes a rare and valuable legacy of the 18th century. " [Translation]

Objets de civilisation, p. 41

FURNITURE IN THE FRENCH MANNER

ARMOIRES

The pine armoires presented in Jean Palardy's catalogue have considerable character and charm. Anyone who is familiar with 18th- and 19th-century French provincial furniture will be able to see not only the many technical, decorative and stylistic similarities between French and Québec models, but also the very original way in which local pieces were designed, executed and finished. Even fairly inexperienced observers can readily identify Québec products by their form, color and ornamentation. With their plain, flowing lines and functional simplicity, New France-style armoires reflect the character of those who inhabited the St. Lawrence Valley, and thus vividly illustrate how the meaning of the vernacular encompasses more than just workmanship and style.

251
Armoire in the Louis XIV manner preserved at the Hôpital Général de Québec. Probably of French manufacture and imported into New France in the early 18th century. Photograph by Ramsay Traquair, ca. 1925.
This piece of furniture, which is still part of the hospital's collections, has never been painted. The Hôpital Général – built in the 17th century and belonging since then to the Augustinian Hospitallers, who arrived in Québec City in 1639 – always emerged unscathed from the many fires that swept through the capital.

252
Plan and elevation showing two façade designs for a Régence-style armoire with an arched cornice, from A.-J. Roubo, *L'Art du menuisier en meuble*, 1772.

253
Armoire framed with moulding and fitted with two doors decorated with linenfold motifs and lozenges. Original color, pine, Québec City area, mid-18th century.
The linenfold pattern is part of the medieval idiom and was rarely found on early New France furniture. In Québec, it was long confused with the concave corner, which is completely different from the linenfold motif and has no stylistic or ethnological relationship with it. This very graceful armoire is well balanced and beautifully carved.

192 FURNITURE IN THE FRENCH MANNER

254
Armoire decorated with diamond points and St. Andrew's crosses. Original color, pine, end of the 18th century.
Like many old pieces of furniture, this armoire has undergone certain alterations. It was sawn in two, for some unknown reason, its cornice moulding was replaced and its color has been touched up to produce a more uniform appearance.

255
Armoire with two doors and twelve panels carved with lozenges, diamond points and St. Andrew's crosses. Original hardware, pine, Québec City area, mid-18th century.
The case of this piece is framed by block-carved moulding and its cornice is embellished with dentil moulding. Magnificent armoire in the Louis XIII manner, clearly reflecting 18th-century French provincial tastes.

256
Armoire with baluster hinges and two doors decorated with "X" carvings. Partially stripped, pine, Québec City area, last quarter of the 18th century.

257
Armoire deriving from the Louis XIII style with two diamond-point doors. Original color, pine, ca. 1775. Both the cornice and base moulding are missing.

258
Armoire with two doors, eight concave-cornered panels and a shaped bottom rail decorated with volutes. Original color, pine, Sorel, late 18th century.

259
Armoire with two lozenge-carved doors. Hardwood, Québec City, mid-18th century.

260
Armoire with two lozenge-carved doors and two drawers at the bottom. Pine, end of the 18th century. The color of this piece has been reapplied over the original burl finish in imitation of exotic wood, and the base moulding has undergone basic restoration.

THE NEW FRANCE STYLE 197

261
Armoire framed with moulding and fitted with two doors with concave-cornered panels, a shaped and cut-out base embellished with a shell carving, and a carved centre post. Pine, early color, Saint-Jacques de Montcalm, end of the 18th century. The feet have undergone basic restoration.

262
Armoire with rat-tail and baluster hinges and two doors decorated with multiple lozenges. Original grey-blue color, pine, second half of the 18th century.
Basic restoration has been performed on the base and cornice.

263
Armoire with two doors carved with lozenges and concentric circles (also called discs or *galettes*). Original color, pine, mid-18th century.
The block-carved moulding that frames this piece displays the same motif as the centre post. The feet are missing.

264
Armoire in the Louis XV manner with two doors, eight shaped panels, recessed side panels and polychrome decoration (green case, creamy beige door frame and cornice, and rusty-brown panels and block-carved panel moulding). Vertical rat-tail hinges, pine, Montréal, late 18th century. Piece of exceptional quality, as was often the case of armoires in traditional rural houses.

265
Armoire with two diamond-point doors, concave-cornered side panels, pick-and-barrel hinges and horizontal base moulding. The case is framed with moulding that forms an integral part of the corner posts, and the centre stile has three panels also surrounded by integral moulding. Original blue color. This outstanding piece of pine furniture has been in the Paul family of Saint-Joseph-de-Sorel since the last quarter of the 18th century.

266
Armoire of Louis XV inspiration framed with moulding and fitted with two doors decorated with simple raised and shaped panels and an attractive cut-out base. Original color, pine, late 18th century.
Intact, well-preserved piece with a well-balanced design.

267
Armoire with two doors carved with multiple lozenges. Pine, first half of the 18th century.
This piece has been stripped down to the bare wood in accordance with once-prevalent restoration and enhancement techniques.

268
Armoire with two doors decorated with raised panels. Original color, pine, Lanaudière region, mid-19th century.
The floral overpainting and fancy cornice, which were added at a later date and possibly derived from the Eastlake style, gave a new look to this otherwise very simple piece of furniture.

THE NEW FRANCE STYLE 201

269
Armoire with two doors embellished with triple raised panels. Red finish over base coat, pine, mid-19th century.

270
Simple armoire with two doors decorated with raised panels. Stripped to original color, pine, ca. 1860.
Furniture is often found in a deplorable state, presenting restorers with the challenge of breathing new life into each piece. In this case, certain panels have been repaired.
It is always very moving for owners to see the true character of a piece of furniture emerge after hours of painstaking work.

TWO-TIERED BUFFETS

After perusing the records of dozens of French Regime notaries, Robert-Lionel Séguin wrote the following about the buffet in his captivating work, *La Civilisation traditionnelle de l'«habitant» aux 17ᵉ et 18ᵉ siècles*: "Buffets were found in just about every kitchen as of the 18th century. They had two single-leaf doors and a drawer above each door, and were in the Louis XIII or Louis XV manner. In February 1703, a resident of Montréal by the name of Alexis Legay owned 'a small pine buffet with two doors locking with a key, valued at six *livres*'." [Translation] (Notaire Adhemar, 6398, Archives judiciaires de Montréal) With regard to the two-tiered buffet, the ethnohistorian added:

> This is one of the most beautiful types of *canadien* country furniture. Consisting of two sections placed one on top of the other, the two-tiered buffet has four doors and two drawers, and was found in *canadien* homes as of the 18th century. In May 1703, an appraiser visited the Joseph Martel family in Montréal to evaluate "a pair of wooden pieces (*un paire bois*) in butternut, in two tiers, with two drawers and four doors locking with a key." The object described was worth the tidy sum of 80 *livres*. [Translation] (Notaire Adhemar, 6433, Archives judiciaires de Montréal)

The term "a pair of armoires" (*paire d'armoires*) was also used in historical records to refer to this type of furniture. Bernard Audet, in *Avoir feu et lieu dans l'île d'Orléans au XVIIᵉ siècle*, discovered seven such references in inventories drawn up in the seigneury of Île d'Orléans during the early days of the colony, prior to 1700-1710. The oldest of these inventories, found in the home of Jacques Paradis, dates from 1679.

Several beautiful examples of two-tiered buffets have survived, and most derive from the Louis XIII and Louis XV styles. As revealed by numerous inventories, these pieces of furniture were used for storing dishes, table linens and cutlery. Over time they became multi-purpose storage units filled with pleasant odors, as described by Rimbaud in the poem quoted at the beginning of this book.

271
Two-tiered buffet, Hôpital Général, Québec City.
Photograph by Ramsay Traquair, ca. 1925.

272
Drawings of the late 18th-century two-tiered buffet shown on the next page. These drawings, which were done in around 1930 by a team under the direction of Professor Ramsay Traquair of McGill University, show the front and one side of the buffet, the profile of its cornice and doors, the panel design, joining details and even the keyhole escutcheon. A baluster hinge and scroll foot are also illustrated. The collection known as the Fonds Traquair contains several drawings of 18th-century Québec furniture.

273
Two-tiered buffet in the Louis XV manner, with original hardware, shaped panels and skirt, and scroll-carved feet.
Pine and butternut, ca. 1775.
Well-balanced, elegant piece of furniture.

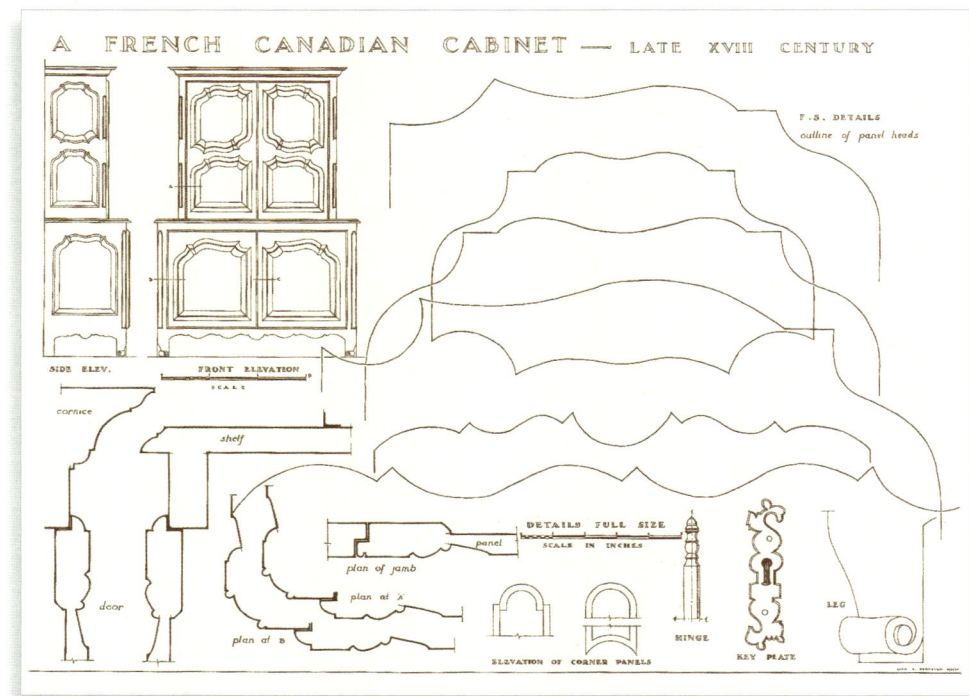

274 to 276
Two-tiered buffet of Louis XV derivation. Fruit wood, Lotbinière region, ca. 1740.
This outstanding piece of furniture must have belonged to a member of the bourgeoisie. With its proportions, height, finishing and workmanship, it conforms to the highest cabinetmaking standards of 18th-century Europe. The piece was assembled with forged nails and still has its original hardware. Throughout its existence, it has no doubt been merely varnished or polished. These photographs clearly illustrate the modular structure of two-tiered buffets; the arched cornice of the piece shown here is detachable. Such objects probably graced the homes of colonial authorities and members of the bourgeoisie in Québec City, the capital of a vast empire during the New France period.

FURNITURE IN THE FRENCH MANNER

277
Two-tiered buffet fitted with four doors and two drawers, and decorated with lozenges. Stripped pine, ca. 1775.
Old pieces of furniture, such as buffets, are always interesting, whether viewed from the side or from the front. The quality of a piece depends on the extent to which all of its details form a harmonious whole. Here, geometric motifs have transformed this buffet into a piece of classical sculpture, as is commonly observed in 18th-century French provincial furniture.

278
Two-tiered buffet with four doors and two drawers of Louis XIII inspiration, decorated with lozenges and diamond points. Original hardware, pine, mid-18th century.
The two upper panels of this stripped piece of furniture have undergone basic restoration. Judging from objects still found in many old attics and information gleaned from interviews with older people, it can be affirmed that storage pieces of similar workmanship graced the homes of prosperous *habitants* during the French Regime.

279 to 282
Two-tiered buffets in the Louis XV manner and three-tiered buffet in the Louis XIII manner. Stripped pine, end of the 18th century.
From 1930 to 1970, old furniture was stripped in accordance with the tastes and "scientific museum" approach of the time. While such treatment highlighted construction and decorative techniques, it destroyed the ethnohistorical dimension of pieces by eliminating their color. Sometimes stripping was so severe that the surface of the wood was permanently affected. Such objects have unfortunately lost a great deal of their interest and value.

283
Two-tiered buffet with four doors and two drawers, decorated with lozenges and surmounted by a dentil cornice. Pine, mid-18th century.
The base of this stripped piece has been reworked and its decorative base moulding was not reapplied.

210 FURNITURE IN THE FRENCH MANNER

LOW BUFFETS AND LOW ARMOIRES

This category includes the simple low buffet, consisting of a single unit with two doors usually surmounted by two drawers, and the low armoire, with two doors but no drawers. On account of their proportions, low armoires resemble low buffets more than they do true armoires, which are always more vertically elongated. However, it is sometimes hard to tell the difference between a low armoire and a real armoire. Nevertheless, all of these pieces are forms of case furniture that were used in the common room or in other parts of the house.

284
Low buffet in the Louis XIII manner, decorated with diamond-point carving. Pine, Charlesbourg, mid-18th century. This piece was photographed around 1940 by architect Sylvio Brassard in the attic of the Villeneuve house in Charlesbourg, a Québec City suburb.

285
Ca.-1930 drawing of a low buffet in a Québec City residence by a team under the direction of Professor Ramsay Traquair of McGill University. This piece of furniture reflects the spirit of the Louis XV style and no doubt dates from the second half of the 18th century.

286
Low armoire with triple raised panels in an excellent state of preservation, with all of its original components still intact. An early stain was uncovered when the piece was stripped. Pine, Québec City area, late 18th century. This photograph captures the spirit of a rural interior during the early days of the British colonial regime.

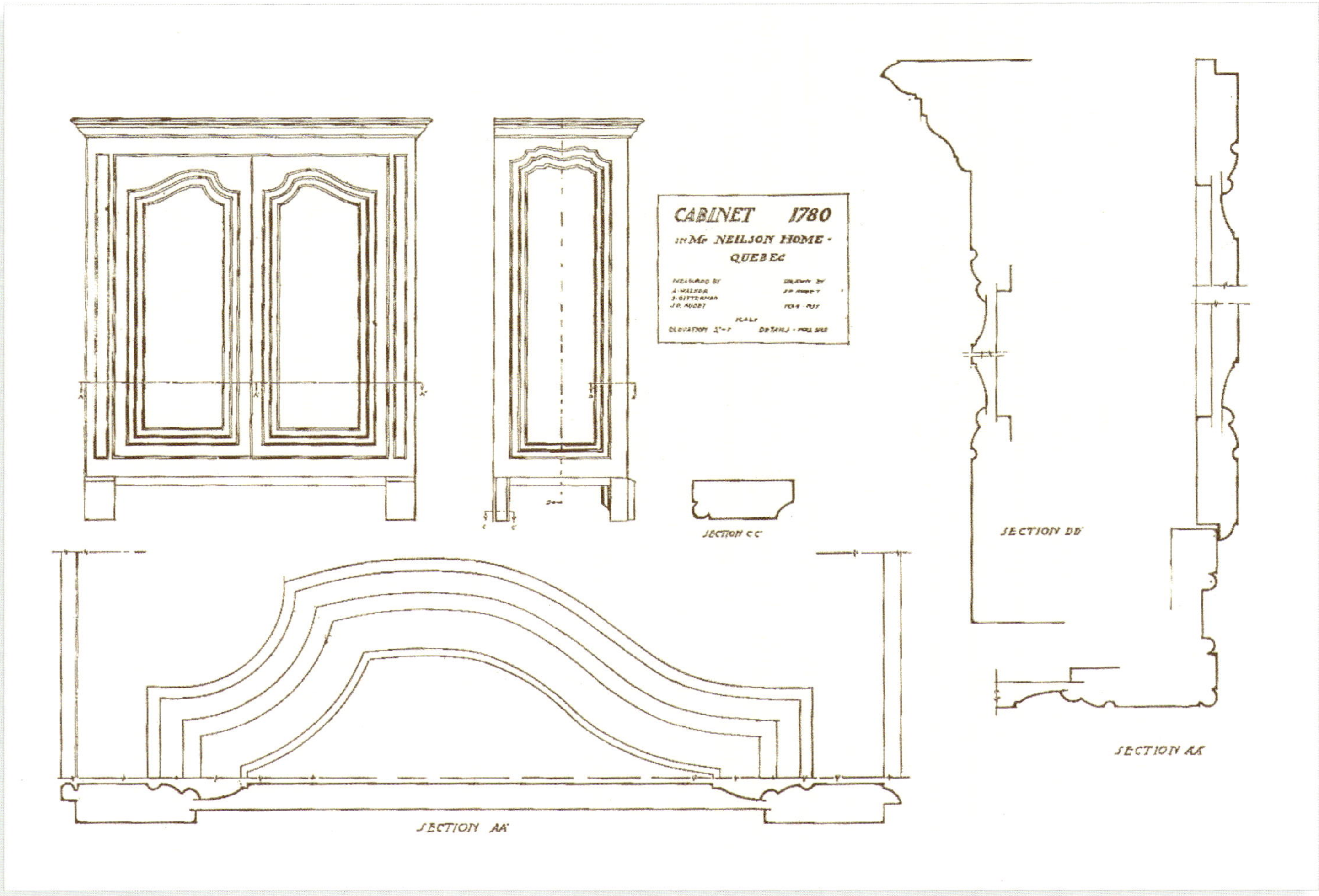

287
Low buffet with two doors and two drawers, decorated with panels with shaped corners and cartouches framed by ogee arches. Bulbous feet, original hardware and color, pine, Lévis (Lauzon), second half of the 18th century.
Intact, well-documented piece in a good state of preservation. Outstanding ethnographic object.

288
Low buffet with two doors and one drawer, embellished with raised panels and an attractively shaped skirt with openwork volutes. Original hardware and knobs, slot above right-hand side of drawer, early color, beginning of the 19th century.
The harmonious design and excellent state of preservation of this buffet make it a very interesting piece.

289
Low buffet with two doors, two drawers and simply shaped recessed panels. Original color, ca. 1825.

290
Low buffet in the Louis XIII manner with two doors, two drawers and stylized concave-cornered panels embellished with discs. Rich block-carved moulding, original hardware, pine, late 18th century. Refinished.

291
Low armoire derived from the Louis XIII and Louis XV styles, with shaped panels and two bottom drawers carved with lozenges. Pine, ca. 1800.

292
Slant-top desk-armoire in the Louis XIII and Louis XV manners, with shaped front panels and lozenge-carved side panels. Pine, late 18th century.
Relief-carved hearts adorn the top of the doors.

293
Low buffet of Louis XV derivation with a very attractive, carved and cut-out base. Pine, mid-18th century.
Finely executed piece of furniture.

294
Low buffet carved with lozenges of Louis XIII inspiration. Pine, late 18th century.
The color of this very simple piece has been touched up to produce a more uniform appearance.

295
Simple low buffet in the Louis XV tradition with two doors, two drawers and pleasingly shaped panels. Early hardware, pine, Québec City area, ca. 1775.
The turned yellow birch chair in pure Louis XIII style still has its original finish and is also from the Québec City area. Attractive ensemble dating from second half of the 18th century.

THE NEW FRANCE STYLE 217

296
Low diamond-point armoire of simple design with raised side panels. Early color, pine, mid-18th century.

297
Low buffet or low armoire in the Louis XIII manner with two arched doors, two drawers decorated with St. Andrew's crosses, raised panels and a pleasingly shaped base. Original color, second half of the 18th century.
The side rails are embellished with linenfold carving.

298 a, b
Low armoire with two doors decorated with diamond-point carving and concave-cornered side panels, richly adorned with rosettes and heart roundels. Pine, end of the 18th century.
Unfortunately, this piece has been stripped.

299
Low buffet of Louis XV inspiration with two doors, two drawers and flush side panels. Original hardware, stripped pine, second half of the 18th century.
This photograph recaptures the atmosphere of an 18th-century rural interior.

300
Low armoire in the Louis XIII manner with two diamond-point doors. Original color, pine, Québec City area, mid-18th century.

301
Low armoire with two doors decorated with St. Andrew's crosses. Stripped pine, ca. 1770.
Both the case and centre post of this piece are framed with moulding. Basic restoration would involve replacing the feet.

CORNER CUPBOARDS

302
Low bow-front corner cupboard of French derivation fitted with a single door embellished with a lozenge-carved panel, butt hinges and forged nails. Early color, pine, Saint-Jean-Port-Joli, beginning of the 19th century.
This piece of furniture has never had an upper section.

Corner cupboards are functional pieces of furniture that make it possible to use what is normally wasted space in a room. In France, low corner cupboards were quite common under Louis XIV and became widespread after his reign. In Québec, they seem to have been very popular as of the end of the 18th century. Since most corner cupboards are Neoclassical in spirit, they are discussed at greater length in the next chapter.

303 a, b, c, d

Bow-front corner cupboard in the Louis XV manner with an arched cornice and an attractively shaped and carved skirt. Its lower section is fitted with two doors decorated with shaped panels, while its upper section has two glazed doors. Butternut, Québec City, ca. 1790.
According to Jean Palardy, this typically French, but locally made, piece of furniture comes from the old rectory of the Québec City Cathedral, which was built between 1773 and 1775. It was undoubtedly the work of a master church carver and cabinetmaker. The cupboard still has its original hardware, and the interior vault beneath its arched top is adorned with a carved shell.
An outstanding, typically Québec piece of furniture highlighting the skill of Québec cabinetmakers in the second half of the 18th century.

TABLES

New France-style furniture included a wide variety of table forms, such as work tables, which could be used in hospital dispensaries; refectory tables, found in the dining halls of religious communities; and console tables, employed in the home or in the choir of a church. Washstands, occasional tables and writing desks were other commonly encountered types. French Regime tables conformed to the tastes of all levels of society during the 17th and 18th centuries.

304-305
Refectory of the Augustinian Hospitallers at the Hôpital Général in Québec City, ca. 1930.
This room, which was fitted out at the beginning of the 18th century, is furnished with refectory tables and serving tables in the Louis XIII manner. The refectory tables, which date from the mid-18th century, have drawers in the apron for storing cutlery and dishes for each place. They are also fitted with baluster-turned legs, firmly joined by a long stretcher. Tables of this type are very popular with collectors because of their solidity, comfort, functional nature and historical significance. They lend a convivial atmosphere to historic homes.

306
Drawing showing two different models for a Louis XV-style console table in Rococo fashion, by Nicolas Pineau (1684-1754), ca. 1735.

307
Québec console table in the same manner as the models illustrated on the preceding page, with cherub-head and *rocaille* ornamentation. Butternut, second half of the 18th century.
This piece probably comes from the choir of a church, where console tables were common.

308
Dispensary table in the Louis XIII tradition from the Hôtel-Dieu hospital in Montréal. Yellow birch, 18th century.
The spiral-turned legs are joined by H-stretchers. The upper part of the table does not seem to be as old or as well executed as the base. A scientific analysis is needed.

THE NEW FRANCE STYLE

309 a, b
Chair-table. Yellow birch, pine and ash, late 18th century. One of the main characteristics of early Québec furniture is its functional nature. Armoires and buffets, for example, were tall and wide but not very deep, while settle-beds, or *bancs-lits*, served as both beds and benches. In addition, certain types of tables could be taken apart (trestle tables) or folded (drop-leaf tables) and stored against a wall, while chair-tables had tops that could be simply lifted back to reveal a handy seat fitted with a storage drawer. This specimen has an H-stretcher and turned legs reflecting the stylistic influences of the two cultures that shaped Québec.

310
Kitchen of the Engineer's House in Louisbourg, ca. 1740. This reconstruction of a French Regime interior provides an excellent idea of what kitchens were like in most bourgeois homes in places such as Québec City during the 18th century. Today, only a few sites like the Ferme Saint-Gabriel and the Château de Ramezay in Montréal still recreate the spirit of daily life during the French Regime. Our cultural memory has suffered considerably as a result, and a determined effort must be made to highlight all traces of that glorious period when immigrants from France were carving out a new homeland in North America.

311 to 317
Tables of Louis XIII and Louis XV inspiration with turned legs and H-stretchers sometimes ornamented with a finial, or with cabriole legs in the Louis XV style. The tops of the Louis XIII tables are rectilinear, while those of the tables in the Louis XV manner are shaped. According to Palardy, the table with ball turnings on the lower left combines the Henri IV and Louis XIII styles and is probably the oldest in Québec. Pine and yellow birch, first half of the 18th century.

318
Reconstruction of the engineer's dining room at the Fortress of Louisbourg, ca. 1740.
Louisbourg was the main settlement on Île Royale, which formed part of French Acadia. Construction on this fortress began in 1714, and by 1752, it was home to nearly 2 600 people, most of whom earned their livelihood from fishing. A colonial administration with a marked hierarchical structure oversaw the fortified town, which was inhabited by a garrison. After France officially lost the colony in 1760, the fortress was demolished. Many of its installations were rebuilt in the 1960s as part of regional economic development measures targeting Cape Breton in Atlantic Canada. Exhaustive ethnohistorical research has made it possible to reconstruct the interior of buildings in detail.

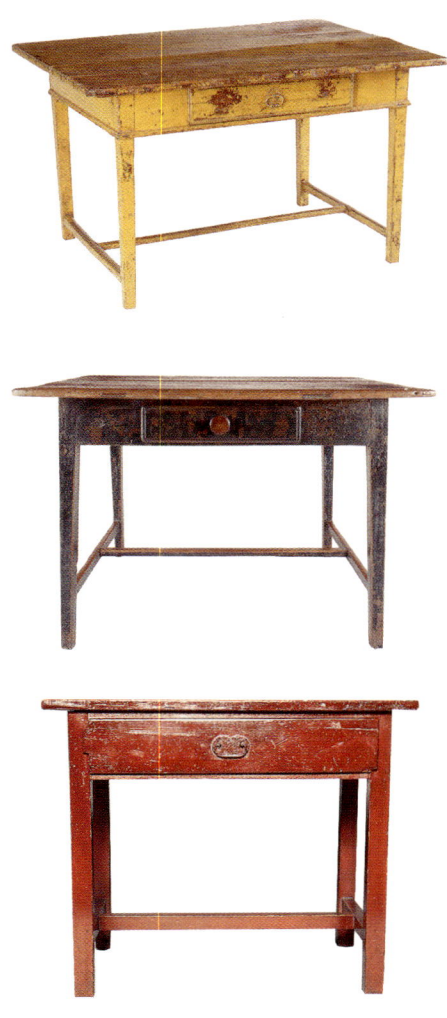

319
Rustic table of French derivation with tapered legs, moulded H-stretcher and moulding around the apron and drawer. Forged nails, original ochre-yellow color, pine, ca. 1790.

320
Exceptional utility table of French derivation with heavily moulded and chamfered legs, H-stretcher, drawer and top. Original color, pine and yellow birch, ca. 1775.

321
Table of French derivation in as-found condition with a full-length drawer, hand-forged heart-shaped pull and forged nails. Yellow birch and pine, 1860.

322
Gate-leg table with tapered legs and a wooden hinge. Original color, pine and yellow birch, ca. 1840.

323
Fine table with a keyed top, H-stretcher, tapered legs and an appliqué drawer. Original knob and color, pine and yellow birch, ca. 1810.

324
Rustic kitchen table with tapered and chamfered square legs and a fairly thick top made of two wide planks. Early color, forged nails, pine, ca. 1840.

325 a, b, c
Gate-leg table in the Louis XIII manner, in both closed and open positions, with a full-length drawer in one side of the apron, a chamfered H-stretcher and rectangular shapes at joints. Original color, yellow birch and pine, mid-18th century.
This seems to have been the most common table form in traditional rural homes. Eloquent piece of furniture.

THE NEW FRANCE STYLE 231

DESKS

The writing desk was reserved for the administrative elite, bourgeois businessmen and church officials. Several pieces from the 18th century have survived to this day. The Augustinian Hospitallers still have the desk of Monseigneur Jean Olivier Briand (1715-1794), photographed by Ramsay Traquair around 1930 (**326**). According to the community's records, this piece was made in 1770 by a joiner named Pierre Émond and was commissioned by the Bishop of Québec. Period tables with a top covered with inlaid leather – as are still found from time to time – were also used as desks.

326-327
Desk of Monseigneur Jean Olivier Briand, Bishop of Québec, 1770.
Photograph by Ramsay Traquair, ca. 1930.
This Louis XIII-inspired piece has a turned H-stretcher decorated with a central finial, a festooned apron and three drawers embellished with concave-cornered panels and quatrefoil motifs. Curly yellow birch, late 18th century.

328
Mazarin-style desk with seven bow-front drawers and eight tapered legs. This type of desk, which was very popular in the 18th century, was named after the famous Italian-born cardinal who played a major role in politics and the arts in France in the mid-17th century.
A piece of fine linen stuck to the back of this desk bears an inscription that reads: "I have given and give to Madame St. Martin, Mother Superior of the Hôtel-Dieu, this bureau or commode as it is, such as it is and to this effect I sign.

At Québec this day August 16, 1768. Chavigny."
[Translation] Yellow birch, Québec City, early 18th century. Made by a skilled cabinetmaker, this desk must have belonged to an important colonial figure. The small leather-covered box on top of the piece, decorated with fleurs-de-lis, dates from the same period as the desk and belongs, along with all the other accessories, including the tapestry, to the museum adjacent to the Hôtel-Dieu hospital in Québec City (Musée des Augustines de l'Hôtel-Dieu de Québec), an institution that has played an active role in the city since 1639.

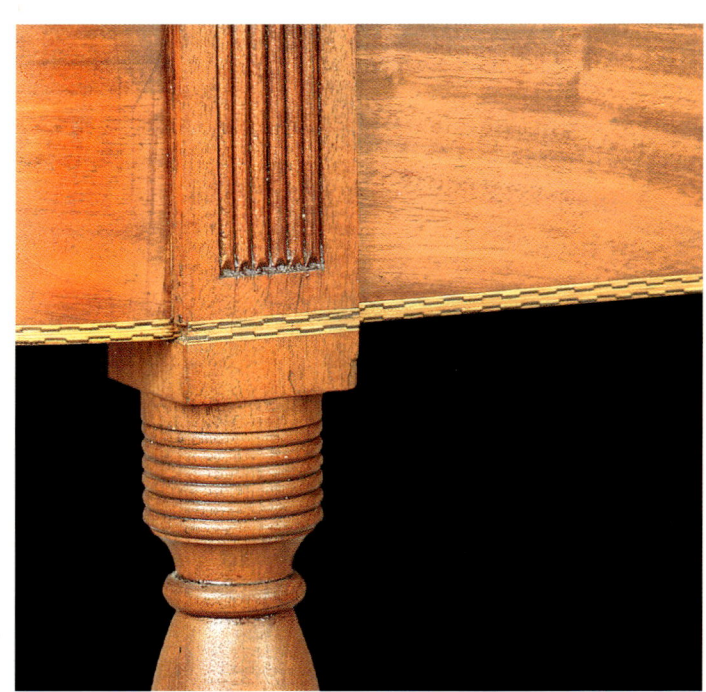

329 to 332
Details of Québec Neoclassical furnitures. Scrolled Regency armrest;
Hepplewhite chair back; clock case with oval marquetry inlay representing
the main symbols of Britain; leg and apron assembly
on a Sheraton mahogany table.

Chapter 3

The Merging and Melding of Cultural Influences

Neoclassical Furniture in the St. Lawrence Valley

1790-1840

THE CONSTITUTIONAL STYLE

THE TRADITIONAL FORMS OF FRENCH CANADIAN FURNITURE evolved slowly through the *ancien régime* until, after 1760, the sudden confrontation with Anglo-American styles led to a reorientation of tastes and the assimilation of new shapes and motifs to the French prototypes and decoration that had been uncontested since the founding of the colony in 1608. The evolution of hybrid forms brought about by the intrusion of these new styles was not unlike the effect that Italian and Dutch influences had had on continental French furniture of the 17th century.

John A. Fleming, *The Painted Furniture of French Canada 1700-1840*

MANY NORTH AMERICAN AND BRITISH ANTIQUARIANS feel that the furniture and architecture of the English late-Georgian age, coinciding with the American-Federal period, represented a high water-mark in human-inspired design. (European antiquarians, conversely, sometimes confuse opulence with elegance.) At the taste-making level of society the excesses of the baroque age had passed, though they were to re-emerge in the ugliness dictated by fashion in the third quarter of the 19th century. The late Georgian and American Federal period was an age both of rationality and understatement in design, and of neo-classical taste based on ancient Mediterranean forms. The furniture of this period was, in a phrase, comfortable, rich and human – pleasing and radiating an enveloping warmth to the eye and the soul. Supreme good taste, for a time, was also fashionable, a most fortuitous benefit which can hardly be considered true of all ages.

Donald Blake Webster, *English-Canadian Furniture of the Georgian Period*

Mahogany clock, Québec City, first quarter of the 19th century.

Neoclassical Furniture in the St. Lawrence Valley

In 1846, Newton Bosworth published the second edition of the first history of Montréal under the title *Hochelaga Depicta or a New Picture of Montreal Embracing the Early History and Present State of the City and Island of Montreal*. Focusing on the city that Maisonneuve had founded at the foot of Mount Royal two centuries earlier, it showed how much this urban centre had changed in just a few decades and how rapidly it had adopted the values of British Neoclassicism. Many of the illustrations in the book, which were signed by the artist John Duncan, depict public buildings – namely, court houses, customs houses, prisons, covered markets, banks, theatres and schools – in the Late Georgian and Regency styles. These buildings were influenced by the work of Andrea Palladio, a Renaissance architect who had drawn considerable inspiration from the sources of Greek and Roman classicism, and whose designs were already highly popular in Britain, and had been so for many years. Buildings bearing the stamp of Palladio were always very elegant, with their tripartite façades and plan, often projecting, central sections adorned with porticos and pediments, gently sloping roofs, and bare, regular surfaces. These ashlar structures had a simple, sober appearance, embellished only by the occasional string course and by quoining at the corners and around doors and windows.

The interior of such buildings, which was always very bright owing to the presence of many large windows, displayed the same distinctive features and orderly arrangement as their exterior. Their symmetrical plan, moulding proportions and outline, ornamentation, entablatures, and fluted columns, surmounted by capitals in the style of the main architectural orders, were all borrowed from the classical vocabulary of ancient Greece and Rome, as it had been reinterpreted in Italy during the 15th and 16th centuries. This taste for the stylistic values of antiquity, which was reflected even in

333
Interior of the Jourdan-Fiset house on Saint-Louis Street in Québec City, ca. 1940. Québec City, the capital of French Canada, has been marked to a significant extent by British culture. English domestic, civil, military and religious architecture radically changed the face of this city founded by Champlain in 1608. Here, more than anywhere else in the St. Lawrence Valley, the values of British Neoclassicism influenced interior design, furnishings and material culture in general. In the mid-20th century, many homes still testified eloquently to the dynamic contribution of British culture.

THE CONSTITUTIONAL STYLE IN QUÉBEC
1790-1840

JEAN-ANTOINE PANET
1751-1815

GUY CARLETON, LORD DORCHESTER
1724-1808

SOURCES: British **Late Georgian** and **Regency** and U.S. Federal styles; French Directoire, **Empire**, Restoration and Louis-Philippe styles, as interpreted in the United States. Return to the values of antiquity and classical simplicity.

WOOD AND MATERIALS:
Vernacular furniture: pine and butternut
Period furniture: mahogany, black cherry, walnut, yellow birch, butternut, and bird's-eye, curly or tiger maple
Veneering: mahogany, walnut and maple

Sideboard, Montréal, ca. 1820.

COLLECTIONS: McCord Museum in Montréal, Royal Ontario Museum in Toronto, Séminaire de Québec in Québec City, and Musée de la civilisation in Québec City.

baseboards, bed and wall mouldings, simple cornices, and elegant, sober mantlepieces, was what fashioned the institutional architecture of Montréal during the Neoclassical period. The style offered tangible proof of how, within less than 50 years, England had left its distinctive stamp on the city that formed the heart of British North America and which, in the first half of the 19th century, played an active role in building modern Canada.

Québec City, the capital of Lower Canada, experimented, like Montréal, with the new cultural influences, integrating them into the architecture of many of its civil and military buildings, including the citadel, city gates, Anglican cathedral, prison, and marine hospital. As in the case of Montréal, its downtown core began to be built up with row houses, while its outskirts were dotted with picturesque villas in the Georgian and Regency styles. Such villas housed the barons of the timber trade and other entrepreneurs active in the colony's burgeoning business sector. As evidenced by the changes being wrought in these two rapidly growing cities, it was in the late 18th century and the first half of the 19th century that the cultural influence of England in the St. Lawrence Valley was not only at its purest but also at its peak. However, this influence would eventually be diluted by the imperialistic tendencies of the United States, which, in its efforts to capture new markets, flooded Canada with its own stylistic trends and cultural values.

During the Napoleonic Wars, England was denied access to the Scandinavian coun-

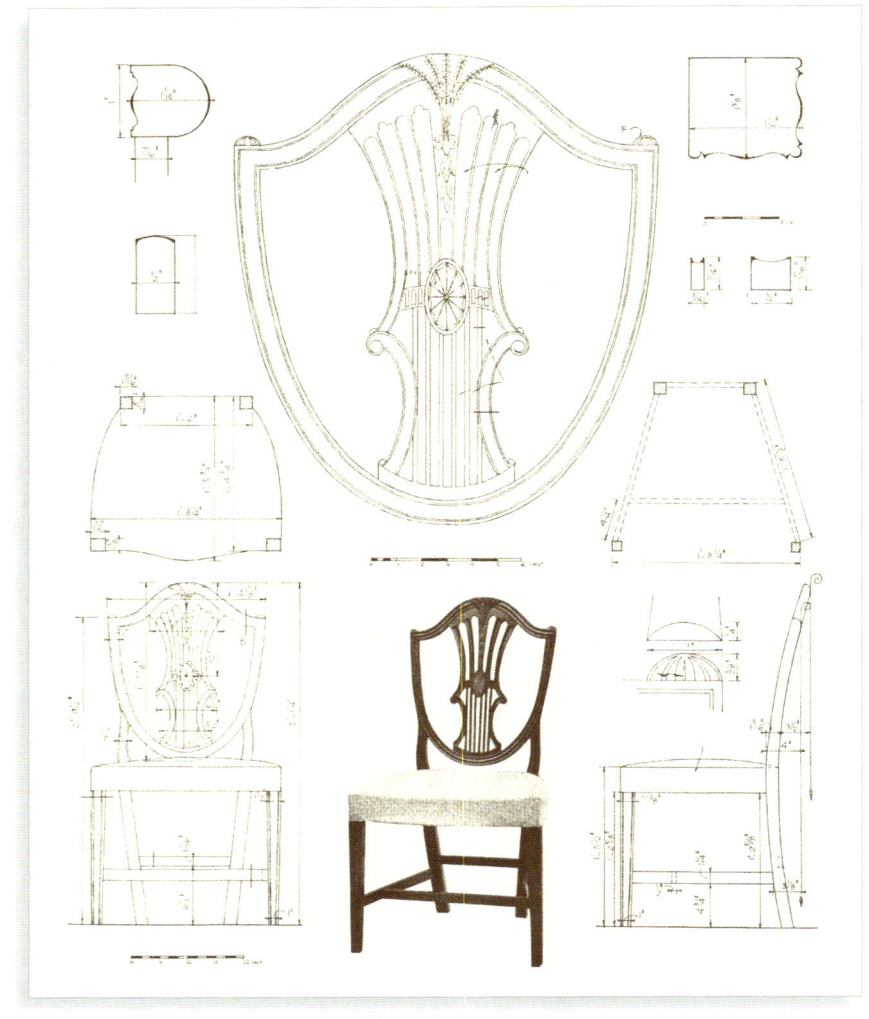

tries, which had traditionally supplied it with wood. Therefore, as of the 19th century, the British started to obtain this essential raw material from the St. Lawrence Valley. Given that the advantageous tariffs of the period favored exports of timber, many Quebeckers sought employment as lumberjacks or raftsmen, since such workers were needed to harvest this precious resource and transport it downriver by raft. The new colonizers readily found local businessmen who, in their quest for economic success, were willing to supervise logging, log driving and sawmill operations. These *nouveaux riches*, who soon embraced the styles and fashions followed by their British bosses, gave free rein to their penchant for progress by building houses and purchasing furniture that would be equated with success. The members of the local elite, who also developed a taste for the new trends, were soon imitated by ordinary citizens, with the result that an entirely new network of influence and authority ultimately had a profound impact on society as a whole.

The Neoclassical period in Québec marked the beginning of a new era, characterized by a flourishing of the arts. Cities were transformed as the colony's economy developed at an unprecedented rate and the English-speaking population grew, playing an increasingly important role in all spheres of activity and having a major influence on social and cultural life. Rural areas also changed radically as they gradually abandoned the medieval practices inherited from the French Regime and adopted more modern ways.

Given that the new fashions were readily espoused by French-speaking painters, sculptors, architects and builders, many churches were rebuilt or renovated with Neoclassical forms and ornamentation. Similarly, house designs in both the countryside and urban areas were completely revamped on the basis of the new forms, layouts and decors defined at the time. The Neoclassical Québécois house was an original expression of this trend. With its roof ending in deep bell-cast eaves extending over a long porch, its framework set high off the ground and its symmetrically arranged windows letting in an abundant supply of light, it was a unique house form that would survive well beyond the chronological limits established for this rich period.

During this dynamic chapter in Québec's history, the Neoclassical style not only had a profound impact on architecture, but on

335
Hepplewhite-style shield-back chair with tapered legs. Black cherry, Québec City, 19th century.
Some of Québec City's older institutions still have hardwood chairs that are very similar to the models proposed by Hepplewhite, Sheraton and other British and U.S. designers of the Neoclassical period. Only careful scrutiny makes it possible to tell the difference between an original period piece and an old reproduction, dating, for example, from the late 19th century.

334
Scale drawing of a Hepplewhite-style chair of U.S. manufacture with straight legs and a shield back comprising an openwork splat of classical design embellished with scrolls and a central medallion-shaped inlay. This type of chair, which dates from the late 1700s, is very similar to pieces that were imported into or made in Québec at the end of the 18th century and in the first half of the 19th century. The drawing is from the collections of the Metropolitan Museum of Art in New York City.

THE SPIRIT OF THE NEOCLASSICAL ERA 1790-1840

At the turn of the 19th century, architecture and the decorative arts were marked by a return to the values and forms of antiquity. Clothing, silverware and furniture incorporated elements borrowed from the stylistic repertoire of Greece and Rome. Quebeckers developed a unique house form with a symmetrical plan, a beautiful doorway in keeping with the classical orders of architecture, a roof with deep bell-cast eaves, and a long covered porch, providing protection from the rain and an excellent view of the surrounding landscape. Clearly, Québec fell sway to the tastes and fashions in vogue in England during the Georgian period.

Silhouette portrait of Ignace-Michel-Louis-Antoine d'Irumberry de Salaberry, 1809.

Silver teapot by Salomon Marion, ca. 1820.

Serving dish belonging to Louis-Joseph Papineau, Davenport, England, ca. 1810.

Bouillotte lamp with metal shades, Québec City, 19th century.

Sheraton dressing table in mahogany, Québec City, ca. 1820.

Embroidery screen, walnut veneer, ca. 1850.

White muslin dress, ca. 1810.

Slant-top desk belonging to Joseph Guillet *dit* Tourangeau of Québec City, mahogany, ca. 1810.

Neoclassical Québécois house owned by France Maranda, Saint-Laurent, Île d'Orléans, 1852.

Québec City, the capital of Lower Canada, ca. 1805, by Georges Heriot.

Hepplewhite-style chair, mahogany, Québec City, ca. 1810.

Sofa in the U.S. Empire manner, mahogany, Québec City, ca. 1820.

Tea caddy with inlaid ornamentation, Québec City, 1810.

Cast-iron double stove from the Forges du Saint-Maurice, Trois-Rivières, ca. 1820.

Bedroom suite, ca. 1840.

PERSONAL ACCOUNT

Neoclassical Elegance

It was because of my keen interest in heritage that I decided to become an architect. My mentor was André Robitaille, who initiated the restoration of Place Royale in Québec City. I was absolutely fascinated with the first scholarly publications put out by Québec's cultural ministry in the late 1960s. My mother, who had studied fine arts, had always taught us to appreciate the values of the past, and she took great pleasure in telling us the history of the family heirlooms in our home. We belonged to the Tourangeau family, who had lived in Québec City for generations, as well as to the Dionne family of Saint-Roch-des-Aulnaies. My childhood and adolescence were marked by visits to distinguished relatives, whose homes were like museums. Perhaps this explains why I later became interested, while doing research in university for a paper that would eventually be published, in the evolution of the interior design and furnishings of old houses in Québec City. My paternal grandmother was the granddaughter of Wilhelmina Dionne, the daughter of Pascal-Amable Dionne, the last seigneur of Saint-Roch-Des-Aulnaies. I remember that she had several objects from the seigneurial manor, including a portrait of St. Cecile, the patron saint of musicians, painted by Chevalier Falardeau; a large silver épergne, or table centre piece; and chairs with sabre legs in the Neoclassical manner. I was fascinated by manor houses, seigneurial life and period furniture. Heritage conservation has now become the focus of my professional life.

Neoclassical furniture is what I like the most, since it is this type of furniture, more than that from the Victorian era, which graced the old manors and beautiful villas of my childhood. The Tourangeau, Dionne, De Bonne, and Panet-Raymond families owned pieces of furniture in the style of the years 1790 to 1820, which constituted a turning point in Québec's history. These objects impressed me because of their light, graceful lines, which were simpler than those of later pieces. I once had the pleasure of restoring the Anglican cathedral, a perfect example of Neoclassicism in Québec City. This building, which is situated close to the Catholic cathedral and even outshines it to some extent, symbolized, through its Neoclassical architecture, the new authority established in the colony since the Conquest. As for Neoclassical furniture, it embodied the new values ushered in along with the change in regime. As I learned during my research, which was based in part on the study of numerous architectural drawings, the interior design of many 18th-century homes was remodelled according to British tastes. Chimneys, mouldings and other woodwork were redone in the new style, leaving only the structure of buildings unchanged.

With its beautiful dark brown color and subtle golden tones, Neoclassical mahogany furniture stood out from the walls behind it, which were painted yellow or pale blue in keeping with the fashion of the day. Woodwork, which was painted white, also offered a pleasing contrast with the colored surfaces around it. I love the elegance and simplicity of the unique polychromatic decor that characterized Neoclassical interiors and that has been preserved in France in buildings designed by certain architects, such as Gabriel. The entire Western world fell under the influence of the Neoclassical idiom, with its decorative vocabulary derived from antiquity. Québec, for its part, fell sway to the Empire style, as it was interpreted in the United States. Some pieces in this style were made of solid wood, while others were finished with thick pieces of veneer. Like furniture built of mahogany, that made from curly, tiger or bird's eye maple, embellished with inlays of mahogany and other woods and fitted with copper knobs, contrasted beautifully with the colors in vogue during the Neoclassical period.

Some of the pieces of furniture that grace my home are family legacies which date from this period. Others come from the homes of certain British families that lived in Québec City, including the Davis family. Although a great deal of Neoclassical furniture was produced in the Saint-Jean-Port-Joli region and on the Côte-du-Sud, such articles are now very rare on Québec's antique market.

Since I am highly aware of the significance of old objects and the information that can be gleaned from them, I ardently hope that the furniture I have inherited from my family will remain in the family. Steps must be taken to preserve this precious heritage, whose intrinsic qualities make it so worthy of such attention.

Georges Leahy
Québec City, June 1999

material culture as a whole, including the decorative and furniture arts. In Britain, this style was known as Late Georgian or Regency, designations which through their association with certain kings and symbolically charged moments evoked the image of an empire on which the sun never set. It is only natural that the first generation of British colonists, who had emigrated to seek success in a land that was theirs for the taking, would strive to surround themselves with the comforts and latest fashions enjoyed in the mother country by the families they had left behind. It is also understandable that, during this period of prosperity, Quebeckers, who were open to the world thanks to their shipping industry and who wished to maintain ties with France, were won over by the latest fashions and trends in vogue in that country. The account of the extremely enthusiastic welcome extended to the frigate *La Capricieuse* in 1855, whose arrival marked France's first official visit to Québec since its defeat in 1760, reflects the admiration inspired by the land from which the first settlers originated.

Newspaper advertisements offer eloquent proof that furniture was among the items imported in large quantities from England during the days when the British colony was first being organized. Many of these pieces were sold by merchants established in Québec City and Montréal.

As demonstrated by Jean Palardy, Elizabeth Collard and Paul-Louis Martin, a number of English and Scottish furniture makers opened workshops in Québec quite early on. In studies that complement one another, these authors have listed cabinetmaking and joinery workshops active during the first half of the 19th century. Similar information has also been provided in the scholarly publications of Donald Blake Webster and John A. Fleming, which, like the above-mentioned studies, are included in the bibliography. Although craftsmen and their workshops as well as the places and period in which they plied their trade have been accurately identified through careful perusal of historical records, very few pieces of Québec-made period furniture from Montréal, Québec City or the Eastern Townships — the three areas where British colonists decided to settle — have been attributed with certainty to a given furniture maker. Unfortunately, such attribution problems are not only confined to the movable and built-in furniture found in ordinary homes but also apply to that made for Québec's many public institutions.

ARCHIVES

The Blending of Cultural Influences in Neoclassical Furniture

Notarial records contain apprenticeship agreements or employment contracts between individuals from the same craft guild. In 1817, two such agreements were concluded by furniture makers in Québec City, the furniture arts capital of the British colony. Preserved in the Québec's National Archives, they provide a fairly good idea of how a range of tastes were embraced by the population at the time and how this situation fostered a blending of cultural influences during the Neoclassical era.

No. 263 – May 23, 1817
Engagement of Etienne Clavet as an apprentice to James Fitzgibbon

Before the undersigned public notaries of the province of Lower Canada, residing in the city of Québec, were present Jean Baptiste Clavet, dwelling in the parish of Ste Foy, who for the benefit and advantage of his son Etienne Clavet, a minor of about eighteen years of age whom he certifies is trustworthy, did acknowledge that he authorized the engagement of the said Etienne Clavet as an apprentice joiner and furniture maker for three full, consecutive years starting the twentieth day of last April unto James Fitzgibbon, master joiner & furniture maker of the city of Québec, dwelling in that city, to serve as his apprentice for the said period and that the said James Fitzgibbon promises and engages and binds and obliges himself to show and teach him the said trades and all that is involved in them, without hiding anything from him, as long as the said apprentice is capable of learning, and to provide him as an apprentice with food, shelter, shoes and lighting, in addition to treating him well and paying him the sum of six pounds current money annually for his personal support, payable at the end of each month the said apprentice promises and engages to learn to the best of his ability all that will be shown and taught to him by the said James Fitzgibbon, his master, to obey him with respect and docility in all that he is ordered to do that is legal and honest, to work for his benefit and avoid him injury, and to inform him of any wrongs he learns that he might suffer, without going absent or leaving to work elsewhere. Should the said apprentice desert his master, the father binds and obliges himself to look for his son throughout the district of Québec and to bring him back to his said master if possible so that he may complete the time he has left to work, and the said master binds and obliges himself to grant him leave to practice his religion freely on Sundays and holidays of obligation only and even to oblige him to attend Church on the said holidays and Sundays.

The whole to be executed under pain of all Costs, damages and interest, the said parties have made election of their domicile irrevocable at their actual residence. Where etc For thus etc Promising etc Obliging etc Renouncing etc, thus done and passed at the city of Québec, in the office of the undersigned notary Mr. Gauvreau on the twenty-third of May in the morning one thousand eight hundred and seventeen, the said James Fitzgibbon having signed together with us the said notaries, the said father Jean Baptiste Clavet and son Etienne Clavet having declared being unable to write or sign when asked. Duly read.

James Fitzgibbon
Charles H. Gauvreau N.P., P. Gagnon not Pub
[Translation]

Source : ANQ
Greffe Charles. H. Gauvreau
May 23, 1817, No. 263
Transcription : Michel Gaumond

No. 331 – September 16, 1817
Agreement, between Alexander Murison and Pierre Parent

On the sixteenth day of september in the afternoon one thousand eight hundred and seventeen, before the undersigned public notaries duly commissioned and sworn in and for the province of Lower Canada, dwelling in the city of Quebec, personally came appeared and were present Alexander Murison joiner and cabinet maker, from Montrose north Britain now residing in the city of Quebec of one part and mr. Pierre Parent of the said city of Quebec, joiner & cabinet maker of the other part which said parties to these presents in the presence of us the undersigned notaries did acknowledge and confess as follows, that is to say, the said Alexander Murison has engaged and by these both engage himself unto the said Pierre Parent accepting hereof the said Alexander Murison for and during to the full end of term of seven months & fourteen days to be computed from the date here of and fully be completed and ended on the first day of may next to serve him the said Pierre Parent in his shop the space ten hours for each and every day of the duration of the present agreement and in his capacity aforsaid do all such joiner and cabinet maker work at the request of the said Pierre Parent or of his employers by his order, the aforsaid work so to be done and performed by him the said Alexander Murison fit for sale in a good workmanlike manner and to the best of his skill and knowledge without selling dealing trafficking, lending, delivering or entrusting the goods and effects of the said Pierre Parent or any part of parcel thereof to any person or persons whomsoever without the actual consent, approbation and instruction of the said Pierre Parent.

It is also by and between the said parties to these presents, that all such time lost by the said Alexander Murison through neglect or otherwise during the continuance of the present agreement shall be deducted of and from the said Alexander Murison's wages, at the end of every week.

And in consideration of the hand labour of the said Alexander Murison in his capacity aforsaid the said Pierre Parent both hereby promise and engage and bind and oblige himself to well and truly pay or cause to be well and truly paid unto the said Alexander Murison, the sum of four shillings & six pences current money of this Province for each and every day's work of him to the said Alexander Murison payable at the end of every week and when and as the same shall become due and owing to him the said Alexander Murison.

And it is further agreed and covenanted that in case the said Alexander Murison, for the better convenience of himself, or of both parties, should take his board at any time during the continuance of the present agreement with the said Pierre Parent and his family, then and from the time he shall commence taking his board with the said Pierre Parent as aforesaid until he shall think proper to board elsewhere a sum of twelve shillings current money aforsaid shall be deducted and retained of and from his weekly wages at the end of every week, and whereas the said Pierre Parent as a Roman Catholic is bound to keep lent days the said Alexander Murison shall and will aim binds and oblige himself to keep all such lent Days as well as the said Pierre Parent and family, and also to provide for himself with his own necessary bedding.

The whole to be executed under pain of all Costs, damages and interest, the said parties have made election of their domicile irrevocable at their actual residence aforsaid. Where etc Notwithstanding etc For thus etc Promising etc Obliging etc Renouncing etc.

Thus done and passed at the aforsaid city of Quebec, in the dwelling house of the said Pierre Parent in St John Suburbs, the day and year first above written, the said parties having to these presents first duly read according to Law set and subscribed their names and signatures together with us the said notaries in faith and testimony of the premisses.

Alexander Murison, Pierre Parent
Et. Boudreault N.P., Charles H. Gauvreau N.P.

Source : ANQ
Greffe Charles. Herménégilde Gauvreau
September 16, 1817, No. 331
Transcription : Michel Gaumond

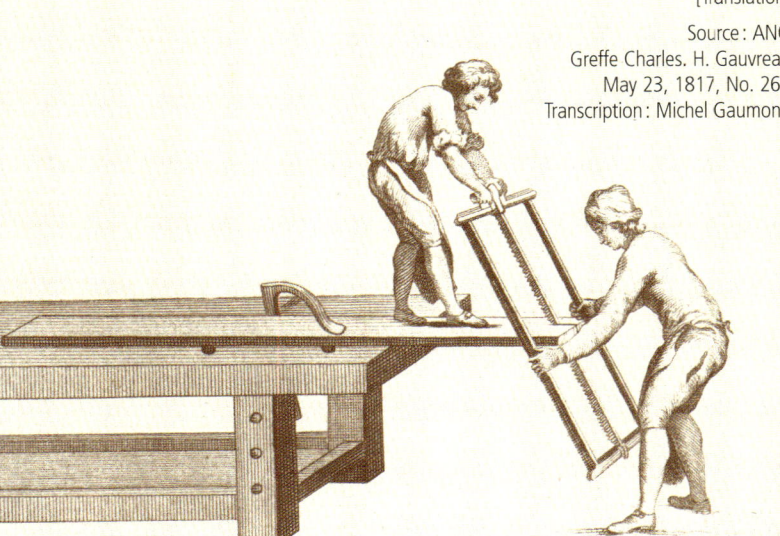

BRITISH AND U.S. NEOCLASSICAL FURNITURE

*I*n the late 18th century and the first half of the 19th century, Neoclassical furniture was defined by publications put out by British architect-designers and through the dissemination of catalogues of models that provided inspiration for cabinetmakers. Québec was influenced by trends from England and the United States, which in turn fell sway to the French Directoire and Empire styles.

a.

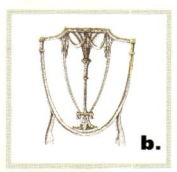
b.

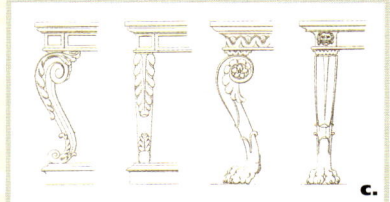
c.

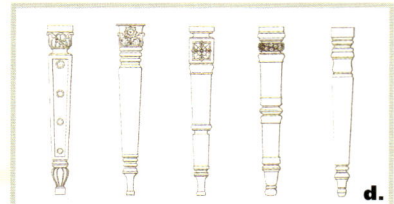
d.

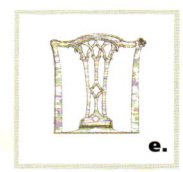
e.

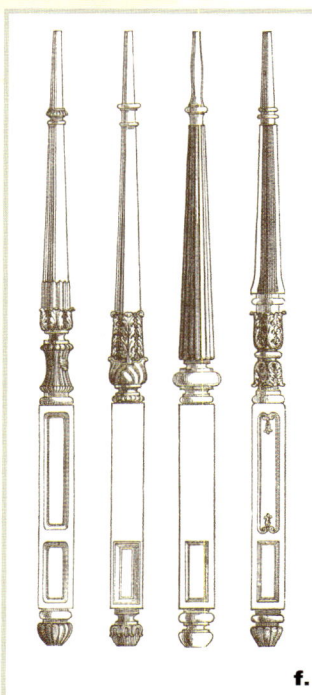
f.

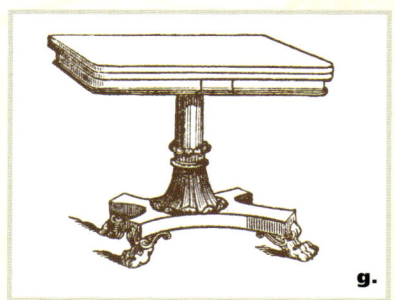
g.

h.

i.

j.

k.

l.

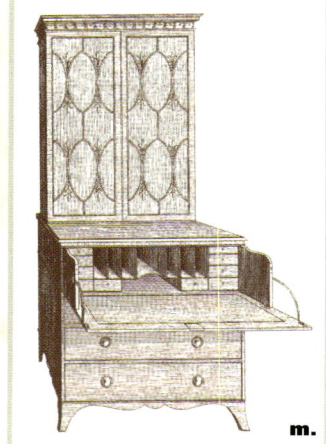
m.

n.

Drawings of furniture from old British and U.S. treatises or catalogues that had an impact on North American and Québec furniture at the end of the 18th century and in the first half of the 19th century.

Thomas King (British), *Modern Style of Cabinet Work Exemplefied*, 1829: **d.** table legs. **h.** washstand with turned legs. **j.** bookcase. **l.** side chair with curved back, sabre back legs and turned front legs. **q.** sideboard. **u-v.** scrolled sofa armrests.

John Claudius Loudon (British), from *Encyclopedia of Cottage Farm and Villa Architecture*, 1833: **f.** turned bed posts. **g.** card table with lion's-paw feet. **i.** caned chair with a pillow top. **p.** sofa. **z.** bedroom suite with a sleigh bed.

George Hepplewhite (British), *The Cabinet-Maker and Upholsterer's Guide*, 1794: **k.** Pembroke table. **m.** secretary. **n.** armchair. **o.** sofa. **r.** dressing glass. **s.** easy chair. **w.** chest of drawers. **y.** desk.

Thomas Sheraton, *The Cabinet-Maker and Upholsterer's Drawing Book* (London: 1791): **a.** tripod tables. **b.** chair back.

Thomas Chippendale, *The Gentleman Cabinet-Maker's & Director* (London: 1762): **e.** chair back.

George Smith, author of another "guide" published in London around 1815: **c.** table legs.

Rudolphe Ackerman (1764-1840), designer of German origin, who immigrated to London: **t.** two récamiers, ca. 1820.

o.

p.

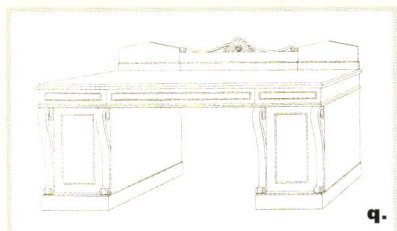
q.

r.

t.

u.

s.

v.

w.

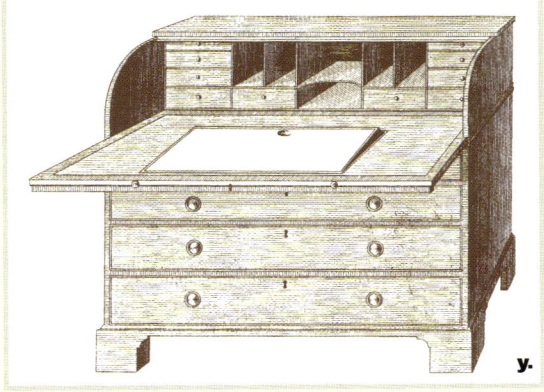
y.

z.

Toward a definition of Neoclassical furniture

Québec Neoclassical furniture is very different from pieces made prior to 1790 with respect to lines, ornamentation and materials. For example, Neoclassical chairs no longer display the baluster-turned legs joined by H-stretchers or the cabriole legs so commonly encountered on their predecessors, but are fitted with straight, square Marlborough legs terminating in spade feet; turned tapered legs, often decorated with various motifs; or sabre legs like those of the *klismos*, an ancient Greek chair form. In general, the surfaces and proportions of Neoclassical case furniture and serving pieces are sober and simple, featuring somewhat austere linear and geometric forms. Chests of drawers and slant-top desks are usually simple box-like structures with large drawers and almost no superfluous ornamentation, and are designed above all to be functional and efficient.

The Neoclassical movement strove to discover the works of classical Greek and Roman antiquity. Doric, Ionic and Corinthian art, with their emphasis on relatively unadorned surfaces, cannot be qualified as very lyrical. The quality of this type of design often stems from its clarity, which allows the structural dynamics of a work to be appreciated immediately. Neoclassical models are pleasing because of the harmonious arrangement of their components, their aesthetic proportions, symmetry and obvious solidity, not to mention their workmanship, which is readily reflected in their construction.

Neoclassical furniture is devoid of mystery. With its structural clarity, utilitarian nature and fine finishing, it has a reassuring, predictable quality, like that of a Greek temple, whose capital-topped columns support the structure's entablature, which in turn supports the roof. Unpretentious, sober and never opulent or ostentatious, this type of furniture is extremely elegant, precisely because of its classical simplicity – a quality that has had universal appeal for thousands of years.

Furniture materials also changed dramatically during the Neoclassical era, given that the new style favored heavy hardwoods and exotic species. Triangular trade with the West Indies made it possible to import large blocks of mahogany, which often served as ballast in the ocean-going sailing ships used to transport this wood. As shown by shipping registers and newspaper advertisements, large quantities of mahogany entered the ports of Montréal and Québec City as of the late 18th century. Trade in this type of wood flourished until the mid 1800s.

Judging from surviving pieces of Neoclassical furniture, the interesting array of hardwood species available in Québec, such as curly and bird's eye maple, yellow birch, butternut and black walnut, also enjoyed a certain popularity as furniture building materials. While the frame and the unseen, utilitarian components of objects, such as drawers and shelving, were frequently made of secondary wood, table tops and the façades and other visible surfaces of case furniture were finished with veneer, often consisting of a thick layer of precious wood. The sides of furniture sometimes received special treatment as well, but they were commonly built with a third species of wood, stained to emulate the grain and color of the type on the front. Many pieces of Neoclassical furniture were made of solid hardwood, which is readily apparent when one attempts to move them. Craftsmen often built objects combining the different wood-fibre patterns of a particular species, using grained wood for the stiles, and heartwood, crotch wood or the fancy figures of burl for the panels.

Period pieces were usually varnished, although they were sometimes finished with imitation graining. Fine ornamentation was frequently achieved with inlay, which involved embedding in the visible surfaces of an object pieces of wood whose grain and color contrasted with those of the surrounding wood. As for the decorative elements found on this type of furniture, they were based on the motifs associated with the main architectural orders of classical antiquity namely, the Doric, Ionic, Corinthian, Tuscan and Composite orders which underpinned the Neoclassical style. They included turned and tapered legs; reeding, fluting and gadrooning; marquetry motifs in the form of ovals, fans, bouquets, allegorical figures and various symbols; dentil mouldings; egg-shaped and palmette motifs; simple scrolls; lyre- and shield-shaped components; geometrical interlacing; and ogee, cavetto and torus mouldings.

Period furniture hardware, in the form of bronze handles, hinges, locks, hooks and feet, was usually of industrial manufacture and imported from England. Objects locking with a key, such as chests of drawers, slant-top desks, armoires and secretaries, were frequently embellished with delicately designed keyhole inlays made of brass and sometimes ivory or even geometric marquetry. Many pieces of locally made furniture had pulls in the form of large turned wooden knobs, while others, produced at the end of the Neoclassical period, were fitted with white porcelain pulls.

It is not easy to identify Québec-built furniture in the Georgian and Regency styles, given that it cannot be readily distinguished from items imported from the Maritimes and certain New England states. This is because furniture makers in those areas used the same materials, designs and ornamentation as Québec craftsmen and thus produced similar chairs, tables, chests of drawers, secretaries, beds and so forth. Although attributing a piece of furniture to a particular workshop or region is interesting, it is even more useful to be able to place the piece in the particular context in which it was used and to identify the people who used it, namely, the family to which it belonged. In this way, a specific ethnohistorical value can be attached to it. Knowing that an English-speaking family in Québec City, Montréal, the Eastern Townships or the Baie des Chaleurs handed down a chest of drawers or a sofa for five or six generations or that a bourgeois household in L'Isle-Vert, Saint-Ours,

336
Chippendale-inspired sofa table made of mahogany veneer over secondary pine, with two cock-beaded drawers, a drop-leaf at each end, ring-turned pendant finials at each corner of the apron, inlay around the top, two false drawers in back and a turned base ending in four feet decorated with zoomorphic motifs. The knobs are replacements. This table, which dates from the 1820s, comes from the Beauce and was made in Québec City. Tables of this type were placed behind sofas in living rooms, where they served as supports for books, candlesticks and so forth. The Sheraton-Regency-style armchair with sabre legs and recessed armrests is built of mahogany and has a pine frame. Also made in Québec City, it dates from around 1820.

Montebello or Saint-Vallier decorated their home with furniture in a specific style can help one to understand a particular decor and to establish links between the various influences exerted at a given period. The use of wood species native to the St. Lawrence Valley, particularly pine and basswood, is sometimes the only clear indication that a piece of furniture was made in Québec.

The main characteristic of Québec-made Neoclassical furniture is its blending of a variety of cultural influences. Although the predominant influence was that of the Smith, Sheraton and Hepplewhite styles developed in England, U.S. interpretations of period designs, which were brought into Québec by the two waves of Loyalist settlers who emigrated from south of the border between 1780 and 1810, also had an impact. However, contrary to what was long believed, ties with France were not severed completely during the Neoclassical period. The Louis XVI, Directoire, Empire and Louis-Philippe styles, which shared certain features with the British styles, also played a role in the hybridization process, by exerting a direct influence on Québec craftsmen or because they were disseminated through furniture designs created in the United States, where French culture was loved and admired. Some workshops, such as that of Duncan Phyfe (1768-1854) in New York City, were largely responsible for this blending of fashions from the Old and New worlds, given that they promoted a Neoclassical style based on French and U.S. tastes.

A study of the furniture produced during this fertile period has made it possible to pinpoint three main trends. The first trend, which was probably the one most marked by British influences, was particularly vigorous in the late 18th century and the first quarter of the 19th century. Featuring mainly English Neoclassical designs, it was characterized by pieces made of solid mahogany or finished with mahogany veneer, and by objects with pure, simple lines built of Québec hardwoods. The second trend, which was slightly later, lasted from 1825 to 1880 and was marked by the influences of the three cultures that were shaping Québec at the time, especially the United States. The heavier, more eclectic pieces produced during this period can be called "Classical Revival," since the manner in which they integrated elements borrowed from the past was quite similar to that observed in the other history-inspired Revival styles which succeeded one another as of the mid-19th century and thus coexisted for a time with Neoclassicism. Classical Revival furniture comprises pieces finished with mahogany or walnut veneers and objects made in the Empire manner from other native species that could be used to emulate exotic woods. Such Empire-inspired furniture includes gaming tables with massive bulbous bases made of ordinary wood, which was painted or stained to give it a more elegant appearance.

The third, but not the least important, trend in furniture from this period was characterized by a wide range of original Québec-made pieces, including armoires, tables, buffets, chests of drawers, beds and cradles, whose designs were based on traditionally informed adaptations or completely revamped versions of pre-1790 furniture. Stripped of their Louis XIII or Baroque motifs, armoires featured lighter, simpler, more geometric lines as well as classical moulding, proportions and ornamentation. As for chests of drawers, both high and low models began to incorporate certain innovative elements such as scrolled columns or ring-turned corner posts into their façades. In addition, as shown by the beds, tables and prie-Dieus produced in the mid-19th century, spool turnings were now a very popular feature. In fact, furniture embellished with such turnings became so widespread that it can be readily considered to constitute a style of its own, which might be called spool-turned Classical Revival.

In the wake of certain major changes in lifestyles and social etiquette, a broad range of new furniture forms appeared, especially in bourgeois households. Card tables, bookcases, slant-top desks and secretaries all testified to the emergence of new domestic, cultural and recreational activities. Drop-leaf side tables, of the Pembroke type for example, and demilune tables were now a common feature of living rooms, while the sideboard, used for storing tableware and serving food, as well as matching dining room suites with extendable tables were frequently encountered in wealthy homes. An interesting array of new chair and sofa designs also emerged, in a multitude of variations on the lines and ornamentation in vogue. All of these changes in furniture form and function also had an impact among the lower middle class, rural inhabitants and certain members of the working class, who produced personal interpretations of Neoclassical furniture in pine and other native species. Painted in the fashionable colors of the day, particularly blue, golden yellow or white and sometimes quite garish hues, and adorned with motifs derived from the vernacular or classical repertoire, such pieces constituted rethought, simplified and originally interpreted versions of the entire range of period forms. They thus reflected the lines and forms favored by the members of Québec's upper classes.

The Neoclassical period in Québec in both the decorative and furniture arts was marked by hybridization and blending, and this phenomenon gained momentum as the 19th century progressed. Although mahogany furniture inspired by the leading English designers of the Late Georgian and Regency periods was not widely distributed among Québec households, the general stylistic values related to this type of furniture, which were espoused by the few privileged members of the bourgeoisie, were embodied in a U.S.-inspired, proto-industrial, Classical-Revival style of furnishings and by original vernacular interpretations.

Since no in-depth studies have been conducted on this period of Québec's ethnohistory, it is not considered very important. Furniture of British inspiration in mahogany or hardwoods, such as maple or walnut, has been removed from Québec by old-stock families of British origin who decided to settle elsewhere in Canada or in the United States. Over the years, the descendants of these families across North America have inherited endearing reminders of the early days of British settlement in the St. Lawrence Valley. Given the stylistic similarity of these pieces with objects from New England, many have ended up in private collections south of the border, where furniture in this style has always been, and still is, highly valued. As a result, a substantial part of our material culture that is typical of Québec's English-speaking community has been lost. And since our government collections unfortunately do not reflect the importance of this heritage, it is difficult to fill the gap at the ethnomuseology level.

The Neoclassical era in Québec is the last period in which all furniture was made in an artisanal manner; thereafter, most pieces were mass-produced in factories. It is also the period when U.S. influences first appeared in the St. Lawrence Valley. Such influences would become increasingly pronounced during subsequent stages in the history of furniture.

As shown by civil architecture and church ornamentation, the full creativity of Quebeckers found expression in the decorative arts during the Neoclassical age. How domestic architecture and the furniture arts were shaped by this creative spirit remains to be assessed. A recent publication by Paul-Louis Martin, dealing specifically with this era, partly answers this question with respect to the interior furnishings of working-class homes. Judging from a brief study of the field, much fertile discussion is sure to follow. Like the various types of furniture dealt with in the other chapters of this book, Québec Neoclassical furniture and the three trends associated with it should be examined in greater depth in order to better understand the characteristics of our society and more accurately evaluate the contribution of British culture to shaping the heart and soul of Quebeckers.

337

Rocking chairs. Yellow birch, Québec City, ca. 1860. Neoclassical designs persisted until the late 19th century. Revival-era rocking chairs dating from the second half of the 19th century thus perpetuated forms that first emerged with the Empire, Georgian, Regency and U.S. Federal styles, which were developed by the main cultures shaping Québec at the time.

THE CONSTITUTIONAL STYLE

ARMCHAIRS

Neoclassical armchairs, whether used at the table, in the living room or in the bedroom, were always very elegant. The delicate design of these sturdy, solid-wood pieces stemmed from their curved back slats; graceful, slender armrests forming extensions of the front legs and arm supports; classical turnings; fluting and reeding; and the fine inlays and relief-carved decoration found on their leg blocks. The skill of furniture makers from the first half of the 19th century was reflected not only in period pieces, but in the simplified vernacular interpretations of these pieces. Made mainly of pine or yellow birch, such interpretations were very original and attractive.

338
Armchair of U.S. Federal inspiration. Québec City, ca. 1815. This piece has a curved back, sabre back legs extending into curved back posts, and elegantly designed armrests forming extensions of the turned front legs and arm supports.

339
Scale drawing of a Neoclassical, Sheraton-style armchair, similar to ones still found in the Québec City area. This early-19th-century specimen belongs to the Metropolitan Museum of Art in New York.

340
Dining room of the Jean-Charles-Chapais house in Saint-Denis, Kamouraska, built in 1833-1834. Founder of the parish of Saint-Denis, Chapais gained political renown as a Father of Confederation. Even though the furnishings shown in this photograph were acquired in the mid-19th century, they clearly reflect the blending of Late Neoclassical values with those of the Revival era. The open-face dish dresser and colors of this room are in keeping with the Québec Constitutional style.

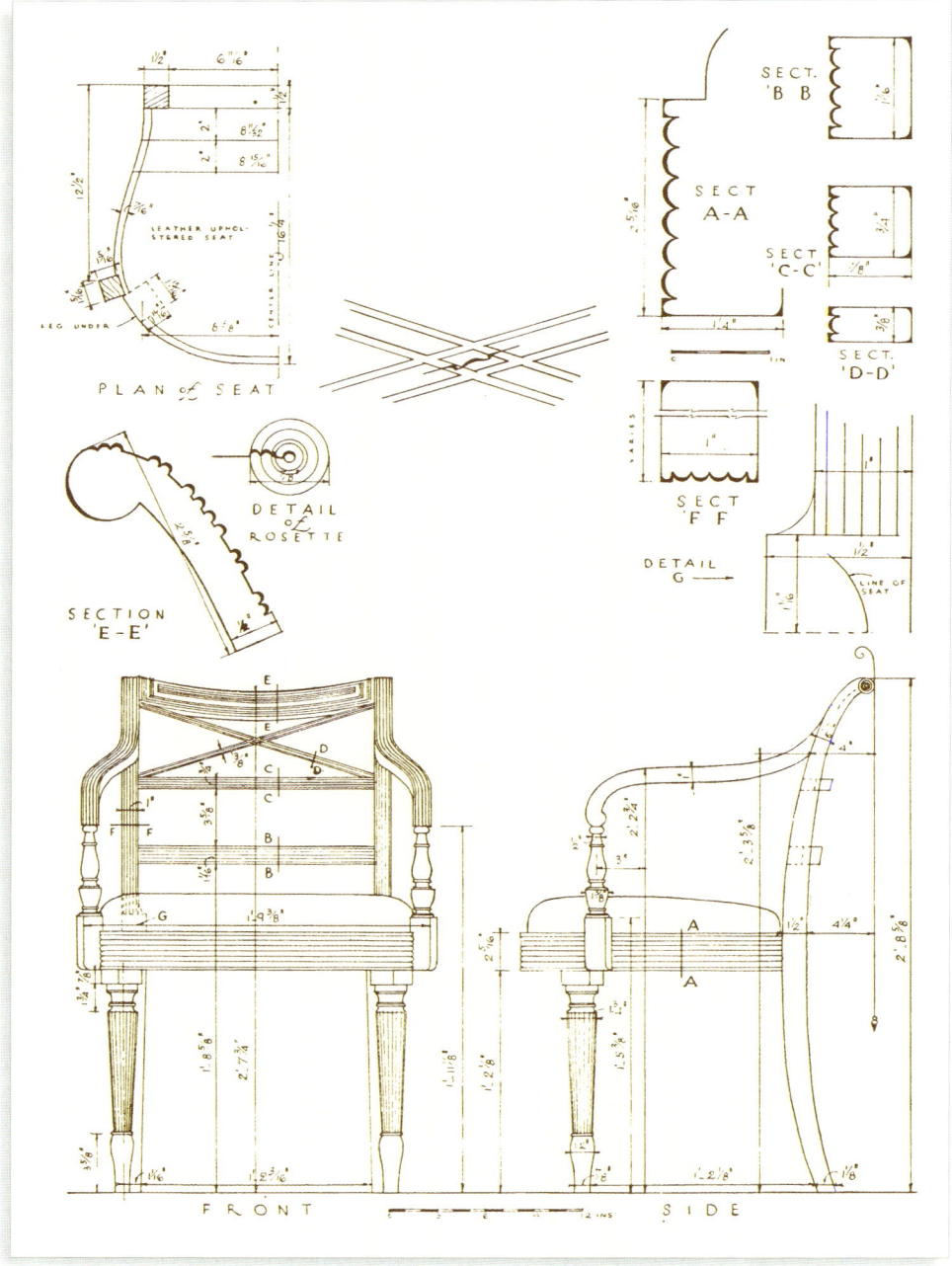

341 to 347
Chairs dating from the first third of the 19th century.

341
Chair in the Hepplewhite manner. Yellow birch, Québec City, Laird family, ca. 1805.

342
Chair of Hepplewhite and Chippendale inspiration. White birch, Québec City, Laferté family, ca. 1800.

343
Balloon-back chair. Black cherry, Québec City, ca. 1840.

344
One of a set of six chairs combining features of the Hepplewhite and Sheraton styles. Maple and yellow birch, signed Healy, Québec City, ca. 1820.

345
Chair with a curved back, sabre back legs extending into concave back posts, and turned, reeded front legs. Mahogany, ca. 1820.

346
Chair of Baroque derivation incorporating features of various styles. White birch and walnut, Québec City area, ca. 1800.
The back of this chair is in keeping with the British Queen Anne tradition, while the curved cabriole legs and turned H-stretcher are typical of the Louis XIII and Louis XV styles.

347
Chair reflecting the transition between the Neoclassical and Revival styles, with a slip-seat, curved slat and crest rail, sabre back legs and turned front legs. Walnut, Thomas Taschereau family, Québec City, ca. 1830.

348
Card table with a bulbous pedestal resting on a platform with scrolled feet. Pine and walnut, ca. 1830. Hepplewhite-style shield-back chairs with sabre back legs and tapered front legs. Yellow birch, ca. 1830. This attractive set dating from the first half of the 19th century is in the Québec Constitutional style and is similar to pieces still found in certain religious institutions.

349
(Pages 254-255)
Living room of the Pelletier house in Beaumont, in the county of Bellechasse. With its well-preserved woodwork and floor covering, this house, which was built in around 1840, has retained its original atmosphere. The sofa, which is upholstered with horsehair, dates from the mid-19th century and reflects the blending of Neoclassical and Revival values.

350-351
"Fancy" furniture set with stencil decoration in the living room of Mr. Pelletier, a notary from Beaumont in Bellechasse county, ca. 1860.
These caned chairs display the style developed by Lambert Hitchcock (1795-1852), a Connecticut chair maker who produced "fancy" chairs. "Hitchcock" chairs have a rolled crest rail, turned front legs and rounded back legs extending upward into flat, curved back posts. These chairs, which are decorated with fruit and acanthus leaves, probably come from the United States. The table has a bulbous polygonal pedestal resting on a platform with scrolled feet, and its top is adorned with gilded and stencilled floral motifs framing a bouquet.

352
Rural Neoclassical interior. Saint-Roch-des-Aulnaies, ca. 1860.
The Létourneau house in Saint-Roch-des-Aulnaies, which has several rooms that have never been painted, clearly reflects rural Neoclassical tastes in the mid-19th century. The arrow-back chairs, which still have their original color, are fitted with stencil-decorated crest rails and bamboo-turned legs. The chest of drawers, with its scrolled columns and seven drawers with porcelain pulls, is slightly later than the other pieces, but perfectly in keeping with the Neoclassical style. Built of ash, this piece of furniture was made by a local craftsman.

353 to 358
Armchairs and stools in the Québec Neoclassical style, 19th century.

353
Regency-style armchair with sabre back legs, a box stretcher, scrolled armrests extending beyond the arm stumps, and a back embellished with painted stringing and two cross-rods connected by a panel. Mahogany, Québec City, ca. 1820.

354
Sheraton armchair with black string inlays on the crest rail and gadrooning on the slat. Mahogany, ca. 1820.

355
Regency armchair with sabre legs. Mahogany, Beauce, 1820.

356
Stool with legs of Baroque inspiration. Black cherry and pine, ca. 1820.

357
Sheraton-Hepplewhite armchair. Yellow birch, signed Healy, Québec City, ca. 1820.

358
Stool with legs of Baroque inspiration. Walnut veneer, ca. 1840.

359
Rustic armchair in the Regency manner with turned armrests and front legs. Original color, pine and yellow birch, ca. 1860.
Good example of the way period designs were interpreted by local craftsmen. Interpretations of period furniture of all forms can be found for every era in the history of furniture.

360
Regency armchair. Mahogany, Québec City, mid-19th century.
This type of gondola chair with deeply scrolled armrests, turned front legs and sabre back legs extending into concave back posts was popular under various stylistic labels in France, England and the United States as of 1830-1840. Québec craftsmen, who were already heavily influenced by fashions from these three countries, made a version of this chair that was a hybrid of French, British and U.S. models.

THE CONSTITUTIONAL STYLE

WINDSOR CHAIRS

The Windsor label applies to a range of furniture forms, including chairs, armchairs and settees, and refers to a style that originated in England and was later adopted in the United States. The Windsor chair is a form in which the legs, back parts and arm supports, if any, are mortised into a saddle-shaped seat, which constitutes the main structural component of the chair. Windsor chairs were probably developed in England in the late 17th century.

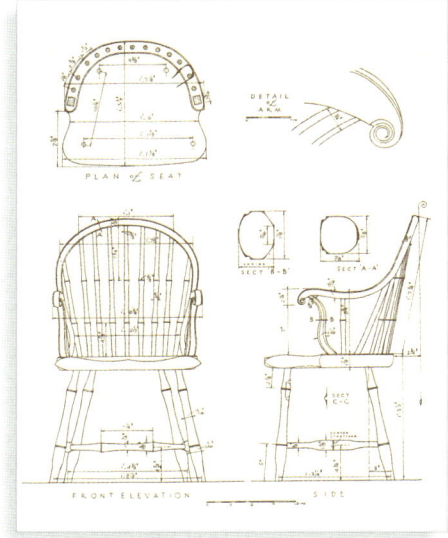

361 to 368
Several different models of Windsor chairs were brought into the St. Lawrence Valley by immigrants from Britain and Loyalists from the United States. They included a wide range of fairly graceful forms, related to specific "styles" and furniture makers, and many were fitted with arched bentwood backs. Their legs, which had a more or less bulbous shape, were always turned and were typically connected by stretchers. Windsor chairs were painted black or some other color and sometimes embellished with stencilling or fine painted stringing.

369
Office of the merchant Sifroy-Guéret *dit* Dumont of Saint-André, Kamouraska.
Located in the large house built in 1840, owned by this merchant, this reconstruction is designed to recapture the interior design of an office belonging to an important rural bourgeois businessman. The slant-top desk with recessed panels, the table with turned legs, the Windsor chair and the arrow-back chairs are typical of the kind of furniture that was found in mid-19th-century Neoclassical interiors. The woodwork, including the board and batten ceiling, is original. Note the unusual curved overhang above each window.

260   NEOCLASSICAL FURNITURE IN THE ST. LAWRENCE VALLEY

370 to 373
Four rustic Québec rocking chairs derived from the Boston rocker, with armrests ending in stylized Regency or Louis-Philippe-style scrolls. Early or original colors, yellow birch, white birch and pine, second half of the 19th century.

374
Two factory-made Boston rockers. Early colors, pine, yellow birch and poplar, last quarter of the 19th century.
This comfortable chair originated in New England in the first quarter of the 19th century. It is characterized by a thick pine seat shaped like a strip of unrolled parchment, curving down at the front and up at the rear. A wide range of models of industrial, artisanal and domestic manufacture existed, and they were often embellished with elaborate turnings and stencil decoration. This type of rocking chair, whose popularity has never waned since it was first designed, has become a classic.

SOFAS

Sofas can seat two or three people and are fitted with comfortably upholstered backs and armrests. Although it is probable that specimens in the Louis XIII and Louis XV styles or with *os de mouton* understructures existed during the French Regime, the sofa did not really become popular in the St. Lawrence Valley until after 1800, when the influence of the British and U.S. Neoclassical styles began to be felt there. An impressive array of models then appeared, ornamented with the motifs in vogue at the time. Some of the most moving examples are those of artisanal or domestic manufacture designed to imitate period furniture.

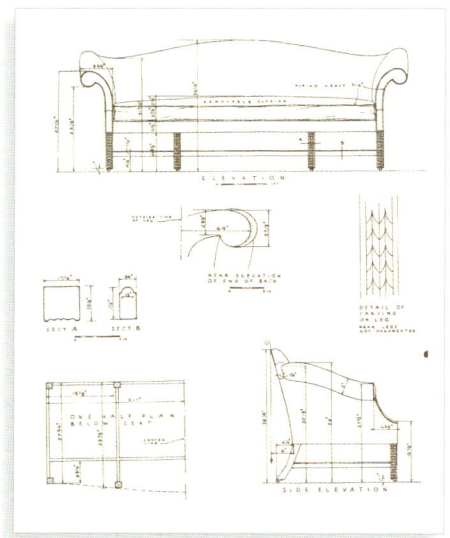

375
Scale drawing of a Neoclassical-style sofa in the Chippendale manner (ca. 1800) preserved at the Metropolitan Museum of Art in New York City. Many of the sofa models found in Québec were inspired by the British, U.S. and French Neoclassical styles. Some very attractive examples in Québec's Constitutional style reflect the blending of these three different interpretations of Neoclassicism.

381 to 388
Different models of Neoclassical sofas, details of which appear on the opposite page.

385
Regency récamier with multiple scrolls, a reeded skirt and armrests, and sabre legs also embellished with reeding and fitted with brass sabots, or toe castors, imitating lion's paws. This récamier, which dates from around 1820 and comes from the John Hall Kelly family of New Carlisle, was originally one of a pair and may have been made in Atlantic Canada.

386
Sofa with a curvilinear crest rail embellished with a shell carving, armrests decorated with acanthus leaves and ending in small graceful scrolls, turned tapered legs, rosette-carved leg blocks and a rope-carved skirt. Yellow birch, Montréal area, ca. 1830.
This piece comes from the Chaussegros de Léry family.

387
Empire-style sofa inspired by models designed in the United States, with a straight back, armrests terminating in lotus flowers, winged lion's-paw feet, and a skirt embellished with rope carving and a central lozenge-carved inset panel. Mahogany, Québec City, ca. 1840.

388
Sofa with a reeded skirt, turned legs and a curvilinear crest rail ornamented with a central cartouche framed with scrolls and surmounted by a bouquet of ferns. Palmettes appear beneath the cartouche and on the scrolled armrests. Mahogany, Québec City, ca. 1840.

THE CONSTITUTIONAL STYLE

389 to 392
Large sofas reflecting the transition between the Neoclassical and Revival eras, with mahogany or walnut veneering; straight or very architectural, serpentine backs; geometric, zoomorphic or phytomorphic ornamentation; plinth, S-scrolled or lion's-paw feet; and armrests ending in scroll, lotus-flower or swan-neck motifs. Québec City and Montréal areas, mid-19th century.

392 a, b
Detail of the sofa shown in the inset, with a mahogany- and walnut-veneer finish, scrolled armrests, and lion's-paw feet profusely decorated with plant-like motifs. This piece comes from the Mauvide-Genest manor on Île d'Orléans, which, in 1998, hosted a public auction that sold a large number of the furnishings collected by one of the building's former owners, Judge Pouliot.

393 to 397

Households in the countryside or in less wealthy areas always managed to obtain furniture in the main styles of the day owing to the availability of simple pieces of domestic or artisanal manufacture that were inspired by these styles. The four Neoclassically informed sofas shown here illustrate this trend and were probably made by a village craftsman or other skilled individual during the first half of the 19th century or slightly later. Like other pieces of this type, they reveal a very endearing side of Québec culture.

393-394

Front and back view of a sofa with a straight back, simple legs, and armrests ending in rudimentary scrolls. Original color, pine and yellow birch, mortise-and-tenon construction, Yamachiche, ca. 1850.

395

Sofa with a rolled crest rail, turned feet, simple upholstering, and armrests terminating in stylized scrolls or lotus flowers. Walnut, Louis-Bertrand house, L'Isle-Verte, ca. 1840

396

Straight-backed sofa with an ogee-shaped crest rail and skirt, and simply scrolled armrests that attractively echo the shape of the feet. McPherson seigneurial manor, Île aux Grues, ca. 1840.

397

Rustic récamier of Neoclassical inspiration with a home-woven slipcover, a cut-out back in a very simplified Eastlake manner, an armrest terminating in a lotus flower, and treble-clef-shaped feet (which have prompted the owner to call this piece his "musical chair"). Stripped wood, Saint-Roch-des-Aulnaies, ca. 1860-1870. Very simple furniture of this type seems to have been common in the Saint-Jean-Port-Joli region.

BEDS AND CRADLES

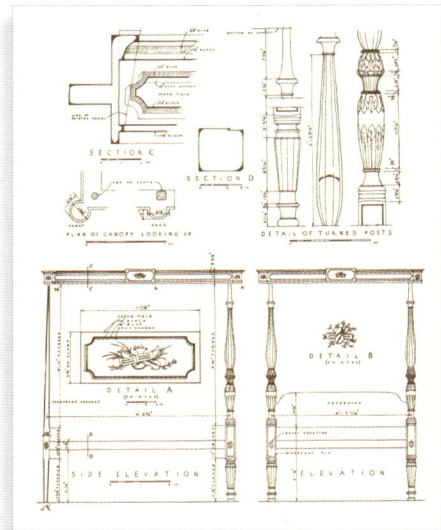

Neoclassical beds came in a variety of forms. Some were tall-post beds with turned and carved hardwood posts, modelled on designs proposed in the late 18th century and first half of the 19th century by British architect-designers or by those who interpreted their designs in the United States. Others were low bedsteads, with curved headboards and footboards in the manner of Empire *lits en bateaux*, which, owing to their resemblance to horse-drawn sleighs, are called sleigh beds in North America. Still other Neoclassical beds assembled with slip-mortise joints had perfectly plain headboards, but more commonly, were fitted with cannon ball finials or rolled headboards and footboards. Beds with spool turnings and a pediment-shaped headboard also appeared during the Neoclassical era and became very popular over the next few decades.

398
Scale drawing of a U.S. Neoclassical tall-post bed with turned and carved posts, ca. 1800.

399
Bedroom of the Louis-Joseph Papineau seigneurial manor in Montebello, ca. 1880.
The side chair reflects the spirit of the decorative arts under Napoléon I, while the bed is embellished with turnings in the English Sheraton style. As for the rocking chair, it is of the Boston rocker type, while the chest of drawers, embellished with columns, reflects the typical Québec practice of amalgamating a variety of influences. Good example of how furnishings exhibiting the stylistic values of three different cultures were often found in the same house.

400
Tall-post bed of outstanding workmanship. Curly maple, Montréal area, ca. 1850.
In the 19th century, when particular attention was paid to the grain of wood, Québec craftsmen chose native species with dramatic figuring, which they finished with clear varnish. This well-balanced, expertly turned piece pleasingly combines French balusters with polygonal rollers of British and U.S. inspiration.

401
Dressing glass. Black cherry, ca. 1830.

402 to 404
Neoclassical-style sleigh beds from the first half of the 19th century.

402
Sleigh bed in the Chapais house in Saint-Denis, Kamouraska. Walnut, ca. 1850.

403
Educational exhibit at the Musée du Québec in 1976 showing what a bedroom would have looked like in around 1830-1850.

404
Bedroom furnishings in the Mauvide-Genest manor prior to the 1998 auction: sleigh bed and chest of drawers, walnut, ca. 1840-1850; Windsor chair, ash and pine, ca. 1840-1850; floor candleholder with a reflector, pine, ca. 1830.

405
Low-post bed fitted with a rolled headboard and footboard of slip-mortise construction and baluster-turned posts ending in cannon ball finials. Yellow birch, original color, L'Isle-Verte, ca. 1850.
This bed is covered with a locally made crazy quilt. Beds often had a red-colored paint or stain finish.

406
Bedroom on the second floor of the Adjutor-Pelletier house in Beaumont, Bellechasse. This room, which was photographed by the author in 1978, is shown in its original state. The three baluster-turned or spool beds date from the transitional period between the Neoclassical and Revival eras. Beds of this type were popular as of 1835-40 and were still offered by J.W. Kilgour & Brothers of Beauharnois in 1880, as shown by the firm's catalogues.

407
Priest's room at the Château Bellevue, built at Cap-Tourmente in the last quarter of the 18th century as a summer residence for priests of the Séminaire de Québec.
Note the spool turnings on the prie-dieu, bed and washstand dating from the mid-19th century. Originally, these pieces came in a range of bright colors or in black or dark brown.

408
Low-post bed with baluster-turned posts and a shaped headboard embellished with wave scrolls. Early color, yellow birch, mid-19th century.
In certain parts of the Maritimes, such as the Gaspé Peninsula, some pieces of furniture, including beds, were adorned with marine-inspired motifs. One of the objects at the museum in Gaspé testifies eloquently to this decorative technique.

409-410
Two corner-post cradles of Neoclassical inspiration. The first has fluted sides, while the second is fitted with a pediment and has retained its original color. Yellow birch, walnut and pine, mid-19th century.

411
Tall-post bed with baluster- and ring-turned posts and an arched headboard assembled with slip-mortise joints. Yellow birch and pine, ca. 1830.
A very simple, pine trundle bed with its original color is located beneath the bed. These furnishings recapture the atmosphere of rural Neoclassical interiors in the middle of the 19th century.

412
Rustic, Hepplewhite-inspired chest of drawers assembled with dovetailing and fitted with a shaped skirt, original pulls and five cock-beaded drawers. Butternut, Côte-du-Sud, ca. 1840.
This piece is located in the bedroom shown on the next page. The walls and floors have never been repainted and are thus still in their original state.

413
Bedroom of the Sifroy-Guéret-*dit*-Dumont house in Saint-André, Kamouraska.
Tall-post bed with turned posts and a simple headboard. Yellow birch, early 19th century. In 1840, Sifroy-Guéret *dit* Dumont (1813-1881), a prominent general merchant, built a magnificent residence on his estate on the banks of the St. Lawrence River to house his family and business. The bedroom of this rural bourgeois home is exceptional in that it has retained its original colors: the walls are ochre, the baseboards Prussian blue, the ceiling and mouldings lead white and the floor orange. After conducting ethnohistorical research for interpretation purposes, the building's present owners refurnished this part of the residence, where the merchant Dumont lived alone at the end of his life.

412
Rustic, Hepplewhite-inspired chest of drawers assembled with dovetailing and fitted with a shaped skirt, original pulls and five cock-beaded drawers. Butternut, Côte-du-Sud, ca. 1840.
This piece is located in the bedroom shown on the next page. The walls and floors have never been repainted and are thus still in their original state.

413
Bedroom of the Sifroy-Guéret-*dit*-Dumont house in Saint-André, Kamouraska.
Tall-post bed with turned posts and a simple headboard. Yellow birch, early 19th century. In 1840, Sifroy-Guéret *dit* Dumont (1813-1881), a prominent general merchant, built a magnificent residence on his estate on the banks of the St. Lawrence River to house his family and business. The bedroom of this rural bourgeois home is exceptional in that it has retained its original colors: the walls are ochre, the baseboards Prussian blue, the ceiling and mouldings lead white and the floor orange. After conducting ethnohistorical research for interpretation purposes, the building's present owners refurnished this part of the residence, where the merchant Dumont lived alone at the end of his life.

414 to 418
Pine chests of Neoclassical inspiration, most with multiple panels and square or turned feet. All still have their original color, except for one piece, which has been stripped, although not very successfully. Pine and yellow birch, between 1830 and 1860. Joining methods and certain characteristics, such as multiple recessed panels, nailed strips of moulding and foot shape, make it possible to associate a chest with the Neoclassical movement.

419 to 423

The settle bed was very prevalent in 19th-century rural interiors. Located in the common room, it served as both a seat and a bed, in addition to reducing the amount of space that had to be heated in winter. Settle beds could sleep two children or one adult. In fact, they were often used to accommodate beggars who came knocking at the door, especially in rural areas, where such individuals were considered to be an excellent source of news. The above photograph, taken by architect Sylvio Brassard around 1940, shows a bed of this type in the old Bédard house on Commune Road in Bourg-Royal on the outskirts of Québec City. The three settle beds shown on the left are all made of pine; two have retained their original color, while one was repainted at an early point in its history. Their crest rails are pleasingly shaped and, in one case, embellished with a spool-turned rod. They have straight backs fitted with splats or turned rods, and simple or panelled box seats. All three date from the mid-19th century.

THE CONSTITUTIONAL STYLE

CHESTS OF DRAWERS

Québec-made Neoclassical chests of drawers were built of solid wood or finished with hardwood veneers of mahogany or walnut. Distinguished by their graceful lines, elegance, careful finishing and inlaid and carved ornamentation, they are among the most attractive pieces of furniture ever made or used here. One can still find pieces which, like other furniture forms, were made to order for members of the elite. While reflecting the fashions of the day, as developed by Hepplewhite, Sheraton, Adam and Duncan Phyfe, such chests also bore the personal stamp of local furniture makers established in Québec City, the Eastern Townships or Montréal. Rural versions of period models were often highly original. Chests of drawers in the Neoclassical style remained in vogue well into the 19th century, at least in the case of those with scrolled columns, which were widely distributed by furniture makers in the St. Lawrence Valley during the second half of the 19th century.

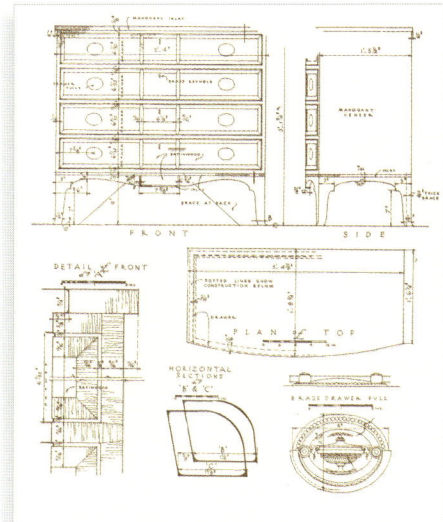

424
Drawing of a bow-front chest of drawers in the Hepplewhite-inspired, U.S. Neoclassical manner (ca. 1800) included in the collections of the Metropolitan Museum of Art in New York. Similar models, adapted to Québec tastes, were made and used here.

425
Chest of drawers with sabre legs, side panels, a pleasingly shaped skirt adorned with wave scrolls and a central shell carving, keyhole inlays and five drawers outlined with string inlays. Original knobs, walnut, Québec City area, ca. 1830.
This solidly constructed, well-balanced chest is a very attractive piece of furniture.

426
Bow-front chest of drawers with flared French feet, four drawers embellished with marquetry inlay, brass keyhole escutcheons, original pulls, a shaped skirt, and string inlays in the top edge. Original state, mahogany, Montréal, ca. 1830.
The arched mirror in a walnut frame with maple string inlays comes from the Québec City area and dates from the same period as the chest.

427
Chest of drawers embellished with walnut and mahogany veneering and fitted with five tiger- or curly-maple cock-beaded drawers. The keyhole inlays are made of black walnut and the sides of pine are stained to emulate mahogany. Davis family, Québec City, ca. 1820.

428
Bow-front chest of drawers with four drawers and rope-carved and ring-turned corner columns. The Chippendale drawer pulls are replacements. Heartwood mahogany veneer over pine, ca. 1820. On top of the chest are two Limoges porcelain objects from the Fabre-Surveillé family of Québec City and a tea caddy with hoof feet. The typical Neoclassical long-case clock dating from around 1840 bears the signature of Pierre Poulin, of Québec City.

429
Room furnished with Neoclassical furniture: bow-front armoire with two doors and one drawer, mahogany, England, ca. 1820; gondola chair, walnut, Québec City, ca. 1830; wing chair, yellow birch, Québec City, ca. 1860.

430
Bow-front chest of drawers with flared feet, five cock-beaded drawers and original hardware. Mahogany, England, ca. 1820.
Many pieces of Neoclassical furniture found in Québec were imported from England. They were usually high-quality items that closely resembled the models proposed by the architect-designers who set the tone of the Neoclassical movement in that country. This chest of drawers and the swing-frame mirror on top of it reflect the spirit of such furniture.

THE CONSTITUTIONAL STYLE 289

431 to 439

Chests of drawers in the Neoclassical manner, with three to six drawers, with or without inlays, original knobs and pulls, and straight or shaped skirts. Butternut, pine, maple and basswood, between 1820 and 1860.
Some of these objects were made by cabinetmakers, while others are the work of joiners. The pieces with an inlaid commemorative date were probably built by Magloire Garon (1808-1860) of Saint-Michel-de-Bellechasse.

440 to 445

Chests of drawers reflecting the transition between the Baroque and Neoclassical styles, with two, three or four drawers, rectilinear or shaped tops, plain or carved fronts, shaped skirts, and straight, scroll or hoof feet. Walnut, pine and birch, between 1775 and 1825.

THE CONSTITUTIONAL STYLE 291

446 to 449
One of the most attractive models of Neoclassical chests of drawers was that with scrolled columns, which appeared in the mid-19th century. Derived from pieces in the Empire style, as interpreted by our neighbours to the south, this chest consisted of two sections, the upper of which jutted out from the rest of the piece and was supported by two scroll-shaped columns. Québec joiners and cabinetmakers made a wide variety of chests with scrolled columns, ranging from very refined pieces finished with precious-wood veneering to very rustic pieces made of ordinary woods assembled with nailed and glued cross-lapped joints.

446
Rustic chest of drawers with ring-turned corner columns, a shaped skirt and five cock-beaded drawers. Original knobs and imitation mahogany color, butternut, L'Isle-Verte, ca. 1840.

447
Chest of drawers with scrolled columns, finished with walnut veneer. Île d'Orléans, ca. 1860.

448
Chest of drawers with scrolled columns designed for a city house. Walnut and mahogany, Québec City area, ca. 1860.

449
Exceptional chest of drawers with scrolled columns extending into scrolled feet and six drawers embellished with carved motifs. Original color, pine and ash, La Malbaie, ca. 1860.

450
Rustic chest of drawers with scrolled columns and five drawers. Early color, butternut and pine, ca. 1870.

VERTICAL CASE FURNITURE

A wide range of case furniture existed during the Neoclassical period. Consisting of armoires, buffets, corner cupboards, dish dressers and bookcases, such pieces were derived from or influenced by the models proposed by the leading British and U.S. designers, who made use of precious wood veneers and varnished solid wood. Most of the painted, softwood versions of this type of furniture were built by joiners working in towns and villages, who succeeded in perpetuating the French provincial tradition by adapting it to the new aesthetic canons and manufacturing methods of the day. The furniture they produced was simpler in both design and construction than that made prior to 1790.

451
Two-tiered buffet of Neoclassical inspiration with raised panels in the French provincial tradition, a dentil cornice, a hand-forged bolt, and a simple, cutout base. Pine, ca. 1840.
This piece of storage furniture was photographed by Professor Ramsay Traquair in 1925 in the living quarters of the Augustinian Hospitallers of the Hôpital Général de Québec.

452
Reconstruction of a ca.-1840 Québec Neoclassical interior exhibited at the Musée du Québec in 1976. It recaptures both the spirit and the stylistic and decorative values of the period.

453
Neoclassical armoire of a type commonly encountered in the first half of the 19th century, with 12 recessed panels and nailed strips of moulding. Early color, original hardware, pine, ca. 1840.

454 to 457

Four models of armoire in the Neoclassical manner, built of pine or poplar. The first two, which date from the first half of the 19th century, have multiple panels with gouge-carved or fluted edges and a classical cornice in the spirit of the Adam style. The second two, which date from the second half of the 19th century, have recessed panels, drawers and attractively shaped skirts and their corner posts are embellished with turned appliqués. The armoire with Gothic-Revival-inspired panels in the shape of lancet arches is from the church in Château-Richer.

458

Armoire with two doors, a long drawer, an attractive cavetto cornice, recessed panels and simple feet. Early color, pine, ca. 1840.
Somewhat austere Neoclassical armoire of English and U.S. derivation, typical of pieces found in Anglo-Saxon homes in Québec during the first half of the 19th century.

THE CONSTITUTIONAL STYLE 297

459 to 466
Various models of vertical case furniture with or without drawers, fitted with nailed mouldings and two doors embellished with recessed panels. Unfortunately, most of these pieces have been stripped. Ash, walnut, basswood, pine, poplar and spruce, between 1840 and 1890. Several of these articles are from the Saguenay–Lac-Saint-Jean region. Although all reflect the values of Neoclassicism, some date from the Belle Époque, or Edwardian era.

467
Very simple low armoire fitted with two doors with raised panels. Original color, pine, ca. 1840.
This well-balanced, Neoclassical-style piece, which is a carry-over from the French tradition, illustrates the transition between two different periods in the history of furniture. It is hard to assign objects of this type to a specific period. Original color, pine, ca. 1840.

298 NEOCLASSICAL FURNITURE IN THE ST. LAWRENCE VALLEY

THE CONSTITUTIONAL STYLE 299

468
Open-face dish dresser with two doors decorated with shaped panels. The construction of this piece of Neoclassical inspiration – with its flush-fitted doors, mouldings and general design – is based on English and U.S. models, while the decorative shape of its panels is borrowed from the Louis XV style. Stripped pine with remnants of original color, Saint-Hyacinthe Road, Saint-Hermas d'Argenteuil, ca. 1830.

469
Armoire fitted with two doors with raised panels, a dentil cornice, a panelled centre post, an attractive cutout skirt and diagonally patterned edging around the case and panels. Early colors, pine, Saint-Eustache, ca. 1820.
Exceptionally well-preserved piece of furniture.

CORNER CUPBOARDS

The corner cupboard was a common furniture form in Québec during the 19th century, and models adapted to the tastes of all levels of society were available. While some were very refined pieces made of exotic woods in the spirit of the designs proposed by the leading English architect-designers, most reflected the popular Québec tradition of producing original interpretations of British and U.S. styles using traditional French joinery methods. Many corner cupboards were architectural pieces of furniture, built into partition walls. The very popular two-piece corner cupboard usually had a glazed upper section, whose window mullion arrangement testifies eloquently to the blending of cultural influences.

470
Corner cupboard of British and U.S. derivation with cut-off corners, early hardware, a shaped base and four flush-fitted doors separated by a long drawer. Pine stained to simulate mahogany, Eastern Townships, ca. 1825.
Like armoires from this period, British- and U.S.-inspired Neoclassical corner cupboards were of very simple design, with flush-fitted doors, recessed panels, nailed strips of plain moulding and unpretentious ornamentation.

471
Bow-front corner cupboard fitted with two glazed doors, two blind doors with simple panels, acorn carvings beneath the cornice and reeded mouldings. This piece, which was made by a skilled cabinetmaker, comes from the Fabre family of Québec " on the cape." Solid mahogany and pine, stained to emulate mahogany inside the cupboard, ca. 1820.
A clear distinction must be made between Neoclassical " town " furniture of British derivation, which graced the homes of certain members of the bourgeoisie, and more lyrical, traditional Québec pieces, which, in keeping with established practices, were built of softwood and painted.

THE CONSTITUTIONAL STYLE 303

472 to 477
Corner cupboards with straight or bow fronts, glazed upper sections, doors with recessed or raised panels, more or less elaborate cornices and bases, and original hardware. Pine or walnut, first half of the 19th century.

478
Corner cupboard with two blind doors and two glazed doors separated by a row of three drawers. The general construction, base, cornice and arched window mullions display English and U.S. influences, while the concave-cornered panels in the doors and drawers are in the pure French tradition. Original glazing, knobs and colors, pine, Valcourt region, ca. 1810.
Attractive piece of furniture combining several different cultural influences, in an excellent state of preservation.

BUFFETS AND CUPBOARDS

Some Québec Neoclassical buffets and cupboards were built by cabinetmakers from native hardwoods, imported solid wood or veneering, while others were made by joiners out of pine or walnut. Buffets and cupboards built by joiners were fairly massive pieces, with multiple panels and flush-fitted doors, and were painted a variety of colors. This type of furniture was used in the common room or the dining room.

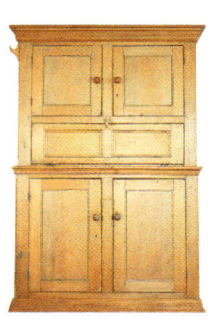

479 to 485
Various models of rustic buffets and cupboards of Neoclassical derivation with glazed or blind doors. Stripped or still covered with original or early color, pine and walnut, first half of the 19th century.

486
Adam-inspired step-back cupboard with multiple panels and four doors. Original color, pine, Beauce, first quarter of the 19th century.

487
Glazed two-tiered buffet with recessed panels, fine decorative fluting, corner columns, a simple base and a well-developed cornice of British Neoclassical inspiration. Solid mahogany and mahogany veneering, England, ca. 1810.

488
Secretary in the U.S. Empire manner, finished with walnut veneering. Adjutor-Pelletier house in Beaumont, Bellechasse, ca. 1850.
The secretary served not only as a desk but also as a bookcase and a chest of drawers or a cupboard. This piece, which is located in an historic house once owned by a notary and containing several rooms that have never been painted, reflects the atmosphere of a bourgeois interior in the second half of the 19th century.

TABLES

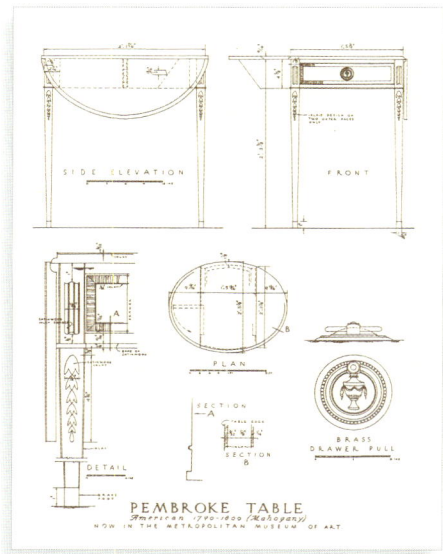

It is no easy task to discuss in just a few pages Neoclassical-style tables intended for bourgeois dining rooms and living rooms and those encountered in working-class homes. Nor is it easy to highlight continuities between these pieces which, in the first case, are solid exotic-wood or finely veneered tables embellished with inlays and other ornamentation consistent with the canons proposed by British architect-designers and, in the second case, pine tables built by Québec joiners and finished simply with a coat of bright paint. Nevertheless, the coexistence of a wide range of models adapted to the tastes and means of all levels of society is an inherent feature of Québec furniture, and it underpins the challenge that had to be met in writing this book — namely, devising a study framework that would apply to furniture styles as a whole. In this particular chapter, the framework also had to take into account not only the highly divergent British and U.S. interpretations of 19th-century influences, but the stylistic concepts of Neoclassicism strictly speaking as well as those of the Classical Revival style, which were closer to Revival-era concepts.

489
Drawing of a Sheraton-style Pembroke table of U.S. manufacture, ca. 1800.
This type of small parlor table of Neoclassical design, fitted with a round top, a drawer and leaves, was imported into or made in Québec. This drawing is from the collections of the Metropolitan Museum of Art in New York City.

490
Lavishly set breakfast table at the Mauvide-Genest manor in Saint-Jean, Île d'Orléans, on the day of Louis-Joseph Pouliot's ordination as a Jesuit priest in 1933. Photograph by A. Laberge, Québec City. Among the other furnishings in the room are a sideboard and a bow-front corner cupboard, both of which are in keeping with Neoclassical taste.

491-492
Extendable gate-leg dining table and demilune parlor table of Neoclassical design made wholly of mahogany and fitted with turned, tapered, rope-carved legs. The two-place dining table, which belonged to the Tourangeau family of Québec City, has a rectangular top, while the parlor table, which is from Montréal, has a shaped top with brass string inlays. Both are period pieces dating from 1820.

THE CONSTITUTIONAL STYLE

493 to 501
Neoclassical-style parlor tables dating from 1800 to 1825, inspired by models proposed by the leading designers of the late 18th and early 19th centuries, with tapered or turned legs, drop-leaf, fold-over or fixed tops, and aprons adorned with inlaid motifs. Some are fitted with castors.

493
Pembroke table in the Hepplewhite manner with turned legs, string inlays and a cock-beaded drawer. Mahogany and walnut, ca. 1820.

494-495
Pembroke-inspired drop-leaf table with an oval top and tapered legs. Curly maple, Québec City, 1810.

496
Drop-leaf table with marquetry stringing around the top, a cock-beaded drawer and turned legs. Mahogany and maple, Québec City, ca. 1820.

497
Card table with a fold-over top and string inlays. Mahogany, curly maple, yellow birch and butternut (inlays), ca. 1825.

498
Card table of Sheraton design with marquetry stringing. Mahogany, Casgrain family, Rivière-Ouelle.

499
Parlor table with two cock-beaded drawers and turned, tapered legs. Tiger maple, Québec City, 1820.

500-501
Hepplewhite-inspired drop-leaf table with tapered legs. Yellow birch and maple, Québec City, ca. 1820.

502 to 505

Various models of card tables, all with fold-over tops. This type of furniture, which was very common during the Victorian era, was usually placed against a wall when not in use and brought into the middle of the room when needed; it could seat four players and its top was generally covered with green felt. Card tables came in a wide range of models (round, square or rectangular), materials and finishings. The models shown here are made of pine, black walnut or mahogany, and, in some cases, are finished with mahogany veneer; they have inlaid motifs in their aprons and are fitted with various types of bases: two have turned bases with four shaped feet fitted with brass toe castors, one a lyre-shaped base and a fourth a pedestal resting on a platform with lion's-paw feet. All date from the first half of the 19th century and reflect the stylistic values of the North American Neoclassical movement, which was influenced not only by British designs but also by renowned U.S. furniture makers' interpretations of the Empire and Louis-Philippe styles.

506 to 516
Round, rectangular or square pedestal tables, candlestands and sewing tables with fixed, fold-over or tilting tops supported by turned central columns resting on "X" supports, tripartite or quadruped platform bases or tripod bases with shaped legs. Some are ornamented with inlaid motifs. Pine, walnut and mahogany, first half of the 19th century. During the Neoclassical period, bourgeois households usually had a few of these useful pedestal tables or candlestands and one of these compact sewing tables. The tilt-top models were placed against a wall when not in use.

517
Gaming table with a bulbous polygonal pedestal resting on a platform with four scrolled feet. Mahogany and walnut, ca. 1840.

THE CONSTITUTIONAL STYLE 315

518 to 527
Various models of parlor tables and washstands with drawers, in the spirit of the Neoclassical style. These pieces, which were probably made by joiners, have either retained their painted finish (early or original color) or have been stripped. Pine, butternut and yellow birch, mid-19th century.

528
Refectory table with turned legs, surrounded by small rush-seat chairs with curved back slats and crest rails. Long serving tables in the same style as this table are placed against the walls. Yellow birch and pine, mid-19th century.
The Neoclassical and Revival values of the 19th century are embodied in this rustic decor at the Château Bellevue in Cap-Tourmente, owned by the Séminaire de Québec, an important institution founded in the 18th century.

SLANT-TOP DESKS

During the Neoclassical period, hardwood slant-top desks were found in institutions and bourgeois homes. Such pieces, which were equipped with pigeonholes, or letter-slots, and often had secret drawers or compartments for hiding important papers, served not only as writing tables, but also as storage furniture, since they were fitted with several drawers. The general design of these pieces was based on classical forms and decorative orders and the models proposed by British furniture makers at the turn of the 19th century.

529
Regency-style slant-top desk with five drawers and concave-cornered panels, embellished with floral-carved ovals, ribbon carving and a large urn surmounted by an eagle. Period pulls, early colour, Saint-Jean, Île d'Orléans, ca. 1820.

530
Slant-top desk. Curly maple, early 19th century.

531-532
Slant-top desk with three drawers, Regency feet and secret compartments behind pillars in the pigeonhole section (see above detail). Original hardware, mahogany, Québec City, 1810.

533 a, b
Slant-top desk in a period decor with a pedestal table and a Hepplewhite-inspired chair. Curly maple and yellow birch, Château Bellevue, Cap-Tourmente, ca. 1820. The upper edge of the letter-slots is pleasingly shaped (see detail) and the fluted columns around the small central cupboard conceal three secret compartments. Original hardware and string inlays.

THE CONSTITUTIONAL STYLE 319

PERSONAL ACCOUNT

A Priest's Photo Album of the Seminary's Clocks

Father Georges Marceau had dreamed of studying clocks ever since he was a little boy. As a child, he loved to secretly open the door of his family's long-case clock in order to admire its golden pendulum as it swung to and fro. However, instead of becoming a clockmaker, Georges Marceau became a priest and pursued this vocation for the rest of his life. When he reached retirement age in 1998, this teacher with the Séminaire de Québec decided to finally devote himself to what interested him the most. He began to study, one after the other, the many old clocks located in the seminary with a view to tracing their history. Father Marceau filled two large notebooks with detailed observations. As he was combing through the institution's archives one day, he was invited by one of his colleagues, Father Laurent Tailleur, to take a look at an astonishing album of photographs that had been sitting in the seminary's vaults for years.

The Séminaire de Québec was founded in the 17th century by Monseigneur de Laval. In 1854, this venerable institution, which had been training priests for decades, gave birth to Université Laval. Its cassock-robed teachers, who all belonged to the same sacerdotal community, were under the authority of a superior, who in turn came under the authority of the Bishop or the Cardinal. The priests lived in rooms lining the long corridors of the seminary, a massive structure that dominated the capital. Each simple "cell" had well-stocked bookcases, a desk, a prie-dieu placed in front of a crucifix, a few chairs, a small bed and a clock. The latter was often a long-case clock or a bracket clock, which had been left to the priest by his family or purchased from a Québec City clockmaker.

In terms of their styles and construction materials, clocks have always been marked by the fashions in vogue at the time they were made. The first page of each of the chapters in this book shows a long-case clock which is representative of the period discussed in that chapter. From the late 18th century to 1860, clock forms and ornamentation were influenced by the values of Neoclassicism. Given that long-case clocks were very popular among the British, these domestic objects became widely distributed in the St. Lawrence Valley. Large, very attractive pieces were even found in the homes of craftsmen like François Létourneau, a master locksmith who lived in Saint-Roch-des-Aulnaies in the early 19th century (see page 327 of my book, *Antiquités du Québec*) or certain farmers such as Joseph Gagnon, who lived in Sainte-Famille, on Île d'Orléans. Mr. Gagnon's clock, along with some of its decorative details, is shown in the photographs to the right.

Québec had a clockmakers' guild which, in the 19th century, included a majority of English-speaking craftsmen. Clock mechanisms were almost always imported from England, although some wooden ones were made in Québec. The *Charlton Standard Catalogue of Canadian Clocks*, by J. E. Connell, provides a complete list of clockmakers and importers. The cases of long-case clocks, most of which were made in Québec, were usually built of solid mahogany, but sometimes they were veneered with precious wood, such as mahogany, laid over pine, or made of an ordinary type of wood. They were painted, stained or finished with simulated graining. When the back of a clock is of oak, there is a good chance that the piece was made in England. Many clocks were embellished with inlaid or painted ornamentation, using motifs from the decorative vocabulary of Neoclassicism.

Long-case clocks are veritable classical temples, devoted to the cult of time. The lower part contains a chamber housing the works, which may be reached through a door locking with a key. This section of the case, which is often adorned with fluted colonettes, is surmounted by a glazed hood displaying the artistically designed face of the clock that solemnly marks the hours. Even the design of the keys used to wind the mechanism is exceptional. As for the clock face itself, its style is always in keeping with one of the architectural orders of classicism and it is typically crowned by a pediment, frequently ornamented with brass ball finials terminating in slender shafts that point majestically towards the heavens.

Amédée-Edmond Gosselin (1863-1941) was ordained a priest in 1890. A teacher of Canadian history, a prefect and an archivist, he was named superior and rector of the Séminaire de Québec on two separate occasions. Like Father Marceau, he loved clocks, and in 1914 he did a photo story on those that regulated the daily activities of his colleagues. He thus highlighted the importance of punctuality, while compiling a moving, visual record of these useful and attractive pieces of furniture, which were so popular in the 19th century.

534 a, b, c, d
Mahogany clock with decorative marquetry motifs on the base, the door and in the upper corners of the pendulum case; quarter columns on each side of the door; and full side columns, brass ball finials and fretwork on the hood. The works are signed Charles Russel, London. Russel worked as a clockmaker at 18 Barbican Street in London from 1787 to 1828.
Stuck to the door of the clock is a yellowed piece of old paper bearing a handwritten note signed by Father Pierre Hébert, which reads: "I, the undersigned, certify that this clock was purchased in around 1820, when it was new, by Joseph Gagnon of the parish of Sainte-Famille, I.O., and was sold to me by his son Pierre Gagnon on July 15, 1904." Father Pierre Hébert, who was born in Sainte-Famille in 1865 and died in 1924, enjoyed a brilliant career as a teacher and senior administrator at the Séminaire de Québec.

535 to 540
Fathers Amédée-Edmond Gosselin, Philéas Fillion, Pierre Hébert, Alfred Paré, Henri Simard and Joseph Narcisse Gignac sitting next to the long-case clocks in their offices. Father Gosselin, who instigated the photo story in which these clocks appeared, placed his clock on a base in order to give it a more stately appearance.

THE CONSTITUTIONAL STYLE 321

541 to 544
Four details of walnut carving on Québec furniture from the Revival era in the Renaissance Revival and Rococo Revival styles.

CHAPTER 4

*Traditional Craftsmanship Meets
the Industrial Revolution*

Revival-Era Furniture in Québec

1840-1890
THE CONFEDERATIVE STYLE

THE DRAWING ROOM IN THE MANOR-HOUSE WAS FILLED WITH MAHOGANY FURNITURE. There were great, well-stuffed armchairs, their wood carved with roses in full bloom, their upholstery of red buttoned velvet. There were also card-tables and whatnots. Two huge, high-backed sofas stood at one end, on either side of the door. In front of the black marble fireplace there was a round table with an "epargne."

This was a strange and complicated object. It consisted of a silver base supporting a number of glass vessels. I never knew what it was supposed to be used for, nor did anybody else. I am inclined to think now that it served no useful purpose at all. It was an "ornament." This showy piece struck me as a very handsome object indeed. Thus, at a very tender age, I showed a taste for useless ostentation and for the poetry of decoration.

ROBERT DE ROQUEBRUNE, *Testament of My Childhood*, transl. Felix Walther, Toronto, 1964.

VICTORIAN TASTE WAS, BY DEFINITION, BOURGEOIS TASTE. It was a manifestation of the gradual opening up of the world that characterized the period, and it reflected the development of knowledge, attitudes and aesthetic sensibility that was the result. The bourgeoisie loved to show off, which explains their penchant for things flashy, flamboyant and ostentatious. For them, taste was bound up with social advancement; but it was also determined by a pre-established code of conventions diffused widely in all sorts of specialized publications (including pattern books, home economics guides and books on etiquette and comportment). To have good taste was to be conventional, for taste was identified with what was proper and appropriate: a degree of luxury quite acceptable for the upper ranks was considered unsuitable for those lower down the scale. Finding the right level, the "happy medium," was a question of propriety and respectability.

CLAIRE DESMEULLES, Art historian, in *Living in Style:
Fine Furniture in Victorian Quebec*, Québec City, 1993.

Revival-era clock.
Oak, ca. 1890.

Revival-Era Furniture in Québec

545

Impressive Renaissance Revival walnut whatnot with a mirror in the Papineau seigneurial manor at Montebello, ca. 1930. Photograph by Edgar Gariépy. Victorian furniture and decor were characterized by opulence and an abundance of ornamentation, in marked contrast to the values of the previous period. In Québec, Revival styles inspired the work of countless furniture makers.

546

(Page 326)
Pencil drawing of a Rococo Revival armchair made in the Québec City workshop of Pierre Drouin and Honoré Roy *dit* Belleau, ca. 1860. This exceptional document is one of several that have survived in a rich archival collection related to these two craftsmen in the capital city. Furniture made in Québec during the Revival period shows as much originality as any produced elsewhere in the Western world and is just as worthy of the attention usually given to both older and more recent furniture by collectors, museums and researchers.

The Revival-era furniture of Québec reflects a period of remarkable fertility. This was made abuntantly clear by the first in-depth study of Victorian furniture in Québec, carried out between 1986 and 1993 by a team of researchers known as MOBIVIQ under the direction of John Porter of Université Laval. The project led to two superb exhibitions, one at the Montreal Museum of Fine Arts and the other at the Musée de la civilisation in Québec City, and resulted in a large book entitled *Living in Style: Fine Furniture in Victorian Quebec* (1993). The incomparable richness of this period has never ceased to impress me as, for some thirty years now, I have devoted myself to fieldwork throughout Québec and made frequent visits to museum storage rooms and antique dealers.

In the previous period, Montréal and Québec City had experienced rapid growth and seen numerous workshops of all sizes spring up, along with several large factories that increasingly turned to new forms of advertising. The marketing era had been born. Manufacturers, both French- and English-speaking, sought to reach a broader clientele. They extended their influence and broadened the distribution of their products through increased use of sea and rail transportation, thus extending their business activities far beyond the cities and towns of the St. Lawrence Valley, to the rest of Canada. Such manufacturers include William Drum and Philippe Vallière, who were both leaders in the Québec City furniture sector in the second half of the 19th century. Certain manufacturers, like Vallière, maintained a large retail store, as well as a factory in the downtown area.

In the towns and in certain villages, elegant furniture in specific styles was produced for an elite clientele. But the new mechanized factories, which tended to be built near the railroads and docks

The Confederative Style in Québec
1840-1890

JOHN A. MACDONALD
1815-1891

GEORGE-ÉTIENNE CARTIER
1814-1893

SOURCES: British Late Regency and British Victorian, U.S. Victorian, Louis-Philippe and French Second Empire. Revivals, especially of Gothic, Louis XV, Rococo and Renaissance styles.

WOOD AND MATERIALS:
vernacular furniture: pine and butternut
period furniture: imported and local fruit woods, mahogany, rosewood, walnut, yellow birch; veneers of figured walnut, maple and yellow birch
secondary wood: pine, basswood and white birch

Revival-era sofa, attributed to Vallière, Québec City, ca. 1860.

COLLECTIONS: Museums of religious communities in Québec City and Montréal, Musée de la civilisation in Québec City, Musée du Séminaire de Québec, episcopal palaces, seminaries and classical colleges in the different Roman Catholic dioceses of Québec.

---

in big cities, mainly turned out ordinary furniture for less affluent customers. At the same time, many local joiners were inspired by fashionable trends and created their own, somewhat humble versions of these styles.

The period was also marked by intense activity in the field of technical innovation and patented inventions. Imaginative approaches led to all kinds of new functional combinations: highchairs that could be transformed into baby carriages or walkers, stepladder chairs, beds built into walls, platform rockers, armchairs whose adjustable backs and footrests could be extended almost to make a bed (ancestors of the famous Morris chair), the amazingly light Hunzinger chair, folding beds and sofa beds. Furniture makers found dozens of ingenious ways to upholster and began to use new materials, such as wicker and papier maché inlaid with mother-of-pearl.

The advertisements run by many businesses in trade magazines never failed to laud the astonishing power of the steam engines that operated the factories. This wonderful invention supplied energy to various new specialized machines, each one more technically advanced and productive than the next. Machines took raw timber and sawed it up, split it, turned it, planed it, sanded it, mortised it and drilled it; machines also made tenons, dove-tails and dowels. In short, machines produced all the components that went into making a piece of furniture. Many operations previously accomplished by hand with manual tools were thus eliminated. Upholstering techniques were greatly improved and chairs were made softer and, above all, more comfortable to meet the new expectations of the public.

Québec furniture makers found inspiration and guidance in trends originating in France, Britain and the United States. Furniture imported from these countries, especially the United States, was well received in the Québec market. As well, there were local, national and international exhibitions, which promoted fashionable trends and provided a showcase for

workshops. The workshops used the exhibitions to vaunt their capacities, proudly displaying their craftsmanship to a broader public and competing for awards that they would be sure to use later in advertising. Many important furniture makers took advantage of exhibitions to pick up original ideas that could be used in designing new models. In a remarkable master's thesis, "Les meubliers du Québec aux expositions provinciales, internationales et universelles 1850-1900" (1992), Daniel Drouin aptly describes the importance of exhibitions to the development of Québec furniture.

Furniture makers also sought inspiration in foreign publications and journals. The importance of such printed sources is made clear by the best monograph to date on a cabinetmaker's workshop — a study of the Québec City workshop belonging to Pierre Drouin and Honoré Roy *dit* Belleau, based on an exceptional documentary collection and written by John Porter, Rénald Lessard and Jean-Pierre Labiau (*Cahiers du CÉLAT* 10, June 1989). Half of the collection, which was discovered in the safekeeping of Honoré Roy's descendants, consists of 64 color plates from the Parisian magazine *Le Garde-meuble* from the 1840-1850 period. Some of these plates have been used to illustrate the present chapter. People in Québec liked to follow trends in both the decorative arts and clothing through the French and U.S. weeklies circulated in the St. Lawrence Valley at the time. Furniture makers had little choice but to adapt rapidly to the new modes made known this way. Manufacturers often claimed in their advertisements that they offered furniture in the latest London and Paris styles. *Le Garde-meuble* had been started in 1839 by Désiré Guilmard, a furniture illustrator who continued to work for publications in this capacity between 1839 and 1885. His furniture magazine remains important. In the article referred to above, John Porter writes that, "One of the most widely distributed magazines in Québec was undoubtedly *Le Garde-meuble*, published by the editor Désiré Guilmard of Paris. Plates from magazines such as this were often used as models by furniture makers." [Translation] The researcher goes on to say that as models were reshaped and adapted, numerous variants were created, ranging from the utterly simple to the most elaborately carved,

547
Rococo Revival bergère used as a bishop's throne, richly carved with plant and animal motifs and with chimera heads projecting from the arm stumps. Walnut, attributed to Philippe Vallière of Québec City, Trois-Rivières, ca. 1880. The wildly imaginative furniture made by Québec cabinetmakers in the Revival era shows enormous artistic skill. Furniture design received impetus from international exhibitions and the work done by other cabinetmakers in Europe and the rest of North America.

THE SPIRIT OF THE REVIVAL ERA 1840-1890

The influence of Victorian fashions in the St. Lawrence Valley can be seen in a taste for densely decorated interiors and extremely ornate objects. New machine tools made it easier to produce furniture inspired by the various historical periods that were successively idealized by society. With their exuberant ornamentation and predilection for somewhat heavy furniture, Revival styles contrasted strongly with the Neoclassicism that had preceded them.

Silver ewer, Hendery, Montréal, ca. 1850.

Daguerreotype of Mr. and Mrs. Smith of Québec City, ca. 1850.

Rococo Revival wall mirror, Québec City, ca. 1870.

Flow-blue Staffordshire ware, signed J. Heath, ca. 1845.

Evening gown belonging to Virginie de Saint-Ours, Montréal, ca. 1867.

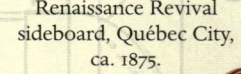

Renaissance Revival sideboard, Québec City, ca. 1875.

Cradle-in-frame, Chicoutimi, ca. 1880.

depending on the expectations, means and tastes of different customers. A drawing in the Drouin and Roy collection shows a sofa made in their workshop that is almost an exact copy of Plate 456 in *Le Garde-meuble*. On April 9, 1870, François Gourdeau advertised in *L'Événement* that "Every three months, he receives plans from Paris illustrating furniture and apartments furnished in the latest French tastes. These plans come from the famous publisher, Guilmard & Company." [Translation]

While furniture making was stimulated by international exhibitions and color plates illustrating the work of master cabinetmakers, many designers sought further inspiration in specialized publications, in particular pattern books from Britain, France and the United States. If the products of a New York workshop, like that run by Alexandre Roux between 1837 and 1881, are compared with the furniture made in Québec in the middle of the 19th century, definite similarities will be noticed in the armchairs, sofas and sideboards. Revival styles exhibited a number of stereotypes when it came to types of furniture, materials, shapes and decoration. Taking this into account, Québec craftsmen showed no less originality than those in the best French or U.S. workshops. Québec furniture from this period of our history is incontestably as worthy of attention and interest as Québec furniture in the classical French manner.

Each Western country experienced the Revival movement in its own way. In the English-speaking world, the period was referred to as Victorian, since the reign of Queen Victoria, extending over the second half of the 19th century, from 1837 to 1901, corresponds quite closely to this period of enthusiastic eclecticism inspired by a pervasive romanticism. In France, the same style is defined by the labels Second Empire or Napoleon III. In many other sovereign nations, the term Revival is used by art historians to designate the period.

For this book, it has been decided to divide the period of time usually covered by these designations into two smaller periods, each distinguished by its own theoretical, aesthetic and formal underpinnings. The first one, referred to here as the Revival period, extended from 1840 to 1890. The furniture of this time drew inspiration from the past, incorporating historic references that were sometimes broadly interpreted. The second covers what is known as the Belle Époque, or Edwardian era, normally regarded as extending from 1890 to the Great War, but for the purposes of this book, viewed as continuing until 1920. This is the period that may be considered to have ushered in the Modern era, rather than simply carrying on with the past-fixated fashions that preceded it. This transitional stage in the development of the decorative arts has thus been detached from the Victorian era and allowed to stand on its own as a stylistic period. It will be discussed in a separate chapter dealing with the trends I have designated as Pre-Modern.

It is impossible to fit the work of certain late-19th-century reformers into the Revival period, with its penchant for imitating historical styles. Such reformers include William Morris (1834-1896), Charles Eastlake (1836-1906) and William Godwin (1833-1886), all of whom sought to renew the decorative arts, interior decorating and furniture making by applying certain values of their time. While William Morris seems to have been entranced by the forms and manner of medieval craftsmanship and thus never made a clean break with history-inspired design, he nonetheless rejected the decorative hodgepodge of grotesque interpretations made possible by new machinery. His ideals were best realized in simple, solid Medieval furniture constructed of local materials. This furniture met Functionalist precepts long before the movement existed; it was almost austere in style and was affordable for

548
Ferrotype portrait of Joseph Routhier and Honoré Roy, two Québec City cabinetmakers specialized in furniture, ca. 1860. Mr. Routhier presents a model rocking chair, while Mr. Roy holds an appliqué bas-relief carving of a beaver, which is still in the family's possession.

549
Rocking chair upholstered with horsehair. Walnut, attributed to the workshop of Philippe Vallière, Québec City, ca. 1870.

THE FURNITURE MAKER

Philippe Vallière (1832-1919), a Québec City Furniture Maker

As a cabinetmaker and furniture manufacturer, Philippe Vallière enjoyed a solid reputation among his contemporaries. There are, however, considerable gaps in our present knowledge of his work. He produced some of the most elegant furniture of his time, constantly adapting it to fashionable trends throughout the half-century of his career. He was also, according to newspapers and trade yearbooks, the foremost furniture merchant in Québec City, from the Victorian era to the end of the Belle Époque.

Philippe Vallière was born to Olivier Vallière and Luce Trahan, of Saint-Vallier Street, Québec City, on September 15, 1832. He was educated at a Christian Brothers' school and then entered Québec City's Business College, the only establishment offering commercial training in the city. His grandfather had been a cooper and his father was a cabinetmaker, furniture maker and coffin manufacturer. Philippe thus learned the rudiments of his trade from his family. In 1853, he became an associate with his father in the J. O. Vallière et Fils firm, located at 28 Saint-Vallier Street. Philippe then went to Europe for further training in cabinetmaking. While he was there, he recruited a number of French and Belgian craftsmen who, according to the newspapers of the day, were considered true artists in their homelands.

On January 28, 1856, he married Ann Scott in St. Patrick's Church in Québec City. The couple had thirteen children, seven of whom died in infancy. In 1866, he became the sole owner of the firm. His business expanded, and by 1871 he was able to engage some one hundred employees, about thirty of whom were specialized in finishing interiors with stairs, moulding and furniture. He also imported luxury materials. He decorated the council room in the city hall with Gobelins tapestry for the the throne, Russia leather for the tabletop, and morocco leather and silk brocatelle for the armchairs. He also sold various funerary items, such as wooden and iron coffins, and rented out a magnificent hearse.

In 1873, the business was making about $100 000 annually and its production was still growing. Since employees earned an average salary of one dollar a day, Vallière's profits must have been considerable. In 1887, a fire destroyed the factory, which, because of the numerous flammable products it contained, was not insured. Although a warehouse full of expensive furniture and the retail store were spared, Vallière suffered an estimated loss of $125 000. A new, larger and better-equipped factory was built of brick, measuring 100 feet by 275 feet and rising four storeys. Its machinery was operated with a 65-horsepower steam engine, and 130 employees, including some fifty sculptors, worked there. Unfortunately, very few of the pieces made in the factory were signed. On April 14, 1967, the factory was razed by a demolition company.

Vallière furnished the most prestigious buildings of his time, including the Québec Parliament Building on Côte de la Montagne in 1867, the new Parliament Building (designed to house all government departments) on Parliament Hill between 1880 and 1897, and the United Canada Parliament Building in Ottawa. In Québec City, he finished the city hall's council room and recorder's office, the reception room in the bishop's palace when Elzéar-Alexandre Taschereau was made a prince of the Church in 1886, and the new Québec Law Court, inaugurated in 1889. His work included many other civil and religious institutions throughout Québec. He also obtained the contract for furniture for the now famous Château Frontenac, which opened on December 20, 1893. The distinguished residences he furnished include that of the Governor General and that of Jean-Charles Chapais, a father of Confederation, at Saint-Denis-de-Kamouraska. The *Canadian Album, Men of Canada*, put out by the Reverend William Cochrane in 1893, stated that Philippe Vallière owned one of the largest furniture factories in Canada, and the largest east of Toronto.

He won numerous first prizes in various national and international exhibitions. In 1890, the government entrusted him with the construction of the Québec pavilion in the Jamaican exhibition. The hall was built with every type of Québec timber. Despite his many business responsibilities, Vallière took an active interest in municipal, provincial and federal politics. In 1890, the City of Québec gave a street near his factory the name Vallière to honor his many successes as a cabinetmaker, his contribution to economic life and his work as a city councillor and alderman. His old residence, at 5 Hébert Street, called the Maison Vallière, would later be used to house Université Laval's social sciences faculty (1939-1968), founded by the Dominican father, Georges-Henri Lévesque.

On January 17, 1919, Philippe Vallière passed away in his home at 126 Sainte-Anne Street. He was 86 years old. His death represented the loss of an eminent citizen not only in Québec City society and but also in the world of trade and politics.

Suzanne Fournier Vallière
Lévis, June 1999

550
Portrait of Philippe Vallière by Ippolito Zapponi, Rome, 1876.

551
The store, offices and rear of the factory belonging to businessman Philippe Vallière, in *The City of Quebec Jubilee Illustrated 1837-1887* (Montréal, 1887).

552
The store entrance at 940 Saint-Vallier Street, today part of "the Vallière block," probably with Philippe Vallière and his two sons, ca. 1890.

SOURCES FOR REVIVAL-ERA FURNITURE

In the 19th century, Québec cabinetmakers used magazines like *Le Garde-meuble*, published by D. Guilmard in Paris, to follow trends in the Western world. Chromolithographs taken from this magazine were found with documents kept by the families of cabinetmakers Honoré Roy *dit* Belleau and Pierre Drouin, who had collected such illustrations. By the end of the 18th century, trends in the decorative arts had begun to influence different countries in the world at very much the same time. After 1851, international exhibitions became a source of inspiration and fostered interaction.

Color illustrations like these, published in the mid-19th century in the French magazine *Le Garde-meuble*, were influential in the spread of furniture styles throughout the Western world.
a., b., c. Rococo Revival easy chairs. **d.** side chair. **e.** Renaissance Revival ladies' worktables. **f.** Rococo Revival dining room table. **g.** Rococo Revival drawing room table. **h.** Rococo Revival prie-dieu. **i.** Baroque Revival borne (circular ottoman) for a formal drawing room. **j.** Renaissance Revival sideboard. **k.-l.** Louis XV Revival sofas. **m.** Renaissance Revival bed.

h.

i.

k.

j.

l.

m.

PERSONAL ACCOUNT

The Joys of Research in the Decorative Arts

I am an art historian and have always been fascinated by the decorative arts and the way people have finished and furnished their rooms in different periods and in various levels of society. Since this somewhat specialized field generally receives very little attention in university fine art departments, I had to learn "on the job." Working on my own research projects opened doors for me, since there is a demand for this type of knowledge in Québec.

In 1986, I had just finished my master's degree when I learned that John Porter, a Université Laval professor, was forming a team called MOBVIQ to trace the history of Victorian furniture in Québec. I went to see him and asked to become a member. I did a great deal for the project and I also learned a great deal. The undertaking led to two major exhibitions, in 1993 and 1994, and resulted in an impressive volume entitled *Living in Style: Fine Furniture in Victorian Quebec*.

We had to begin from scratch. Nothing had been done on Victorian furniture in Québec. We systematically went through notarial records in every region of Québec, selecting those that corresponded to different trends within this period and specific social categories. Equal attention was given to farmers, members of the liberal professions and the wealthy middle class, both in the country and the city. However, Revival-style furniture seems to have been a luxury enjoyed by the more affluent classes, which explains the critical reaction of reformers like Morris, Eastlake and Stickley in the following period.

At the same time that we were progressing on this front, we also perused countless documents related to lifestyles, closely examining the books, magazines and brochures that circulated in Québec at the time. The whole manufacturing sector was analyzed and classified according to workshop and region on the basis of advertisements, promotional material and newspaper articles describing industries and workshops, or reporting on the participation of furniture makers in local, national and international fairs and exhibitions. Census records and comparative statistics were also gone over with a fine comb.

We also sought the assistance of parish priests and their collaboration proved invaluable. They opened many doors to us by reassuring parishioners whose homes still held their original Victorian furnishings that these strangers passing through their regions were indeed conducting legitimate research. Each team member filled out thousands and thousands of filing cards. I was with the project for six years. Part of my responsibilities involved going through every piece of iconographic material to be found, and a number of wonderful photographs were discovered this way. The resulting iconographic collection is now stored in the archives of the Musée du Québec. The final report, to which every team member contributed, was inspired by both art and science.

Encouraged by this experience, I then worked on furnishing the main floor of the Dionne seigneurial manor in Saint-Roch-des-Aulnaies, a bourgeois home that is open to the public. The work I had done with MOBVIQ was very useful for this project in terms not only of the research method used but also of documenting and elaborating a final proposal. The building, constructed in 1850, had kept its original appearance and all its divisions were intact. The task was to give the rooms a spirit that corresponded as closely as possible to the ethnographic truth. This objective was attained by recording and interpreting source material obtained from old documents and interviews with elderly people who had known the site.

Quite recently, I was asked by Parks Canada to provide expertise in the renovation of the Montebello residence owned by Louis-Joseph Papineau, a hero of Québec history. Like the Dionnes' grand house, this seigneurial manor was originally decorated at a time of stylistic transition, and developing such a site is always a challenge. Papineau moved into his new home in 1850, which represents a pivotal moment in the history of the decorative arts in Québec — a time when Neoclassical and Revival values overlapped. Furthermore, he brought with him from Montréal a certain number of articles purchased after his marriage to Julie Bruneau and they were in the pure Empire style. Once again, my research and proposal were greatly advanced by the detailed study of primary and iconographic sources already conducted by Parks Canada. Related correspondence, probate inventories and family photographs proved infinitely useful in developing a proposal for the interior decoration.

Papineau blended the Neoclassical and Revival styles with skill. His son Amédée was a great collector and later stuffed the rooms with all kinds of bric-a-brac. The proposal was to bring the period of Louis-Joseph back to life. In this period, the meeting of two stylistic movements affected everything from forms of furniture and its arrangement to interior decoration, including colors and wallpaper.

Several pieces of furniture that once belonged to Louis-Joseph were tracked down and returned to their original setting. However, as is always the case in this kind of project, many important items, such as the bed and other bedroom furniture, seem to have disappeared forever.

Reconstituting the original setting and lifestyle in which a person and a family lived presents an extraordinary research challenge and one that really never ends. Surprises always await around the bend.

Claire Desmeules
Art historian
June 15, 1998

most households — or, at least, that is what Morris hoped. Eastlake and Godwin were part of a new group of British designers who called themselves the Art Furniture Movement, which to some extent promoted the same views as their contemporary, Morris. They too were weary of superfluous, stuffy ornateness and proposed innovative, elegant and simplified furniture designs with linear forms, often decorated with incised motifs. They went further than Morris in promoting industrial furniture that everyone could afford. While they differed from him in their advocacy of industrial mass production, their basic ideas were similar to his. Both movements made considerable efforts to educate the public.

True Revival-era furniture was inspired by certain periods in the past whose symbolic significance, stirring contexts or evocation of national pride lent themselves to idealization in different societies. Generally speaking, architecture and the decorative arts tend to adapt easily to a society's ideological movements. In England, idealization of the Gothic period gave rise to the Gothic Revival and admiration for classicism produced a reinvented classicism — not to be confused with the preceding Neoclassical period. In France, the values of the Renaissance, Baroque and Rococo were favored and the Revival era saw the emergence of the movements known as

553

Reconstruction of a Baroque Revival bedroom in the Dionne seigneurial manor at Saint-Roch-des-Aulnaies. The padded foot of the sleigh bed is decorated with phytomorphic motifs and a beaver holding a maple branch in its mouth. The same type of carving adorns the washstand with scrolled feet and columns, as well as the chest of drawers with a mirror shown on page 367. This walnut and mahogany suite comes from the Jourdain-Fiset house in Québec City and dates from 1870. According to oral tradition, it was ordered from Philippe Vallière's workshop in the capital city. Here it is used to recreate the spirit of an era.

554
Victoria, Queen of England, photographed by Mayall. This monarch's reign lasted for 64 years, from 1837 to 1901 — one of the longest in the history of humankind. The period in the history of art roughly corresponding to her reign is generally referred to as the Victorian era.

Renaissance Revival, Baroque Revival and Rococo Revival. Britain and France acted as the prime cultural movers influencing North American fashions. At the same time, some designers found inspiration in the material culture of the East and borrowed decorative elements such as certain interlacing forms, the bamboo motif, glossy lacquer-like finishes and various inlay techniques.

In their passion for the past, designers sometimes turned to a pure period style, producing furniture that is clearly identifiable as Jacobean, William and Mary, Louis XV, Baroque or Rococo. However, at other times, especially after 1860, the fashion was for a mixture of styles combined in the same piece of furniture or in the same building.

In 1851, Québec's total population had reached 890 261. Montréal had 57 715 residents and Québec City 42 052. Forty years later, in 1891, these figures had grown respectively to 1 488 535, 215 650 and 63 090. These significant changes in the population were the result of immigration from English-speaking countries and an influx of rural people to the cities, attracted by the many opportunities offered by industrial production, especially in Montréal, which was in full economic expansion at the time. By the end of the Revival period, according to the 1891 census, there were 8 334 people living in Trois-Rivières and 10 110 in Sherbrooke. In 1851, 311 furniture makers were active in Québec, but 30 years later, in 1881, they numbered 1 359. In 1851, Québec City had 87 furniture craftsmen and Montréal 81; by 1881, these figures had increased respectively to 214 and 464. Cabinetmaking and joinery, whether artisanal or industrial, were particularly vigorous sectors of the economy in the regions of Témiscouata, Dorchester, Saint-Maurice and Maskinongé, as well as in the Hochelaga suburb of Montréal. Between 1851 and 1881, Montréal overtook Québec City and emerged as the centre of the furniture industry. Most furniture makers employed only two or three workers at the time. Considerably more manpower was needed by large firms that had the means of acquiring powerful steam engines and new, highly productive machinery. The Québec City market was dominated in this period by two businesses, one of which continued to prosper in the following period as well. The first was a factory belonging to William Drum (1808-1876), which operated from 1834 to 1873. In 1870, 120 workers, including 100 men, 12 women and 8 boys, were employed there. The other business was the factory run by Philippe Vallière (1832-1919) from 1853 to about 1912. In 1889, Vallière's firm had 130 employees, some fifty of whom were sculptors, according to an unpublished article by Suzanne Vallière entitled "Philippe Vallière, 1832-1919, ébéniste et manufacturier de meubles à Québec" (Lévis, 1992, 154 p., illus.). In Montréal, a factory operated by John Hilton from 1845 to 1872 catered particularly to the Anglophone market. For a time, this business competed with the Irishman, Owen McGarvey (ca. 1821-1897), who associated with his son to become Montréal's biggest furniture manufacturer in the last quarter of the 19th century; this factory closed in 1897. Other important workshop owners include Charles E. Pariseau, Azarie Lavigne, J. A. I. Craig, George Armstrong, Noël Pratte, Adolphe Bélanger and H. P. Labelle. More has been learned about certain workshops over the past few years, as ethnohistorians discover archive collections and sets of furniture that can be attributed to a maker with certainty. Such discoveries have shed light on the Québec City workshops of Pierre Drouin, Honoré Roy and François Gourdeau.

In Québec, those who made furniture in Revival styles preferred to work with black walnut, yellow birch and mahogany. It is also possible to find pieces made in maple, oak, basswood, ash, pine and cherry, as well as in several exotic woods like rosewood, but walnut and mahogany remained by far the most popular.

Furniture makers in this period made abundant use of veneering techniques to satisfy a demand for dramatic wood grains, which had also been prized in the preceding era. New machine tools made it possible to cut thin layers from the hardest of local and imported wood efficiently and at low cost. In 1850, a Quebecker named Onésime Saint-Armand used newspaper advertisements to promote an instrument that could produce bird's-eye veneers to rival those of "West Indies wood," as he put it, with a touch of nationalist pride. There were good profits to be made by veneering experts who could produce sometimes quite startling visual effects from the fanciful wood patterns hidden beneath a tree's bark: the swirling crotch grain of branch nodes in trees like walnut, the figures in burls growing on the trunks of elms, the straight-grained sapwood of oak, and the astonishingly luminous golden fibre of bird's-eye maple and curly maple. Cabinetmakers sometimes turned to 18th-century French treatises on the subject. Sideboards, bedsteads and chests of drawers were finished with layers of wood that gave them a distinctly luxurious air, adding to the effect of complex forms, rich moulding, decorative turnings and carved appliqués.

The technological revolution that marked the second half of the 19th century freed craftsmen from the tasks of sawing, surfacing, and preparing joints, for these were now done by machine tools of all sorts. Craftsmen could thus devote more time to adorning their work with either block-carved or appliquéed decoration. The traditional mortise-and-tenon joint was gradually replaced by dowelling, a technique whereby wooden pins were inserted into holes made in each of the parts to be joined. This construction method produced quite fragile pieces of furniture because the area of junction was sometimes very narrow. The furniture's fragility was further aggravated by the use of animal glues, nails and screws, and by the furniture's imaginative shapes (for example, the sweeping curves of cabriole sofas with medallion backs) and, despite their apparent solidity, such pieces often do not age well.

Carving, both in bas-relief and high relief, was much admired, especially when integrated with turning and moulding in the structure or decoration of pieces such as chairs. However, much of the furniture produced in this period was actually quite simple in its ornamentation; for example, the decoration of certain Renaissance Revival sideboards and beds consists of interesting shapes that were cut out of walnut veneer and then glued or screwed in place, accented with stereotypical appliqués carved with a modicum of skill. Industrial hardware, on the other hand was always carefully made and is exemplified by drop handles in various motifs.

As Patrick Albert, a furniture restorer at the Centre de conservation du Québec, points out in a book entitled *Le Meuble de goût* (p. 433), when it came to heavily carved and ornamented cabinetwork, "black walnut was the most popular wood. It was readily obtained and its discrete grain and deep warm color was well suited to trends in taste. It was also easy to carve and took a fine polish. Other types of wood were of course used, but there was a noticeable preference for somewhat dark wood, and stains were sometimes applied to maple, ash, butternut and yellow birch to give them the appearance of other woods. For example, yellow birch was particularly appropriate for imitating mahogany because of its wavy grain." [Translation].

This leads us to the subject of surface finishes on furniture in the Revival era. Finishing coats were transparent, semitransparent or opaque, depending on whether the goal was to let the natural grain show through, deepen or change the wood color, or cover it completely to produce a new color or an effect that looked like wood grain. Imitation grain was obtained with ingenious techniques and often quite simple tools. Natural wood was finished and protected with linseed oil, tung oil, wax, and oil or spirit varnishes. Spirit varnishes contain dried resins such as lacquer and produce an attractive glossy finish. This type of varnish was preferred above all others because of its shine and easy maintenance, since simple polishing restored its lustre.

Each sequence and movement in the Revival era had its own type of decoration and own stylistic rules based on the older ones that inspired it. In the Gothic Revival period, furniture was decorated with finials, crockets, scrolls, trefoils, quatrefoils, gables, and ogival or ogee arches. In the Rococo Revival era, chairs were adorned with *rocaille* motifs, curves and countercurves and cabriole legs. The Renaissance Revival was marked by pediments, special turnings and architectural compositions whose form and decoration displayed the symmetry and balance of monumental works.

Influenced by the dictates of numerous treatises on the subject, notions of interior decorating changed quite radically from those of the previous period. The methodically organized simplicity of Neoclassicism was replaced by profusely decorated walls and floors, heavily draped windows, and rooms crowded with furniture whose cushions and deep upholstery reflected a growing preoccupation with comfort. Special chairs, like armchairs but without armrests, were designed for women in order to accommodate the voluminous crinoline skirts they wore in accordance with the "generous" style of the age.

SOURCES FOR REVIVAL-ERA FURNITURE

Developments in Revival styles can be followed through a number of treatises by British and U.S. architects and decorators as well as countless North American sales catalogues, pattern books and publications. These styles held sway in the St. Lawrence Valley between 1850 and 1900, especially among cabinetmakers in Montréal and Québec City. Networks of influence are revealed in the illustrations that inspired these furniture makers.

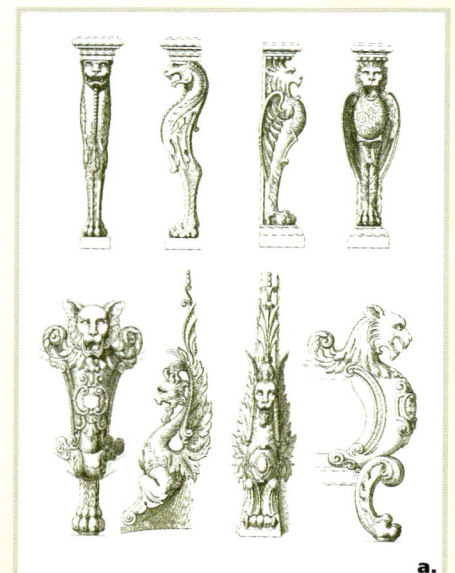

Illustrations taken from various 19th-century British and U. S. publications showing the type of Revival-era furniture found in the St. Lawrence Valley.
a. chimera-decorated legs on furniture at the Great Universal Exhibition of 1851, published in *The Victorian Cabinet-Maker's Assistant* by Blackie and Son of London (1853). **b., c., f., i.** various "new style" and Rococo Revival tables published in *Cabinet Maker's Album of Furniture* by Henry Carey Baird of Philadelphia (1868). **d.** Renaissance Revival sideboard, (Baird, 1868). **e.-l.** cast-iron lawn settee and chair by the William Buck Store Company, Brantford, Ontario, ca. 1895. **g.** black walnut chair and sofa by J. & W. Hilton of Montréal, presented at the 1851 Exhibition in the Crystal Palace in London. **h.** two-doored cupboard with corner columns, (Blackie, 1853). **j.** chair legs, (Blackie, 1853). **k.** Renaissance Revival sideboard (Blackie, 1853). **m.-n.** whatnots by the Archer Manufacturing Company, Rochester, N. Y., 1880. **o., p., s., t.** hall chairs (various sources, 1840). **q.** portrait by the Notman Studio, Montréal, 1863. **r.** Rococo Revival sofa (Blackie, 1853).

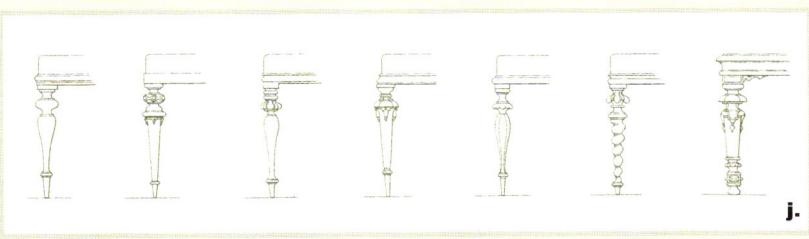
j.

k.

l.

q.

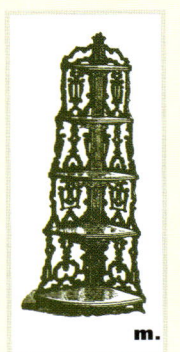
m.

n.

o.

p.

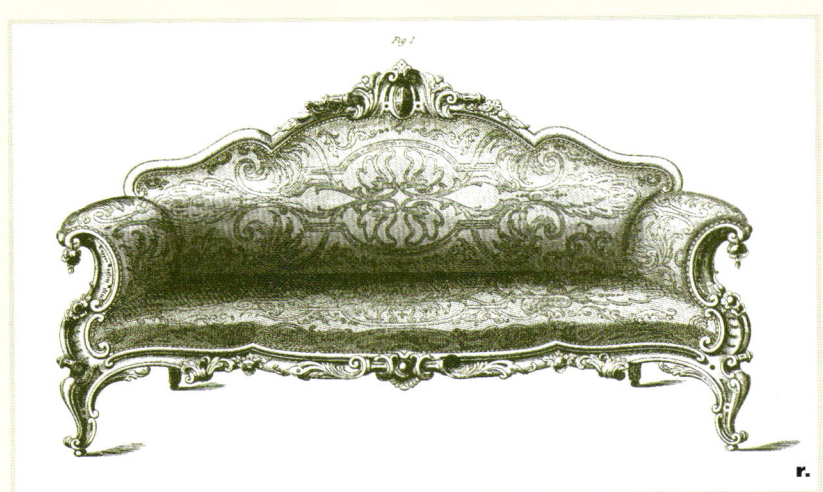
r.

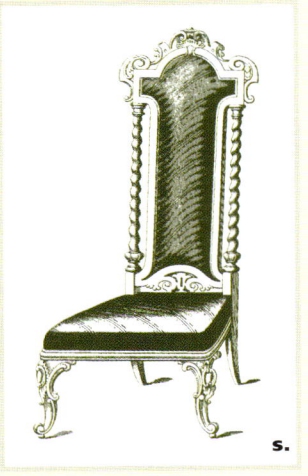
s.

t.

Three trends in the revival period

Gothic Revival (1830-1860)

The Revival movement was marked by different stylistic trends that overlapped in time and sometimes blended. Pattern books published in England, the United States or in France in the second half of the 19th century show that there was a succession of fashions for the Gothic, the Baroque or Rococo, and finally the Renaissance. At the same time, the values of Neoclassicism were never entirely abandoned, reappearing in North America in a Neoclassical Revival of a somewhat massive nature, quite far removed from the Georgian, Regency and Empire styles of the early century. This type of furniture, inspired by Neoclassicism, is dealt with in the preceding chapter.

The characteristics of Gothic Revival were inspired by the great medieval period, and the style borrowed every Gothic feature imaginable, combining them freely and sometimes producing flamboyant effects. The movement was especially marked by verticality, ogival forms, spiral and ball turnings, gable crests and pinnacles with finials and crockets.

555
Drawing of a Gothic Revival chair of a type found in Québec between 1840 and 1870. Illustration in Loudon's 1833 catalogue.

556 a, b, c
Three armchairs in blend of Gothic Revival and Eastlake styles, crowned by gables decorated with crockets and finials and bearing the French words for "well-being," "economy" and "justice." Les Coopérants (formerly the Société des artisans canadiens français). Walnut and burl walnut with leather, Montréal, Demers et Riopel, 1886-1889.
Gothic Revival furniture was not especially popular with the French-speaking population. The style was better received in the English-speaking community, where it was particularly used in the decoration of churches and rectories. Certain foundries in Montréal and the United States offered garden furniture in this style.

Rococo Revival (1850-1865)

In the middle of the 19th century, there was a renewal of interest in the 17th- and 18th-century Baroque and Rococo styles, which had been especially popular in France during the Régence and under Louis XV. French and U.S. furniture makers in particular drew inspiration from them. Attractive catalogues were distributed by French cabinetmakers who had adopted this fashion, with its curves and countercurves, cabriole legs and generous scrolling. Elaborate decorative carving echoed Baroque themes but might update them to some extent, or gave local themes a Baroque interpretation. The demand for fine walnut and mahogany furniture in this style was supplied by dozens of Québec cabinetmakers.

557
Drawing of a Rococo Revival sofa published by Blackie & Son in *The Victorian Cabinet Maker's Assistant*, London, 1853.

558-559
Rococo Revival sofa, bearing a bust of Jacques Cartier and decorated with motifs of seaweed, *rocaille*, lattices and seabirds. Note the curvilinear back, armrests and skirt, deep-buttoned upholstering and scroll feet. Walnut, attributed to the workshop of Philippe Vallière, Québec City, ca. 1880.
This exceptional piece is kept in the throne room of the Archbishop of Québec City. The entire room was furnished by Vallière for the consecration of Québec's first prince of the church, Elzéar-Alexandre Taschereau, in 1886. It was a fitting homage to this important figure and is well worth seeing. The Musée du Saguenay—Lac-Saint-Jean, in Chicoutimi, possesses equally impressive examples of this type. The Revival-era furniture of Québec abounds in items that are truly unique and are no less representative of Québec furniture production than the diamond-point armoire.

Renaissance Revival (1860-1880)

This style was marked by triangular, arched or broken pediments, decorative medallions in geometric shapes that were glued or screwed in place, semicircular arches, generous use of cyma curves and arched or concave-cornered panels. Always highly architectural, Renaissance Revival furniture in Québec was very popular for bedroom and dining room suites; it is perfectly exemplified by the great sideboard with rounded corners and carved braces of game birds or other representations of local wildlife.

560
Pencil drawing of a Renaissance Revival sideboard from the workshop of Pierre Drouin or Honoré Roy, two Québec City cabinetmakers, ca. 1875.

561-562
Renaissance Revival bed and sideboard. Walnut and figured walnut, Québec City and Montréal, ca. 1875.

563
Renaissance Revival sideboard in a reconstructed mid-19th-century setting in the Dionne manor at Saint-Roch-des-Aulnaies.
The table and chairs show something of the Neoclassical style with Empire influences. In homes occupied by the same family for several generations, rooms were seldom decorated in a single style.

THE DRAWING ROOM SUITE

In the Revival era, furniture for the drawing room, dining room and bedroom began to be offered in suites. This gave interior decoration much more stylistic cohesion. Previously, pieces of furniture were often sold individually and interiors were more diverse.

344   REVIVAL-ERA FURNITURE IN QUÉBEC

564
Pencil drawing of a Baroque Revival armchair from the archives of the workshop belonging to Pierre Drouin and Honoré Roy of Québec City, ca. 1860.

565 to 568
Rococo Revival walnut drawing room suite made in Philippe Vallière's Québec City workshop and purchased in 1866 by Mme Jean-Charles Chapais, born Georgina Dionne (1830-1888), to furnish the drawing room of the family home in Saint-Denis-de-Kamouraska. An archived invoice attests to these facts.
This exceptional suite consists of furniture in the Louis XV manner, with cabriole legs, deep-buttoned horsehair upholstering, curvilinear backs and carved relief decoration in the form of foliage, fruit and flowers on the skirts and padded armrests. The suite includes a sofa, a rocking chair, a gentlemen's armchair (with armrests), a ladies' chair (without armrests) and side chairs (not shown). This graceful furniture, with its unbroken flowing lines, shows the signature of Vallière in the sinewy carving of the knuckle on the armrests.

569
A corner of the drawing room in the Dionne manor in Saint-Denis-de-Kamouraska, with some of the furniture bought in Québec City from Philippe Vallière in 1866. Photograph by Neuville Bazin, 1950.

The gentleman and lady of the house could enjoy a piano recital seated in their own chairs; the type of chair called a gentlemen's chair had armrests, while a ladies' chair lacked them in order to accommodate her crinoline skirt.

570
(Pages 346-347)
The drawing room in the Chapais house in Saint-Denis-de-Kamouraska today, after restoration and redecorating. Furniture by Philippe Vallière still graces this formal room. On the open card table lies an album of old family photographs.

THE CONFEDERATIVE STYLE

571 to 576

Drawing room suite in the Baroque Revival style with Louis XV influences. Note the curvilinear backs with upholstered medallions topped by carved decoration, curved and cabriole legs, and sinewy arm stumps in the manner of Philippe Vallière. Walnut, Lévis, ca. 1870. Furniture in Revival-era drawing rooms tended to be arranged in small groups associated with certain activities. Since people could walk about a piece of furniture, it was like sculpture in the round. An article's back was therefore as important as its front. Upholsterers were only too happy to cover furniture in matching color and pattern combinations that complemented the interior decorating fashions of the time.

577
This studio portrait of an unknown woman by E. B. Hodge, of Waterloo, near Granby, was used on a visiting card. Such photographs from the 1860-1870 period typically show Revival-style furniture. To please their customers, photographers have always ensured that their settings include accessories in the latest fashions.

578 to 581
Walnut suite with shaped backs, decorated with plant-inspired motifs. The sinewy carving on the supports of the padded armrests is continued on the curved and cabriole legs. The side chairs have distinctive three-part backs and the ladies' chair is embellished with leafy consoles on either side of the seat. Attributed to the Vallière workshop in Québec City, ca. 1870.

THE CONFEDERATIVE STYLE

582 to 585
Revival-era drawing room suite combining elements of Renaissance Revival and Rococo Revival, attributed to furniture maker and upholsterer François Gourdeau (1840-1920) of Québec City, ca. 1870.

This craftsman was the son of a furniture maker and learned his trade from his father, working with him in Saint-Jean-sur-Richelieu. He perfected his craft first in the United States and then in Québec City, with the sculptor Jean-Baptiste Côté (1832-1907). In 1864, he established himself in this city and worked as a cabinetmaker for the next 50 years. Gourdeau developed a business with high standards of excellence, according to contemporary newspaper articles on economics and trade. These articles also reported that he employed a staff of 15 craftsmen in 1871 and produced furniture in mahogany, black walnut, butternut, ash, oak and pine.

The articles shown here are attributed to this workshop on the basis of their style; they are part of a suite of 12 items, including a table and chairs, belonging to a Québec City family. This furniture is inspired by Elizabethan art and is decorated with garlands and flowering rose branches, volutes and scrolls, Rococo fleur-de-lis-shaped leaves, bulbous Renaissance Revival turnings and Baroque crests with cartouches framing the head of a man or a woman carved in high relief. The walnut frames have been reupholstered. An excellent text on Gourdeau has been written by John Porter and Yves Lacasse in *Le Meuble de goût*.

586
Visiting card portrait of a child standing on a Revival-style chair, William Ellison, Québec City, ca. 1865.

587-588
Reconstruction of Revival-era interiors in the Sir-George-Étienne-Cartier house in Montréal.

This father of Canadian Confederation has received special attention in the political discourse underlying historical interpretation projects carried out by the federal government. A team of professionals working at the Québec city branch of Parks Canada produced these attractive rooms, which reflect the impact of the Revival movement on the decorative arts of Québec.

THE CONFEDERATIVE STYLE

589
Portrait of the Garneau family of Québec City by J.-Ernest Livernois, ca. 1890.
The family members are posed around a Rococo Revival sofa in the style of Vallière.

590 to 592
Upholstered medallion sofas by Québec City furniture makers. Walnut, ca. 1880.
Québec furniture in the Confederative style reflects the boundless imagination of the cabinetmakers who produced it. Each piece was treated as unique, and while rough work and joining was performed with efficient machine tools, decoration was finished by hand. The craftsmen working in the same shop must have had very lively discussions about models, compositions and sources of inspiration.

593
Revival-style decoration of a room in a beautiful house on Guénette Street, in Lévis.
Here is another example of the fine work done by certain enthusiasts who have painstakingly restored a Confederative-style Québec house and devoted themselves to recreating the spirit of an age when the decorative and furniture arts were in full flower in our country. Once again, it is individuals who preserve and safeguard this aspect of Québec's cultural history.

594 to 596
Other models of 19th-century walnut sofas in Revival styles.
Cabinetmakers made liberal use of carved decoration in floral motifs such as the rose, a symbol of England. Human figures were given all sorts of interpretations and appeared frequently in the decoration of Confederative-style furniture. Certain parts of furniture were adorned with grotesque mythological creatures, inspired by medieval art. The example shown here is the head of a chimera or lion holding a ball in its teeth, decorating the scrolled arm stumps of the sofa in the upper photograph.

597 to 599
A remarkable Rococo Revival walnut sofa. The carving is attributed to the sculptor Jean-Baptiste Côté (1832-1907) of Québec City. This unique sofa was made in 1859. A bust of Napoleon is enthroned in a cartouche in the middle of a crest constituted of plant-like forms. The crest rail, armrests, skirt and curved legs are carved with flowers, lattices and full or partial acanthus leaves. The two eagles with spread wings, symbols associated with Napoleon, reinforce this tribute to the much venerated historical figure. Judging from Québec family trees, Napoléon was a very popular given name in the 19th century.

600 to 610
Various models of Confederative-style walnut chairs. An infinite combination of motifs and models is mirrored in gentlemen's easy chairs, ladies' chairs, side chairs, hall chairs and fireside chairs, most of them with curved and cabriole legs, carved skirts and curvilinear or balloon backs.

THE CONFEDERATIVE STYLE

BEDS AND CRADLES

The Confederative-style bedroom was furnished with the same opulence and diversity as the drawing room and dining room were. Beds became very architectural, inspired by Baroque and Renaissance styles, and were given highly elaborate shapes. They were decorated with veneers and carved motifs borrowed from a variety of stylistic conventions.

611
Drawing of a pattern for a Revival-style bed from a book by Downing, a U. S. designer, 1850.

612
Revival-era cradle-in-frame with a turned, scrolled and carved base, and openwork balusters. Walnut, ca. 1880.

613
Renaissance Revival bed with arched pediments, rounded corners, finials and consoles. Walnut and figured walnut veneer, ca. 1875.
The decoration of monumental Renaissance Revival furniture often included lavish moulding that formed geometric shapes. The contrast between the fine-textured wood of the structure and the extravagant burl and crotch-grain patterns of the veneer panels produced an harmonious and soberly elegant effect.

614
Renaissance Revival bed with Baroque influences. Walnut and burl walnut veneer, ca. 1875.
The headboard is topped with superimposed semicircular arches crowned with plant-like carving. This Revival "monument" is also embellished with consoles, volutes, rounded corners and panels in a variety of shapes.

THE CONFEDERATIVE STYLE

360 REVIVAL-ERA FURNITURE IN QUÉBEC

617-618

Renaissance Revival bed manufactured by Jacques & Hay of Toronto to furnish a bedroom in the Montréal home of Sir John Rose when he received the Prince of Wales in 1860. The son of Queen Victoria had come to the colony to celebrate the 100th anniversary of the British victory on the Plains of Abraham. Curly and bird's-eye maple and basswood, 1860.

Furniture makers' advertisements and articles in newspapers, magazines and trade directories make it clear that furniture manufacturers in Québec, Ontario and the Maritimes often did business together. The English prince slept in a bed made not just of maple, the vernacular emblem of Québec, but with the finest parts of this tree, showing beautiful curly and bird's-eye figures.

619-620

Renaissance Revival half-tester bed and bedside table. Curly maple and bird's-eye maple, ca. 1870. After 1860, the previously ubiquitous tester bed fell out of favor, mainly for reasons of hygiene and comfort. The French Empire-style bed, known as a sleigh bed, with its out-curving footboard and headboard soon took the place of the old-fashioned high-poster. Beds with modified canopies continued to be used for a while, especially among the English-speaking population, but soon the open "French" bed with its relatively low headboard became the norm.

615-616

(Page 360)
A Revival-era bedroom, belonging to Mme Joseph Masson, of Montréal, in 1898.
These two photographs taken by the Notman Studio, in Montréal, show a typical master bedroom in a wealthy middle-class home of the Revival period. The room is dominated by a Renaissance Revival bed in ash and walnut. To one side of it stands a small matching bedside cabinet and on the other is a bedside table in the 19th-century Aesthetic style. The large wardrobe and chest of drawers both have mirrors and are in the same Renaissance Revival style as the bed. Each piece has an arched pediment decorated with geometrical plaques and is crowned with a spine-like crest bearing a stylized palmette.

621 to 626

Bedroom suite. Ash, Chicoutimi, ca. 1880.
The furniture made in large urban workshops for the wealthy middle class was paralleled by furniture inspired by the same dramatic style but less opulent in its construction and materials.

This vernacular furniture was characterized by its plain surfaces, ordinary wood, decorative appliqués of carved or moulded wood, and joints held together with glue and nails. Made in joiner's workshops, such furniture usually does not weather the passage of time well.

This complete bedroom suite was the work of Joseph Grenon, a joiner in the Saguenay—Lac-Saint-Jean area. The pieces are finished with stain and varnish.
The handles on the storage furniture are carved, and the chest of drawers and panelled headboard are both crowned with crests of scrolled openwork. The bed is decorated with carvings of fruit and a plunging duck, as well as a holy water basin surmounted by a cross. The bed also has rounded corners.

627 to 629

Bed and chest of drawers inspired by the Baroque Revival style. Walnut, ca. 1880. The foot of the bed presents a charmingly allegorical sculpture of two birds billing amid flowering branches. The chest of drawers with carved scrolled columns is an elegant version of the serpentine-front commode, as it is called by antique collectors. This model, with its numerous drawers, enjoyed great popularity with a broad spectrum of the population in the last third of the 19th century. The varnish on these pieces has been rejuvenated.

THE CONFEDERATIVE STYLE

630 to 634
Chests and Service Furniture

Chest in the Revival manner. Oak, Chicoutimi, 1918. This large dark oak chest, with its carvings inspired by German styles in the second half of the 19th century, bears a highly informative dedication: "To my friend Dubuc, the homage of an admirer. A. Lemieux, January 1st, 1918." [Translation] Another inscription, on the cover, reads: "J. E. A. Dubuc, Knight of St. Gregory the Great, Chicoutimi, 1904." [Translation] The chest was a commemorative piece made by a craftsman named Lemieux and offered as a sign of friendship to J. E. A. Dubuc, the well-known timber magnate from the Saguenay—Lac-Saint-Jean area, on the occasion of his admission to the Pontifical Order of St. Gregory the Great in 1903. On the side panels, the carving represents various scenes from the lumber camps — a lumber jack at rest, smoking his pipe; teams of horses drawing sleighs loaded with logs; jovial men enjoying a meal inside a round-log camp; and Midnight Mass in the village. The scenes are framed with bands of classical motifs. This piece is an example of how functional folk-art furniture in a specific stylistic trend could be used to commemorate and honor an event. In the Belle Époque, chests were still popular with certain segments of society. They were usually made in their simplest form.

364   REVIVAL-ERA FURNITURE IN QUÉBEC

635 to 638
Revival styles affected every article of furniture and, during this period, new items were introduced.

635
Whatnot decorated with openwork trim and turned spindles. Walnut, ca. 1875.

636
Rococo Revival tapestry screen. Walnut, Québec City, ca. 1870.

637
Renaissance Revival hall tree. Walnut, Québec City, ca. 1875.

638
Renaissance Revival prie-dieu, decorated with an angel's head and crowned with a niche for a statue. Walnut, Québec City, ca. 1880.

THE CONFEDERATIVE STYLE

DRESSERS AND CHESTS OF DRAWERS

The Revival-era bedroom suite had a bed of course, but also included a chest of drawers, one or more bedside tables and a type of dresser with a mirror, that one used standing up. These pieces were made in the same style and with the same materials as the bed and matched its decoration. However, such articles could also be purchased separately.

639 to 644
Revival-era dressers and chests of drawers — most with their own fixed or swing-frame mirror — inspired by Baroque Revival and Renaissance Revival styles, as well as the return of Neoclassicism. Drop handles, knobs and moulded or carved handles. Walnut, ash, maple and basswood; between 1870 and 1885.

645-646
Chest of drawers in a combination of Baroque Revival and Neoclassical styles, with a swing-frame mirror, stiles adorned with elegant scrolls, rectilinear base and carved decoration. Walnut, ca. 1860.
This piece belongs to the suite seen in the inset photograph, which is presented in a larger format on page 335.

THE CONFEDERATIVE STYLE 367

647
Chest of drawers with an arched and scrolled backboard and five drawers. The column-shaped stiles are decorated with phytomorphic carving and the central arch of the backboard is topped with a double scroll that forms a shell-like ornament. The drawers have carved handles and are trimmed with cock-beading. Oak, walnut and yellow birch, ca. 1875.

648
Revival-era bedroom furniture: a bed with French-inspired turned posts, a dresser-wardrobe decorated with Gothic Revival panels, and a Sheraton display case. These pieces are housed in the interior of the 18th-century Mauvide-Genest manor in Saint-Jean, Île d'Orléans. This photograph recreates the atmosphere of the period and illustrates how a variety of styles might be found in the same room at a given time.

REVIVAL-ERA WARDROBES AND CUPBOARDS

Bourgeois homes in the Revival period contained various pieces of storage furniture, some of which continued to convey the functional and aesthetic values of the previous era. Bookcases with glass doors were fairly common, as were wardrobes, which were sometimes two-tiered. This massive furniture was in keeping with the grandeur of the vast rooms in the most sumptuous residences, where three-metre-high ceilings were not uncommon.

Storage pieces were frequently Neoclassical in their general lines, but they were decorated with Revival elements borrowed from the Baroque and the French or English Renaissance styles. Some of the more monumental of these articles are found today in the venerable religious institutions to which they were donated during the period when fine bourgeois houses built in the second half of the 19th century were demolished or renovated in Montréal and Québec City.

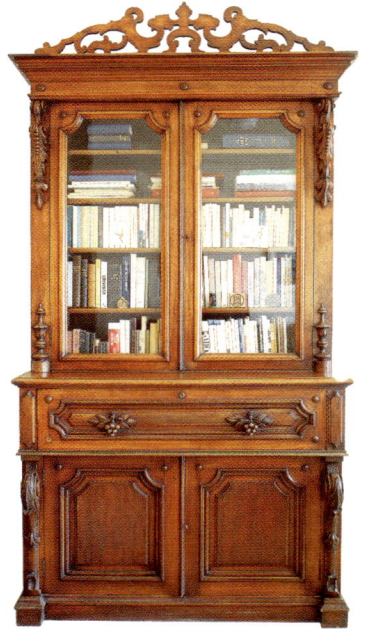

649 to 654
Revival-era bookcase, wardrobes and cupboards in Renaissance Revival and Rococo Revival styles. Walnut with curly maple, mahogany and walnut veneer, Québec City, ca. 1875.
The wardrobe in curly maple and bird's-eye maple (near left) is crowned with the three-feather emblem of the Prince of Wales. It was made by the Toronto company, Jacques & Hay, for the bedroom used by the son of Queen Victoria during his visit to Montréal in 1860.

THE CONFEDERATIVE STYLE 371

THE CONFEDERATIVE-STYLE SIDEBOARD

The dining room in a great bourgeois house in the last third of the 19th century always had a massive sideboard, with a back quite as elaborate as the headboard of any fashionable bed. The sideboard held a place of honor in the room that was the scene of much convivial socializing. Shelves displayed Revival-style tinted crystal lamps, while candlesticks and elegant silver and glass articles were placed on the top. The sideboard held the fancy tableware that was set out on fine linen, but also created an opulent backdrop for elegant diner parties.

655
Renaissance Revival dining room sideboard, Papineau manor, Montebello, ca. 1880. Photograph by J. G. Parks.

656
Pencil template drawing of a still life of fish inspired by a French model illustrated in the Parisian publication, *Le Garde-meuble*, in about 1855 and used by the workshop of Pierre Drouin or Honoré Roy, in Québec City. The paper is perforated with little needle holes along the outlines of the fish, indicating that it served as a marking template.

657
Renaissance Revival sideboard with a brace of partridge on its backboard's central panel, a broken pediment crowned by a fruit-bowl finial and flanked by fruit-like crockets, concave-cornered panels with disks and scrolls, and carved handles in fruit shapes. Walnut and figured walnut, Lévis, ca. 1880.

658
Strongly architectural Renaissance Revival sideboard. Walnut, figured walnut and maple, Québec City, ca. 1880.
The arched pediments are crowned with palmette finials, and the highest one ends with ears on either side. A brace of game birds decorates the central panel with its Mannerist pediment and volutes. The three drawers are fitted with brass drop handles. The concave-cornered panels on the doors have plaques shaped with Baroque pediments above a plinth base. This piece is flanked by side chairs in the Hepplewhite style.

THE CONFEDERATIVE STYLE

659 to 662
Renaissance Revival sideboard and details. Walnut, Lévis, ca. 1870.
This sideboard is crowned with a Baroque-inspired pediment carved with a hunting scene. Both levels of the piece are decorated with acanthus leaves, scrolls and panels carved with game birds and fish. Such sideboards, whose decoration was inspired by the country's abundant wildlife, became very popular between 1860 and 1880.

THE FURNITURE MAKER

Mr. Drum's Factory
[As described in 1873]

The largest of the furniture factories in Québec and even in Canada is that of Mr. William Drum, on Saint-Paul Street.

It is an immense four-storey building, with a surface area of 15 000 square feet, constructed on a quay that extends into the Saint-Charles River, with a landing stage on one side. Behind the main building lies the steam engine that supplies motor power to nearly one hundred brand new machines of all sorts. This machinery cuts, splits, turns, planes, polishes, mortises and pierces wood, as well as making tenons; in short, it prepares every element used to make a piece of furniture.

All this equipment is operated by the 100-horsepower steam engine. It was constructed by Mr. McDougall of Montréal and integrates the many improvements made to steam engines over the past few years. The boilers were built by Mr. Neil, of Palace Street, with specially imported iron.

Mr. Drum is one of the founders and benefactors of Québec industry. Starting out as a simple craftsman, he was constantly propelled by his energy and aptitude for business to further advancement. He has never ceased to expand the establishment that he opened on his own in 1832 with four workmen; today he employs almost two hundred workers, who earn an average of one dollar per day.

It goes without saying that Mr. Drum produces furniture of every description, from the most luxurious to the least expensive. With the exception of black walnut furniture, which is sold less dearly in Upper Canada, especially in Oshawa, Mr. Drum's production is sold at prices that defy competition. He controls and supplies the market in the Maritime provinces and sells the greater part of his furniture in St. John's, New Brunswick, and in Halifax. The rest is shipped to Montréal or to the Eastern Townships.

To give some idea of the establishment's operations, it suffices to say that around a thousand chairs can be produced there every week.

Furthermore, we have rarely seen such a well-organized factory. The first floor houses the saws and other instruments for shaping the wood, which comes in from the riverside entrance. The process begins with a big circular saw, five feet in diameter, that can handle 50-foot-long timber.

This is where the wood is prepared and turned into plank timber for use in the factory. A great deal of wood is also sawed for ship building. Leaving the sawmill area, the timber is shaped and passed through various machines before being transferred to the next floor up.

Mr. Drum is the very model of a benevolent employer who looks after his workers. Some of his employees have worked with him as apprentices or journeymen, and he treats them as brothers. His sons, who help him run the business, are equally kind and good men. Like their worthy father, they never allow harsh words, bitter criticism or reprimands to be addressed to their employees. They therefore keep their workers forever. The employees are so well treated that they are as interested in the concern as they would be if they owned it themselves.

The different buildings that compose Mr. Drum's factory form a complex of about 150 feet by 50 feet with three floors. The factory sits on a quay extending into the Saint-Charles River. The quay and buildings together are worth at least $20 000, which brings the total value of the factory property to nearly $100 000.

Apart from the factory where wood is prepared, Mr. Drum also has kept his old workshop at 193 Saint-Paul Street, facing the market, as a store and paint room. It is an immense three-storey building measuring 80 feet by 40 feet. He has his business office and sample room there as well.

Well-informed sources say that Mr. Drum's business makes $200 000 annually. It would not take many such establishments to earn Québec City an important place in the manufacturing world.

A. Frechette, in *Annuaire du commerce et de l'industrie de Québec*, Québec City, 1873

663 to 666
Renaissance Revival sideboard and details. Walnut and ash, Québec City, ca. 1870.
No two sideboards in this style ever had exactly the same shape and decoration. Although otherwise relatively simple, they are imaginatively carved with all sorts of animals, plants and human figures: swags of fruit and vegetables, braces of game birds and fish representing regional wildlife, foliated scrolls, grape-vine branches, boughs or bouquets of flowers, shells, interlacing leaves and heads of women (Columbia).

667 to 671

Renaissance Revival sideboard and details. Walnut and ash, Québec City, 1870.
Many of these pieces have elaborately carved cresting with openwork plant motifs. They were often fitted with bevelled mirrors that reflected the Revival-era cut-glass and silver-plate articles displayed on the top.

THE CONFEDERATIVE STYLE

672 to 678

Three Renaissance Revival sideboards with Baroque-influenced touches (details on page 379). Walnut, ash, basswood and pine; between 1860 and 1880. These strongly architectural pieces, each with its own distinctive shape and Naturalistic decoration, are small masterpieces of Québec cabinetmaking. The Revival furniture made in Québec displays as much originality and imagination as any that evolved elsewhere in the second half of the 19th century. The carving on these pieces reflects an important development — sculptors had begun to apply their art to secular objects rather than devoting it exclusively to churches, as had been the case for the past two centuries. The furniture decoration that resulted, inspired by the land's natural resources, is not confined to a single stylistic canon.

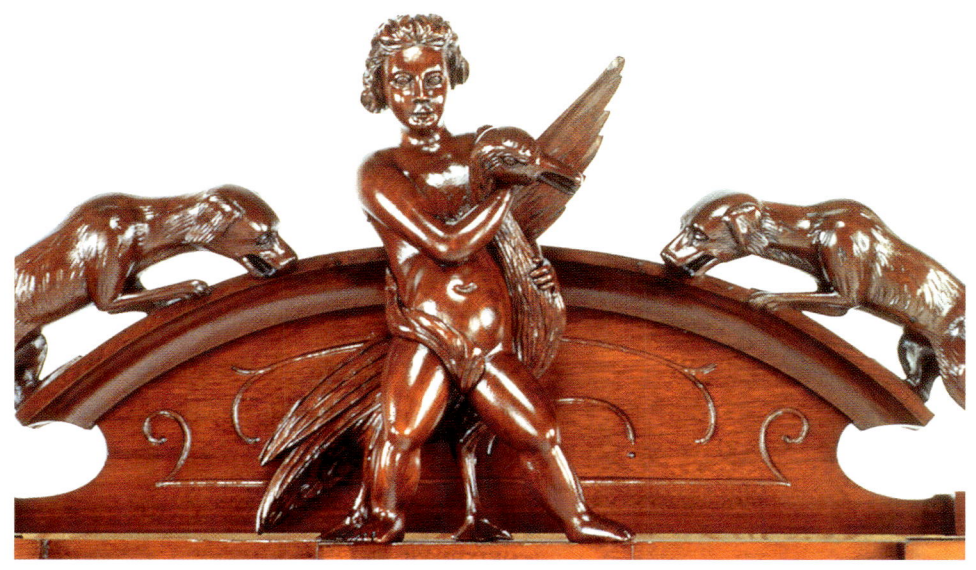

THE CONFEDERATIVE STYLE

NEOCLASSICAL SIDEBOARDS

While certain households favored massive walnut sideboards decorated with Naturalistic motifs, many others preferred a more Neoclassical style for their dining rooms and opted for elegant sideboards with somewhat sober lines, inspired by the previous era. Sideboards of the latter type appear in notarial inventories from the 1820s.

679
Sideboard combining Neoclassical and Revival styles. Papineau manor, Montebello, ca. 1880. Photograph by J. G. Parks of Montréal.

680
Baroque Revival davenport. Walnut, ca. 1875.
The word davenport was at first used for a small slant-top desk with a series of drawers on one side. This one is embellished with large foliated consoles and a semicircular arched panel. The drawer handles are of carved wood.

681
Baroque Revival sideboard. Walnut and mahogany, ca. 1870.
In general, Neoclassical sideboards had two or three doors with drawers above and backboards with relatively simple decoration. A certain variety of models was offered by Québec cabinetmakers and import retailers.

682
Sideboard reflecting the transition between the Constitutional and Confederative styles in Québec. Walnut and mahogany, ca. 1850.
An exceptional piece, with multifoil arched panels, three projecting drawers with a cyma-curve profile, supported by two columns, and a backboard whose central rectangle is flanked by two elongated foliated consoles.

TABLES

Every type of table used in the dining room or bedroom was affected by the Revival fashions of the Confederative period. Drawing room tables, console tables, gaming tables, light serving tables and dining room tables were made in Baroque or Rococo Revival styles, often with Louis XV touches displayed in their cabriole legs and generous decoration. Gracefulness took precedence over solidity in this furniture, which often had fragile joints.

683
Studio portrait of Henry Empey of Montréal, Notman Studio, 1865. Portrait photographers always liked to pose their subjects with the latest fashions in furniture. When photographs first began to be used on visiting cards, the Rococo Revival mode was in style, as is shown by the table and chair in this setting.

684
Drawing made by the Parks Canada restoration service of an old Rococo Revival table attributed to Honoré Roy *dit* Belleau, a Québec City cabinetmaker, ca. 1860.

685
Rococo Revival table. Walnut and mahogany, Québec City, ca. 1855. Elegantly carved *rocaille*-style cyma curves and scrolls lend movement to the lines of this table's skirt, cabriole legs and serpentine X-stretcher with a finial.

686
Rococo Revival gaming table. Mahogany and walnut, ca. 1860. Plant-inspired motifs adorn the knees and feet of the cabriole legs; the serpentine X-stretcher is topped with a finial on a plinth. The skirt is decorated with incised hatching and has a central medallion carved with fruit and leaves. Québec furniture makers' workshops produced such pieces in a wide range of models.

687
Dining room in Louis-Joseph Papineau's seigneurial manor, ca. 1880. Photograph by J. G. Parks.
The meeting of two periods is reflected in this interior, its furnishings blending the Québec Constitutional and Confederative styles. The sideboard, table, chairs and interior decoration show a mixture of the two aesthetic worlds respectively associated with these periods.

688-689
Rococo Revival gaming tables. Mahogany and walnut, Québec City, ca. 1860.
These pieces, with their curvilinear tabletops, skirts, legs and X-stretchers, are generously decorated with sculpted birds, bunches of fruit and ram's heads. The great variety of motifs used by cabinetmakers in Québec City and Montréal attest to these craftsmen's boundless imagination when it came to embellishing their work.

690
Rococo Revival dining room suite in the Château Bellevue, Cap-Tourmente. Walnut and mahogany, Québec City, ca. 1860.
It is hard to imagine monumental furniture such as this anywhere else but in the great formal rooms of bourgeois homes. Many such exceptional pieces made in the workshops of Montréal or Québec City were donated to religious institutions and are found today in their buildings.

384 REVIVAL-ERA FURNITURE IN QUÉBEC

CAST-IRON FURNITURE

The first ironworks in Québec were developed at the Forges de Saint-Maurice in the first half of the 18th century. A wide range of stoves in the Neoclassical style were soon being produced by this enterprise and a number of others also in the Trois-Rivières area. The Pierre-Boucher museum in Trois-Rivières has a bed in the Louis XIII manner, made entirely of cast iron, with slim baluster-shaped posts. The metal is stamped with the date 1799. Both this museum and the Québec City branch of Parks Canada own other cast-iron beds in the extravagant Rococo Revival style, similar to those offered by certain U.S. foundries in the mid-19th century. It is tantalizing to think that Revival-era beds of this type could have been produced by foundries in the Saint-Maurice area too, but none have come to light so far.

691
Line engraving of a cast-iron lawn settee with a grape-vine motif produced by the Clendinneng & Son foundry in Montréal and offered in their 1894 catalogue. Québec foundries sold a wide range of Revival-style garden furniture with flamboyant ornamentation.

692
Illustration of cast-iron beds in an 1857 catalogue put out by the Wickensham foundry in New York. Examples of quite similar beds are occasionally found in the St. Lawrence Valley.

Garden furniture has existed ever since people began to landscape their surroundings. Such furniture has been discovered by archaeologists at Herculanum and Pompei. During the French Regime in Québec, it is quite possible that gardens belonging to institutions and influential families had chairs, benches and armchairs in Louis XIII or Louis XV styles so that people could sit out in the sunshine and enjoy the fresh air, admire fine views and smell the flowers. Old French furniture treatises present models for furniture of this type. In the 19th century, creating a garden was a fashionable pastime for the wealthy middle class. The Picturesque villa was not complete without its conservatory and gardens. Foundries in Britain, the United States and Québec offered excellent cast-iron pieces in Gothic Revival and Rococo Revival styles, heavily ornamented with plant and animal motifs. Examples are found in the 1894 catalogue put out by William Clendinneng's foundry in Montréal.

After 1860, garden furniture made of bent branches nailed together became so popular that several photographers used tables and chairs of this type as fashionable props in their studio portraits.

Québec has a rich history of garden furniture, whose styles in each period reflect the values of the great movements and the interaction of cultural influences.

REVIVAL-ERA GARDEN FURNITURE

693
Rococo Revival cast-iron bed. Original green color, ca. 1860.
A very rare model in metal, with interlacing, scrolls, foliated scrolls and lion's-paw feet; the head and foot are both shaped to resemble the stylized outline of two chimeras joined with a fleur-de-lis at their wing tips. A similar bed has been found in the Trois-Rivières area, along with other examples consisting entirely of intricately twisting plant forms.

694
Portrait of Willy Tempest of Montréal in 1963 by the Notman Studio. The props include a twig chair, which was the latest fashion at the time.

695
Rustic twig chair, late 19th century.
Between 1860 and 1890, twig garden furniture was very popular.

696
(Pages 388-389)
The garden at George Hague's 25 Redpath Street residence in Montréal was an island of calm, where at tea time one was comfortably seated in a twig chair or on a solid lawn settee made by a cabinetmaker. Notman Studio, 1895.

THE Confederative STYLE

THE LOUIS-BERTRAND HOUSE AT L'ISLE-VERTE

A Lingering Fragrance of the 19th Century

Certain houses seem to exist in a timeless world. As if by magic, their original nobility remains unscathed by changing eras. They seem filled with a spirit of remembrance that clings tenaciously to them like perfume.

For a person who loves old houses, there is nothing quite like stepping into a historic building that has been scarcely touched by the passage of time. One is suddenly plunged into an environment where the past lives on in period furniture arrangements, colours, wallpaper and the many accessories used in everyday life. At such special moments, the mysteries of the past beckon to the lucky visitor, who feels almost overwhelmed by the historical reality captured by the imagination and the senses. Such a moving experience is to be found in the Louis-Bertrand house, which stands in the middle of the village of L'Isle-Verte, to the east of Rivière-du-Loup and Cacouna. The house is like a time capsule, full of delights for the eyes and richly rewarding for anyone with a thirst for knowledge — an unforgettable place.

A Notable's Residence

Louis Bertrand (1779-1871) belonged to the French-speaking rural bourgeoisie of the 19th century. Born in Cap-Santé, in Portneuf county, this merchant settled in L'Isle-Verte in 1811, at the age of 32. Five years later, he married Appoline Saindon, with whom he had eight children. From 1819 to 1849, he leased the L'Isle-Verte seigneury and, a few years before the abolition of the seigneurial regime in 1854, he obtained title to a considerable amount of it. Bertrand made most of his money running a general store and post office set up in his residence in 1831, but he also did very well financially with his sawmill. He was associated at this time with William Price and

697
The monumental entrance to the Louis-Bertrand house at L'Isle-Verte.
A flight of stairs leads invitingly to the Neoclassical portal and into the vestibule, illuminated by the door's transom window and sidelights. A journey through time is about to begin…

698
Upholstered fireside chair with cabriole legs. Original fabric, walnut and yellow birch, ca.1865. The Louis-Bertrand house is full of old furniture from the Neoclassical, Revival and Pre-Modern periods.

699
The Louis-Bertrand house is a monument to the Québec Constitutional style, which expressed the Neoclassical values of the time. The living quarters stand well above the ground and are surrounded by a wide verandah. The windows, door, functional elements and even the layout are all arranged symmetrically. The elegant family home is crowned with a bell-cast roof that deeply overhangs the front and back walls. See page 23 for an old photograph of the house.

700-701
Inside, the house is laid out symmetrically on either side of an entry hall with its stairs leading to the two upper floors. In the drawing room a painted portrait of the lady of the house hangs from the wall moulding between two doors on the north side and facing it between two sunny windows on the south side is a portrait of the master of the house. Beneath each picture are balloon-back chairs and a gaming table with a turned base. The colors, drapes and carpets all date to the Revival period, when the house was young.

Henry Caldwel, wood barons making huge fortunes out of the colony's timber resources, for which Great Britain had an avid need.

Louis Bertrand always combined public service with his professional life. A year after settling at L'Isle-Verte, he became chief of the militia, a position that he continued to occupy for a long time. Then, from 1832 to 1848, he served as the National Assembly member for Rimouski and supported the cause of Louis-Joseph Papineau's patriots, going so far as to sign the Ninety-two Resolutions in 1834, just before the historic uprising.

Louis Bertrand played a determining role in the socio-economic development of eastern Québec. He was succeeded by his son, Charles-Frédéric-Adolphe (1824-1896), who, as well as continuing to run the general store and post office, expanded the family business by purchasing other sawmills. In 1865, he acquired a foundry that was famous for its farm implements and stoves. The Bertrand family brought an astonishing cultural life to the village, founding a literary society in 1859. Unfortunately, however, at the very end of the 19th century, financial problems brought an end to the activities of this prolific family, whose authority and leadership had been felt for nearly a century.

The house that now bears his name was built by Louis Bertrand in 1853 on the ruins of his second home, which had burned down. After he died, three more generations lived there: Louis-Achille as of 1880; Aimée, who was married to Charles Eugène Michaud, from 1914 to 1938; and Fathers Robert and Pierre Michaud from 1938 on. An aura of timelessness envelops this heritage home; it is a true museum, as absolutely authentic as anything one could dream of finding.

A Museum-Home

The Louis-Bertrand house is one of several gracious bourgeois residences in the Québec City area and in the counties and seigneuries to the southeast — Bellechasse, Montmagny, L'Islet, Kamouraska and Rivière-du-Loup. These elegant homes contrast with most rural architecture, having more in common with large presbyteries or seigneurial manors. Generally built of wood in the 1840-1870 period, they were all designed in the Neoclassical style, which marked the architecture of the St. Lawrence Valley from the beginning of the 18th century. Examples of such houses, built by notables to meet their domestic, commercial, administrative and professional needs, include the Jean-Charles-Chapais house in Saint-Denis, Kamouraska (built in 1833 and renovated in 1866), the Sifroy-Guéret-*dit*-Dumont house in Saint-André, Kamouraska (1840), the Amable-Morin house in Saint-Roch-des-Aulnaies (ca. 1840) and the Amable-Gosselin house in Saint-Laurent on Île d'Orléans (1852).

The Louis-Bertrand house sits on the north side of the village's main street, a stone's throw from the parish church. It is a large, graceful building, with a sloping roof overhanging wide verandahs in front and back. An unpretentious, Neoclassical portal with Gothic Revival touches is surrounded by numerous, symmetrically organized windows. The rhythm of these openings is continued on the side walls and back wall of the house. Paired chimneys crown the roof. The combination of these many details and the balance between functional and aesthetic elements show an amalgamation of French heritage, British influences and U.S modes. The Neoclassical effect is accentuated by the plaster that was applied to the wood-panel exterior and made to look like ashlar, with quoins at the corners. To make the trompe-l'oeil stonework more realistic, the plaster was skilfully covered with a coat of grey paint thickened with sand. Between 1830 and 1880, this was a customary finish for luxury homes and monumental buildings; the Papineau house in Montréal is another good example.

702-703
The very scent of the Revival period seems to permeate the Louis-Bertrand house. Some pieces of furniture have never been repainted. An example is this built-in cupboard on the ground floor, near the kitchen and family dining room, still full of dishes and tableware from the Confederative era.

With its many windows, wide covered verandah, shutters and summer-villa look, the Louis-Bertrand house is a splendid representative of the Picturesque style, a happy blend of architecture and nature. In its shape and layout, the building presents all the characteristics that define the vernacular Québec house, which gained immense popularity with every level of society throughout the first half of the 19th century. While the ground floor was used by middle-class owners as business space, kitchens and servants' quarters, it could also serve as a workshop for craftsmen and as a summer kitchen and root cellar for farmers. Such storage space was especially needed now that farmers had begun to market their vegetables, particularly potatoes, which became a basic food.

Stylistically, the vernacular house borrowed characteristics from both the Neoclassical and Revival fashions of the time. It was well adapted to the seasonal extremes of summer and winter. Depending on its size and layout, it could meet the special needs of various social classes. Such cultural, geographical and sociological qualities underlie the interest accorded to this consummate architecture, which ceased to evolve after 1860, having matured into a state of formal and functional perfection. Such a house is often represented in the winter scenes painted by artists like Cornelius Krieghoff and Clarence Gagnon. A

704
A tiny dark attic holds beds, toys, children's sleds, portable stoves for cold weather and a thousand other curiosities that tell the story of a family that left its mark on this eastern region, which is less well known than the neighboring resort areas of Kamouraska and Rivière-du-Loup counties.

705
(Pages 394-395)
A square piano has a place of honor in the drawing room. The Bertrand family played an influential role in the cultural life of L'Isle-Verte in the Confederative period. They held a "salon," as it was called then, and formed a very active village literary society with its own legal charter.

Interior Decoration with a History

The interior of the Louis-Bertrand house, which faces south for practical reasons, is organized symmetrically around a central axis in the manner of the Roman and Italian Renaissance villas inspiring the tradition that came to influence British domestic architecture in the 18th and 19th centuries. The ground floor has four solid doors and male servants' quarters. The second floor, which is bright and built well off the ground, is incontestably the "noble" floor of the house. On either side of a vestibule with a central staircase, there is a vast room: on one side, a drawing room full of Victorian splendor, with a 3.5-metre-high ceiling, and on the other, a dining room that was later converted into a living room. In back, the northern side is occupied by mouldings and colors to the 19th-century curtains, wallpaper and carpets and from the furniture and decorations to the accessories and articles used at home every day. Anyone who is curious enough to peek into chests of drawers and the many closets (a novelty at the time) or cannot resist opening cupboard doors and poking about the attic is rewarded with

further delights that add even more pleasure to this memorable journey through time.

The furniture in the Louis-Bertrand house is partly in the Neoclassical style, as is the interior finishing, and partly in Revival styles. The work of local or regional joiners mingles with that of professional cabinetmakers. The furniture in the drawing room mirrors mid-19th-century fashion, showing the strong historic references of Baroque Revival and Rococo Revival styles. Certain bedrooms are furnished in the Renaissance Revival style. In contrast, other bedrooms as well as the library and living room on the third floor are clearly influenced by the British Neoclassical mode and borrow from Late Georgian and Regency styles, to use terms based on European eras. The photographs of the house, taken with the gracious permission and generous co-operation of the Michaud family, speak for themselves.

710
A corner of the main drawing room, opening onto the guest room. In the Revival period, interior decorating meant walls covered with paintings, chromolithographs and various commemorative elements, which were hung from wall mouldings. Whatnots and small tables displayed all kinds of bric-a-brac and dozens of studio portraits of family members in highly decorative frames. Such pictures might also be organized in thick leather- or velour-bound albums, which sometimes had their own lecterns. It was a time of nostalgia and romanticism.

711
On an upper floor, a chest of drawers with scrolled columns stands between two doors with their original paint. The pine floor, also with its original finish, is covered by a rug woven locally in the Confederative period. The chest of drawers is made of ash, pine and walnut, with carved handles on its eight drawers and a shaped base. A few everyday accessories and mementoes are placed on top.

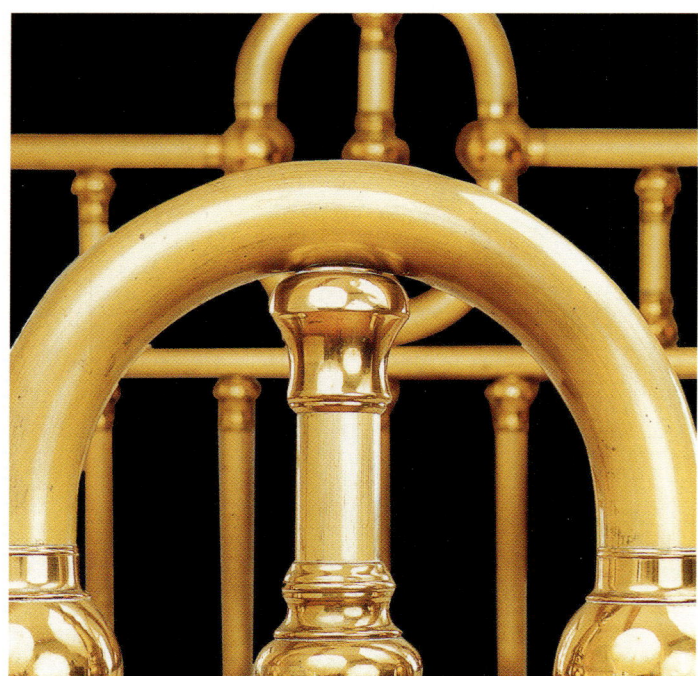

712 to 715
Details of furniture influenced by the ideas of Pre-Modern reformers, ca. 1895. Thonet bentwood chair; back splat of a chair steam-embossed with the effigy of Sir Wilfred Laurier; door on a Mission sideboard; the tubular patterns of a brass bedstead.

CHAPTER 5

*Between Historicism
and Industrial Functionalism*

Pre-Modern Furniture in Québec

1890-1920
INDUSTRY AND REFORM

Over all the furnishings the dust holds sway,
The Venetian mirrors have shed their charm;
There lingers still, like old Parmese perfume,
The bitter sweetness of a long-known sachet.

And never more across the silence flow
Piano tunes in a rhythmic lullaby;
Mozart and Mendelssohn, wed in sweet harmony,
Are but heard in dreams in sleepy evening's glow.

But the poet, wandering in gross ennui,
Opening windows to the night's clear force,
Alone, fists clenched, and with the wildest glance

Suddenly imagines, haunted by remorse,
A solemn great ball, evolved from fantasy,
Where he thought he saw his dead parents dance.

ÉMILE NELLIGAN,
Montréal, ca. 1899
[Translation of *"Le Salon"*
by Fred Cogswell in
*The Complete Poems
of Émile Nelligan*]

Arts and Crafts clock,
ca. 1900.

Pre-Modern Furniture in Québec

Between the Revival period and the Modern era there came a time of transition in which all sorts of new principles were developed in aesthetics, sociology, techniques and trade. These principles would strongly affect the decorative arts and furniture production in the 20th century. Imaginative ideas were put forward by reformers like William Morris, George Eastlake and William Godwin in Britain, Victor Horta in Belgium and Émile Gallé in France. Their ideas were adapted to a North American context by Gustav Stickley, who took certain Arts & Crafts values and, combining them with a new approach to creating and marketing furniture, became the most influential designer of Mission furniture in the United States. These men were just a few of the many great designers — briefly presented in the first chapter of this book — who influenced different movements at the end of the 19th century. During this transition period, furniture in Québec followed the same trends that predominated in neighboring Ontario and the United States. It was a time of unprecedented inventiveness. New materials and techniques, some of which had been timidly experimented with in the preceding period, were now used to design furniture and mass-produce it. Previously unimaginable styles developed out of materials such as bentwood, oak, brass and iron. These styles were promoted in an extremely well-orchestrated way, mainly through widely-distributed sales catalogues that reached consumers even in the furthest corners of the continent and kept them up to date with the latest developments. Québec, fascinated with U.S. fashions, marketing and ways of doing things, enthusiastically entered the age of merchandising.

716
Living room in the summer home of Senator Rodolphe Forget at Saint-Irénée-des-Bains in the Charlevoix region. Photograph by Quéry Frères, Montréal, 1906. The interior of this recently-built house was decorated in the cluttered style of the Revival era. Nevertheless, individual pieces of furniture reflect Pre-Modern trends embodied by the Mission and Arts & Crafts styles and the fashion for wicker.

PRE-MODERN TASTES 1890-1920

The sales catalogues that circulated in Québec during the Belle Époque provide a good idea of the type of vernacular furniture that was available on the market. Manufacturers, wholesalers and retailers used catalogues to present furniture that reflected the reform movements in the decorative arts. The new ideas presented by people like Morris, Eastlake, Godwin, Stickley and Thonet led to the appearance of simple, unadorned furniture. The furniture industry also vaunted the advantages of plain oak furniture, as well as brass, iron and wicker furniture in all kinds of innovative styles.

PRE-MODERN STYLES IN QUÉBEC 1890-1920

WILLIAM MORRIS
1834-1896

HECTOR GUIMARD
1867-1942

SOURCES: English reformers William Morris, Charles Eastlake and William Godwin, initiators of Art Nouveau Victor Horta and Émile Gallé, U.S. manufacturer Gustav Stickley and the Grand Rapids businesses in Michigan, bentwood specialist Michael Thonet and numerous innovators in the North American metal- and wicker-furniture industry.
WOOD AND MATERIALS:
handcrafted furniture: pine and butternut
industrial furniture: oak, white ash (Ontario), elm, basswood and white birch, wicker
metal: brass and iron bars and iron tubing

Eastlake sofa, Québec City, 1885

COLLECTIONS: Museums and religious institutions
AUTHOR'S NOTE: At the turn of the millennium, this facet of the decorative arts in Québec is poorly represented in the public collections of regional and national institutions. Pre-Modern furniture in Québec has been ignored by such institutions.

THE INFLUENCE OF THE REFORMERS ON QUÉBEC FURNITURE

Arts & Crafts and Mission (1900-1930)

The 1904 spring-summer mail-order catalogue distributed by the department store belonging to Zéphirin Paquet (1818-1905) presented five models of solid oak Morris chairs, some of which were described in the accompanying texts as being richly carved. The 1901 edition of Eaton's illustrated catalogue, distributed from Toronto throughout much of Québec, offered four variants of this chair. In fact, the furniture for drawing rooms, living rooms, dining rooms and bedrooms presented in the sales catalogues circulated by both general retailers and furniture businesses from the end of the 19th century to the early 1930s normally included items whose functionality and somewhat austere lines reflected the influence of the Englishman William Morris. Numerous U.S. firms began to make this type of furniture in an even more sober form, which became known as the Mission style. The name was given to the style because its supporters, notably Gustav Stickley and the Roycroft Community, devoted themselves to promoting an essentially functional design, bare of superfluous ornamentation, and this pursuit was considered to be a true mission. The movement was most definitely a precursor of the Functionalist theories that would be advanced a few decades later.

The principles of the Arts & Crafts movement, born in 19th-century Britain, reached the shores of North America between 1895 and 1900. The new artistic movement had a marked influence on the St. Lawrence Valley at the beginning of the 20th century. This is evident from a series of photographs taken in 1906 by the Quéry brothers to document the elegant shingle-style villa built the previous year by Sir Rodolphe Forget as a summer home at Saint-Irénée-des-Bains in the Charlevoix region. The drawing room and living room were furnished mainly in the Arts & Crafts style, although a good deal of wicker furniture was also used.

The name Arts & Crafts refers to a move-

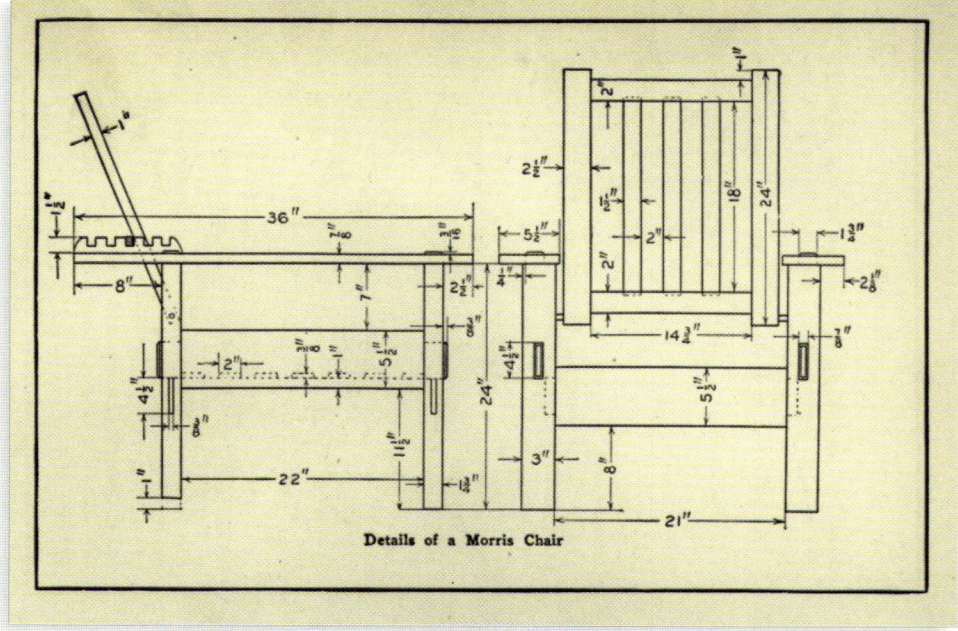

Details of a Morris Chair

ment in the decorative arts that began in Britain in the second half of the 19th century. It grew mainly out of the theories and ideas of John Ruskin, the art historian, and was given form above all by William Morris and his associates. The school's adherents idealized the creative processes of the Middle Ages and the objects produced by the trade guilds of this period. They embraced the idea that furniture should be handmade, constructed out of local materials and based on simple, sturdy designs. At the same time that France was seeking modernity in the flowing, nature-inspired curves and swirls of Art Nouveau (mockingly called *style nouille*, or "noodle style"), the Anglo-Saxon world turned to a functional, geometrically austere design. Although sinuous lines appeared in certain fields, applications and movements, these never caught on as the Arts & Crafts style did. This movement might be said to have formed a link between the "minor arts" of the 19th century and the designs of the next era.

Initially, the Arts & Crafts movement was neither a new approach to forms and decoration nor a stage in the sequence of styles. It was rather the artistic expression of an ideological ground swell of protest in reaction to the tremendous changes that marked Britain as it developed from an agricultural society into an industrial one. According to Ruskin and Morris, factories and machine tools were responsible for a host of social evils, with whole segments of the population, including children, cooped up for long hours. Families fell apart as people were obliged to work far from home, employees were forced to accept often degrading conditions of work and communities degenerated, their members suffering increasingly from disease and poverty. Furthermore, industrialization made people unhappy because they became mere cogs in the manufacturing process, with none of the satisfaction that comes from seeing the end product of one's work. The concern for human dignity felt by England's social reformers was matched by a belief in the importance of aesthetics. The artistic formulas and architectural orders of classicism were to be rejected, as was the ever-popular showiness of Victorian eclecticism, because these fashions were considered to be artificial, lacking veracity and limiting creativity. The reformers also thought that products should be made by the person who designed them and, insofar as it was possible, constructed of natural local materials. They called for homes that would be designed and fitted out according to true

717
Scale drawing of a Morris chair presented in a 1910 Popular Mechanics publication intended for non-specialists.
Mission furniture was so simple, both stylistically and technically, that people were encouraged to make it for themselves. In spreading this style, the furniture industry faced serious competition from a considerable number of ordinary handymen and local joiners.

718
Morris chair. Fumed quarter-sawed oak and leather, Lévis, ca. 1895.
This piece, with its trefoil arches and quatrefoil motifs borrowed from the Gothic vocabulary, gives true expression to the Arts & Crafts style, which favored the use of decorative motifs from the medieval period. This chair was used in the presbytery of Saint-David-de-l'Auberivière, a parish which now belongs to Lévis. The hinged back can be adjusted with a chain that may be attached at various lengths to a hook.

THE PRE-MODERN PERIOD 1890-1920

By the end of the 19th century, both designers and the public had grown weary of historic allusions in architecture and the decorative arts. Inspired by the possibilities opened up by mass-production and machine tools, a few reform-minded ideologists proposed that interior decoration and furniture should be simplified and given lighter forms. Part of this innovative movement heralding the Modern era found expression in new materials, such as iron, wicker and brass.

Silver-plate butter dish labelled "Mériden," in the English Aesthetic style, Montréal, ca. 1880.

Art Nouveau electric lamp, brass, Québec City, ca. 1900.

Men's winter fashions in a catalogue put out by Simpson's of Toronto, 1914.

Fancy oil lamp, Trois-Rivières, ca. 1900.

Belle Époque evening wrap, Montréal, ca. 1915.

Cylinder phonograph, ca. 1895.

PERSONAL ACCOUNT

A Passion for the Arts & Crafts Style

I have lived in Québec City for the past 23 years. I work there as an economist in the civil service. Soon after I arrived in the city, I had to find furniture, just as anyone else would. One weekend, quite by chance at a flea market, I came across an armchair and a rocker whose simple lines and solidity struck me at once. My friends admired my new purchases so much that I decided to do some research in books and identify their style. This is how I discovered that they belonged to the Arts & Crafts movement. I became particularly interested in the Englishman William Morris and his school of thought, as well as in the American Gustav Stickley, who helped to launch the Mission style that was so popular in the United States. I learned a great deal about the influence each of these men had and how their thought had enriched different branches of the decorative arts in sometimes quite revolutionary ways. There are numerous catalogues and several excellent studies dealing with this style, which our neighbours to the south are especially fond of.

Today, after some twenty years of patient research, my collection holds over 100 articles from this period, including ceramic objects and diverse accessories. In my experience, it is fairly rare in Québec to come across collectors' items bearing the mark of Stickley's firm or the Roycroft Community, both of which used an easily recognizable logo. I don't believe that the movement really ever caught on in Québec. Even though the manufacturers who made furnishings in this style intended them for the general public, it was the members of the bourgeoisie who were won over by the pleasing lines of the new fashion. It is possible that the innovative aesthetics of the Arts & Crafts style represented too strong a break with old ways and seemed too avant-garde, with the result that the originally targeted clientele offered a certain resistance. This possibility remains to be investigated.

Arts & Crafts furniture is increasingly difficult to find on the Québec market. The dearth of these objects is explained in part by the enthusiasm with which American collectors snap them up. It would be ill-advised to insinuate that they do not have a legitimate claim. They guard their heritage jealously and I find it quite understandable. Mission furniture is probably one of the first true manifestations of American taste that was free of European influences. Although the movement at first borrowed from British modes, Stickley gave his designs such simplified lines that the end result was something entirely different: modernity before the Modern era. Americans invented a bare type of furniture, reduced to its essential function, stripped of ornamentation and designed to last. It seems normal to me that this style arouses such interest among collectors in New York City, and throughout the United States for that matter, since from a cultural viewpoint, it is essentially part of their identity. The prices asked by Québec antique dealers are determined by demand in the United States and this, along with the strong American dollar, means that items in the Mission style are extremely expensive, sometimes exorbitantly so — a piece of ceramic may go for $3 000 and a signed armchair in good condition can fetch $5 000 or more. A third of my collection is the result of numerous visits to flea markets, where someone who knows a field can make wonderful finds. The other two thirds comes from antique stores.

I love oak furniture and am particularly fond of the grain of this wood. When it is quarter-sawed, an astonishing meshing of fibres is made visible. Quarter-sawing, which involves cutting planks from the oak log like wedges of pie, reveals the distinctive ligneous structure of this venerable tree. The patina is important, as are the signs of wear on varnish and on leather seats. I try to clean new acquisitions thoroughly, but no more than that. I never go so far as to strip them down to the bare wood, which would only diminish the spiritual beauty of these mute witnesses to history. Looking at the condition of a piece — the wear marks on its armrests or the scars left by a pipe or cigar — I have no trouble imagining scenes in the life of the object.

Since the style first became popular in Québec among the English-speaking population, it is not surprising that the best examples of these goods are found today in old resort areas. This furniture for living rooms, verandahs and villas is very comfortable — it evokes the soul of an era. I like things that are simple, sober, durable and endowed with a certain elegance; I dislike empty show. When I look around at the furniture that I live with, the object that gives me the most pleasure is an attractive folding screen. It is an unusual object and, with its discreet aesthetic, it is almost like a painting. It is made with vertical strips of oak and has an upper section that is ruled out in rectilinear forms. I am deeply moved by the simplicity of its touching beauty.

With time, I have learned a great deal about the Arts & Crafts movement and the North American market for related products. I have also discovered much about the way the style came to Québec and developed here. I am always on the lookout for a rare object. Nowadays, unfortunately, I have no more space for new acquisitions. If I am to keep on nourishing my curiosity about this style and my passion for it, I must consider the possibility of exchanging some of my pieces or to get rid of one to make room for another.

Alain Rivest
Québec City, July 27, 1999

programs, in which architecture, decoration, furniture, lighting, curtains, fabrics, accessories and kitchen or service equipment would all be harmonized into a cohesive whole. In other words, the reformers promoted the concept of interior design before the term actually existed.

The people who espoused these ideas saw themselves as artists, rather than simply craftsmen. Taking the medieval craft guild as an ideal, they sought a means of working together and sharing their skills and knowledge. In 1871, Ruskin founded the St. George's Guild, the first creative community to pursue these objectives. It was only somewhat later that the movement became a runaway success, following the establishment of the Guild of Handicraft and the founding in 1888 of the Arts & Crafts Exhibition Society, from which the new style took its name. From 1890 on, there sprang up all kinds of artists' groups working in various fields within the Arts & Crafts movement, at first in Europe and then in the United States and Québec.

In 1906, a group of Montréal women obtained a charter to found The Canadian Handicrafts Guild with the goal of reviving craft work and particularly home textile making. In 1929, when Jean-Marie Gauvreau published *Nos intérieurs de demain*, arguing for the use of native wood in a natural state, he was, somewhat belatedly, aligning his ideas about furniture and other areas of creative craftsmanship (such as textiles, ceramics and wrought iron) with the reformist thinking of many other Modern artist-designers, including William Morris, C. R. Ashbee and M. H. Baillie Scott of England, Charles Rennie Mackintosh of Scotland, Joseph Maria Olbrich and Joseph Hoffman of the Wiener Werkstätte, in Austria, and Hector Guimard and Victor Horta of Belgium.

In the United States, the movement was well received, but was adapted to meet the precepts of capitalist efficiency. As Leslie Green Bowman points out in *American Arts & Crafts:*

Virtue in Design (Los Angeles County Museum, 1990), the movement's U.S. proponents did not elevate craftsmanship to the level of fine arts as their European counterparts had, but rather modified it to satisfy industrial requirements. In England, Morris himself eventually had to admit that it was a Utopian dream to expect the ways of the old guilds to be respected. If solely handicraft methods were used, it would be impossible to attain the movement's cherished goal of winning a large share of the market. In the United States, a number of intellectual leaders took up the ideas of Ruskin and Morris. One of these leaders was a friend of Ruskin's, Charles Norton, the first professor of fine arts at Harvard University and an influential critic. It may also be argued that the school of architecture at McGill University, in Montréal, was strongly influenced by this movement in the first quarter of the 20th century.

U.S. academic societies and workshops claiming kinship with the Arts & Crafts movement appeared at this time, first in Boston and Chicago and then soon in other cities as well. This newly fashionable trend proved to be a boon to previously uncompetitive manufacturing concerns. These businesses reinvented themselves by installing efficient machine tools, streamlining their operations with shrewd mass-production methods and selling simply designed furniture through a solid marketing strategy.

The first person to adapt Arts & Crafts ideals to the context of the merchandising and mass-production age was Gustav Stickley (1857-1942). A veteran of the furniture industry, he was already well acquainted with the movement's theories but, on a trip to England in the 1890s, he was struck by the depth of its social and aesthetic values. By the end of the decade he had come up with an admirable interpretation of this fashion, which previously could be afforded only by an elite that prized sturdily built, artistically decorated

719
Mission bookshelf-desk, chair and lamp. Québec City, ca. 1910.
The values of this North American movement affected the role of furniture in every corner of the house, including the study, where people read and did paperwork.

THE U.S. MISSION STYLE 1900-1920

The Arts & Crafts movement started by William Morris and his school in Great Britain inspired creative minds in the United States to explore the principles promoted by these reformers in the fields of architecture and interior design. U.S. adepts of the style proposed a version of furniture that was even plainer and more simplified than that favored by the original reformers. The new style was baptized "Mission" because its promoters felt that paring furniture down to its essential utility had to be undertaken as a mission. They believed in functionalism before the Functionalist movement existed.

Furniture presented in the catalogue published by the Bishop Furniture Company of Grand Rapids, Michigan. The copy of the catalogue used for these pages was found in Québec. Fieldwork and comparative studies make it clear that these items are very similar to those produced by Québec manufacturers or imported into Québec from Ontario, for cultural trends tend to affect broad swaths of North America. The inset portrait is of Gustav Stickley, who started the Mission style on this continent.

MISSION STYLE, QUÉBEC VERSION 1900-1925

The catalogues distributed by Québec and Ontarian furniture manufacturers and retailers in the first quarter of the 20th century presented furniture suites and individual pieces in the aptly named Mission style. The Stickley or Roycroft Community furniture so popular on the U.S. market at the time was echoed in the lines of these catalogues' drawing room and bedroom suites and individual chairs, armchairs and tables, offered in golden or fumed quarter-sawed oak, surface oak and elm with an imitation oak finish.

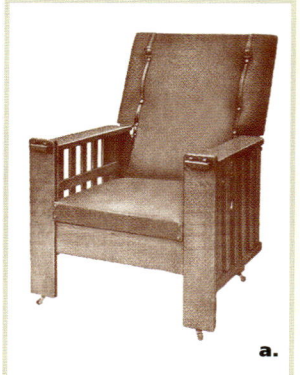
a.

b.

c.

d.

e.

f.

Various items of factory-made furniture in the Mission style offered by catalogues in Québec between 1900 and 1930.
b. T. Eaton Company, Toronto, 1920-1921. **a., c., d., e., f.** P.-T. Legaré of Québec City, from 1910 to 1925.
g., h., i., j., k., l. Victoriaville Furniture.
A number of Québec firms offered Mission-style furniture that varied in the quality of its workmanship. Photographers, who always kept up with the latest fashions, naturally equipped their studios with this type of furniture, as is evidenced by the portrait of an unknown Québec City woman, taken in about 1900.

g.

h.

i.

j.

k.

l.

723
View of the large living room in the summer home of Senator Rodolphe Forget at Saint-Irénée-des-Bains, in the Charlevoix region, showing Arts & Crafts-influenced Mission furniture in the foreground. This style was particularly popular in Québec for furnishing homes in resort areas.

724
Mission-type sideboard with a mirror, original brass hardware, central doors decorated with leaded glass in a stylized flower pattern and outer doors decorated with intaglio motifs. Oak, Montréal, ca. 1900.
This piece, which was made in Montréal, once stood in the Château Meunier on Anticosti Island. A number of photographs show that the furniture in this mansion reflected the Art Nouveau, Arts & Craft and Mission styles.

INDUSTRY AND REFORM   421

725 to 730
Set of rush-seated chairs. Dark-stained yellow birch, ca. 1915. This set comes from the Mauvide-Genest manor in Saint-Jean on Île d'Orléans. The Mission and Arts & Crafts styles favored great simplicity, solidity and the use of traditional handcrafting techniques and procedures.

731 to 735

Settee, armchair, rocking chair and side chair, all in the Mission style. Yellow birch, oak, basswood and leather, ca. 1920.

In the first quarter of the 20th century, P.-T. Legaré's catalogues and the promotional material distributed by various furniture merchants in Québec offered pieces of furniture — some better made than others — that were described as being in the Mission style.

736 to 739
Mission armchair and suite consisting of a sofa, rocking chair and armchair. Oak and leather, ca. 1920.
In the 1920s, factory-made vernacular furniture in the Mission style tended to be heavy. Québec and Ontario companies became specialized in this type of furniture, which was well promoted, for example, in P.-T. Legaré's catalogues. Furniture makers showed no lack of imagination in their constant search for new forms.

740
Advertisement for Valiquette, a large furniture store in Montréal, *La Presse*, August 1913. The Mission style was the height of fashion.

424   PRE-MODERN FURNITURE IN QUÉBEC

741 to 746
Mission tables, rocking chair, armchair and plant stand. Oak, yellow birch, maple and elm, ca. 1915-1920. The square table and the armchair were made by Joseph Bouchard of Pointe-au-Pic. The Morris rocking chair comes from the Beauce area.

INDUSTRY AND REFORM

747
Elzéar Beaulieu of Lévis, in 1902, standing beside a Mission-style Morris chair in his bedroom.

748 to 751
Mission screen, china cabinet, table and shelf. Oak and yellow birch, ca. 1915.

752
Gaming area furnished in the Mission style in the Mauvide-Genest manor. Oak, ca. 1915.

THE EASTLAKE STYLE 1880-1910

At the end of the 19th century, Québec, like the rest of North America, was strongly influenced by the proposals made by the English architect Charles Locke Eastlake (1836-1906) with respect to architecture, decoration and interior design. Industrial furniture intended for every budget was made in this style and appeared on the market in North America, including Québec. In the St. Lawrence Valley, firms like the J. W. Kilgour & Brothers Company of Beauharnois offered furniture suites and individual items that were inspired by Eastlake's models.

a.

b.

c.

f.

g.

h.

d.

e.

i.

j.

Charles Eastlake and William Godwin were British reformers in the field of aesthetics and the decorative arts in the last quarter of the 19th century.
The Art Furniture Movement launched by Eastlake and Godwin in London sought to eliminate everything superfluous from furniture, while favoring geometrical forms and Japanese-inspired elegance. Except for **b.**, **k.**, **l.** and **q.**, which came from U.S. manufacturers, all the furniture shown here was made in the workshops of the J. W. Kilgour Company of Beauharnois in around 1890.
The studio portrait shows two students from the Séminaire de Québec, Émile Bélanger and his brother, dressed in the seminary's school uniform and comfortably installed in Eastlake furniture in Anselme Romuald Roy's studio in Lévis, around 1890.

k.

l.

p.

m.

n.

o.

q.

r.

754 to 757

Industrial Eastlake bedroom suites and sideboards in elm and walnut, offered in the catalogue distributed by the Beauharnois Steam Cabinet Factory, of the town of Beauharnois, in 1885. Sideboards, with their bevelled mirrors, might be painted brown, yellow or red, or given an oil or imitation oak finish; bedroom furniture could be painted brown or red with yellow highlights. During the Belle Époque, the J. W. Kilgour & Brothers Company of Beauharnois, which remained a thriving business for almost a century, put out sales catalogues of several dozen pages, presenting its production with fine line engravings that give a very clear idea of the merchandise offered. The catalogues published by the company's competitors are equally informative. Eastlake furniture, designed for industrial production-line methods and the use of machine tools, was distinguished by its horizontal lines and decoration consisting of grooving, festoons on crest rails and incised floral or abstract motifs sometimes inspired by Japanese art.

INDUSTRY AND REFORM

Art Furniture

One of the people who marked the last decades of the 19th century, at the threshold of the Modern era, was the architect Edward William Godwin (1833-1886). Along with Eastlake and a number of others, he belonged to the British Art Furniture Movement, but he also participated in a broader aesthetic reform movement that sought to educate the public in the appreciation of "good taste" and a new vision of beauty in the home. Godwin, like several other architects of his day, proposed furnishings and interior decoration plans that were an integral part of the buildings he designed. By the dawn of the 20th century, architects would be increasingly involved in the decorative arts and furniture design. Godwin, like many reformers, rebelled against the excessive historical borrowings of the previous era and he offered his own global vision of modernity. He sought reform while remaining strongly rooted in his own time. The concepts he proposed were abundantly inspired by the art, and therefore the culture, of Japan, which had become accessible to the rest of the world only in the middle of the 19th century and now attracted great interest. *Japonisme* was combined with the Queen Anne style to produce truly novel, avant-garde furniture, and it was one of the sources of inspiration for the Functionalist movement that developed in the first decades of the 20th century.

For Godwin and the proponents of the Art Furniture Movement and the Aesthetic Movement, artistic sensibility was no less essential to furniture design than it was to the more traditional academic fields of painting and sculpture. The furniture industry had little choice but to take this outlook into account and adapt its normal production accordingly.

In *Living in Style: Fine Furniture in Victorian Québec*, John Porter writes: "From 1880 to the start of the First World War, the term Art Furniture was applied to a wide range of productions, which, depending on the manufacturer, could be in either simple or complex shapes, with flat and angled planes or generous curves, using styles and ornamentation of historical or exotic inspiration. [...] A number of contemporary documentary sources indicate that the latest fashions in Aesthetic furniture had their influence in Quebec."

At the 1876 Philadelphia World's Fair, *Japonisme* made a tremendous impression on people. Five years later, D. S. Rickaby of Québec City advertised drawing room furniture in the latest fashions, "Japanese and American." In the Belle Époque, the label Art Furniture covered almost everything that was not in the styles of Revivalism, Arts & Crafts or Mission, Art Nouveau, Eastlake, industrial oak, Thonet bentwood and metal (as in brass beds). The winds of reform stirred by the Art Furniture Movement in Europe and North America would clear the way for a totally new functional aesthetics.

758-759
Bedroom suite combining the Eastlake style with Renaissance Revival tastes. Walnut and mahogany, Québec City, ca. 1895.

760

Handcrafted bed in the Eastlake manner. Painted yellow birch and basswood, Beauce region, ca. 1895.
This bed, with its horizontal lines and fairly flat surfaces, was built by Charles Barbeau, the father of anthropologist Marius Barbeau, and he signed his work by carving his initials on the headboard. The headboard crest is festooned with scallops and beads, while bands of plant-inspired motifs adorn the stiles.

761-762

Bed and dresser with a mirror and three drawers in the manner of the Art Furniture Movement. Walnut and figured walnut veneer, marble and glass, by Owen McGarvey, Montréal, ca. 1880.
This exceptional, very architectural suite has a monumental air. A highly decorative effect is produced by the dense ornamentation on the geometrically composed pyramids of the headboard and backboard, the rhythm of the turned elements that make up the openwork and the combining of rectilinear patterns with more lyrical motifs. Furniture in the Eastlake style or influenced by the reform proposed by the Aesthetic Movement in the last quarter of the 19th century was made for all levels of society, including the grand bourgeoisie. In this case, the craftsman seems to have enjoyed playing with disks, rings, diamond points, finials, festoons and veneering.

763
Eastlake dresser with three drawers, a mirror and original hardware. Walnut, Québec City, ca. 1880.
In the Revival and Pre-Modern periods bedroom storage furniture often had marble tops.

764
Rural bedroom with a vernacular bed of industrial manufacture in the Eastlake style. Ash and basswood, ca. 1890.
The Létourneau house in Saint-Roch-des-Aulnaies contains rooms that have never been painted. They have retained the very perfume of the Belle Époque. Widths of homemade *catalogne*, or rag rugs, cover the floor.

765
Furniture expressing the values of the Pre-Modern period. The Eastlake bed, made of yellow birch and walnut, is extremely simple, with a headboard topped by a scalloped crest. The bookcase is in the same general style, but is tinged with Neoclassicism.

766-767
Three-legged tables with curvilinear feet in the Anglo-American Aesthetic manner of the late 19th century. Pine and walnut, ca. 1880.
The lower table was designed and made by a cabinetmaker. It served as a model for the upper, country-made table, still bearing its original color. The two articles demonstrate that in every era, even in the Pre-Modern period, ordinary people and joiners were inspired by furniture fashions to make their own versions of new styles.

768 to 771
Upholstered Eastlake drawing room suite consisting of a sofa, platform rocker, armchair and chair. Walnut and oak, ca. 1880.

772
Eastlake sideboard with a mirror. Walnut and figured walnut veneer, Québec City, ca. 1885.
This sideboard displays all the characteristics of Eastlake furniture, including a festooned crest, intersecting horizontal and vertical lines, grooving and gouge-incised floral and geometrical motifs. The piece once had a place of honor in the dining room of Dorimène and Alphonse Desjardins' house in Lévis.

773
Belle Époque prie-dieu showing the influence of the Aesthetic Movement. Yellow birch, walnut and mahogany, ca. 1890.
The Eastlake style and the reformers' proposals affected all types of furniture.

INDUSTRY AND REFORM 441

774
Factory-made Belle Époque drawing room suite showing the influence of the Aesthetic Movement. Walnut and yellow birch, Québec City, ca. 1900.
The buttoned back is topped by a balustrade with a shell-shaped crest and the front legs are turned. It is not impossible that furniture in this style was produced by local firms such as Vallière's Québec City factory, which was one of the largest of its kind at the end of the 19th century.

775
Drawing room in the home of Alphonse Desjardins in Lévis, with interior decoration dating from around 1885 and expressing the values of the Eastlake style and the Aesthetic Movement in the Belle Époque.

Machine-Made Oak Furniture (1880-1920)

So far, we have looked at Pre-Modern furniture from the viewpoint of its stylistic values and their ideological underpinnings to identify certain movements that influenced both industrial and handcrafted production. However, the form of some of the period's furniture was conditioned directly by the advent of modern manufacturing methods and procedures. The popularity of the materials used for this furniture and the spread of new techniques justify placing it in a category of its own.

Almost everyone has seen the type of chair that is made of oak, or given an imitation oak-grain finish, with the crest rail bearing stylized steam-embossed decoration. Such chairs came in an infinite variety of models. Not so very long ago, in the classical colleges run by religious institutions in Québec, such chairs used to line the walls of the rooms where Sunday visitors were received. Another well-known item in this vein is the adjustable swivel chair, a solid piece of oak furniture that used to be a standard in old administrative offices, placed throne-like behind a massive desk made of the same material. And many readers will have sometimes lingered for a moment in front of an old hall rack, with its combined chest and bench surmounted by a large mirror inviting a glance from anyone entering or leaving the house.

From about 1880 until the Roaring Twenties in North America, every piece of functional furniture for the modern home was available in oak, or an imitation of this noble wood, which for centuries has been prized for its sturdiness, its resistance (even to salt water) and its attractive grain in patterns that vary depending on how the wood is sawed. Oak was generally given one of two finishes. A golden finish brought out the wood's natural tones, while a fumed finish was darker and emphasized the interesting grain characteristic of oak. Suites of furniture for the drawing room, dining room and bedroom were offered in a wide range of models.

These models might be inspired by sim-

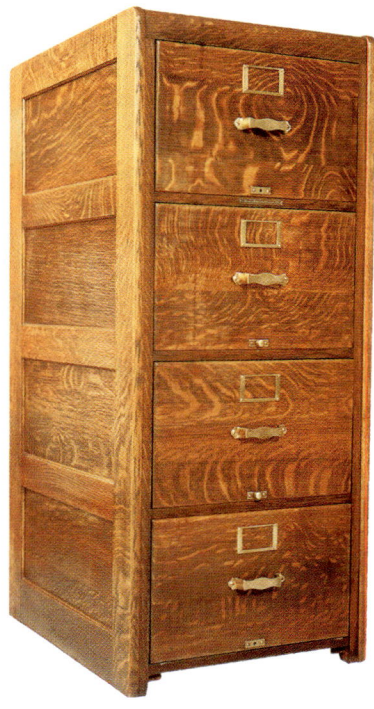

782
Filing cabinet. Oak, ca. 1890.

783
Interior of an office. Québec City, ca. 1900.
At the end of the 19th century, secretarial and office work underwent a veritable revolution. Men gradually left such jobs and women began to take their place. At the same time, the organization of space was completely changed. In keeping with current fashions, the new places of work were furnished in oak, with roll-top desks, filing cabinets, modular bookcases and swivel chairs whose backs curved into armrests. With the arrival of this convenient furniture, the modern office took shape.

784
Pre-Modern combined desk and display case. Oak, ca. 1890.
This multifunctional piece of furniture, reflecting the values of the Revival period as well as those of the reformers' Aesthetic Movement and early North American industrial design, blends a number of trends in design and production at the dawn of the Modern era.

OAK FURNITURE IN NORTH AMERICA 1880-1920

After 1880, oak furniture became common throughout North America. At the dawn of the merchandising era, large Chicago stores like Sears Roebuck and Montgomery Ward used catalogues to boost their sales of an entirely new kind of industrial furniture, reflecting the major stylistic trends in the Western world at the time. The town of Grand Rapids specialized in a vernacular type of furniture that became extremely popular with North Americans.

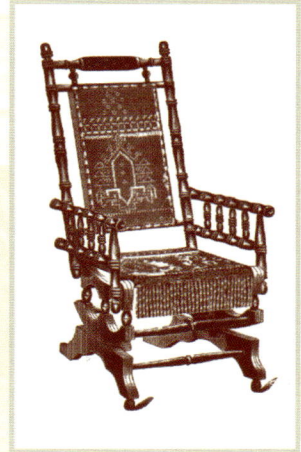

Various pieces of furniture in fumed oak from the 1895 catalogue distributed by the Bishop Furniture Company of Grand Rapids, Michigan, one of the North American firms that set the tone for this furniture style. The copy of the catalogue used for these pages was found in Québec. Similar furniture suites and articles were manufactured in Québec as well.

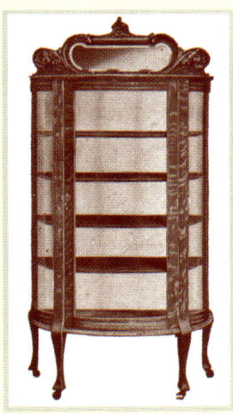

OAK FURNITURE MADE IN QUÉBEC 1890-1920

Throughout the Belle Époque, Québec furniture manufacturers and retailers published catalogues offering customers all kinds of suites and individual pieces in oak. This furniture, which was remarkably similar in form to goods produced in the United States and Ontario, was made of solid oak or of other woods given an "oak finish."

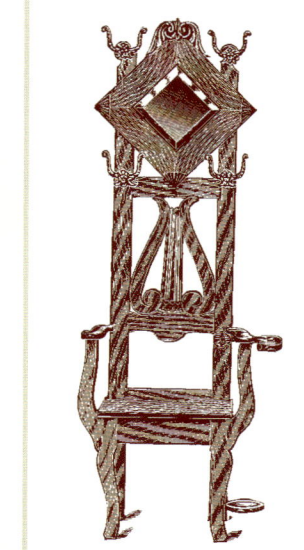

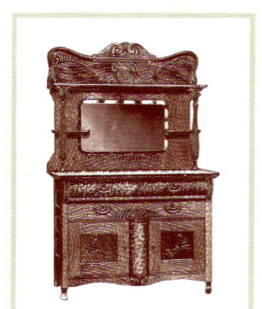

Various articles in golden or fumed oak shown in the catalogues published by P.-T. Legaré between 1910 and 1925 and by J. W. Kilgour of Beauharnois between 1890 and 1910.

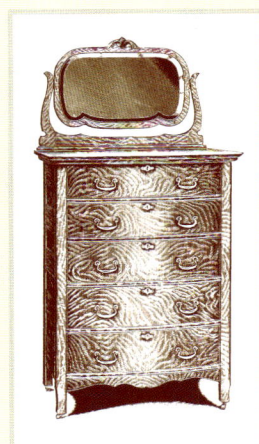

785
Mission chair. Oak, ca. 1895.

786
Coffer-bench showing Art Nouveau influence. Oak, ca. 1900.
Mass-produced industrial oak furniture, appearing during the Belle Époque, between 1875 and 1914, and widely distributed through modern marketing methods, was designed in all kinds of styles, drawing inspiration from both traditional modes and contemporary reformist ideals.

plified versions of the great styles of the past or by fashionable trends of the time, including Arts & Crafts and Mission, Art Nouveau and the Art Furniture Movement of the reformers Eastlake and Godwin. Pieces of furniture might also show a blend of two or more of these styles. Industrial designers were well aware of contemporary fashions and expressed them with a certain amount of originality in furniture that could be produced efficiently with machine tools.

In the 1880-1920 period, it was possible to furnish an entire house in oak. Interior decorating was harmonized with this wood. Some of the furniture in this style is extraordinarily inventive. The telephone had just entered people's lives, and with it and other new devices came all kinds of specialized furniture, always in oak. There were cupboards to hold player piano rolls, phonograph cylinders, sheet music and records. There were the phonographs and record players themselves, sewing-machine tables, iceboxes and laboratory-style kitchen cabinets for storing food and preparing meals efficiently. And there were modular bookshelves and filing cabinets for offices; harmoniums, pianos and piano benches; long-case clocks and wall clocks; and various forms of roll-top desks and slant-top desks. Windows, doors, flooring, staircases, chimney mantles and moulding were all made of oak as well. It was truly the age of oak.

The magnitude of this fashion that swept through all of North America in the Belle Époque can be measured simply by perusing the catalogues published by the various firms that made or sold furniture in Québec. Antique stores are also full of these goods. The oak fur-

niture produced in Québec was modelled on that made in the Midwestern states and displayed in the thick catalogues distributed by Montgomery Ward or Sears Roebuck of Chicago. The St. Lawrence Valley seems to have been strongly influenced by the production of the United States and particularly Ontario. The Eaton's store in Toronto sent its English-language catalogues throughout Québec. In any case, there is a strong stylistic similarity between the products made in these different places.

The market was full of furniture for every taste and every pocketbook. Some furniture was made specifically for less well-off households. Such goods could be somewhat shoddily constructed of inferior materials or wood that was crudely camouflaged with imitation-grain finish. The joints were often just hastily nailed or glued. However, for those who could afford better quality, there were elegant, well-made dining room and bedroom suites in this style. Much of the manufacturing work was now done by machine tools such as mortising machines, which made slotted holes, and turning and sculpting machines. These new tools gave rise to massive furniture with lion's-paw feet, griffons, chimeras and all kinds of decorative elements inspired by the most exuberant moments in the history of furniture. Anything that could be drawn could now be carved. Since oak is a very resistant wood it could be decorated using a variety of techniques, including steam embossing. Although some oak furniture presented completely plain surfaces, it was often enhanced with glued appliqués. The appliqués were produced by specialized firms that published fat catalogues full of motifs borrowed from every stylistic vocabulary. Other furniture was given striking outlines, with generous scrollwork and curved fronts, like the glass-doored china cabinets that could display silver-plate and cut-glass ware. At the time, all sorts of decorative canons were mined for unusual elements. Competition spurred businesses to constantly renew the products on the market. Every year, indeed every six months, it was necessary for them to offer a new product and to promote their innovation. Manufacturers vied with each other to show off their talent and originality in the furniture fairs and exhibitions that were held from time to time in various large cities in the United States, Canada and Québec.

The industrial movement that gave oak its special status seems to have originated in the Chicago area and, more particularly, in Grand Rapids, Michigan, which was seen as the world capital of furniture manufacturing. After the fire of 1871 that destroyed Chicago, the town known as the Windy City was rebuilt, an enterprise that called on the energy and innovative spirit of the entire continent. A great number of audacious designers came from Europe as well as from Canada and Québec to be part of this renewal. The material used for their creations was oak, which was available in seemingly inexhaustible quantities. The two major mail-order companies, Montgomery Ward and Sears Roebuck, set up business in Chicago and obtained their supplies locally. At this time, cities were growing rapidly in North America; between 1880 and 1920, most cities doubled their population. This factor, along with the fact that catalogues could reach every region, meant that the new fashion spread like wildfire. Québec soon joined the movement, both as an importer and a producer of goods.

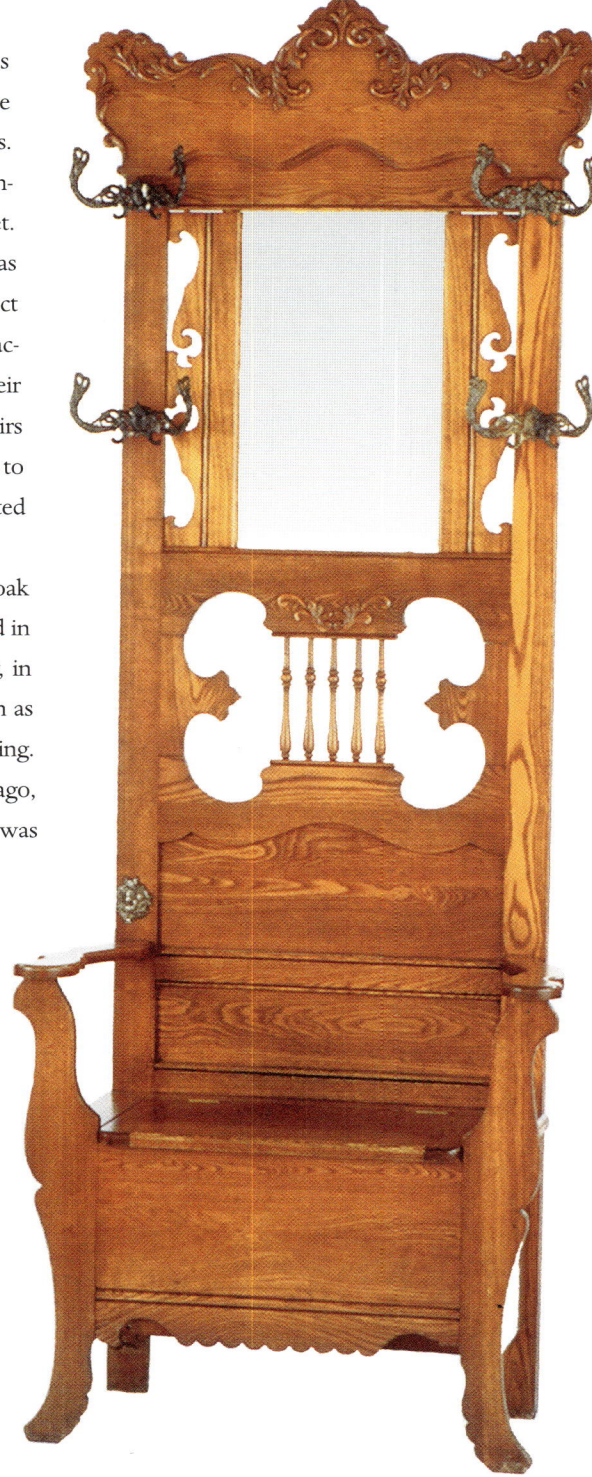

787
Hall stand. Ash and oak, ca. 1900.
There were countless variations on the hall stand, a practical piece of furniture that combined the functions of coat rack, bench and chest, and was often equipped with a mirror. Hall stands were made of ash, golden oak and dark oak, and might reflect industrial Revival styles or the avant-garde notions of reformers in the last quarter of the 19th century.

INDUSTRY AND REFORM

454 PRE-MODERN FURNITURE IN QUÉBEC

788 to 790
Industrial bedroom furniture in the Empire Revival manner. Quarter-sawed oak, Québec City, ca. 1900
The round mirror on the chest of drawers stands on the stylized legs of an eagle or bird of prey. The chest of drawers has the same type of feet on cabriole legs that flow seamlessly into the projecting corner stiles. The brass handles are original.

791
Morris chair. Oak and ash, ca. 1900.
Oak was a very popular material for making simplified Revival, Mission and Arts & Crafts furniture, including the famous Morris chair.

792
Industrial dining room suite. Golden oak, Lévis, ca. 1910.
The extension table is supported by heavy turned and reeded legs. The vertical lines of the feet harmonize nicely with the slender bars on the sloped, curved backs of the chairs. The suite reflects the values of the Arts & Crafts and Mission movements in a manner that would be used with great success by Frank Lloyd Wright and others in the Modern period.

793 to 795
Three models of glazed china cabinets manufactured industrially and reflecting the precepts of Belle Époque reformers and innovators, especially those related to the Art Nouveau, Arts & Crafts and Mission styles. Fumed oak, ca. 1895.
Oak could be given a number of different finishes, as is made clear by the advertisements of this period. China cabinets for displaying fine tableware, silver and crystal came in countless forms and sizes, with flat or curving fronts. There was a model for every pocketbook, depending on the amount of decoration and the quality of construction.

Some Oak Furniture Finishes

Fumed oak

Golden oak

Quarter-sawed oak

Old English oak

796
(Page 456)
Wardrobe with two mirrored doors and a drawer, decorated with glued appliqués and a curvilinear crest. Quarter-sawed fumed oak, ca. 1900. During the Belle Époque, manufacturers used oak to produce every type of household furniture.

BENTWOOD FURNITURE (1870-1930)

The fashion for bentwood launched by Michael Thonet (1796-1871) in the late 19th century is reflected in distinctive furniture that can be found throughout Québec, in homes, antique stores and religious institutions. If one takes the trouble to look underneath these side chairs and armchairs, or the occasional hat tree, the paper label with maker's name is often still in place, making it possible to attribute a piece to the Austrian firm established by Thonet in Vienna in 1842 or to one of his competitors. This furniture maker and talented businessman had begun his career many years earlier. In 1830 he had started to experiment with ways of curving wood and eventually developed a method for bending red beech or white birch rods with steam. At the first World's Fair held in London's Crystal Palace in 1851, at a time when a heavy style with historical references was the height of fashion, Thonet presented his disconcertingly light and innovative furniture. It received mixed reviews. With the help of his five sons, he further improved his product. He directed his marketing efforts towards the lower-middle classes, where the canons of fashion had less weight, and targeted cafés and public spaces, considering them ideal for his type of furniture. The famous little side chair known as model No. 14 was the Thonet brothers' glory. Just before the First World War, the Thonet company employed nearly 6 000 workers and produced over two million pieces of furniture each year. Each item, intended for export, consisted of a bundle of a few bent rods and some screws. The company was something like a 19th-century IKEA. Every major city in the Western world had its Thonet representative. In Québec City, D. S. Rickaby was the official agent. In Montréal, McGarvey advertised his store's fine selection of Thonet and Kohn furniture in newspapers like *L'Électeur* of November 10, 1890, and *La Minerve* of December 6, 1889. When Thonet's patent expired in 1869, numerous European and North American industrialists started their own bentwood furniture companies. One of the leaders among these new competitors was the Viennese firm run by Joseph Kohn. In Québec, labels bearing his name are sometimes found on small side chairs with cane seats. There was at least one Québec enterprise that applied bentwood techniques to chair manufacturing. This was the Beauharnois furniture company belonging to the Kilgour family; it will be presented in the following chapter.

The Thonets' innovations affected not only woodworking techniques and marketing strategies but also the shape of furniture. In many respects these furniture makers were precursors, more in tune with the Pre-Modern era than most of their contemporaries. Some of their amazingly light, solid and comfortable models have become classics. Over a century after these pieces were first made, they remain just as attractive, despite changing tastes. Thonet was always seeking new ways of doing things. His firm was the first to seek patterns and produce furniture belonging to the universe of industrial design and the Functionalist style that would mark the 20th century. The bending techniques and functional designs used by the Thonets for beechwood were eventually applied to chromed metal tubing and this furniture was perfectly suited to the purposes of people like Adolf Loos, Josef Hoffmann, Otto Wagner, Marcel Breuer and Ludwig Mies Van der Rohe. The company, however, was always able to adapt to the great aesthetic movements. When Art Nouveau was in fashion, for example, bentwood furniture was offered in quite original interpretations of this lyrical style.

797
A view of the Thonet workshop in Austria, showing the steam chambers used to prepare the wood for bending. The rods were treated at low pressure (10.7 psia) and a temperature ranging from 90° C to 100° C. A few Québec firms, such as the J. W. Kilgour Company, borrowed these techniques for making chairs.

798 to 801

Bentwood Thonet chair and hat stand. White birch and beech, Québec City, late 19th century.
It is clear, both from fieldwork and exploring the antique market, that in the Belle Époque many Quebeckers acquired furniture produced by the Thonet factory or by the European and North American manufacturers who later adopted the bentwood technique to make their own models in this style.

BENTWOOD FURNITURE 1880-2000

Bentwood furniture, particularly chairs, are found quite often in the St. Lawrence Valley. As of the mid-19th century, Michael Thonet and his Viennese business made this type of furniture in beech, using economical production-line techniques. With its innovative lines, this style spread like wildfire throughout the Western world. When Thonet's patent expired in 1869, several competitors began to make similar products. Some of them, like the J. W. Kilgour Company of Beauharnois, were Québec firms.

a.

b.

c.

d.

e.

f.

g.

h.

i.

a. portrait of Michael Thonet (1796-1871). **b., c., d., e., f., l., m.** furniture incorporating bentwood made by the J. W. Kilgour Company of Beauharnois, ca. 1910. **h.** chair in P.-T. Legaré's 1917 catalogue. **g., i., j., k., n., o., p., q.** articles from Thonet's general catalogue, end of the 19th century. **r., s., t.** models for plywood seats, Thonet's general catalogue, ca. 1900.

j.

k.

l.

m.

n.

o.

p.

q.
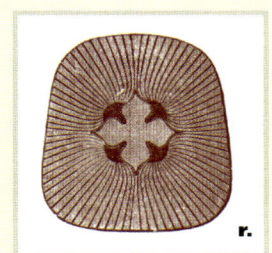
r.
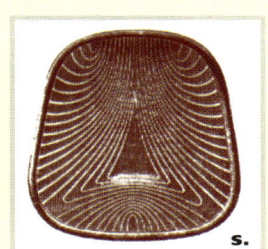
s.
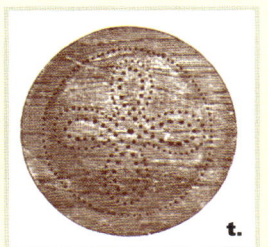
t.

METAL FURNITURE

The 19th century was incontestably the age of iron. This resistant material was found to have advantages in a wide range of fields and was used to make machinery, railroad tracks, bridges, ships and modular sections that formed building façades. Iron even began to be used for building structures after the Crystal Palace was constructed in London in 1851. Iron could be produced in tremendous quantities thanks to technological advances that radically improved the efficiency of blast furnaces. Steel and brass, as well as cast iron, were used in the furniture industry.

In the 19th century, city parks and park cemeteries became a normal part of the landscape. These spaces were furnished with cast-iron furniture, consisting mainly of benches and seats made specifically for this purpose and reflecting the Naturalistic styles of the Revival age or the Pre-Modern reform movements. Many such seats are presented in the catalogues of William Clendinneg, of Montréal. Cast iron was also used for the wood stoves that had kept homes warm from the earliest days of settlement in the St. Lawrence Valley and these pieces of furniture were updated as well. (See Chapter 2 of my book, *Objets anciens du Québec. La vie domestique*.)

The manufacturers of cast-iron goods offered bedsteads in this material. Some of these beds

802
Ice-cream parlor chair. Twisted iron, Chicago, ca. 1890. In the last quarter of the 19th century, North American firms began to manufacture chairs and tables, along with a range of other items, made with steel rods and bands. Garden furniture in this material was produced in many forms and became very popular with Quebeckers.

803
Bedroom with a brass bed. Québec City, ca. 1915. Old photographs rarely intruded into the privacy of the bedroom. This picture showing a bedroom in an ordinary family home reveals a layout that seems to echo the three-part iconographic pattern of the altar area in a Roman Catholic Church — like an altar, the bed, representing every sacrifice and joy, dominates the room, while above it hangs a crucifix; and on either side, where reliquaries would sit atop altar tabernacles, are portraits of the family's ancestors.

804
Brass bed with medallions. Beaumont, ca. 1900. Different models of this type of bed, which was so popular in the Belle Époque, are still used to furnish interiors today. They often belong to people who collect old furniture.

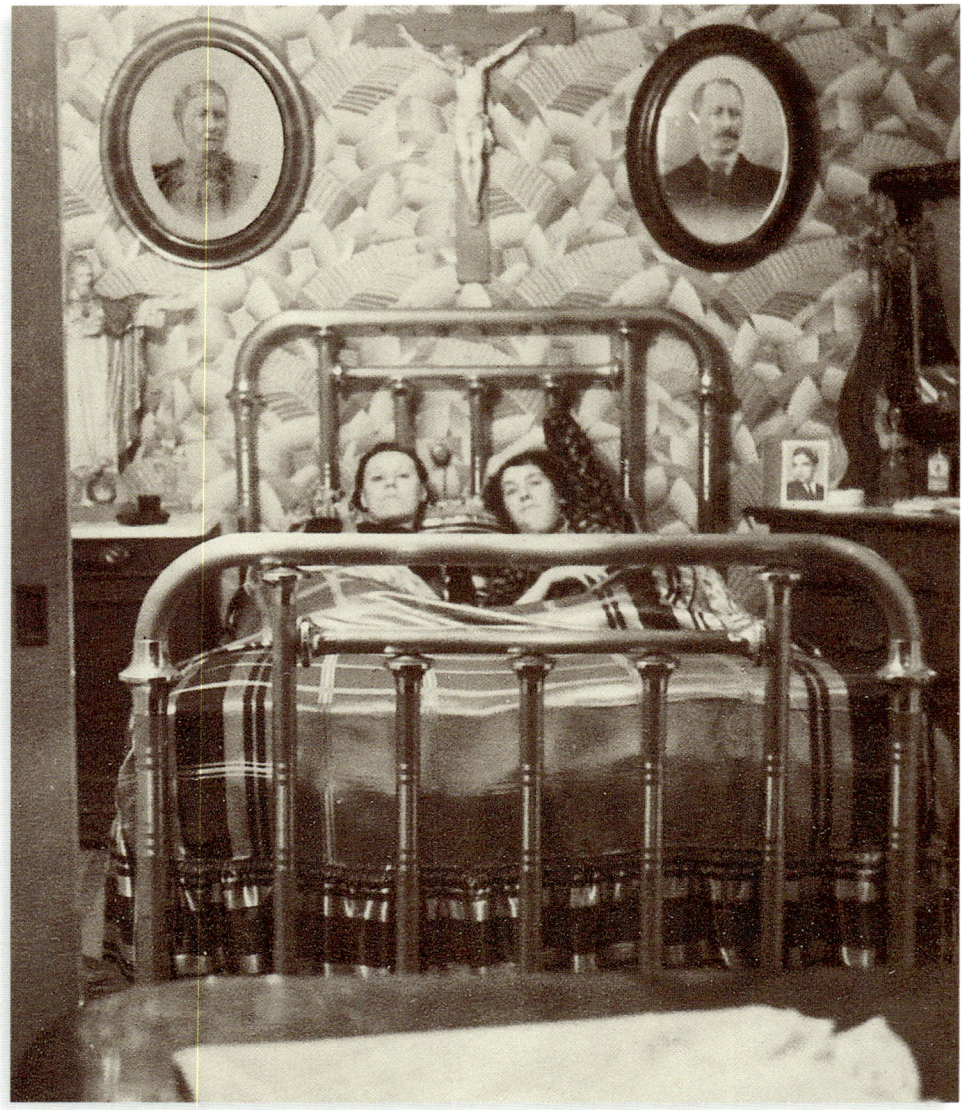

had high posts that could be fitted with curtains but ordinarily they were folding beds adorned with Revival-fashion lyres and lattices. The most elaborate of these beds borrowed decorative elements from the Gothic style or the Naturalistic motifs of the Baroque. Items cast in British or U.S. foundries no doubt served as models for the sand moulds used in Québec ironworks.

According to a persistent ethnohistorical rumor, one of the Trois-Rivières foundries operating in the 19th century may have produced cast-iron beds. Beds made of this material and probably manufactured in Québec in the 19th century are kept in the Pierre-Boucher museum in Trois-Rivières and in the store rooms of Parks Canada in Québec City. These beds are very similar to the finest products manufactured in the United States. One of them, presented at the end of the preceding chapter, is embellished with paired roosters or griffons with lion's-paw feet and wing tips linked in a fleur-de-lis.

The last quarter of the 19th century was marked by the appearance of the brass bed. By the Belle Époque and the Roaring Twenties, industrial advances had made it possible to produce bedsteads whose lines, form and finish were reminiscent of marching-band instruments. Thick, shiny tubing was bent into extravagant curves, interrupted by decorative bulbous collars in brilliantly polished brass, echoing the shape of the large knobs fixed to the tops of bedposts. The most sought-after pieces today have openwork brass plaques with foliated scrolls on the headboard and footboard, joined with lengths of angle iron that act as side rails. It is clear from the fanciful decoration that these beds' designers gave free rein to their imaginations.

A number of Québec firms specialized in manufacturing brass beds, which are today a mainstay of the antique market in Québec. Robert Gale, an inventor of the box spring and the inner-spring mattress, produced these articles in his factory in Waterville. The business, George Gale & Son, enjoyed a solid reputation and principally employed young women for assembly operations. In Montréal, some of the most successful brass-bed companies were the Parkhill Manufacturing Company Limited, situated at 400 Saint-Antoine Street; the Dominion Bedstead Company, with its factory to the east of Cornwall, Ontario, and an outlet at 300 Atlantic Avenue; and the Ives Bedding Company Limited, whose parent company was a Montréal hardware business. Ives Bedding produced the popular "Regal" bed, which was widely marketed in Québec through P.-T. Legaré's catalogues in the 1910s and 1920s. The popularity of brass beds is made clear by a glance at sales catalogues and advertisements for such items in newspapers and magazines. Brass beds were shown with golden or fumed oak bedroom suites consisting of washstands, chests of drawers and dressers, which were also promoted in such publications. I have found material for the study of brass beds in numerous Belle Époque catalogues put out by Québec manufacturers and retailers, and by Ontario firms that did business in the St. Lawrence Valley.

The 1917 catalogue published by the Parkhill Manufacturing Company of Montréal included photographs that showed how its furniture was manufactured. The 128-page catalogue, which contains over 100 illustrations of brass-plated, steel and enamelled-iron furniture, begins with an introductory explanation of the articles' advantages: "1. Absolutely the best shellac; brass-plated by electricity according to our special procedure; smooth, attractive and long-lasting finish. 2. Rigid construction. 3. A variety of elegant artistic designs. Any woman would be proud to own an *Alaska* brass bed. 4. Elegant, attractive trim and finish. Something to please every taste. 5. High-quality, smooth-rolling castors, making these beds extremely easy to move." [Translation]

The passage summarizes a number of facts about this type of bed: almost every component of a brass bed received its finish through electrolysis, although some parts were made of brass sheets or, in luxurious models, of cast brass; the brass surface was given a shellac coating to protect it from tarnish; the beds were solidly constructed in a variety of wildly imaginative designs; and metal furniture was seen as very hygienic and easy to keep clean, being promoted as ideal by the authors of a number of books on home economics. The same Parkhill catalogue gives a sample of the types of finishes offered; buyers had a choice of glossy, ribbon, "polette," and satin finishes. The ribbon finish had a matte surface with bands of glossy finish, while the term "polette," which seems to have been the firm's notion of an amusing way to say things in French, was used to refer to a satin finish with glossy panels. The Parkhill company also sold bassinets and

805
Postcard showing the façade of the City House Furnishing store on Saint-Laurent Street in Montréal in around 1908. The windows are full of different models of brass beds.

806
The catalogues published by Québec companies that made brass beds might run to over 100 pages showing dozens of models and often presented pictures of factory production. This photograph is of a section of the Parkhill Manufacturing Company on Saint-Ambroise Street in Montréal. A worker, wearing his Sunday best for the occasion, is operating a bending brake. Numerous old photographs provide valuable information about the organization of space and use of tools in factories and workshops.

swinging cradles, single beds and three-quarter beds in the same finishes. A catalogue put out by the Dominion Bedstead Company offered a series of box springs and mattresses as well as hat trees in the Thonet manner. Some brass beds had square posts and spindles and were adorned with openwork panels in the same material.

The bed companies also offered iron beds finished in white enamel and trimmed with decorative brass knobs, spindles and collars. These beds were available in the same models as the brass beds.

From 1870 to about 1930, metal beds became the fashion among all levels of society. While solid brass and brass-finish beds were extremely popular, iron beds were not as expensive and found favor with the working classes (a parallel might be made with the ferrotype photograph, which made portraits available for a song). Several pages devoted to these articles could always be found in the annual or biannual sales catalogues put out in this period by retail merchants with a market in Québec. These included large department stores like Eaton's of Toronto, Morgan's of Montréal, Paquet limitée and Julien of Québec City as well as the Legaré mail-order company. P.-T. Legaré controlled a network of over 1 000 agents in different towns and villages throughout Québec. The U.S. firms Montgomery Ward and Sears Roebuck also marketed metal beds in this fashion.

The 1902 Sears Roebuck catalogue claimed that in the cities, which were experiencing unprecedented growth at the time, nine households out of ten owned iron beds. An impressive selection of these articles was presented in the pages of the thick catalogue. The beds were recommended not only for their low cost and easy maintenance but also because they were enthusiastically endorsed by doctors as being well adapted to the antiseptic measures that became common following Pasteur's discoveries. They wrote that no other bed should be used in the sickroom. Iron beds were systematically employed in hospitals and sanatoriums. According to one catalogue description, they were "cleaner, neater, healthier and more stylish" than wooden beds. Québec boarding schools generally used them in their dormitories. While most of these beds were finished in white, they were also offered by the catalogues in black, navy, pink and olive green. There seemed to be no limit to the number of fanciful designs for headboards and footboards. While some of them were relatively plain, decorated with only knobs and cast-iron spindles, others presented a profusion of scrolls and lacy filigree figures of all kinds, accented by brass knobs and collars in contrasting colors. Certain models were decorated with fleur-de-lis.

By the end of the 1920s, brass and iron beds were no longer in fashion. Sales catalogues instead increasingly promoted steel beds with round or square tubing. Legaré offered this type of bed with an imitation walnut finish, embellished with medallion-like caned panels.

BRASS BEDS 1890-1920

The new trends that influenced furniture design in the Belle Époque gave rise to many imaginative forms, but the brass bed stands out among them for its exuberant decoration. During this period, a number of firms in Québec and Ontario produced and distributed an impressive array of bed models in unprecedented forms. Catalogues promoted the idea of decorating bedrooms by combining these beds with washstands and dressers made of golden or fumed oak.

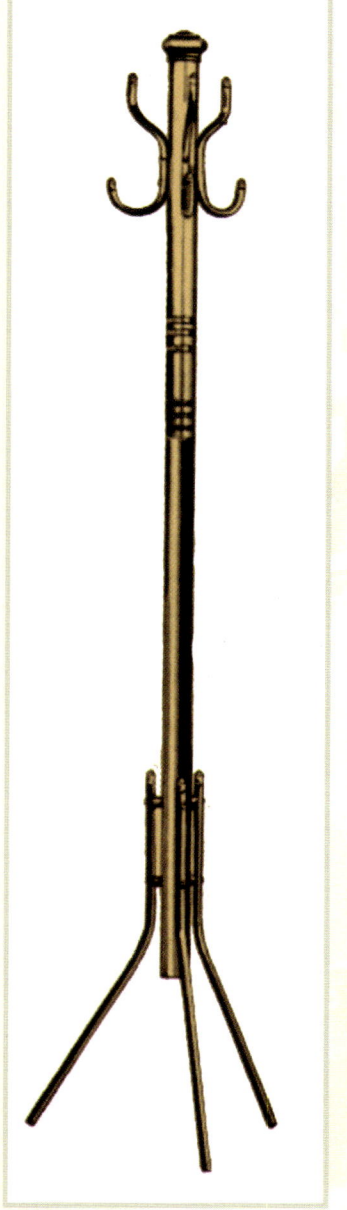

A few models of brass beds made and distributed in Québec during the Belle Époque, taken from the catalogues of three important manufacturers: the 1922 catalogue put out by the Dominion Beadstead Company, a Montréal firm; the 1890 catalogue published by the Ives Bedding Company, a well-known hardware-foundry business that had operated in Montréal since 1859 (its brass bed factory was located in Cornwall just to the west of Québec); and the 1917 catalogue published by the Parkhill Manufacturing Company, illustrating dozens of "Alaska" brass and iron beds made by its Montréal factory.

WICKER FURNITURE (1870-1930)

The fashion for wicker furniture developed towards the end of the Revival era and continued throughout the Pre-Modern period. Wicker is a generic term that covers a variety of plant fibres, including osier, bamboo, cane and machine-made twisted paper fibre. These materials corresponded to the industrial prerogatives and ideological concerns that marked the last quarter of the 19th century. Wicker furniture was extremely affordable and presented numerous advantages: it was light, well-suited to mechanized manufacturing techniques, comfortable (despite the cracking noises it made when one sat down), and relatively solid, for a considerable number of such articles made in the 19th century are still in use today. Wicker also met the criteria proposed by those who preached for reform in the decorative arts or who celebrated a new art of living in highly popular books that took a critical look at contemporary interior design. Wicker added a touch of exoticism in a romantic era, when the world was becoming more open and far-off lands were becoming more accessible; it came from natural sources; and, being airy and easy to keep clean, it corresponded to the hygienic ideals that were accepted following the introduction of Pasteur's procedures.

Light and airy, wicker furniture was at first seen as particularly suitable for verandahs and covered porches. Since wicker began to be used at about the same time as the idea of the summer vacation became widespread, it is only natural that the oldest traces of this furniture are found in

807
The extravagant curlicues of wicker furniture were prominent in the settings used in studio portraits. Photographers always sought out the very latest fashions. This picture by Philippe Gingras, who worked in Québec City during the Belle Époque, shows little Rosario Faucher enthroned amid wicker tendrils.

808
Mrs. Arnoldi and her family on their verandah. Montréal, 1919.
Wicker was especially popular for verandah furniture and for certain items used in summer homes or country villas. After 1920, it became common for ordinary living rooms and drawing rooms to be furnished in wicker.

809
Wicker rocking chair in the ornamental style of the late 19th century. Saint-Laurent, Île d'Orléans, ca. 1890.
Wicker furniture like this rocking chair, with its immensely imaginative and eclectic decoration, was produced throughout the Belle Époque.

WICKER FURNITURE 1880-1930

In the Revival and Pre-Modern periods, there was a fascination with the exotic and an idealization of nature that found expression in a new type of furniture made of plant fibre and generally known as wicker. At first, the Québec market was supplied by the United States. The "mechanization" of manufacturing procedures encouraged several Québec firms to specialize in this type of production, although much of the weaving work had to be done by hand. With such a flexible material, designers could give their imagination free rein. Wicker furniture, initially associated with resort areas, was soon available in every fashionable style and used in drawing rooms and living rooms in ordinary homes.

a. workers weaving chairs inside a wicker workshop in the J. W. Kilgour factory in Beauharnois in 1926. **b.** girl dressed for her First Communion in Samuel Belle's studio, Rivière-du-Loup, ca. 1895. **c., d., e., f.** fancy articles offered by the Haywood Wakefield Company of the United States, ca. 1900. **g., h., j., l.** pages from the 1893-1894 fall-winter catalogue published by Henry Morgan & Company of Montréal. **i.** boy dressed for his First Communion in Napoléon Montreuil's studio, Saint-André-Avelin, ca. 1900. **k.** page from P.-T. Legaré's 1925 catalogue.

g.

h.

i.

k.

j.

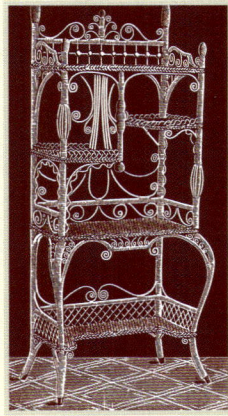

l.

the resort areas of Kamouraska, Charlevoix, the Eastern Townships and in the countryside around Québec City and Montréal, where the custom of spending summer by a river or lake was well established. At the end of the 19th century, wicker furniture began to appear in the drawing rooms of the middle classes, probably because it was associated with the pampered lifestyles the bourgeoisie were accustomed to when on holiday. In around 1905, for example, a certain Joseph Lessard of Vallée-Jonction bought a wicker suite for his family's drawing room. Manufacturers also offered utilitarian articles intended to facilitate various household tasks. Sewing tables, shelves for plants, plant stands, hall chairs in dramatic shapes and all kinds of other furniture was available in wicker.

The exotic shapes to which wicker lent itself seemed to express everything fresh and modern in the Belle Époque. Throughout Québec, photographers installed wicker tables and chairs in their studios in order to appear up-to-date and provide ultra-fashionable settings for their clients to pose in. The old photo albums of Québec families are full of such pictures.

The production of wicker furniture can be divided into three periods in Québec. The first one, extending from 1880 to 1900, corresponds to the "Ornate Revival" style. This style includes chairs in sometimes quite whimsical shapes, richly decorated with fancy weaving, varied patterns, coiling and elaborate scrolls. The second period, which lasted from 1900 to 1920, is referred to as "Pre-Modern" and was inspired by the art of the reformers in the last quarter of the 19th century. It followed the same general lines as the furniture that came out of the reform movement. The third period was strongly marked by the values of Art Deco and the Functionalist philosophy of the 1920s and 1930s. Incorporating color and bright motifs, this period produced "Modern" wicker.

Between 1870 and 1930, the period in which this furniture was especially popular in North America, there were over a hundred U.S. firms that imported or manufactured wicker goods. A half dozen such businesses existed in Québec. The largest of the U.S. concerns was undoubtedly the Haywood Wakefield Company, started in 1897, when two major firms founded in the previous decades joined forces. The new company increased its control of the market by buying up many U.S. firms in the first quarter of the 20th century. By 1920, with its 7 factories and 13 warehouses, it employed over 5 300 workers. The Haywood Wakefield catalogues are exuberant. The catalogues put out by Philippe Vallière of Québec City and Owen McGarvey of Montréal at the end of the 19th century advertise the wicker furniture made by this U.S. company. J. D. Gagné of Bagotville, near Chicoutimi, learned how to make wicker furniture in a factory in Saint-Romuald, located in the vicinity of Lévis, and then, in 1911, set up the Canadian Rattan Company in Victoriaville. This business put out numerous catalogues, many of which were consulted for this book. The catalogues published by Morgan's of Montréal in the late 19th century are also very informative. The store used this means to sell fancy chairs and other articles in the Ornate Revival style, both imported and of domestic manufacture. An inventory of Québec wicker-furniture manufacturers remains to be made, but even in the absence of such a study, it is clear that a number of companies must have specialized in producing this style of furniture, which was so enthusiastically promoted in catalogues and magazines.

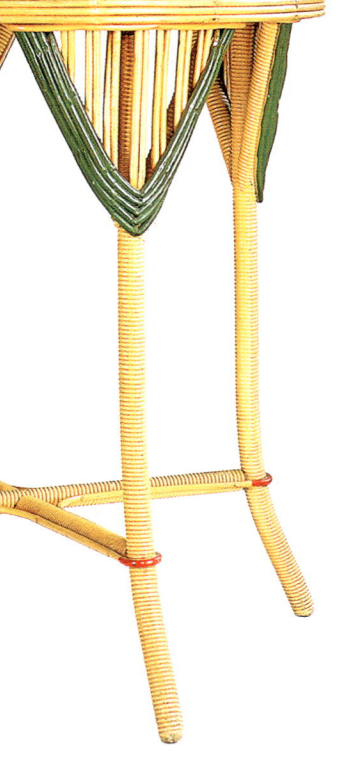

810 to 812
Wicker furniture suite, ca. 1925.
In the last quarter of the 19th century, co-ordinated suites of wicker furniture became available on the market. Although the materials, weaving and finish might be inspired by various sources, they were harmonized for each suite. In the 1920s and 1930s, color was used to add highlights to wicker furniture, which was now influenced by the Art Deco and Mission styles.

813

Wicker furniture advertisement by the J. W. Kilgour Company of Beauharnois in 1936. The text accompanying this picture states that the company had been working with this material since 1863.

For the Summer Home

" Discover the harmonious effect of furniture made of a material that is naturally decorative. Kilgour verandah chairs and wicker furniture have served this purpose for the past 73 years. The 1926 models maintain the fine quality of our previous production. " [Translation]
Even radio cabinets, newly arrived in Québec in the 1920s, were made in wicker to match verandah suites.

814-815

Wicker plants stands and rocking chair, ca. 1900.

816 to 820

Chairs and sewing table displaying the values of the Art Deco and Mission styles. Wicker and bamboo, ca. 1910. A great deal of wicker furniture was produced in Québec. Merchants also imported such goods from the United States, where both medium-sized and large businesses tried to outdo each other with imaginative models. Numerous catalogues from Québec and the United States attest to this production and the trade it engendered. The stylistic movements that shaped furniture design also affected wicker. Cushions were covered in the floral prints that were popular at the time.

INDUSTRIAL VERNACULAR FURNITURE 1870-1920

Thousands and thousands of chairs, armchairs and rockers were made in this period. From the second half of the 19th century to the outbreak of the First World War, countless models of ordinary items were offered by the Québec furniture industry, made up of various-sized businesses in every region. The antique market is full of these solidly built old objects, made of hardwood and often decorated with turned elements, stencilled motifs or steam-embossed patterns.

d.

e.

a.

f.

g.

h.

i.

b.

c.

j.

k.

l.

Various pieces of furniture intended for the general public in Québec. From catalogues published by the J. W. Kilgour & Brothers Company between 1880 and 1900, as well as by P.-T. Legaré between 1915 and 1920.
a. verandah rocking chairs, ca. 1910. **b.** "Louis Cyr," or jumbo rocker, ca. 1900. **c.** wide-backed rocker, 1890.
d., e., l. children's highchairs, one of which converts into a stroller, ca. 1900. **f.-j.** simple kitchen chairs, ca. 1880.
g., h., i., k. various rocking chairs, ca. 1890. **m., t., u.** parlor tables, 1915 to 1925. **n.** factory-made cradles, 1880. **o.-s.** kitchen tables with turned legs, 1890. **p.-q.** factory-made spindle beds, ca. 1880. **r.-x.** washstands, 1880. **v.** factory-made desk, 1900. **w.** serving table with turned legs.

m.

n.

o.

p.

q.

r.

s.

t.

u.

v.

w.

x.

821 to 832

Factory-Made Chairs, Armchairs and Rockers from the Belle Époque

Anyone who looks through old issues of furniture maker's catalogues or peruses newspapers for furniture advertisements is invariably struck by the enormous variety of industrial chairs, armchairs and rockers made during the Belle Époque, in the Pre-Modern era. This impression is only strengthened by fieldwork in the different regions of Québec. Furniture companies tried to surpass each other with imaginative forms, turnings, finishes and decoration. These myriad chairs, including the New England Shakers' simply designed polychrome verandah rockers, show the influence of the great aesthetic movements originating in France, Britain and the United States in this period. Viewed as a whole, these chairs announce Québec's entry into the Modern era.

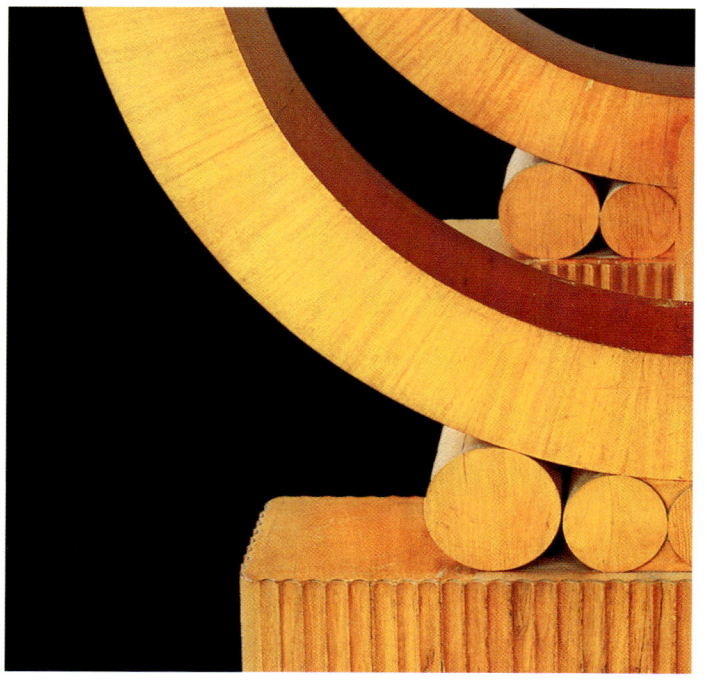

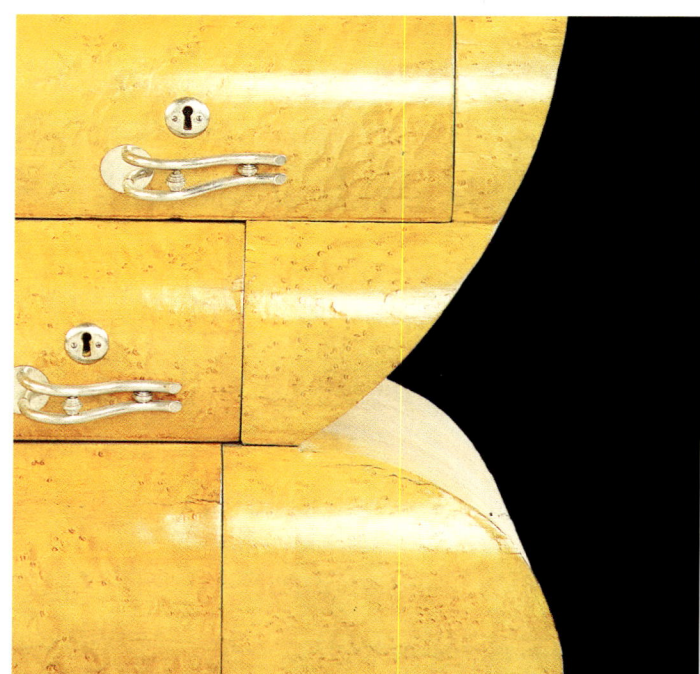

833 to 836
Details of Modern furniture found in Québec.
Leg on a maple and yellow birch table by the École du meuble de Montréal; back
of a chromed tubing chair made in Québec; part of a reclining chair by Le Corbusier; corner
of a bedroom dressing table in bird's-eye maple, probably from Québec.

CHAPTER 6

Mass Production and Studio Design

Modern Furniture in Québec

1920-1960

ART DECO AND INDUSTRIAL DESIGN

WE HAVE come to a turning point in our history. We are increasingly seen by the rest of the world to be no longer a colony but a nation. We must affirm our ethnic character in every domain.

JEAN-MARIE GAUVREAU
[Translation] *Nos intérieurs de demain*, 1929

I ROSE UP against certain forms of an invasive Americanism that seemed to me would eventually manage to appropriate everything that remains of our tradition and individuality as a people of French stock.

JEAN-MARIE GAUVREAU
"Commentaires et impressions en marge d'un voyage à New York" in *Technique*, February 1938

LET US LOOK TOGETHER, if you will, at a piece of old *Canadien* furniture made of white pine or butternut. Admire its elegant, well-balanced proportions. Examine its handcrafted fluting and its mortise-and-tenon or dovetail joints. The vibrations of the craftsman's hand can be sensed in each tool mark, in the beautiful diamond-point panels and in the mouldings shaped with a grooving plane.

JEAN-MARIE GAUVREAU
[Translation] Undated manuscript

OUR MAPLE, ELM and ash trees, our yellow birch, white birch, oak and cherry trees are not any more misshapen than trees in other countries. And if they were, what luck it would be for cabinetmakers. For then our crotch grains and burls would no longer be used simply for our own consumption, but their renown would spread to every market in the world and to famous decorators, always on the lookout for new and rare materials.

JEAN-MARIE GAUVREAU
[Translation] "Bois et meubles du Québec," lecture, April 2, 1935

CABINETMAKING, properly speaking, is not just a craft. A cabinetmaker, in the true sense of the word, is not simply a skilled worker — which is in itself quite excellent — but also a man of taste. Cabinetmaking is an applied art. If a craftsman is to interpret a decorator's sketch, he must understand the underlying spirit of this sketch and give it form, while exploiting the possibilities offered by the chosen material. He does not submit to this material; it must submit to him. This is an important distinction. Constructing a piece of furniture is actually somewhat like architectural work on a reduced scale; the lines and proportions count for as much as the nuances and colors.

JEAN-MARIE GAUVREAU
[Translation] *L'Enseignement de l'ébénisterie à l'École technique de Montréal*, 1931

Long-case clock by Alphonse Saint-Jacques. Maple and yellow birch, 1936.

Modern Furniture in Québec

837
Dining room furniture by Louis Jaque (Beaulieu). Bleached oak and babiche seats, Montréal, 1945.

838
"Bench" chair by Louis Jaque. Oak and babiche, 1945.

Québec furniture produced between 1920 and 1960 — during the 40-year period ending with the Post-Modern period, which is treated briefly in the concluding pages — can be divided into two major categories, corresponding to the production methods involved. The first category includes industrial furniture produced on a vast scale and generally in fairly large series. This furniture was supplied in part by numerous businesses established throughout Québec and in part by firms in Ontario and the United States. The other category involves furniture that was made for an elite clientele by various woodworkers and cabinetmakers who, as has always been the case throughout the history of Québec, maintained workshops in cities and villages. These craftsmen's work includes their own interpretations of new styles and versions of furniture seen in sales catalogues, as well as special orders placed by architect-designers and interior decorators or by individual clients who wanted their surroundings to include pieces they had seen in the pages of a magazine, in a store or in someone's home. Often the pieces that inspired such work came from abroad, for example, from Europe. Another type of furniture that belongs to this handcrafted category consists of the work of the teachers and students at technical colleges and at the École du meuble in Montréal. As well, there were small industries that employed a few specialized craftsmen for work in avant-garde niches. An example is the

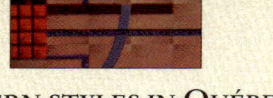

MODERN STYLES IN QUÉBEC
1920-1960

F. LLOYD WRIGHT
1867-1959

WALTER GROPIUS
1883-1969

LE CORBUSIER
1887-1965

SOURCES: Trends in industrial design from France, Britain and the United States, Art Deco, Bauhaus, École du meuble de Montréal…
Functionalist geometric lines, sparse decoration, color, new materials.

WOOD: maple, pale and dark yellow birch, elm, ash, oak, cherry, butternut, pine
Veneers: mahogany, figured walnut, figured elm, "birnut"
Metals: hammered wrought iron, metal tubing

Sideboard by Henri Beaulac, 1945.

COLLECTIONS: Montreal Museum of Fine Arts, Musée de la civilisation in Québec City, Musée des arts et des traditions populaires in Trois-Rivières, Musée du Saguenay—Lac-Saint-Jean in Chicoutimi.

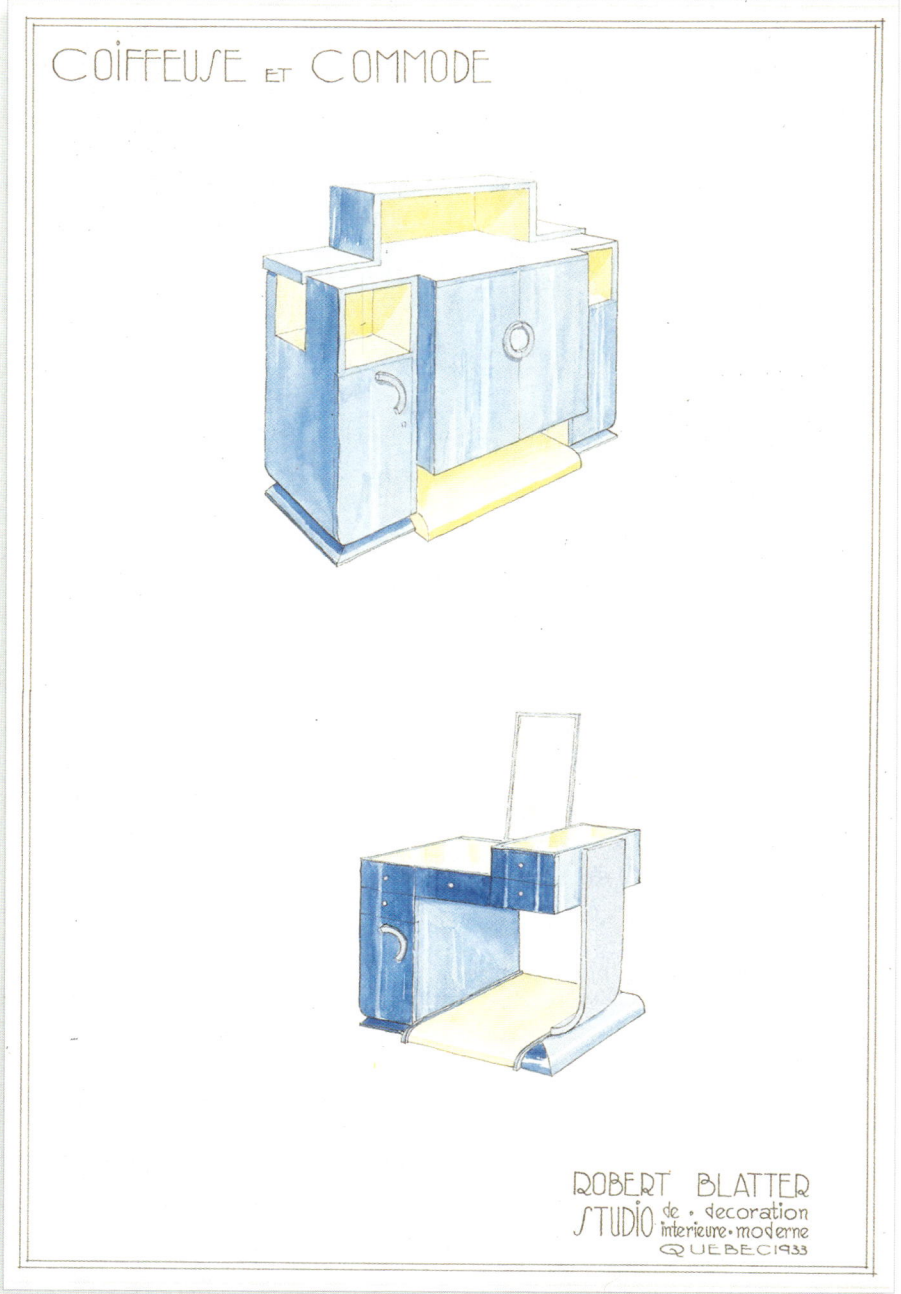

Montmagny Furniture Company Limited, in operation on the south shore of the St. Lawrence River in the 1940s; it produced original furniture inspired by French Art Deco and the Waterfall style.

Handcrafted furniture was largely influenced by a fairly small number of architects who, true to the philosophical tendencies of the period, refused to isolate decoration from interior design, which now encompassed furniture design. Such architects included Robert Blatter and Jacques Rousseau in Québec City and Ernest Cormier, Omer Parent and Jacques Carlu in Montréal, all of whom helped to lay the foundations of Modernity in Québec. Architect-designers with this outlook tended to fall into one of two Art Deco "camps." The first attracted traditionalists, who borrowed

certain conventions from the past and reinterpreted them with bold new lines, while the other called for truly innovative work, exploring the frontiers of design. The two groups also differed with respect to their intended clientele: the first group of architect-designers — for example, Robert Blatter — concentrated on luxury products for a privileged class, while the other group displayed a more "populist" philosophy and took into account the potential of their designs for mass production.

Robert Blatter (1899-1998) was a self-taught designer of Swiss origin. He took an active part in the Exposition des Arts Décoratifs et Industriels Modernes held in Paris in 1925. This event was a magical moment in the history of the new style known as Art Deco, which had been developing since the beginning of the century, although interrupted by the Great War. The Parisian exhibition in some way marked the apogee of this artistic movement, which, through the efforts of Jean-Marie Gauvreau and the École du meuble de Montréal, continued to dominate Québec design until the time of the Quiet Revolution in the 1960s, when the style began to be contested as being too traditional. No fewer than 21 countries took part in the Paris exhibition. Every leading architect and decorative artist

839
Drawing, highlighted with watercolor, of a chest of drawers and dressing table for a bedroom by Robert Blatter. Québec City, 1933.
Some of the architect-designers and interior decorators who were active in Québec in the Modern period left eloquent drawings of their designs for furniture and interiors. Blatter, who worked mainly in Québec City, was one of them.

840
Dressing table by Jean-Marie Gauvreau. Ebony and amboyna, ca. 1930.
The founder of Montréal's École du meuble, which opened in 1935, made this very French Art Deco piece in the 1920s when he was completing his studies at the École Boulle in Paris. Gauvreau remained true to the values of the Art Deco movement throughout his life and kindled enthusiasm for it among his students.

THE MODERN SPIRIT 1920-1960

*A*t the turn of the 19th century, the winds of change blew through the arts world. Architecture and the decorative arts were radically altered by the principles of rationalism and Functionalism. Furniture was stripped of all artifice. Design was characterized by geometric clarity, pure colors, clean lines and subtle decoration. Modern art is international. All the industrialized nations in the world were affected by this movement and its stylistic principles were applied to everything, from living quarters to silverware. New materials led to innovative design concepts.

Vase by Jules Bazin, ca. 1948.

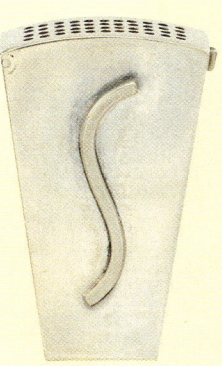

Salt and pepper shakers by Georges Delrue, ca. 1948.

Le Port de Montréal, Adrien Hébert, 1924.

Emerson radio, 1940.

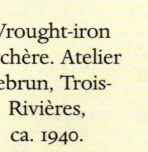

Evening gown, ca. 1925.

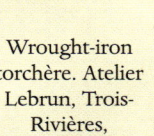

Wrought-iron torchère. Atelier Lebrun, Trois-Rivières, ca. 1940.

Fish lamp by Hubert Boyer, ca. 1945.

Hall chair. Atelier Lebrun, Trois-Rivières, ca. 1935.

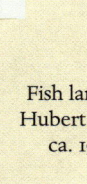

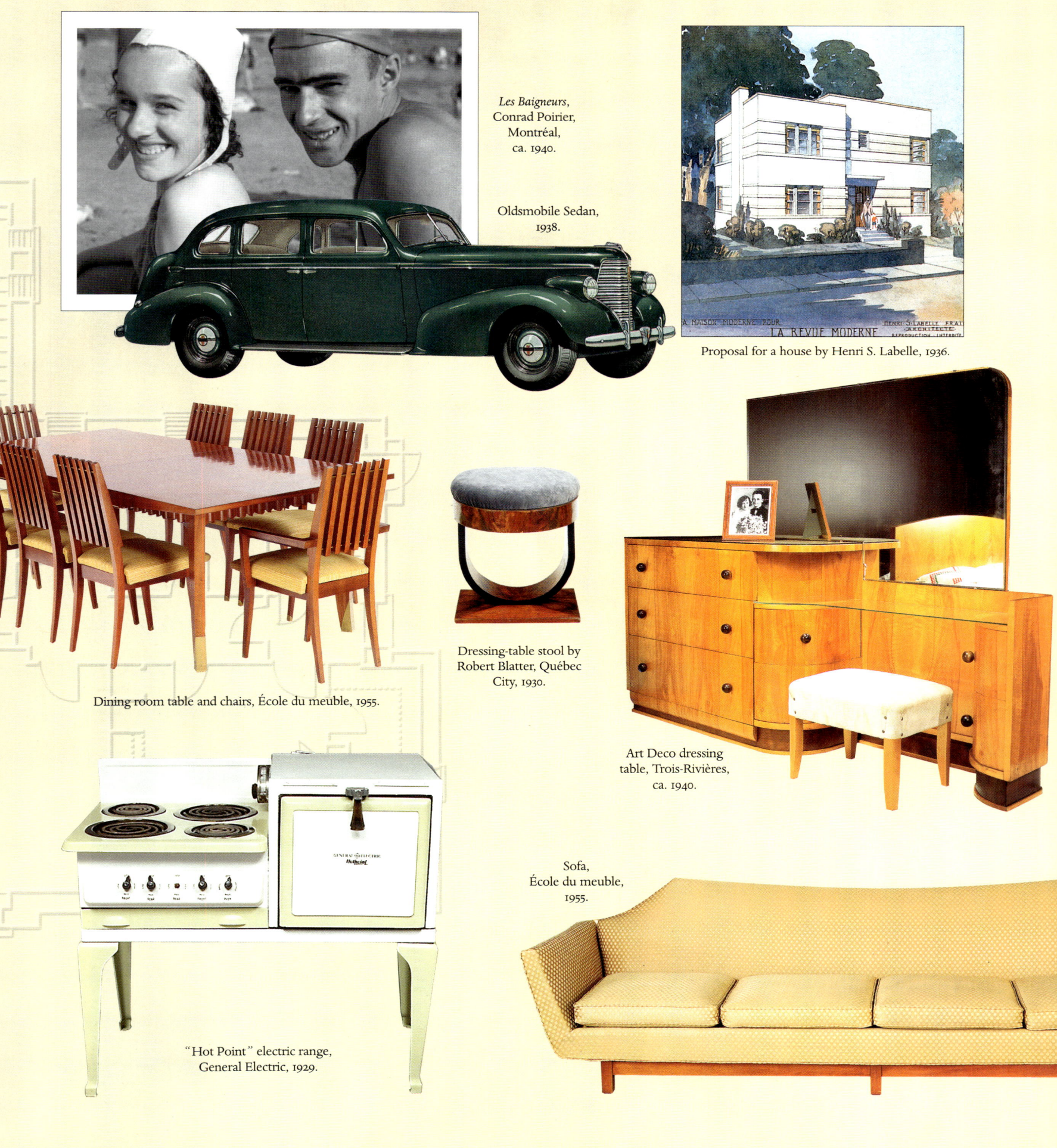

Les Baigneurs, Conrad Poirier, Montréal, ca. 1940.

Oldsmobile Sedan, 1938.

Proposal for a house by Henri S. Labelle, 1936.

Dining room table and chairs, École du meuble, 1955.

Dressing-table stool by Robert Blatter, Québec City, 1930.

Art Deco dressing table, Trois-Rivières, ca. 1940.

"Hot Point" electric range, General Electric, 1929.

Sofa, École du meuble, 1955.

THE CABINETMAKER

Antoine Rousseau, a Québec City Cabinetmaker

"I am more of a craftsman than a businessman, and it's through work that my workshop grew into a business." E.-Antoine Rousseau thus sums up his cabinetmaking career with well-deserved pride, stressing the word "craftsman," with all its connotations of creativity and artistry.

The E.-A. Rousseau cabinetmaking firm, located at 317 Dorchester Street in Québec City, is owned by a man whose father and grandfather both made a name for themselves as turners in the city. He is a sharp-eyed, energetic-looking man of around 50. I met him in his office beside the vast, recently constructed workshops that stand at the entrance to Pointe-aux-Lièvres. Despite the early hour, he was already at work, receiving customers, arranging business meetings and distributing the day's most urgent work among his staff. Antoine Rousseau has got off to an early start like this, day after day, for the past 25 years. When he began, he had just one apprentice but he was gradually joined by more assistants; he now manages a staff of 28, some of them specialized carvers who work wood with skilled hands and practised eyes.

It was in 1922 that young Rousseau left his father's shop, where he had apprenticed for a few years, and opened his own workshop. He had decided to break with the family tradition of wood turning, for he wanted to find a way of putting his natural artistic talent to good use. The field that offered him the most latitude and a promising future was cabinetmaking.

His grandfather, Louis Rousseau, had run a turning shop for nearly half a century, first on Saint-Joseph Street and then on Dorchester Street. Louis Rousseau's sons, Louis, Philippe and Ulric, inherited his small enterprise, whose value lay in the reputation of the Rousseau name rather than the size of the business.

There is little documentation on the first Rousseau turnery on Saint-Joseph Street. It was sold in about 1860 for the sum of $1 500, which was "an advantageous transaction," according to contemporary reports. The grandfather then set up shop at 40 Dorchester Street, where Laurentide Automobile inc. now stands. Québec City residents had found that Mr. Rousseau could be relied upon for "a job well done." Customers entering the shop might order a complete stairway or simply buy a few small balusters to repair a highchair for a new baby. But in general the business seldom dealt with customers directly, since most work was carried out by building contractors who ordered goods for their clients. The Rousseau sons eventually took over the business and ran it until the city made plans to widen Dorchester Street in 1931. The brothers, who were getting on in age, decided to sell everything instead of demolishing their workshop and setting up elsewhere. The Rousseau business ceased to exist as a turnery, but the name was beginning to become known for the cabinetmaking done at the E.-A. Rousseau workshop.

E.-Antoine Rousseau established his first workshop in an old building at 158 Roi Street. Mr. Rousseau lived on the second floor. He did not make a great deal of money but through hard work he managed to make ends meet. After a long day in the workshop, the young cabinetmaker would spend his evening preparing drawings for the furniture that had been ordered. He worked only to order, whether it was to make cupboards or furniture for a dining room, bedroom, living room or study. These drawings, as Mr. Rousseau explains, required and still require a certain natural aptitude for interior decoration, since a piece, regardless of its intrinsic value, must harmonize with its immediate surroundings — the room and its decor. To respect this fundamental principle of interior decorating, Mr. Rousseau would go to his clients' house to study the setting and determine what the owners wanted. He would make a sketch on the spot, make a few suggestions and then finish the work back at his place. At different stages, he would act as a draftsman, artist, architect and builder, and sometimes even as a sculptor. It is not surprising that he considers himself a craftsman first and foremost.

Admittedly, working conditions had greatly improved for cabinetmakers. Modern machinery had replaced his grandfather's rudimentary tools, and electricity had relegated the horse, which supplied power in 1860, to other activities. Nevertheless, Mr. Rousseau was still without an essential piece of equipment — a lumber drying kiln. The absence of this equipment caused the young cabinetmaker's first nightmares. He recalls how customers would often call up a few months after he had delivered a piece of furniture, complaining that a door or drawer had shrunk and that the catch no longer worked. Even though the wood had been left to dry for several months, hanging from the workshop ceiling, it still contained too much moisture when it was made into furniture and the evaporation process continued after the piece had been delivered. Since the other technical aspects of cabinetmaking presented Mr. Rousseau with no problems, this was the only real difficulty he had to face in the early years of his business.

A few years after starting out, Mr. Rousseau was obliged to expand the premises. In 1928, he had the old building on Roi Street demolished and on the same site built a two-story building that would be entirely occupied by his workshop. At the same time, he installed the drying kiln that he had so badly needed at the beginning of his career. This piece of equipment could prepare more than 2 000 feet of wood at a time. Today his drying chamber can handle 6 000 to 7 000 feet of wood. Business improved in the new workshop. Scarcely two years after it was constructed, there were so many orders to be filled that the cabinetmaker was obliged to add a third floor to the building and hire new employees. For the most part, these workers were former students of Québec City's École technique. Mr. Rousseau considers the training offered in this technical school ideal for a career in cabinetmaking, since the regular program is the equivalent of two years of apprenticeship. To be sure, success in the field also depends on a person's natural aptitudes, but the theory taught in technical schools takes the place of training that no-one would have time to give in a workshop, in Mr. Rousseau's opinion. The workshop he runs is the only one of its kind in Québec City, but he believes that the École du meuble in Montréal will attract an increasing number of young people to cabinetmaking and that, as a result, the trade will attract more candidates than it has in the past.

When asked about the public's tastes, Mr. Rousseau emphasizes their diversity, for a number of different styles are popular. According to him, the style adopted by people is dictated more by necessity than by whims or trends. Today people turn to him for space-saving solutions in their tiny apartments. In many cases, it is quite difficult to follow the rules of style to the letter. There are always some who, because of their notion of cabinetmaking — or more often of art — or their underestimation of the work that goes into building a piece of furniture, ask for an item that is identical to one that is produced in series, but "at a reasonable price." But a cabinetmaker's reputation rests on the original and exclusive nature of his work and the luxurious appearance of his furniture. It's as if someone were asked to build a Rolls Royce and sell it at the price of a Ford, simply because it was built elsewhere than in the prestigious car maker's factories.

Many people hold their heritage dear and, for them, old pieces of furniture are symbols of a past filled with memories. Mr. Rousseau says that these people are ready to pay considerable sums to conserve their old furniture, for maintaining and repairing it often requires the skills of a specialist, generally a talented wood carver. Mr. Rousseau has frequently been called upon for this type of delicate work from the early days of his workshop to the present. He has also been entrusted with numerous patternmaking contracts for manufacturing concerns, notably for Atelier & Chantiers du Saint-Laurent inc. Mr. Rousseau began to practise this trade in addition to cabinetmaking long ago and employs three patternmakers at present.

Two years ago, in 1946, Mr. Rousseau set up his workshop in an immense building at 317 Dorchester Street and, in doing so, realized an old dream. He now has two floors with a total surface area of over 10 000 square feet; in comparison, the old shop on Roi Street had only 2 200 square feet. This expansion is a good illustration of how the E.-A. Rousseau cabinetmaking business has grown in 25 years. The first floor is occupied by all the machinery, including planing machines, trimmers to straighten planks, circular saws, band saws and sanders. Finishing and repairs are carried out on the second floor, which also houses a drying chamber.

Even though his business is flourishing, Antoine Rousseau remains above all a craftsman who loves his chosen trade of cabinetmaking. He far prefers manual work and the hubbub of the workshop to administration. His son, Paul-André, is in charge of accounting and one of his brothers, Maurice, who shares his passion for cabinetmaking, works with him in the shop.

Adapted from Léa Pétrin "E.-A. Rousseau ébéniste"
Le Soleil, Québec City, Sunday, December 5, 1948

851 to 854
Art Deco bedroom suite attributed to Robert Blatter of Québec City. Yellow birch and split figured walnut veneer, probably made in the workshop of the cabinetmaker A.-E. Rousseau, Québec City, ca. 1930.

Montréal and at the end of that year received a government grant that enabled him to per-

period from 1935 to 1945 was his institution's golden age, largely because of the exceptional

PERSONAL ACCOUNT

A Teacher of Cabinetmaking at the École du meuble

ued to head this institution until 1968, when it closed and the old master retired.

Gauvreau wrote throughout his life. His published work includes books, such as *Secrets et ressources des bois du Québec*, and numerous articles, particularly those written for the magazine *Technique*. As Louise Chouinard points out, he wrote "nearly 200 books and articles, dealing mainly with handcrafted work, the École du meuble, specialized teaching, techniques, Québec wood species, cabinetmaking, the history of furniture in the world, French Modern furniture and Québec country furniture." [Translation] In addition, Gauvreau participated in every major exhibition, conducted methodical surveys on the general situation of handcrafting in Québec, gave lectures, worked as a critic and taught. He was an institution in himself — tireless, inexhaustible and involved in every facet of his profession.

The École du meuble de Montréal owed its existence to a government policy, announced at the beginning of the 20th century, of setting up a network of technical schools. Its immediate predecessor, the École technique de Montréal, was established in 1907 as the first institution intended to meet this purpose.

As is well demonstrated by Louise Chouinard and the few other researchers who have explored this period — whose productivity is well evidenced by fieldwork — Gauvreau was guided in his many enterprises by three main objectives: first, to establish a tradition of high-quality cabinetmaking; secondly, to encourage the emergence of an authentic type of Québec furniture; and finally, to promote the use of Québec's wood in furniture making. This last goal was one that he held especially dear.

The work of someone like Gauvreau, with his passion for wood, handcrafting and the furniture arts, fitted in very well with the ideological temper of the times. In the interwar period, the entire planet was caught up in zealous nationalism and a search for origins. In the wake of the Art & Crafts movement, vernacular material and handwork continued to be highly valued. The aesthetic movement

quality of its teaching staff. The École du meuble became a place of artistic and cultural effervescence without parallel in the history of Québec. It was seen as a revolutionary hotbed by the government of the day. Paul-Émile Borduas taught freehand drawing there, the architect Marcel Parizeau taught furniture composition and interior architecture, and Maurice Gagnon, a well-respected art critic, gave courses on the history of art.

In 1958, the École du meuble became the Institut des arts appliqués. Gauvreau contin-

859
Watercolor-highlighted perspective of a proposal for a Modern bedroom drawn by Alphonse Saint-Jacques for his cabinetmaking diploma from the École technique in Montréal. The furniture, which is strongly influenced by the French Art Deco movement, is made with yellow birch veneer. [Translation]
Technique, November 1935, vol. 10, no. 9.

860
" Study area with furniture made of maple from the Province of Québec, trimmed with black walnut trim. Indirect lighting from niches in the corner cabinet and from the frame above the sofa. Designed by Jean-Marie Gauvreau, a teacher. This suite was the first to be made in 1930 by the students at the École technique de Montréal. " [Translation]
Technique, November 1935, vol. 10 no. 9.

861
" Modern drawing room suite in the French Art Deco style, made of zebrawood and black walnut in 1933-1934 in the cabinetmaking workshop of the École technique de Montréal. The chairs and sofa are designed by Jean-Marie Gauvreau and the rest of the furniture is designed by Alphonse Saint-Jacques, who was then a fourth-year student and who went on to become a designer and teacher with the École du meuble founded in 1935. " [Translation]
Technique, November 1935, vol. 10 no. 9.

862
" Office with furniture in " birnut " (stained Québec yellow birch) with inlay of black walnut, yellow birch and black cherry made in 1934-1935 in the cabinetmaking workshop of the École technique de Montréal. Indirect lighting is provided by ceiling fixtures made of turned and inlaid wood. Note the practical storage area for papers and books under the desk top. The chairs are covered with cream-colored leather. " [Translation]
Technique, November 1935, vol. 10 no. 9.

ART DECO AND INDUSTRIAL DESIGN 499

that marked the period was Art Deco; its influence was felt throughout the world and naturally affected North America and Québec.

A growing nationalism was reflected in numerous publications paying honor to Québec's historic roots and campaigns to encourage people to speak "good French" and buy locally made products. The École du meuble was actively concerned with many aspects of this movement and was involved in surveys on handicrafts and traditions, interpretations of various traces of Québec's material past and setting up collections of old objects, including furniture. Gauvreau's school had a "museum of furniture" from the time it opened. The value given to the traditions and the craftsmen of the past found expression in a reinterpretation of older styles and the promotion of ancestral French techniques, which constituted the basis of training and production in Québec. In this spirit, Gauvreau encouraged his fellow citizens to treat their old furniture with great care. He fiercely criticized the way Québec's furniture was allowed to be siphoned off from its homeland. He was the first in Québec to propose an approach to conservation intended to guide furniture restoration, which he strongly supported. He offered precise instructions for finishing and advocated stripping old finishes off wood and polishing it with a protective wax.

Gauvreau devoted much energy to promoting the use of Québec's vernacular wood; for him, the achievements of early woodworkers demonstrated the potential of this material for Modern furniture. In any case, this was a period marked by renewed interest in the use of local resources and in manual work inspired by traditional crafts. Ramsay Traquair, a professor of the history of architecture at McGill University, liked to teach his students about the clever solutions used by early *Canadiens* who had to rely exclusively on the bounty of their natural environment when it came to building their homes and churches. During the Modern period, spinning and weaving, especially with wool and linen, were held in high respect in Québec, as were all the old methods in the domestic arts, now seen as under threat from industrial production. These traditional activities were encouraged by people like Oscar Bériau, a founder of the Cercle des fermières du Québec. Gauvreau's enthusiasm for this trend is evident in works like *Artisans du Québec*, published in 1940, in which he lauds the nobility of wood, clay, metals and textiles, as a vital factor in the renewal of traditional practices such as joinery, sculpture, cabinetmaking, pottery, forging and weaving. He believed that Québec wood was eminently suitable for dramatic veneering that would make a name for the grains and figures offered by local species.

863 to 865
Modern bedroom furniture made at the École du meuble de Montréal. Yellow birch veneer, ca. 1940.
The chest of drawers, bed and dressing table strongly reflect Art Deco aesthetics.

Gauvreau and the École du meuble wholeheartedly accepted the aesthetics of Art Deco and the Modernism of France, an artistic approach that adapted and grew as it attracted new talents and ideas. It was natural for the school to favor this approach, given the founder's training and his close links with the École Boulle, as well as the frequent invitations he extended to his former masters to teach or lecture and the coverage given to their work in many of the articles he wrote, especially in the magazine *Technique*. Furthermore, the library at the École du meuble was well supplied with periodicals and other publications that kept staff and students abreast of developments in the Modern movement, while the teachers themselves had often trained abroad, particularly in France, in the best art schools.

Following the paths opened up by Gauvreau and the École du meuble, a number of former students set up studios that specialized in the production of avant-garde furniture. However, most graduates were drawn to designing rustic furniture inspired by traditional styles. Louis Chouinard's thesis on the École du meuble concludes with the following passage:

"Furthermore, by training the first generation of designers, Jean-Marie Gauvreau made it possible for an industrial aesthetic to develop in Québec. In 1963, there were three or four industrial design offices in Montréal. Today the city has over 200 firms specialized in this field. The Interior Decorators' Society of Québec has more than 500 members, while its industrial counterpart, the Association des designers industriels du Québec, founded in 1968, has nearly 200. After the Institut des arts appliqués closed in 1984, training in this field continued to be offered by industrial design departments in the Cégep du Vieux-Montréal and Dawson College and by the design faculties at Université de Montréal and the Université du Québec à Montréal (UQAM).

[…]

"This study leads to the following conclusions: Jean-Marie Gauvreau was partially successful in training students to produce handcrafted furniture that would create a tradition of excellence in cabinetmaking; he failed to reach his goal of developing an "authentically *Canadien*" style, but succeeded in making furniture out of the wood found in Québec's forests and put the richly decorative quality of this material to good use; and he was influential in the development of industrial design in Québec." [Translation]

866
Sketches of Art Deco furniture drawn in France. These sketches illustrate the strong influence of French cabinetmaking on the academic work done by students like Jean-Marie Gauvreau when training at the École Boulle in Paris.

867
Old photograph showing the first furniture made by Jean-Marie Gauvreau on his return from the École Boulle, ca. 1930.

868
Chiffonier by Jean-Marie Gauvreau. Ebony, figured amboyna and glass, ca. 1930.

869
Industrial Art Deco dining room suite made in Québec. Yellow birch, ca. 1940.

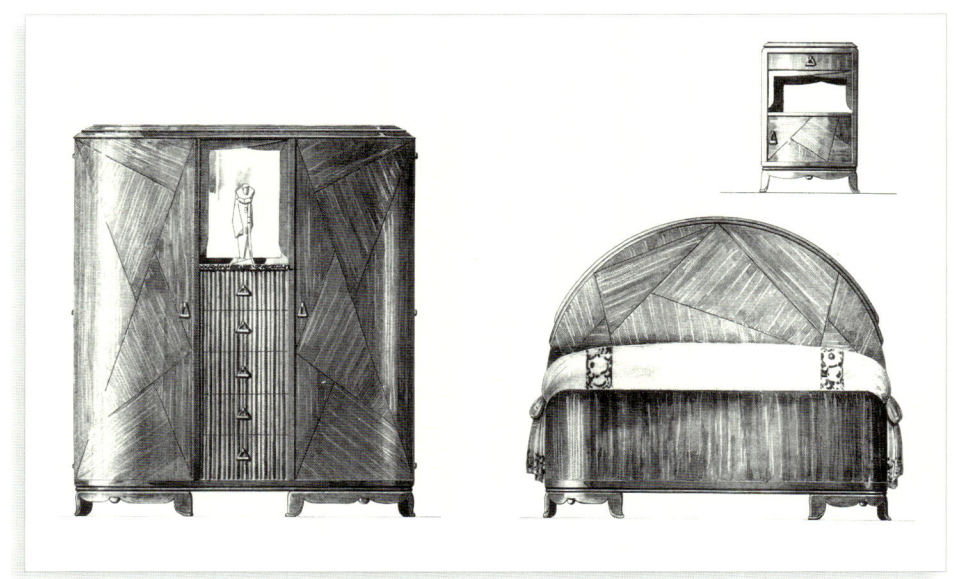

PERSONAL ACCOUNT

The Birth of a Piece of Furniture

You start by making all sorts of sketches on paper to capture the idea that has germinated in your head or in your imagination — quick, freehand sketches. Sometimes it takes over 20 tries before one of them expresses the character you want for the piece. When the shape has been decided, the next stages are to make a full-sized plan and determine the techniques and joining methods that will ensure solidity and that are feasible with the tools and machinery available. It might be decided to give the piece a stained finish, but natural wood is generally preferable.

The process of designing a piece of furniture is guided by several factors. There is the material — the wood with its grain and color, which may contrast with other types of wood. There are elements made of metal, ceramic and glass. And there are projections creating patterns of shadow and light, the massiveness or airiness of the moulding in various shapes and the textures of openwork and carving. All these elements are at the disposal of the designer-draftsman. The design may be sometimes influenced by clients' tastes or even be a direct expression of their desires. It can take several days and nights before the designer is satisfied with the final drawing.

The piece of furniture should be drawn in perspective and highlighted with color before it is presented. This is what I have always done.

Alphonse Saint-Jacques

ART DECO AND INDUSTRIAL DESIGN 503

870
Dressing table with brass knobs and fabric-upholstered stool by Henri Beaulac (1914-1994). Bird's-eye maple and mahogany, Montréal, 1947.

871
Dining room suite by the École du meuble de Montréal. Mahogany, brass and leather, ca. 1955.

872 to 877
Sofa table, occasional tables, coffee table, sideboard and sofa by the École du meuble. Teak and yellow birch, 1958.

WROUGHT IRON

Encouraged by Jean-Marie Gauvreau, two men, Jean-Cyrille Lebrun (1910-1963) and his brother Hugues (1913-1985), both of whom had received technical training in several fields at the École technique in Trois-Rivières, decided in 1933 to establish their own blacksmith's shop. Two years later, their shop, called "La P'tite Forge," was set up on Niverville Street. In 1945 the business moved into modern quarters designed by the architect Maurice Denoncourt. By this time, the two disciples of St. Eloi, the patron saint of metalworkers, had specialized in architectural and hand-wrought iron.

The Lebrun brothers designed their own, often unique, pieces, although they also sought the collaboration of designers such as Henri Beaulac, Jean-Jacques Spénard, Jacques Beaulieu, Albert Nielson and Raymond Lasnier. The Lebruns received impressive orders for lighting fixtures, grilles, railings and banisters for churches and other buildings. Between 1947 and 1949, the brothers took part in numerous exhibitions and displayed their products, which included furniture. Many craftsmen also trained at the forge, which closed its doors in 1967.

In Québec, the 1940s and 1950s might be called the golden age of hammered iron and ornamental iron. During this time, renewed interest in handcrafting and a demand for very diverse products gave metal craftsmen throughout Québec an opportunity to put their inventiveness and skill to good use. Their production consisted mainly of hall chairs and mirrors, torchères and chandeliers, telephone and drawing room tables, coat racks, umbrella stands, table lamps, plant stands and ashtrays. Certain companies promoted these household furnishings through catalogues. The cover on a catalogue put out by the H. L. Ironcraft Company Limited, a Saint-Hyacinthe firm, bore the words "Le maître forgeron au service de l'art" ["An iron master in the service of art"] — an inscription that eloquently reflects the popularity of wrought iron at the time.

Father Grégoire Tessier (1928-1998), a history enthusiast who for several years managed the collections at the Musée Pierre-Boucher in Trois-Rivières, had a real passion for the wrought iron hammered out by the craftsmen of Québec. Over a period of 40 years, he acquired hundreds of pieces attributed to 11 well-known iron smiths, including the Lebrun brothers, Charles Martin, François-Xavier Morin of Lévis, and Émile Juneau. His collection, the only one of its kind in Québec, is extremely well documented, providing a basis for ethnographical research and has also been used to produce a fascinating exhibition.

The craftsmen of this period worked their iron bars to the core, tirelessly hammering out scrolls, spirals and plant-like forms to decorate buildings. For the most part, their work may be classified as belonging to the Art Deco style.

878 to 884
Various pieces of furniture in wrought iron by Québec designers in the Modern period.

878
Top view of a rectangular coffee table with feather motifs by François-Xavier Morin, ca. 1948.

879
International style torchère attributed to the Lebrun brothers. Atelier Lebrun, ca. 1940.

880
Round table with plant-like decoration. Atelier Lebrun, ca. 1950.

881
Telephone table by Roland Levasseur. Trois-Rivières, ca. 1945.

882
Hall chair. Atelier Lebrun, 1935.

883
Rectangular coffee table with feather motifs by François-Xavier Morin, ca. 1948. (Top view on facing page.)

884
Coat rack and umbrella stand. Atelier Lebrun, Trois-Rivières, ca. 1950.

INDUSTRIAL MODERN FURNITURE

The furniture produced industrially during the period defined as Modern in this book was influenced by various trends springing from the schools of thought that shaped the decorative arts at this time.

As is evident from numerous catalogues distributed by manufacturers and retailers, the 1920s saw a continuation of the fashion for the U.S. version of the Arts & Craft style, known as Mission, which in some cases became excessively heavy. In the next decade, many consumers were drawn to furniture in somewhat simplified interpretations of historical styles. Suites for the dining room (table, chairs, sideboard and glass-doored china cabinet) and for the bedroom (bed, dressing table, chest of drawers, chiffonier and bureau with swing-frame mirror) were made with solid walnut, multi-ply walnut veneer and yellow birch given an "antique" or "French" walnut finish, according to advertisements. Examples of this updated Revival furniture are presented on pages 518-519.

In the middle of the 1930s, there began to appear vernacular industrial furniture that was marked by curves and fluid lines, showing the influence of the Art Deco style. This was the first industrial furniture to venture into the realm of Modernity. Pieces for bedroom suites were made with rounded corners and façades veneered with wood in geometric shapes or dramatic patterns. Veneers were especially used to produce the Waterfall style, much promoted by the advertisements of the time; the upper edges of Waterfall furniture curved smoothly from horizontal to vertical, like flowing water. This furniture was also often decorated with grooving, imaginatively combined plaques, and strips of inlaid wood with contrasting grains. Round or square mirrors became popular. Dining room furniture underwent a similar transformation. Plain chairs had upholstered seats and their simple, sturdy lines were softened by vertical fluting or horizontal grooved rings around their legs. Tables were given a new look with squarish legs rounded on their outer corners and smooth-edged, veneered tops. Each piece took on an air of reassuring solidity. Sideboards, the most attractive items in these suites, integrated the forms, lines and vocabulary of Art Deco, with their bold geometric decoration and symmetrical design characterized by doors flanking a central element. Legaré's 1939 sales catalogue (no. 140) presented typical examples of this sort of furniture.

Industrial furniture was also made in the chromed tubing that had gained popularity with the introduction of the Wassily chair designed by Marcel Breuer in 1925 and the cantilevered chair launched by Mart Stam the following year. By the mid-1930s, a number of North American firms, including some in Québec, were producing their own versions of living room sofas, armchairs and rockers in this new material. A tubular steel frame was provided with stylized wooden armrests and upholstered with fabric whose motifs echoed the abstract aesthetics of many artists of the day. Advertisements showed this furniture sitting on similarly patterned rugs and linoleum.

The shapes, finishes and fabrics used for upholstered sofas and easy chairs, wicker furniture and enamelled tubular steel beds were updated to harmonize with the Art Deco or International styles. Sales catalogues were full of furniture that echoed the new movements. All kinds of over-stuffed seating furniture — chesterfields, armchairs and sofas — were made with spring-coil upholstering covered with jacquard velvet, mohair, friezette or silk, in either solid colors or bold floral designs in fashionable shades. Soft, firm cushions and scrolled armrests made this furniture very inviting. Consumers seeking comfort were quite taken with these features, and the lines of this furniture became emblematic of the period.

In the 1950s, a number of Québec firms began to use chromed tubing for quite startling kitchen furniture with seats covered in brightly colored vinyl. Middle-class living rooms were furnished with somewhat mechanically simple furniture whose geometric shapes were upholstered with pastel-toned fabrics incorporating metallic threads; for example, lime green might be shot with charcoal accents.

In 1953, when my mother and father finally built the bungalow of their dreams after the war, they furnished their kitchen in chromed tubing and bought a lamé-upholstered suite for their living room. The old wooden dining room suite in the Art Deco style was traded in and the wicker living room suite was relegated to the basement.

885
Industrial drawing room furniture, Lévis, ca. 1935. In the 1920s, some businesses began to adopt the simplicity of Art Deco, but others turned to certain Revival styles, combining the old with the new. This led to increasing heaviness in vernacular drawing room furniture.

INDUSTRIAL ART DECO 1930-1950

The furniture industry has always produced its own versions of the artistic movements promoted by designers and workshops in a given period. In the Art Deco period, suites for the drawing rooms, dining rooms and kitchens of ordinary homes were given an updated look. Even the chest was reinvented. Art Deco-influenced industrial furniture was marked in particular by geometrical shapes, clever veneering in linear or chevron patterns, the smoothing out of all angular elements — in the Waterfall style — and round or square mirrors.

a.

b.

c.

The extent to which industrial production in Québec was influenced by Art Deco can be seen in numerous catalogues distributed by manufacturers or retailers of vernacular furniture.
a. Waterfall cedar chest with fancy seven-ply veneer, Ontario, 1935. **b.** Waterfall dining room suite with walnut veneer, some of it in chevron pattern, P.-T. Legaré, 1939. **c.** Waterfall kitchen furniture in natural wood with a choice of red, green or brown trim, five-ply maple veneer, P.-T. Legaré, 1939. **d., e.** armchairs and sofa, Simons, Montréal, 1936. **f.** Waterfall bedroom suite with black walnut and Oriental walnut veneer, Montmagny Furniture Company, 1943. The upper drawers are veneered in chevron patterns on either side of a figured walnut central panel and are topped by marquetry moulding. The company was one of dozens of similar businesses in Québec at the time, and its catalogue for this year included numerous suites like the one presented here. **g.** Coil-spring upholstered drawing room furniture covered with velvet, in lines inspired by Neoclassicism, Krohler, Stratford, Ontario, 1925. This company's catalogue contained 150 pages showing furniture in this style, which was very well received in the St. Lawrence Valley, judging from the furnishings seen in fieldwork. **h.** Waterfall bedroom suite with walnut and Oriental walnut veneer, P.-T. Legaré, 1939.

d.

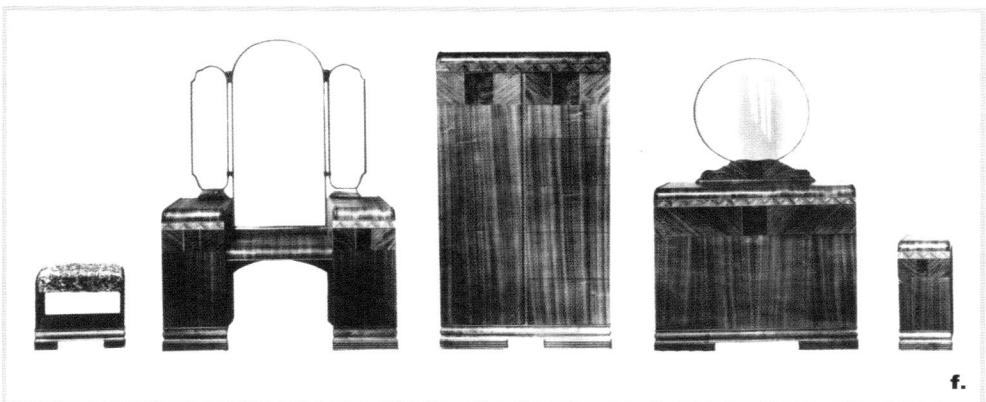

f.

e.

g.

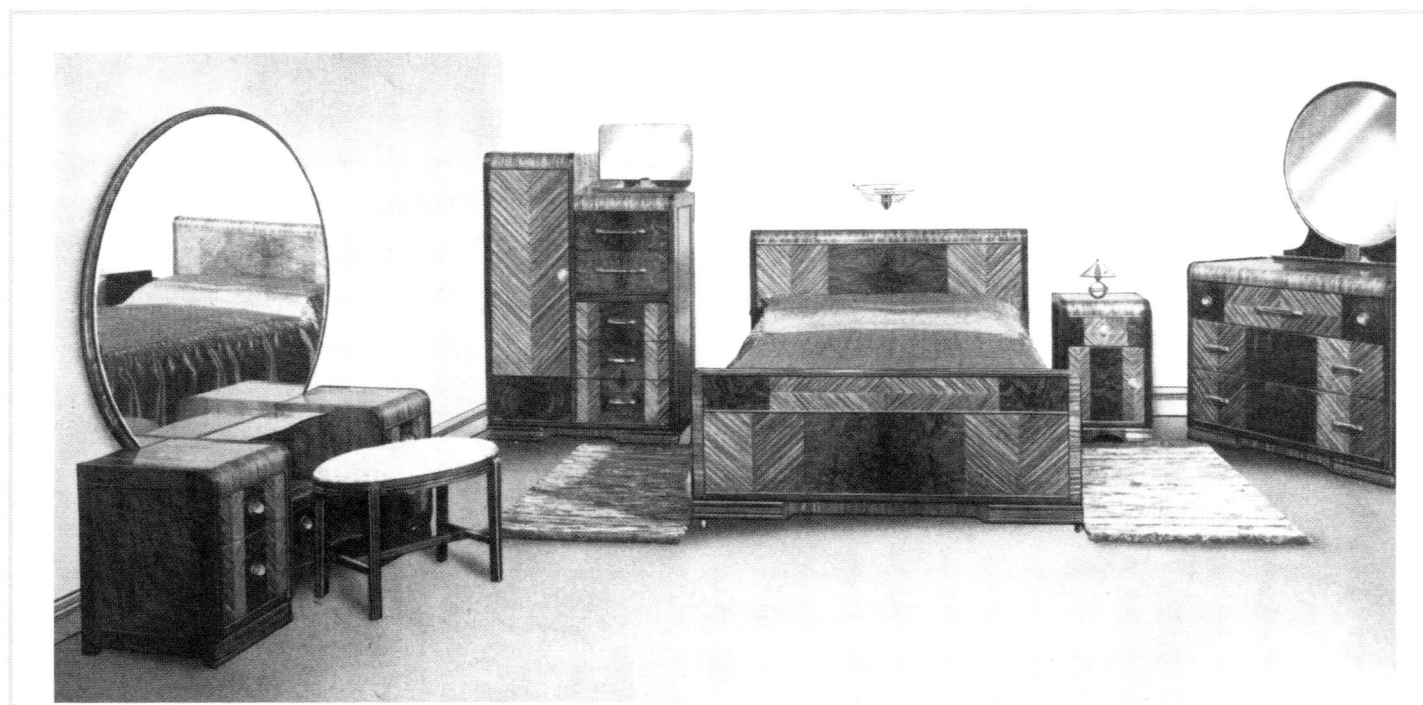

h.

INDUSTRY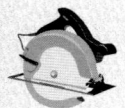

The Story of a Québec Manufacturer

J. W. Kilgour & Brothers Limited of Beauharnois

[…]

J. W. Kilgour, a Protestant Scotsman, founded [his furniture company] in 1863. He began by making furniture by hand for the local market and developed his business by adding new machinery every year, as well as new facilities to house it. By 1941, the Kilgour firm employed nearly 500 workers. Wood is the most important material used in the factory. The company no longer purchases lumber and has not done so for several years, but, on the contrary, possesses its own timber limits and sawmills, which now prepare the wood needed for furniture making.

The company has three factories, two of which are located in Beauharnois, while the third one is in Coaticook. It also owns two sawmills, with one in Taché in the county of Témiscouata and the other in Scottstown, 50 miles from Coaticook.

[…]

The employees normally work for 55 hours each week and no more. There is no overtime work of any sort whatsoever. Both the employees and the employers consider that the implementation of this way of working provides great benefits from both a social and economic point of view. For it enables all involved to maintain their physical and moral well-being and prevents sudden changes in the rate of production.

[…]

The traditions established by the company's founder are continued at present by a number of people, including Mr. Kilgour's nephew, Mr. R. W. Kilgour, who is now president; his only son, who is vice-president; and Mr. Euclide Théoret, the secretary-treasurer. These men are in reality the soul of the company. It is certainly rare to find such different talents and mentalities united in one firm. The first two men are Protestant English Canadians while the third is a Roman Catholic French Canadian. As well, the company's staff has five Protestant English members while the remainder are of Roman Catholic French Canadian origin. It may seem astonishing, but *the company has never experienced a single conflict based on race or religion, nor has it suffered misunderstandings or strikes of any nature whatsoever*. This fact is so singular that it should be set up as an example for all the manufacturers, whether large or small, that are established in our province and even in our whole country.

A friendly agreement has always existed between the workers and the employers, as it has between the English directors and Mr. Théoret. The latter is responsible for financial operations and for establishing and maintaining relations with customers. Thanks to the pervasive influence of these three administrators and the intelligent attitude of the staff, the company's French Canadian workers have always been treated not only benevolently, but even paternally, by the managers and foremen.

The two English Canadian directors, whose fortunate role I have just mentioned, have always dealt with their French Canadian workers in a spirit of understanding.

[…]

It must be acknowledged that certain basic factors have evidently always been respected. Among these, the most important are no doubt *wages* and *work carried out* in excellent physical, psychological and social conditions.

An effort has been made (and successfully made) *to never hire a married woman*. Furthermore, no-one is accepted as a worker unless they are at least 16 years old.

Men on night shift (numbering 15 at the most) work for only 8 hours and *no young women* are allowed on this shift. The salary for night work is the same as that for men on day shift, which lasts for at least 10 hours.

Those on day shift work from 7 a.m. to noon in the morning and from 1 p.m. to 6 p.m. in the afternoon. On Saturday, work stops at noon. This company was one of the first to end the working week on Saturday afternoon; it has been doing this for 30 years now.

Wages are determined in the following manner: about half a worker's total hourly pay is calculated according to a fixed rate, which gives the *basic pay*; the other half is based on the quantity and quality of the work done in the same hour.

[…]

At the beginning of this social monograph, mention was made of the role played by Mr. Euclide Théoret, the present secretary-treasurer of the Beauharnois company. He was engaged by the company in 1895, at the age of 24, as an accountant. He gained proficiency in his work, ceaselessly improving himself and upgrading his knowledge, and was rewarded with his present position in 1910, the year the business was turned into a *limited company*. When Mr. Théoret married, he established his permanent residence in Beauharnois. He has raised 15 children, 11 of whom are still alive.

Mr. Théoret, who has been the secretary-treasurer since 1910, deserves all the credit for the founding of a benevolent society in 1901, intended for the workers and run entirely by them. In 1901, the society provided weekly relief in case of illness, but in 1927, its scope was expanded. It now offers each member: 1/ an allowance of 10.00 at the birth of a new child; 2/ 25.00 for the marriage of a permanent employee; 3/ 25.00 on the death of a member of the society; and 4/ 6.00 per week for a period of up to 10 weeks each year if a member is ill. All this is obtained through a small contribution of 0.50 per month.

[…]

This is brief summary of the social conditions that make life liveable in the factories run by K. W. Kilgour & Brothers Limited. There can be no better proof than one of the workers, who at the age of 68, has been working at the company for the last 54 years. In 1939, two thirds of the 275 workers were less than 40 years old. Further proof of the workers' satisfaction and the job stability they enjoy comes from the fact that, on average, workers remain with the factory of some 275 employees for over 15 years, except for those who leave within the first three years. This shows that the workers feel secure there and like to live and work there for a long time.

[…]

Before ending this unfortunately all too brief sketch, I would like to emphasize the religious aspect of these numerous activities. Thanks to the spirit of good will that reigns throughout the factory, no blasphemous speech has been heard in the workshops for many years.

[…]

J. St-Geo. Morriset, lawyer
Taken from *Le Mouvement ouvrier*, 1943
(Italics as in the original text)

886
The J. W. Kilgour Brothers Limited factory in Beauharnois, ca. 1940.

887
Vernacular dining room furniture. Yellow birch, ca. 1940. In the 1930s, Québec manufacturers were won over to the Art Deco style and offered furniture suites that were strongly inspired by its aesthetics. Many firms made their versions of this furniture in wood from Québec.

ART DECO AND INDUSTRIAL DESIGN

MODERN METAL FURNITURE 1925-1970

*I*n the Modern period, there were remarkable developments in metal furniture. The new proposals made by designers like Marcel Breuer at the end of the 1920s triggered a fashion for chromed metal furniture, which grew increasingly popular. This eventually led to the flashy kitchen suites of the 1950s, with their loud-colored Arborite tabletops and vinyl seat covers. From about 1935 on, wrought iron experienced a sort of resurrection. Enamelled iron tubing, whether square or round, was often used for bedroom furniture. Metal garden furniture was also made in the Art Deco style.

Various articles of metal furniture offered in the catalogues distributed to Québec consumers between 1935 and 1960 by retailers and manufacturers based in Québec and elsewhere.
a., e., g. Royal Chrome, N. Y., 1936. **b., f.** H. L. Ironcraft, Saint-Hyacinthe, ca. 1950. **c.** P.-T. Legaré, 1939. **d.** Eaton's of Toronto, 1956. **h.** Chromed tubing dining room suite offered by Germain Larivière, a retailer in Sainte-Rosalie, in 1973.

d.

e.

f.

g.

h.

888 to 894

Chromed tubing furniture, with Formica tops and vinyl upholstering, ca. 1950. The table, chairs and sideboard are distinguished by the decorative use of buttoned upholstery. The stool shares their stylistic features. From 1945 to 1970, the catalogues offering vernacular furnishings were full of chromed tubing kitchen furniture that included all kinds of chairs and functional items, ranging from stools to rockers and stepladder chairs. This type of furniture, particularly in bright colors, was extremely popular.

MODERN REVIVALISM 1920-1940

After the First World War, the Mission style continued to be in fashion, but there was also a resurgence of historical styles in the industrial furniture manufactured for the middle classes. The forms adopted at this time were fairly simple in comparison with those of the true Revival period. Dining room and bedroom suites were made of varnished wood with plenty of veneering and turning. Catalogues described this furniture as inspired by any number of styles, from Spanish or Italian Renaissance to Tudor, Elizabethan, William & Mary and Georgian, and sometimes even the Modern style, with touches of Arts & Crafts and Art Deco.

Dining room and bedroom suites in the Modern Revival style found in Québec. The illustrations all come from catalogues distributed by P.-T. Legaré in the 1930s. Most of the furniture has a veneer finish and is inspired, to some degree at least, by older French and British styles.

SPECIAL LEGARE

MORCEAUX 9 PIECES
$88.50
FRET PAYÉ
FREIGHT PAID

895
" Arcade " chair by Céline Laperrière. Steel and vinyl, Montréal, 1993.
Post-Modernism broke away from the doctrine of hard-line Functionalism
and has been more accepting of history and a certain lyricism.

Post-Modernity at the Turn of the Century and the Millennium

Québec Furniture at the Threshold of a New Era

1960-2000

An ideal way to follow the history of Québec furniture over the 40 years leading up to the turn of the century and to the new millennium is to leaf through back issues of *Décormag*, a magazine that is still published and that was launched in August 1972, just one year after the North America's first Roche-Bobois store opened in Québec. In the editorial for the first issue, to which I made a complimentary contribution, Ginette Gadoury wrote: *"Décormag is above all a magazine for ordinary Quebeckers, reflecting our lifestyles… It will be full of articles presenting furniture makers and their creations, projects by students of architecture and design, and the generally little-known artists and craftsmen who strive to improve our everyday environment. Each month, there will be a report on a visit to a factory where the furniture of Québec designers is manufactured. Antique collectors will be delighted to find a series of articles on the discoveries to be made in antique stores and how to integrate old objects with contemporary decors."* [Translation]

From the start, *Décormag* used regular features, reports, advertisements and, above all, unpretentious thematic articles to present all types of furniture produced in Québec, always showing it in Québec settings. Until the appearance of this magazine, Quebeckers had to rely on publications from elsewhere, and these often offered products that were unavailable, costly and *"sometimes of lesser quality than our own,"* according to Mme Gadoury.

An even fuller picture of Québec furniture in the latter part of the 20th century is obtained by consulting the many other decorating magazines that have appeared in the wake of *Décormag* over the past decades, as well as promotional material and sales catalogues published by furniture distributors and retailers either based or doing business in Québec. Precious information about recent furniture also comes from interviews with those who have worked in this field and whose memories of it are still fresh. The interviews reported in this chapter — with Benoît Côté, Gilles Vaillancourt and Sylvain Faucher — demonstrate this avenue. All of these many references represent an inexhaustible source of knowledge about the field, which I will only skim over in the next few pages, dealing with it under the categories of furniture of traditional influence, general-market furniture and designer furniture, and concluding with a word on recent developments in the field of training.

896 a, b
The first issue of the magazine *Décormag*, launched in August 1972, and the April 1973 issue, presenting boldly designed kitchen furniture made with silvery vinyl over canvas.

PERSONAL ACCOUNT

Modern Furniture Arrives in Québec City

When I was young, I wanted to be an architect. But it would have entailed moving to Montréal, and that was beyond the financial means of someone like myself who had lost his father at the age of 15. What I really liked to do was to draw and paint — I loved pencils and brushes. I finally decided to follow a career in administration: it was easy. I finished my master's degree at Université Laval in 1953. I had made the right choice. In the 1950s, bond trading and other activities of that nature provided me with a decent living and interesting contacts, but at the same time left me plenty of time for painting. I mostly painted landscapes in Québec City and the surrounding area, and I soon became fairly well known. The Zanettin gallery organized an exhibition that was visited by Jean-Paul Lemieux and his pupils. The critics were full of praise. I was part of a circle of friends that included Denis Morisset, Edmund Alleyn, Claude Picher and many others. It was a magical time.

In 1959, I was invited to manage a contemporary furniture store. At the time, the heavy, massive French provincial style was ubiquitous. Two years earlier, Jacques Guillon and Harry Ross had opened a new store in Québec City, hoping to repeat the success of their Montréal store, Pego's, which sold Scandinavian and contemporary designer furniture exclusively. A few months before I arrived, it was decided to call the store, whose business was slow, " Le mobilier international, " after a famous Parisian store specialized in avant-garde furniture.

I was not at all familiar with the contemporary style. In fact, I had for several years been enamoured of traditional Québec furniture. I was among the "precursors" in the heritage field. When Jean Palardy published his album in 1963 (see Bibliography), I had been won over to this furniture long before and was already well aware of styles, forms and techniques. I have to say that I was quite disappointed when I leafed through the book. It contains beautiful photographs, to be sure, but the choice of items remains debatable and the text is colorless. I learned almost nothing from this book.

As soon as I started at the store, I began to mix the old with the new. I showed that a lovely pine armoire can be very harmonious with living room furniture made of chromed tubing and that combining beautiful objects in different styles can produce a pleasing effect. I have always preferred such combinations. I have constantly said that one can live in a 18th-century *canadien* house — like the house I live in now, built by the first generation of the Leclerc family on Île d'Orléans — and decorate rooms with the furniture of the best contemporary designers, while still respecting the building's ancestral roots. I used to obtain the store's furniture from De Foy; touts would come and see me too, when they had something interesting to sell.

Soon, I decided to offer my services as an interior decorator. My clientele consisted mainly of architects, art lovers and young professionals. Most of them were very familiar with the clean lines of Scandinavian furniture in teak or rose wood. As a decorator, I could at last make use of my "repressed" talents for architecture and design, and apply my sense of color. I had a natural knack of being able to place objects in a three dimensional space at just a glance. I learned the trade quickly and became even more appreciative of contemporary furniture and more knowledgeable about design. Consulting international magazines and books on the Bauhaus, for example, or on the production of the foremost designers opened my mind to new ideas. In 1962, Simon Dresdnere, one of my friends in Toronto, introduced me to Oriental rugs, both old and new, and I at once integrated them into my store and into my decorating business.

The possibilities of blending avant-garde design with Oriental rugs and old Québec furniture is the message I have been communicating with passion and pleasure in Québec City. I was the only one to offer furniture by the best-known designers, such as Knoll, Herman Miller, Le Corbusier-Perriand, Breuer and Eames, and to put it on display. The other stores continued to sell only French provincial and American Colonial furniture. Being a well-known artist and having good contacts helped a great deal. And one has to like the work. I have always enjoyed communicating with people and teaching. In the 1960s, everything went through a renewal. It was time of great excitement. Politics, art, design and furniture — everything had to be rethought and be given a new look. The Quiet Revolution actually reflected a worldwide movement and Québec simply fell into step. I continued like this for some ten years. In 1971, Roche-Bobois set up a store in Québec City. I wanted this franchise. But I didn't get it. The day that this was decided was the saddest of my life. I wanted so much to harvest what I had sown. All the energy I had put into making my fellow citizens aware of Modern styles had paved the way for Roche-Bobois. In 1972, I met Britt, the companion with whom I now live… Today, my happiness depends on just a few things — painting, painting snow geese, painting the wind, painting movement, painting energy, painting the passage of time, painting.

Benoît Côté, painter
Saint-Pierre,
Île d'Orléans
October 1999

897
Two-doored buffet with shaped panels and frame moulding. Original color, Québec City region, second half of the 18th century. Benoît Côté Collection.
Modern and traditional furniture can be very effective together. Even in the late 1950s, Benoît Côté liked to integrate these two styles in his interior designs and in the merchandise offered in his store.

898
"Egg" chair and footstool by Arne Jacobsen (1907-1971), Copenhagen, 1957. Wool, plastic shell, foam rubber, aluminum, painted and chromed steel and plastic for the foot pads.
Montreal Museum of Fine Arts Collection.

In its very first issue in 1972, *Décormag* announced that it intended to present readers with both contemporary and traditional furniture produced in Québec. People were encouraged to mix the old with the new in their interior decoration. In the 1960s, Benoît Côté, who managed a furniture store called Le mobilier international in Québec City, and who introduced the general public there to Modern furniture, was already presenting floor displays that combined 18th- or 19th-century armoires, buffets and chests in pine and walnut with Breuer chairs and suites signed by Le Corbusier-Perriand or other famous contemporary designers. There was a fashion for traditional country furniture throughout the Western world. Québec, which was going through the period known as the Quiet Revolution, found part of the answer to its search for identity in its furniture heritage. Jean Palardy's book (see Bibliography), published in 1963, stimulated general interest in old furniture. By the end of the 1960s, when sources of original pieces began to wear thin, a plethora of craftsmen started to offer their own productions or articles inspired by Palardy's illustrations. These pieces, sometimes produced at an almost industrial rate, were signed works, and they were made according to the rules of the ancient arts of cabinetmaking and joinery. They were generally styled in the French manner, as presented in Chapter 2 of this book, borrowing early shapes, decoration, joining methods and hardware and were finished with colors and patinas that could appear quite old. In adopting this style, Québec was following a path taken by many other societies at some point in their histories, when a search for roots took on a crucial importance.

Another major axis in the field of Québec furniture in this period is represented by what I have termed general-market furniture. This category, ranging from standard, low-budget products to upscale goods, includes the elaborate, history-inspired furniture imported from Ontario and the United States and marked by classic Anglo-American styles, such as William & Mary, Queen Anne and Scottish Revival. In the wake of this furniture's success, Québec companies began to produce their own versions of past styles. First, in the 1950s and early 1960s, there was the French Provincial style, inspired largely by the graceful lines of Louis XV. After this came the U.S. Colonial fashion in the 1960s and early 1970s, followed by the Spanish and Mediterranean styles. In the 1990s, pieces in the so-called Louis-Philippe style dominated the retail market throughout Québec.

At the same time, several Québec businesses made their name with general-market furniture that the makers themselves termed rustic. Such furniture production is exemplified by the Thibault company in Sainte-Thérèse, whose mainly oil-finished suites literally conquered the hotel- and motel-furnishings market in Québec. A good number of firms scattered throughout Québec offered furniture in this heavy style, which gave consumers the impression of getting their money's worth — and something that would last.

The third category that marked the production of this period was designer furniture. In the 1950s, stores specializing in contemporary furniture opened in Québec's two largest cities. An example is Pego's of Montréal, whose owners also operated Le mobilier international in Québec City. These enterprises offered clean-lined Scandinavian furniture in teak or palisander, as well as original work by the best-known International-style designers or goods inspired directly by them. In 1971, Roche-Bobois of Paris set up stores in Montréal and Québec City. There was an ever-growing market in Québec for avant-garde furniture from France, Scandinavia, Italy and the United States. As more stores followed suit, there developed a healthy competition that benefitted Quebeckers taken with the new concepts. All these stores advertised in *Décormag*, whose monthly issues can be consulted in full in Québec's university libraries.

The term "Post-Modern" was first applied to a type of 1960s architecture that made unapologetic references to the past and put a certain distance between itself and the pure Functionalism of the International style, which had dominated the previous period. The new tendency did not make itself felt significantly in furniture design until the end of the 1970s. In 1981, Ettore Sottsass, an Italian designer who had already developed an innovative style, joined commercial designers to form the Memphis group, with the goal of rethinking contemporary design. In the United States, the architects Michael Graves, Charles Jenkins and Robert Venturi have also collaborated with industrial interests to explore the new approach, favoring "joyful" objects, bright colors and sometimes startling shapes that go against established aesthetic norms by borrowing ornamental and formal elements from the styles of older works. The furniture proposed by these people has contrasted sharply with that belonging to the Pop Art style of the 1960s and 1970s — a youthful, revolutionary movement that encouraged designers to look for inspiration in Kitsch, the esoteric and mass-consumption and to produce items with a fairly short life expectancy. Post-Modern furniture is instead designed to be solid and durable, and it is made with high-quality materials following sometimes quite sophisticated handcrafting procedures. As Pierrette Grondin judiciously remarks in "Cyberculture et objets de design industriel ou Comment l'usage de l'ordinateur a influencé la forme des objets produits industriellement," an admirable master's thesis in Art Studies obtained in 1999 from the Université du Québec à Montréal, "The complexity of Post-Modern objects, combined with their production in limited editions, favors a return to handcrafting and, consequently, renewed collaboration between designers and craftsmen." [Translation] A number of Québec cabinetmakers and designers, some of whom are presented in these pages, continue to work in such a framework at the beginning of the new millennium.

In 1966, the Quebec Furniture Manufacturers' Association, which takes part in major exhibitions and actively promotes Québec products, launched an annual furniture design

PERSONAL ACCOUNT

Late-Century Trends

I have been in the furniture business for 35 years now. My father opened La Galerie du meuble in 1959. This Québec City furniture store has seen all the many styles and movements that have come and gone in most of the last half-century. One of my sisters is a decorator.

The only market I know well is that in Québec City. In the 1950s and for a good part of the 1960s, people mainly bought French provincial furniture inspired by the Louis XV style. This furniture was made of hardwood with walnut, cherry or mahogany finishes and came from the Montréal region, Victoriaville or certain towns in Ontario, such as Kitchener. Some items were imported from Italy in an unfinished state and were completed in factories here. The style maintained its popularity with the introduction of suites in pastel shades, highlighted with gilt. This somewhat heavy historic fashion was followed briefly by the so-called Spanish and Mediterranean styles.

Next came the golden age of the American Colonial style. It was all the rage in the 1960s and early 1970s. Most of this furniture was sturdily made of solid maple or some other hardwood and came from factories in the Eastern Townships — for example, from Cowansville — or was imported from Ontario. Of course, this style had nothing to do with our own traditional colonial furniture, whether French or British. Our factories modelled their furniture on U.S. products. This furniture was just varnished at first, but was later decorated with gilt highlights and stencilling. Finally, it was made with some parts in a natural finish and others in bright colors, and this extended the life of the style. People could vary their decor and set themselves apart from their brothers-in-laws and their friends who had furnished their homes in exactly the same fashion.

At the same time that the Québec middle classes systematically adopted these styles, there developed a better-informed, more intellectual clientele who were won over by the Scandinavian furniture that arrived in the late 1950s and by avant-garde designer furniture. The American Colonial style had little in common with our own culture. The clean lines of Scandinavian furniture belonged to the aesthetics of the Modern International style and what might be termed the "rebirth of artistic taste." For Québec during the Quiet Revolution, interest in Swedish or Danish Functionalism was part of an openness to the rest of the world. In Québec City, Benoît Côté was a precursor, an initiator and an educator. As a well-known painter, he belonged to the artistic avant-garde of the time. He was close to architects, artists and other creative people. In his store, he presented the finest, purest furniture, made by all the great international designers. Our store followed his example but, because of our market, we sold reproductions and less expensive originals.

It was after La Galerie du meuble had become involved in this movement that it was chosen as an agent for Roche-Bobois. On September 12, 1971, the great French business opened its doors in Montréal. The next day, it launched its Québec City branch in our store. For Roche-Bobois this represented a foothold from which it could set off to conquer North America. European design from France, Italy and the Scandinavian countries enjoyed unprecedented popularity, stimulated by attractive catalogues — that were often small masterpieces of promotional material — and advertising to die for. The company had first made its mark in Paris with products imported from Copenhagen, Denmark, and then from the other Scandinavian countries.

In the 1950s, the cheapest furniture was made of Formica or imitation wood-grain Arborite with metal tubing. In the 1980s, Melamine became popular. On the Québec market, there has always been a demand for rustic-looking furniture.

The 1970s and 1980s were marked by the appearance of Italian design. This furniture had interesting lines and glossy lacquered finishes, and the prices were competitive.

The recession of 1990-1991 signalled a swing of the pendulum to some degree, as happens every 20 or 25 years. Once again historic revivals became fashionable. The vogue for Louis-Philippe brought back Gondola chairs and chairs with heavily scrolled armrests as well as Empire-style sleigh beds. Around 1996, this conservative trend reached a pinnacle in North America. Even the fabrics were heavy, as if to reassure customers that they were getting their money's worth, with something made to last.

Now, over the past two or three years, as we enter a new century and millennium, there has been a movement towards the avant-garde again. Furniture is simpler, with bold but graceful lines, and is made of light-colored wood and more sophisticated materials.

In the 1970s and 1980s, Québec City was like a standard for businesses that distributed Modern or avant-garde furniture. People came here to see how things worked. They were filled with admiration. Over the last 10 years, the city has become more conservative. To deal in contemporary avant-garde furniture today, a business has to operate in a large, culturally dynamic city and must find a special but sufficiently broad clientele of intellectuals and people who are aware of innovative trends. In the 1980s, Québec manufacturers did not adapt to the new movement — I'm thinking of centres of production like Victoriaville. They continued to make heavy furniture and thus either lost a share of the market or quite simply disappeared. As a result, a whole branch of Québec's economy collapsed. Today, a weak Canadian dollar has given manufacturers a certain boost, but one has to be realistic. What with globalization and the need to conquer markets, it is not enough to just mimic — creativity and inventiveness must be allowed to grow.

If I were to interpret Quebeckers' taste in furniture over the last 35 years, I would say that they favor gentle shapes, the presence of curves and the absence of sharp angles. They want everything to be rounded, bevelled and full. Quebeckers like furniture to be lyrical and warm. These traits can guide the design of avant-garde furniture in every type of material.

Gilles Vaillancourt, La Galerie du meuble
Québec City, September 1999

899
Modular seating elements sold by Roche-Bobois and presented in its Québec catalogue in 1970.

competition to encourage and co-ordinate closer collaboration between industry and designers. Entries were judged on the basis of form, function, durability, originality of design and potential for manufacturing applications. The initiative aroused great interest and stimulated several designers to create prototypes that they somewhat over-confidently attempted to produce and market on their own. Their efforts met with mixed success. Most of the workshops and small industries persuing this vein enjoyed only a brief existence, due to a lack of financial resources and marketing experience. Once again, a look at *Décormag* and the bulletins put out by the Quebec Furniture Manufacturers' Association gives some idea of these designers' originality and audacity, as well as the versatility they showed in using and combining the most diverse materials. Manufacturing agents like Sylvain Faucher, who gave an interview for this book, acted as intermediaries between designers and business, thus aiding distribution.

Many of the people involved in these movements came from the École du meuble de Montréal, which in 1958, 23 years after its founding, became the Institut des arts appliqués. At the end of the 1960s, major changes were made in the way cabinetmaking was taught. Manufacturers found that students were insufficiently trained in industrial production methods. At this time, the École québécoise du meuble et du bois ouvré was opened in Victoriaville, where many companies had factories. This school of woodworking offers handcrafted cabinetmaking courses in collaboration with Montréal's Institut des métiers d'art at the Cégep du Vieux-Montréal, while a diploma in architectural cabinetmaking and joinery can be obtained from the Montréal branch of the Cégep de Victoriaville. Since 1992, the Institut d'ébenisterie de Québec has offered training in the furniture arts at the Cégep de Limoilou in Québec City. With the exception of one or two courses, this training is almost identical to that available at the Institut des métiers d'art at the École québécoise du meuble in Montréal. As well, the design departments in Montréal's universities are instrumental in the training of designers who are actively involved in the furniture arts.

904
"Berceuse" by Jean-François Dugal, Saint-Basil-le-Grand, 1999. Exotic wood (Bolivian coubaria and Brazilian lourofaya), ergonomic shape and traditional mortise-and-tenon and dovetail joints.
This cabinetmaker reinvented the famous Boston rocker, versions of which have been used by Quebeckers for relaxation over the past two centuries.

900-903
(Facing page)
Photographs appearing in *Décormag* and promoting Provincial, French, Colonial and Modern suites offered by Villas, Thibault and Vallière in the 1970s. These styles were extremely popular with the general public.

THE DESIGNER

In the Thick of Things

I am the chairman and chief executive officer of Dismo International. I'm 36 years old and was trained as a cabinetmaker. I've been active in the furniture field for some twenty years. I started out with my own workshop and then joined the Atelier du bois d'oeuvre, a Montréal firm specialized in made-to-measure products. By the end of this chapter in my life, I had two partners and 20 to 25 employees.

I have always been attracted to design. I was 15 when I bought my first magazine, an Italian publication that cost 12 dollars. It was a lot of money at the time. I've always been very close to the design community. I even tried my hand at the craft when I designed a series of pieces that were chosen by the present-day Le Château store. But I realized that design really wasn't my forte. I decided that, with the experience I had acquired, I would develop products in collaboration with designers and see that these products were manufactured and marketed. I saw myself as a good interpreter of creative work, with an excellent knowledge of both manufacturing procedures and the financial challenges facing manufacturing contractors. I also had great respect for designers. Confident in these qualities, in 1989 I launched Dismo International, a name that combines two words: "distribution" and "mobilier" (which is French for "furniture").

To prepare my project, I spent four and a half months in Milan, Italy. During my stay, I met manufacturers and leaders of Italian industry, visited factories and design studios, and tried to understand the Italians and their immense commercial success. As someone who had previously managed a business, I was very much interested in studying businesses that had conquered the world. Civil servants in the federal and provincial governments that I met over there were a little baffled by my enthusiasm. I also undertook a one-month training course in Barcelona, Spain. There I learned about very dynamic and effective ways of making partnerships that bridged furniture design, manufacturing and distribution. I would have liked to visit the Scandinavians, who live in a northern country as we do and have always had good ideas. However, despite their great success from the 1930s to the present, there are only a few firms that have managed to make a name for themselves on this side of the Atlantic. Simplicity is not well accepted in North America. People like things to be cosy and well-padded; they want to feel that they are getting their money's worth. In this respect, Quebeckers represent a very distinct market; as customers, they are more open-minded and ready to accept new ideas. But Quebeckers are also North American. In North America, consumers of high-quality products represent about 7% of the entire population. And within this group, a great deal of education will still be needed before the notion of simplicity is widely appreciated.

I came back from my Italian trip with my head full of ideas. But I came back to a very different cultural context. The most difficult problem to overcome in Québec is related to its business culture. I had prepared my project while I was in Europe. I wanted to take advantage of the Free Trade Agreement that had just been signed. My program was therefore adapted to the situation in North America. In my first year, I acted as an agent for designers. I sold designer services to manufacturing firms throughout Québec. I went everywhere. But the response was poor. After a whole year, I had succeeded in having one chair made. Fortunately, I still had a small reserve of funds. And then I taught. The products I offered weren't suitable for the firms I approached since they sought another clientele.

The role that developed for Dismo was the following: instilling new ideas among manufacturers, ensuring that these ideas materialized within each firm's structure and distributing the resulting products on the North American market. Products such as these cannot be supported by the local market alone, since it is too small to absorb avant-garde work at the prices asked and would thus make the whole enterprise unprofitable. The general public, which is well served by industry, seeks less costly products. As of 1991, I therefore developed superior, high-quality designer products in collaboration with manufacturers, adopting the model I had closely observed in Spain. Twelve private designers, paid in royalties, and seven manufacturers took part in the project. I was paid a percentage of sales, somewhat like a manufacturing agent. Within this network, I attempted to heighten my partners' awareness as much as possible. I had to tour the United States. I talked with all the upper-range sales people in North America and took part in numerous fairs, above all targeting a specific niche that included the consumers our products were intended for. We received excellent press coverage in the United States and in Europe. Initial expenses could be absorbed, since they were spread out among the group's members. I even went to Japan. In 1993, we obtained a contract for furnishing the Montréal Casino. This gave us the needed boost, which is what public commissions are supposed to do. For this contract, eight designers and six manufacturers took part in supplying 13 products.

None of this has been easy, especially when it comes to maintaining relations with our partners. Once the network is set up and solid contacts are established, our lack of business culture allows manufacturers to get rid of their distributors. Simply to save a percentage of their expenses. They just walk away, pocketing the fruits of your efforts without so much as a backward glance.

Today, I have my own store, where I sell products made both in Québec and in the rest of the world. I will always continue to promote Québec designers, but not necessarily products manufactured in Québec. Once burned, twice shy, as they say. Québec has remarkably talented designers. These people, so full of ideas, deserve to be recognized by industry and integrated with it. The development of the manufacturing industry is intimately linked with the vigor of the design sector. At the moment, the weakness of the Canadian dollar gives production an advantage, but in this era of globalization, it is the quality of our products, the originality of their lines, their solidity and their competitive prices that constitute a guarantee for the future. I have always said that there is as much educating to be done among manufacturers as there is among designers. I like to be in the thick of things.

Sylvain Faucher
Montréal, October 15, 1999

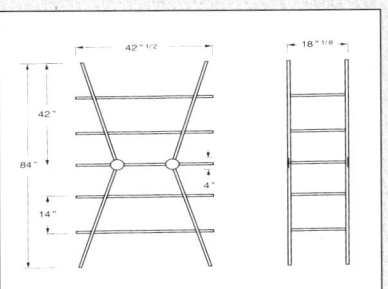
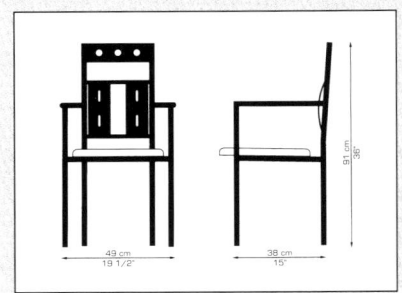
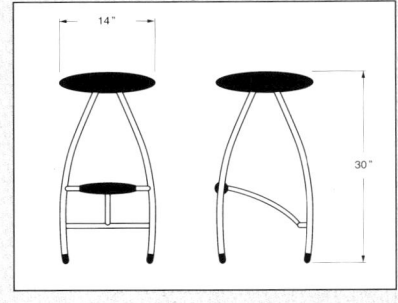
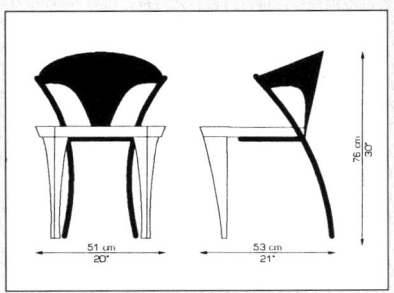

905 a, b, c, d
Designs made between 1992 and 1999 by various designers in the Montréal area for furniture distributed by Dismo International.

906
"Baby Face" chair by Jean-François Jacques. Moulded ash and steel, Montréal, 1993.

907
"Dyonis" table by Anick Blais. Moulded aluminum and steel, Montréal, 1996.

908
"Charlotte" stools by Alain Desgagnés. Steel and yellow birch, Montréal, 1996.

COLLECTION

Québec's National Collection of Furniture

The Musée de la civilisation has been entrusted with the responsibility of establishing and conserving ethnological collections and making them better known. In a recent publication, *Trésors de société, les collections du Musée de la civilisation*, I have traced the history of these collections. As the director of collections from 1987 to 1997, I had the privilege of being closely involved in the exciting period during which this Québec institution came into existence.

The museum's mission is to promote understanding of the history of our civilisation and its principle elements, with particular emphasis on the material and social culture of the people who have occupied Québec's territory or who have enriched Québec society. Since the museum's inception, it has been shaped to some degree by the generous contributions of hundreds of donors. These people share the museum's priority of making our heritage better known and have shown their interest in the preservation and development of Québec's collections.

Furniture Collections, the Legacy of Different Lifestyles

In various periods of Québec's history, the way people lived and inhabited their homes has been shaped by either France, Britain or the United States. Today the network of such influences is more widespread. Québec is part of North America but has its own particular background, and its history brings together the great cultures that have shared its shores and its lands. The museum's furniture collections reflect this history. The furniture of course elicits admiration but it also holds secrets that are fascinating to discover.

From 1927 to the present, the development of the furniture collections has paralleled Québec's history from a purely chronological viewpoint, leading from the period of New France and French North America to that of the British colony and from there to the establishment of Canada, with the English and U.S. influences of today. The earliest acquisitions consisted of furniture in the French manner, echoing the Louis XIII, Louis XIV, Régence and Louis XV styles that marked the period between the birth of New France and the Treaty of Paris. The effects of this original influence persisted throughout the 19th and 20th centuries and are evident in collections of old furniture.

The Canada Steamship Lines Collection or Coverdale Collection

Québec's furniture collection was initiated in 1968, with the purchase of the Canada Steamship Lines Collection, also called the Coverdale Collection. The collection is best known for its 350 pieces of furniture, 75 of which appear in Jean Palardy's *Furniture of French Canada*. These pieces represent the most important periods of our history, starting with the French Régime under Louis XIII, Louis XIV, the Régence and Louis XV and continuing with British rule, during which French, British and American influences mingled. The furniture comes from the homes of habitants, seigneurs, craftsmen and merchants, as well as from religious institutions.

The Chapais-Barnard Collection

In 1968, the Québec government acquired the Thomas-Chapais house and its contents. Jean-Charles Chapais was a politician who built a house in Saint-Denis, Kamouraska, in 1833. In 1866, the house was renovated and Chapais asked his wife, née Georgina Dionne, to redecorate it. She took care of the purchases and wrote letters to her husband to keep him up to date as to what she was buying and which merchants she had met. This correspondence provides precious information on the period's furniture makers, including Philippe Vallières in Québec City (25, 553, 565, 568, 570). Later, their son Thomas, a historian and politician, lived in the house until his death. In 1950, the Québec government acquired the archives and artwork in the Chapais Collection and, in 1967, the furniture and other objects in the house were purchased.

Furniture in the Lucie-Vary Collection

In 1969, furniture from the Lucie-Vary Collection became part of Québec's national furniture collection. The Lucie-Vary furniture includes some 30 armoires, about 15 tables, 13 Louis XIII chairs, chests, rocking chairs, cradles, tester beds and tall-post beds, representing 75 items, in addition to about 100 rustic chairs. There are 13 items of Louis XIII furniture, five of which are armchairs. Since it was customary to strip old furniture in the 1960s, it is interesting that five of the armoires or cupboards still have their original colors.

Other pieces were added in 1972, when the Wilfred-Caron Collection was acquired, and again in 1980, when 80 pieces of furniture and objects from the Batiscan manor and presbytery were transferred by the the Québec ministry of recreation, hunting and fishing.

Collections in Process

When the Musée de la civilisation was founded on December 19, 1984, the collections that were officially transferred to it at the time contained 1 100 pieces of furniture. Since the end of 1987, when the acquisition process was reactivated, over 500 pieces have been added as a result of the museum's inaugural exhibition and the many succeeding exhibitions that focussed on these rich collections.

A great number of donors also chose to offer fine pieces of furniture to the museum and these pieces were a natural complement to its old and contemporary collections. These donations include: two panels from a late 18th-century built-in armoire, painted with floral motifs, from Suzanne Morin-Raymond; a set of Regency dining room furniture, intended as "a donation to the heritage of Québec" from the estate of Madeleine Simard, the granddaughter of Félix-Gabriel Marchand, who was prime minister of Québec from 1897 to 1900; a black cherry sideboard by Louis Jaque (Beaulieu) of the École du meuble de Montréal from Simone Aubry-Beaulieu and Paul Beaulieu; drawing room furniture made by Charles-Olivier Bédard in 1884 and belonging to Zéphyrin Pâquet from Éric Aubin; Rococo Revival and Eastwood drawing room suites belonging to the Déry and Marcotte families from Marguerite Déry-La Follette; and a decorative Hepplewhite-inspired butternut chest of drawers made for a marriage and inscribed with the date "April 6, 1846," a notary's writing desk and a tilt-top gaming table with mother-of-pearl inlay from Huguette Rémy. In 1994, Martine and légor de Saint Hippolyte donated a set of six mahogany chairs made in Paris by "Jacob Frères rue Meslée" in around 1803, a donation that enriches our knowledge of the Empire period and the influences it had on Canadian furniture styles.

More than 10 years ago, the Musée de la civilisation and other institutions in Québec's museum network, particularly its historic houses, began a policy of working together to make optimal use of the national collections through such measures as long-term loans of furniture. Some of this furniture can be found in the house Chapais in Saint-Denis, Kamouraska, the Saint-Roch-des-Aulnaies seigneury, the Étienne-Paschal-Taché house in Montmagny, the Batiscan manor and presbytery, the Manoir Le Bouthillier in Anse-au-Griffon, the Niverville manor in Trois-Rivières and the Domaine Cataraqui in Sillery.

Since 1989, a number of exhibitions have highlighted furniture collections. These have included *A Sense of the Past*, *Memories*, *Objects of Civilization* and *Living in Style: Fine Furniture in Victorian Québec for 1840 to 1900*. Such events underline the main focus of the various collections and clarify the directions to be taken in order to consolidate and develop them.

Contact with the Oldest Collections

The exhibition *A Sense of the Past* at the Maison Chevalier in Place Royale gives visitors a chance to discover what daily life was like in Québec homes long ago. The exhibition is presented in a setting that reflects the history of New France. On the ground floor, people can view the rooms of an 18th-century merchant in Place Royale, while the upper floor displays furniture in reconstructed late-18th-century and 19th-century interiors. These furnishings and other items evoke both a rural and urban past, and their styles echo the fashions associated with the French and British monarchs who ruled over the destinies of the North American colonies. Certain pieces were made in original ways that show a combination of influences (120-131, 136-148). This type of furniture is characterized by the use of local wood for its construction and is often painted red ochre, greenish blue or white tinted with yellow ochre.

Memories

Mémoires is a thematic exhibition on Québec in the past and present. The first part takes a somewhat nostalgic look at earlier days. One of the displays is a household kitchen that reflects the way this much-used room has been transformed over time. It contains hundreds of objects and some dozen pieces of furniture belonging to several eras, but the whole is unified by an atmosphere of nostalgia. The kitchen looks as though it has gone through many periods, which the visitor is invited to recognize. The furniture from old collections contributes to the impression of a room in which things have gradually accumulated, like the many little remembrances that make up our memories.

Objects of Civilization

The exhibition entitled *Objects of Civilization*, which ran from 1988 to 1999, was intended to explain the significance and influence a museum's collections can have (89, 90). The furniture in the exhibition represented some of the most important pieces from the Coverdale and Vary collections as well as recent acquisitions in the Late Georgian (15), Empire (17) and Neoclassical styles. An exceptional sideboard displayed the talents of a cabinetmaker and church builder from the Beauce area (165). The exhibition also made it possible to present an Art Deco dining room from the collection of the Jacques Simon estate (36-40), furniture from the Bélanger-Blatter Collection (37) and Chinese furniture from the Jesuit donation (48, 909).

In the 1930s, the Québec government supported the founding of the École du meuble, which grew out of the École technique. In this school, cabinetmakers were trained to produce original Québec furniture that reflected traditional craftsmanship and incorporated Canadian wood. The Jacques Samson Collection includes dining room and bedroom furniture that was designed by Alphonse Saint-Jacques, a teacher at the school, and was built by his students.

The Bélanger-Blatter Collection represents the work done by the architect Robert Blatter when he designed and furnished a house entirely in the Art Deco style for the surveyor Henri Bélanger. All the furniture, decorative accessories and ornamentation in the house were designed by the architect-decorator. He had these designs executed by the Maison de décoration intérieure moderne (DIM) in Paris. In 1987, the museum acquired seven pieces from the Bélanger house. Thoroughly documented and illustrated, these pieces are representative of the decorative arts in the 1920s.

The Jesuits' Chinese Museum

The Jesuits' impressive Chinese collection comprises nearly 2 000 objects, most of which date from the late 19th century and the early 20th century. It includes large pieces of furniture, screens and decorative objects made of carved wood, jade, ivory, bronze, ceramic and glass. There are also liturgical vestments, paper artifacts, a collection of miniatures representing Chinese crafts and scenes of daily life, and books on Chinese culture and art.

The collection contains over 50 pieces of furniture, including a very special bed. Known as the "Empress's bed," this piece is an imposing assemblage of 51 components, including panels carved with rosettes and lace-like fretwork. Documents reveal that the bed belonged to the dowager empress Ts'eu-Hi, who reigned in China from 1862 to 1908.

The Jesuit Collection is exceptional not only for the cohesion, provenance, richness and diversity of its contents but also for its significance as a reminder of a specific cultural practice that developed in society. In making this extraordinary donation, the Jesuit community has encouraged the meeting of two cultures and reinforced the historic openness of Québec to the rest of the world.

Living in Style: Fine Furniture in Victorian Québec from 1840 to 1900

This exhibition, organized in 1993 in collaboration with the Montreal Museum of Fine Arts, presented some thirty pieces of furniture from the Musée de la civilisation. The furniture on display included Rococo Revival and Renaissance Revival pieces produced by the Québec furniture makers Charles-Olivier Bédard, Philippe Vallière and Francis-Pierre Gauvin. Certain of the recently acquired items in the exhibition had never before been shown to the public. These items included a monumental 1860s Renaissance Revival sideboard from the Cataraqui villa; a Naturalistic sideboard carved with hunting scenes and braces of game birds and fish by Francis-Pierre Gauvin; a Rococo Revival wedding bed decorated with bird, flower and fruit motifs, donated by Alfred Savard; a stained-glass window from the home of Lord Atholston in Montréal, donated by the Jesuit community; an ingenious wicker rocking chair made with ash splints; and a New Raymond sewing machine cabinet made with walnut and figured veneer.

Preparations for this exhibition led to the discovery of the Jourdain-Fiset Collection (333), which contains over 1 000 everyday objects, including a considerable quantity of furniture — much of it in the Empire, Regency and Rococo Revival manner — such as a fireside chair, a *crapaud* chair, a late-19th-century drawing room suite and a bedroom suite with a sleigh bed, chest of drawers and washstand. The Jourdain-Fiset Collection also holds writing desks, bookcases, occasional pieces and gaming tables. All this furniture came from bourgeois residences of the Victorian period, when living at home was an art in itself.

Sharing Québec's Collections

Over the past 10 years, furniture collections have grown rapidly. Serious attention has been devoted to the their maintenance and development, with consideration given to the complementarity of the various public collections. The notion of a "national collection" covers collections held by the government, as well as by the agencies and institutions that help to shape a society. Our collective heritage also encompasses the many and varied collections preserved by families and different groups. An institution like the Musée de la civilisation has a responsibility to develop large collections that represent society and to ensure their continuity and enhancement through the thematic exploration of diverse subjects. The collections attest to the ongoing fulfilment of this mandate.

Richard Dubé
Québec, juillet 1999

909
Chinese bed. Carved mahogany with openwork, ca. 1860.
Québec's national collection includes treasures like this bed, known as the "Empress's bed." It is part of a rich collection consisting of almost 2 000 items of Chinese furniture and other objects donated by the Jesuit community to the Musée de la civilisation in 1990. Until then, this missionary order in Québec City had maintained an impressive museum specialized in the great civilizations of China.
The story of the bed on this continent began in 1888 in the port of Québec City, where it was given to the customs office for 100 dollars. *Le Soleil* of August 7, 1901, reported that a ceremonial bed once belonging to the imperial family of the Celestial Empire was now with the Sisters of Charity of Québec. It was said that "the bedstead [...] is a veritable miracle of openwork carving, a marvel of cabinetmaking, a masterpiece." It was revealed through letters and documents that the bed probably belonged to the dowager empress Ts'eu-Hi, who reigned in China from 1862 to 1908. Throughout the early 1900s, the bed was owned by various wealthy Québec City families. Eventually, in the 1930s, it was bequeathed to the Jesuits, who integrated it with their museum.

910
Large chest of drawers by Kino Guérin, Montréal, 1995.
Veneer of figured madrona, sipo, bubinga and gogo; MDF support, "Perform" plywood and solid maple with brass handles. Constructed with biscuit assembly, lamination, moulding and rivelling. 156 cm x 46 cm x 115 cm.

The Story Behind the Book

As previously mentioned in the introduction, each chapter in this book deals with a subject that merits its own in-depth study in a separate book. In particular, the 20th century suffers from a lack of serious research.

This overview nonetheless confirms that Quebeckers have been involved at every stage in the history of the decorative arts in the West, either as producers with a keen awareness of current trends or as consumers of goods imported from outside, reflecting an undeniable openness towards the world. Québec and Montréal enjoyed an early strategic advantage, since their ports were relatively deep inside the continent, enabling them to become distribution centres for North America. With the development of the railroads in the middle of the 19th century, trade relations were established between the St. Lawrence Valley and Boston, New York and Chicago. The household furnishings market has also been well supplied by industries in Ontario, with which Québec business people have always maintained special relations.

Québec society has developed at the crossroads of three great cultures. Whether in turn or simultaneously, the cultures of France, England and the United States have shaped Québec. It is therefore not surprising that Québec's furniture heritage includes Louis XIII diamond-point armoires, round-backed *duchesse* armchairs in the Baroque manner of Louis XV and pieces reflecting Georgian and Regency styles with French Directoire or Empire influences (sometimes filtered through the United States, which has periodically adopted a fashion for all things French). This mixture of cultural influences made it natural for furniture makers in the St. Lawrence Valley to produce their own original and skilful interpretation of the new history-inspired styles that dominated Europe and North America in the second half of the 19th century — British Gothic Revival, French Renaissance Revival, Baroque Revival and the Naturalistic Rococo Revival. When the reformist architects of the Victorian era became social critics, particularly in Britain, and proposed that furniture should be truly reinvented, Québec was not long to join the ranks of the Arts & Crafts and Mission movements. It adopted the Art Furniture proposed by Eastlake and Godwin, as well as the Art Nouveau style that followed. The St. Lawrence Valley became increasingly reliant on industry to supply furniture in these modes, which were often adapted to U.S. tastes. The United States' proximity and sometimes overwhelming influence in Québec is reflected in the fashion for industrial oak furniture and the Mission style, both of which represented Pre-Modern movements that marked the decorative arts during the Belle Époque. In the 20th century, Québec continued to take interest in outside trends, following the European, North American and Asian movements that gave impetus to Art Deco and the International style; Québec has also embraced the Post-Modernism that grew out of these movements in the 1960-2000 period, at the threshold of the "planetary" era. The Modern and Post-Modern styles have been brilliantly interpreted by Québec designers associated with the École du meuble founded in 1935 by Jean-Marie Gauvreau or with studios that explore contemporary trends.

Foreign products, mainly from France, Britain and the United States, have been welcomed by Québec as a society for nearly four centuries. Today, this interest in the outside world is reflected in an appreciation on the part of certain Quebeckers for contemporary trends in an industrial arts market supplied by the best workshops and most reputable industries in Europe and North America. Fieldwork for this book has sometimes given me the occasion to admire Québec interiors furnished with avant-garde pieces signed by such masters as Ruhlman, Le Corbusier, Wright, Rietveld, Aalto, Bertoia, Eames, Wegner and Sottsass, to name but the best-known of them. Considering Québec's private and public furniture collections, some of which include items of Asian design, it is clear that people here, both as producers and as enlightened consumers, have displayed open-mindedness and great curiosity towards the many movements marking the history of furniture. The furniture in these collections, whether produced industrially or designed individually in workshops, constitutes a treasure that benefits all, and this book seeks to do it justice.

This study is the third in a series that began with *Objets anciens du Québec. La vie domestique*, which came out in 1994, and *Antiquités du Québec. Objets anciens. Vie sociale et culturelle*, published the following year. It constitutes the first serious effort to integrate Québec's material culture as a whole with developments in the decorative arts in the West. Logically, the next goal for this research should be a history of domestic architecture and an overview of interior decoration and design, which would ideally be accompanied by an illustrated dictionary of old objects found in Québec.

Throughout this long project, I have always sought to situate furniture in its context and show how it has related to the general production of a given period. This approach demonstrates the degree to which the great aesthetic movements have affected every field of production, whether artistic or functional, and regardless of the social level of the maker or the user. In this way, I have attempted to offer more than simply a collector's album; my goal has been to give these inanimate objects a soul and bring them to life in the interiors they once graced. To do this, I have sought out various iconographic sources and visited furnished interiors that have been preserved in certain heritage homes or reconstituted in private homes, historic sites and museums. I believe that the real significance of furniture

lies in its role in family or institutional life; this role is even more important than definitions based on aesthetic, technological or commercial movements.

It is deeply hoped that this book will lift a veil from the wonderful story of the furniture made and used in Québec over almost four centuries. I would like to think that it will shed light on the true cultural forces that have shaped Québec's identity and foster pride and recognition with respect to the craftsmen and manufacturers who made our living spaces comfortable and functional, while giving original interpretations to the great movements in the history of the decorative arts.

It is also hoped that this fascinating field of material culture will be given a higher profile in the field of museology. Although Québec's national collection is considerable — as demonstrated above by Richard Dubé, a former director of collections — more attention should be paid to certain styles and products intended for specific socio-economic classes. In the same vein, it would be well to encourage donations and stimulate research. As well, there is a need to establish a register that would record all pertinent information and in particular that related to collections belonging to the state and to regional museums. This inventory could be consulted at any time to provide precise details about the conservation of Québec's furniture heritage and would constitute an ideal complement to the national collection. The task of setting up and maintaining such a register should be entrusted to competent specialists who have received serious training in the field and whose enthusiasm for the endeavor equals that of the collectors.

At the beginning of a new century and a new millennium, marking the arrival of what might be called the "planetary" era and thus the appearance of a "planetary" style, the market for historic objects in Québec is turning its attention to the products of the 20th century. Much of this production is industrial in nature and belongs to international stylistic movements. Québec society is comfortable with otherness, having always been fundamentally open to cultures from elsewhere. For its first 150 years, Québec was like a province of France under the Ancien Régime. Then, with a certain admiration and generosity, it accepted Anglo-Saxon culture and thus the benefits of a strong and prosperous civilization; 19th-century Britain, with its empire on which the sun never set, transmitted every major Western style, including Neoclassicism. By the 1860s, the United States was developing in ways that would eventually make it a superpower. In the late 19th century, many Quebeckers emigrated to this "fertile" nation, enticed by the promise of a better future. Demographic statistics show that the descendants of those who settled New France are now more numerous in the United States than they are in Québec.

Québec's openness to the world can only become more marked as immigration increases and means of communication continue the explosive growth that began in the 1950s. So far, in this mixture of cultures, Québec has managed, with a population of no more than 7 000 000, to maintain its identity by showing remarkable inventiveness in every field of art and culture. Its dynamic approach can only arouse admiration and kindle deep feelings of pride. While the spirit of commercial initiative is at present the glory of the furniture industry, it is to be hoped that in the coming era Québec will make good use of its extraordinary woodworking heritage, so esteemed by Jean-Marie Gauvreau, and once again integrate its many cultural influences to create a prosperous, stimulating environment for innovation and creativity.

911
Dining room furniture by Robert Ducharme, Montréal, 1996. Large oak table, six chairs and a sideboard in the simple lines of the International style that marked the Modern era.
Since 1960, worldwide trends in the decorative arts have found expression in the furniture suites made by Québec's cabinetmakers and designers, whether trained in specialized schools or self-taught. Making a living in this field has not been easy. Although businesses producing this kind of furniture are often short-lived, many of them have offered high-quality design.

Glossary

Terms related to furniture may vary from one author to another, and this can sometimes lead to confusion. To establish a consistent vocabulary for the original French-language book, *Meubles anciens du Québec*, the author turned primarily to three references: *Dictionnaire de l'ameublement et de la décoration depuis le XIIIe siècle jusqu'à nos jours* (Paris: Maison Quantin, 1887-1890) in four volumes, *Dictionnaire de l'histoire de l'art* de Jean-Pierre Néraudau (Paris: Presses universitaires de France, 1985, 521 pages), and *Dictionnaire du mobilier* by Marie-Claude Lespérance (Montréal: Les Éditions Logiques, 1996, 316 pages). The author also recommends two English-language reference books: *Dictionary of Furniture* by Charles Boyce (New York: Roundtable Press Inc., 1985) and *The Dictionary of English Furniture* by Ralph Edwards (London: Country Life, 1954) in three volumes. For the English-language version of the book, the translators relied primarily on the above-mentioned *Dictionary of Furniture* by Charles Boyce, as well as a number of specialized works, some of which are listed in the bibliography.

Acanthus leaf: decorative leaf motif inspired by the acanthus, a Mediterranean plant, and characteristic of capitals in the Corinthian order. Its first use is attributed to Callimachus, a Greek sculptor living in the 5th century B.C. The motif appears in the decoration of Neoclassical, Revival and Pre-Modern furniture in Québec.

Appliqué: carved or moulded decorative element, fixed to the surface of a piece of furniture. In North America, after 1870, the production of appliqués developed into a specialized industry that supplied furniture makers with a great variety of motifs borrowed from diverse stylistic movements. Moulded appliqués were made of an aggregate that was tinted to imitate certain types of wood. Such products were offered in well-illustrated catalogues.

Apron (or Skirt): horizontal member on which a tabletop or chair seat rests and to which the legs are fixed. The term also applies to the lowest horizontal member of a piece of case furniture, such as an armoire.

Arabesque: decorative motifs consisting of plant-like, asymmetrical curves and scrolls, whether painted, carved or moulded. As the name implies, the origin of this type of decoration is Arabian.

Arbalète (*à l'*): term used to describe a type of chest of drawers that appeared during the Régence period in France and was very popular under Louis XV. The front followed the profile of an *arbalète*, or crossbow; on either side of a central recess, the front curved outward and then inward.

Armoire: type of large French cupboard, closed by two full-length doors and often elaborately panelled. The two-tiered armoire has an upper and lower section, both of which are closed by doors.

Arm pad: small fabric- or leather-covered upholstered section set into the upper surface of the arm of a sofa or chair.

Arm stump: vertical member rising from the apron of a chair to support an arm.

Babiche: fairly thin strip of leather (such as buckskin, caribou hide, moose hide or eel skin) used to weave chair seats. The technique was first developed by Amerindians who used it for a variety of purposes, including the fabrication of solid but light snowshoes.

Baluster: vertical support that is often shaped like a slender vase and decorated with carving and turning. It sometimes takes the form of a small column, with a pedestal, shaft and capital. With its great variety of shapes and ornamentation, the baluster has been widely used as a decorative element in Québec furniture.

Bas-relief: decorative carving that projects somewhat from the background without being undercut in any place.

Bead moulding: moulding with a hemispherical profile, often incised to look like a row of beads on a string. Inspired by antiquity, it was especially common in the Neoclassical period.

Bergère: armchair with upholstering and wings on either side of the back. In Québec, rustic chairs constructed entirely of wood were sometimes modelled on this style.

Bombé: used to describe a type of 18th-century chest of drawers that swells outward, so that its front and sides are wider near the middle than they are at the top or bottom.

Bonheur du jour: ladies' writing desk that appeared around 1754. Small and elegant, it had a top with drawers and cubby holes.

Bow-fronted: used to describe cabinet furniture that has an outward-curving front.

Bracket foot: support consisting of two similarly shaped pieces, each with a straight side that meets the other at right angles, usually with a mitred joint, at the lower corners of case furniture.

Buffet: French term for a type of cupboard used for storage. The buffet was a piece of medieval furniture that evolved in successive periods. By the Neoclassical period, buffets were usually two-tiered and had glazed doors.

Bun foot: support that looks like a slightly flattened sphere at the lower corners of case furniture.

Burl: outgrowth on a tree, sometimes caused by an insect or by an injury and most common on maple, ash, walnut and elm. When cut, the wood is dramatically figured and is therefore very desirable for cabinetmaking. Also called a gnarl.

Cabriole chair: upholstered chair appearing in the 18th century, with a curved back for improved comfort (compared with the straight-backed *chaise à la reine*).

Cabriole leg: front leg of seating furniture following the lines of an elongated cyma curve, bulging outward from the apron and then curving inward before ending in an out-turned foot. This type of leg was popular on Rococo and Rococo Revival furniture.

Caning: method of making chair seats or backs with strips of rattan bark woven into geometrical patterns. In Québec, a number of techniques were used and certain materials, such as babiche and elm or ash splint, were adapted to this purpose.

Cartouche: decorative motif shaped like a partially unfurled scroll and often containing words, numbers or initials.

Centre post: stile in the middle of the façade on case furniture with two doors and on which these two doors close.

Chaise à la reine: French term for an 18th-century upholstered chair with a straight back.

Chamfered: bevelled, or having a corners cut or planed to produce a narrow slanting surface. As one of the easiest ways to give a decorative touch, it is often found on rustic furniture.

Chesterfield: comfortable sofa with coil-spring, deep-buttoned upholstering and no exposed wood. The back curves smoothly into the arms. This piece of furniture, whose name is of unknown origin, appeared in England in around 1830 and became extremely popular during the 20th century, when it was produced industrially in versions influenced by every stylistic movement of the time.

Cheval glass: large swing-frame mirror, often oval in shape and mounted between two fairly ornate posts. It appeared in the Napoleonic period and became very popular in bourgeois homes, before it was replaced in large part by the swing-frame mirrors that sat on top of industrially produced dressing tables during the Belle Époque.

Chevron: decorative motif consisting of repeated V-shapes that form a herring-bone pattern.

Chiffonier: small table or cupboard with shelves and drawers used for serving food or drinks. The term also may refer to a tall, narrow chest of drawers.

Chimera: fabulous animal represented in various forms and found on 19th-century Revival furniture.

China cabinet: piece of vernacular dining room furniture manufactured industrially after 1875 and used to store and display fancy chinaware, crystal and silver plate, which was also chain-produced in the Revival era. Such storage pieces were often made in simplified historical styles.

Chinoiserie: fairly complex decorative motif inspired by Chinese styles. In Québec certain pieces of furniture were adorned with Chinoiseries in the 19th century.

Claw-and-ball foot: foot carved to resemble an animal's foot or bird's claw clutching a ball. This foot was inspired by Chinese furniture and was used on English furniture such as chairs, tables and piano benches from the 18th century on.

Cock-beading: narrow moulding with a convex profile, used to edge a drawer front.

Coffer-bench: see Settle.

Colonettte: small decorative column on furniture.

Column: vertical structural element consisting of a base, or plinth, a shaft and a top, or capital. The decoration of columns is determined by conventions that were established in antiquity and continued to be used throughout the history of the decorative arts. These conventions correspond to the five orders of architecture: the Greek orders — Doric, Ionic and Corinthian — and the Roman orders — Tuscan and Composite. A column may by extension be any turned or ornamental vertical support.

Composite: incorporating several materials or styles, used together. A composite piece of furniture may be made of metal and wood, or of several different sorts of wood, and may display a combination of elements from diverse styles.

Concave-cornered: used to describe a square or rectangular panel with its corners cut back and replaced by inward-curving lines.

Console: decorative bracket between two surfaces at right angles to each other. It may be used to support a cornice, a shelf or a small table against a wall. It is usually given the shape of a cyma curve.

Crapaud: 19th-century French upholstered chair that takes its name from the French word for "toad" because of its squat shape.

Crocket: bronze or carved wood appliqué placed on the outer edges of a stile on a piece of furniture, or on its corners, for both decorative and protective purposes. Crockets were seldom used in Québec-made furniture, but they are found on older pieces that were imported.

Crosier: carved decorative element consisting of straight line ending in a scroll and reminiscent of a crook, or crosier, carried by a bishop.

Crotch grain: the swirling-patterned grain displayed by wood cut from the place where the trunk of a tree intersects with a major limb.

Cyma curve: S-shaped curve used either in decorative carving on furniture or in the profile of the furniture itself. Elongated cyma curves applied to the corner stiles of chests of drawers are typical of the Neoclassical and Revival periods.

Demilune: having the outline of a half-moon when viewed from above. Used for a type of table that was popular after 1775.

Dentil moulding: moulding consisting of a row of square or rectangular blocks that alternate with similarly shaped recesses. In use from antiquity, dentil moulding is found on various types of furniture but is typical of cupboards from the Neoclassical era.

Diamond point: decorative motif belonging to the Louis XIII style and common on the panels of armoires. The motif has the appearance of a tetrahedron-cut diamond, sometimes with truncated points.

Dish dresser: two-tiered case furniture for storing tableware. The lower section typically has doors, while the upper section has shelves on which dishes can be displayed, sometimes behind glazed doors.

Disk: decorative motif consisting of concentric circles used on the panels of sideboards and armoires.

Dovetail joint: means of joining two pieces of wood at right angles by fitting one or more wedge-shaped extensions at the end of one piece into matching wedge-shaped cavities in the other piece. The wedge-shape resembles the flaring tail of a dove.

Dowelling: joinery method in which pieces of wood are drilled with matching rows of holes where they are to meet and are then held together by small cylindrical bits of wood inserted in the holes.

Dresser: in medieval times, a piece of furniture with shelves for storing food and kitchen equipment and furnished with a flat surface for food preparation. In modern times, a cupboard for storing tableware, or another name for a chest of drawers.

Dressing table: table usually fitted with small drawers and a swing-frame mirror and used for grooming.

Egg-and-dart: decorative motif consisting of a row of alternating ovals and darts. The motif was used in antiquity.

Escutcheon: decorative plaque or inlay in various materials, protecting the wood around a keyhole or a handle.

False centre post: vertical convex moulding along the open side of one door on a two-doored cupboard or armoire. When the doors are closed the moulding looks like a centre post.

Figured wood: wood that has been cut in a way that reveals distinctive patterns that lie perpendicular to the grain. Bird's-eye, tiger-striped and curly figures are common examples.

Finial: decorative vertical element on top of a stile or crest, or in the centre of an X-stretcher. Finials may be made of turned or carved wood or of cast metal and are found especially on the crest rails of chairs and on bed posts. Brass finials often top clock cases. The most common shapes are the ball finial, the urn finial, the flame finial and ball and steeple finial.

Fire screen: fabric-covered frame placed in front of a fireplace to protect people near the fire from excessive heat. Its shape and decoration evolved with changing fashions. One type of firescreen slid along a pole to various heights.

Fluting: decorative carving consisting of even, parallel grooves cut into the surface of columns, legs, stiles and aprons. Different patterns are formed depending on the depth, profile and spacing of the grooves.

Foliated scroll: decorative motif in the form of an intricately curving shape adorned with leaf-like motifs.

Frame: the joined elements that provide the basic structure of a piece of furniture.

Frieze: ornamental border forming a band around an apron on a table or under the cornice of a piece of storage furniture.

Furniture: generic term for any item that generally stands on the floor of a house or a work space and is used for people to sit or rest on, or for supporting or storing objects.

Gadrooning: decorative motif that looks like a row of overlapping ovals, obtained by intaglio or relief carving.

Gnarl: see Burl.

Gondola chair: chair whose back curves around on either side so that the lines of the back flow smoothly into that of the armrests.

Grain: longitudinal organization of the fibres composing a material and the resulting pattern visible on the surface of the material when it has been cut in the same direction as the fibre. Wood grain is an important factor in the aesthetic value of a piece of furniture.

Greek Key pattern: decorative motif consisting of single continuous line that delineates a series of small, repetitive right-angled shapes. It was first used in antiquity and became popular again in the Neoclassical period. Also known as meander.

Grotesque decoration: motifs representing fabulous animals (chimeras), grimacing anthropomorphic figures and foliated scrolls, originating in the Middle Ages and reintroduced by Revival furniture.

High relief: decorative carving that projects relatively far out from the background and that may be undercut in places.

Hoof foot: furniture foot carved to look like the foot of a hoofed animal. The foot may represent a solid or cloven hoof.

Inlay: decoration obtained by making an intaglio pattern in a material and filling the recessed areas with another, contrasting material.

In the round: type of carving that is entirely undercut and is attached to its background solely by its pedestal.

Japonisme: fashion for furnishings inspired by the Japanese imports that became available in the West in the mid-19th century. This type of furniture, with simple, asymmetrical lines, reflected the general enthusiasm of the Revival age for exotic goods. The movement was particularly strong in Britain and the United States.

Joinery: the techniques by which pieces of wood are assembled for the purposes of carpentry and cabinetmaking. The main types of assembly, or joints, are the dovetail joint, the mortise-and-tenon joint, the cross-lapped joint, the mitred joint, the dowelled joint and the tongue-and-groove joint (See illustration on page 109).

Lacquer: extremely glossy finish given to furniture. Originally lacquer was made from the resin of an Asian tree.

Leaf: section that can be added to a table to increase the surface area of its top. A leaf may be hinged or sliding or may be entirely removable.

Leg block: squarish enlargement on a chair or table leg at the point where the leg is joined to a horizontal element, such as a stretcher.

Linenfold: carved decorative motif in the shape of a length of cloth or parchment folded in on itself at either side. The linenfold motif appears on Gothic and Gothic Revival furniture.

Lion's-paw foot: foot carved with toes to look like a lion's foot.

Listel: slender flat or convex moulding used for picture frames.

Lloyd loom: device for producing imitation wicker furniture, patented in 1917 by Marshall Burns Lloyd of the United States. The loom made it possible to weave furniture out of paper ribbon twisted around metal threads.

Lozenge: diamond-shaped decorative motif characteristic of regional furniture in the French manner and widely used in inlay and marquetry patterns during the Neoclassical period.

Mask: decorative motif consisting of a human face.

Medallion: circular or oval motif that held various types of decoration and that was popular in the Neoclassical era.

Mortise-and-tenon joint: means of assembling two pieces in which one piece is provided with a (usually rectangular) extension, called a tenon, that fits into an identically shaped cavity, called a mortise, in the other. If the cavity extends through the entire thickness of the second piece, the end of the tenon is visible, and the resulting joint is referred to as an exposed mortise-and-tenon joint. This joining technique dates back to antiquity.

Moulding: decorative band with a uniform profile, generally combining elements of concave or convex curves, reeding or fluting, and flat surfaces. There are many varieties of moulding, ranging from the very simple to the very complex, and a number of mouldings may be placed alongside one another.

Nesting tables: set of tables in different sizes, fitting one under the other when not in use.

Ogee: S-shaped profile in moulding or S-shaped upper outline of a pediment.

Openwork: decorative carving in which spaces are cut through the entire thickness of a material to produce a pattern.

Os de mouton: French term for a type of sinuous wooden chair leg said to resemble a mutton bone and used in the early 18th century.

Palmette: decorative motif in the shape of a stylized palm. It was used in very ancient cultures (Egypt and Mycenaea) and became extremely popular in the decorative arts of the 17th and 18th centuries.

Patented furniture: piece of furniture that was patented by its inventor during the heady period of industrial innovation experienced in the West between 1860 and 1900. Certain patented furniture was novel in the way it worked; an example is the platform rocker. Other such furniture combined several functions in the same object, such as a child's highchair that could be converted into a stroller, or a space-saving sofa bed that could be folded into a three-place seat.

Patina: shiny surface acquired by wood with use over time, or similar surface obtained through artificial means.

Pediment: triangular or semicircular ornamental element at the top of a piece of case furniture. Borrowed from the classical architecture of antiquity, the pediment first appeared in furniture during the Renaissance. In the broken pediment, the two upper edges do not meet and often end in scrolls. Different types of finials may be placed at a pediment's centre or at its extremities.

Perfume burner: decorative motif in the shape of a bulbous vase, used on Neoclassical furniture.

Pilaster: vertical column-like relief element set into the façade of a piece of furniture, either for support or for decoration, and showing the same components and styles as a column.

Pin: slender cylinder of solid metal, sometimes with baluster-like extremities, that passes through the loops of a hinge and around which the hinge pivots.

Plastic furniture: furniture moulded out of a synthetic material. Such furniture has been available since the Second World War. The first use of plastic for vernacular furniture is attributed to the designers Eero Saarinen and Charles Eames.

Plinth: base of a column. Also, projecting or recessed base of a piece of case furniture.

Quatrefoil: decorative motif composed of four arcs of a circle joined at their extremities to form a four-petalled outline. The motif arose in the Middle Ages and was borrowed by the Gothic Revival style in the 19th century.

Rail: horizontal member used in the frame of panel and case furniture, or adding support to the structure of seating furniture and tables. Rails are joined to stiles and legs.

Récamier: French daybed with a shaped back and scrolled headboard and footboard. The récamier is a Neoclassical piece of furniture that takes its name from Juliette Récamier, a Parisian celebrity whose portrait by the painter David shows her reclining on this type of daybed.

Reeding: decorative carving consisting of slender, parallel convex ridges sometimes fashioned in stiles, rails and aprons.

Rocaille: manner of combining decorative motifs in the Louis XV Rococo style and characterized by asymmetrical arrangements of stylized rocks and shells combined with volutes and curves. In Québec, this type of decoration was used a great deal for church-related artwork in the 18th century.

Rope moulding: ancient form of moulding that resembles a thick cable and which was very popular in the Neoclassical period.

Rosette: decorative motif in the form of a stylized rose, usually contained by a circle.

Sabre leg: front leg of a piece of seating furniture, having a rectangular cross-section and curving inward from the apron and tapering somewhat towards the foot.

Sabot: metal sheath encasing a foot, sometimes provided with castors. Lion's-paw sabots characterize the furniture designed in the Duncan Phyfe style.

Scotia moulding: moulding with a deep concave profile.

Scroll: decorative form resembling a rolled piece of paper or its cross-section. A C-scroll is a single curve with scroll-like extremities, while an S-scroll is a double curve with scroll-like extremities.

Scroll foot: foot carved to look like a rolled ribbon, curving outward from the front of the piece of furniture.

Secrétaire: French term for various types of writing desks with either slant-tops or flat tops.

Secretary: slant-top writing desk with drawers in its lower section and a bookcase above.

Settee: piece of seating furniture resembling an armchair extended lengthwise, often with upholstering. Associated mainly with the 17th and 18th centuries, it has continued to be used especially as a piece of lawn furniture.

Settle: bench with high back and arms, dating from the Middle Ages. The settle is associated with rustic furniture and may be combined with other functions. The coffer-bench is a settle with a seat that lifts up to reveal a chest, a settle-bed opens up to become a bed and a settle-table has a back that folds over to become a tabletop.

Shaped: carved or cut into decorative curves. This term is especially applied to panels with curved sides and to the bottom rails and aprons of tables, chairs and case furniture.

Shaft: body of a column or colonette between the base and the capital. A shaft may be fluted in various ways and the fluting itself may be decorated.

Shield-back chair: chair with an open back in the shape of the type of medieval shield used to show a coat of arms. In the Neoclassical period, a variety of models were offered by furniture makers in Britain and the United States.

Skirt: see Apron.

Sofa: upholstered seating furniture for more than one person, first appearing in the 17th century and becoming particularly popular in the Revival period.

Spade foot: furniture foot in the form of a block that tapers somewhat towards the bottom.

Spindle: piece of turned wood, swelling gently towards the middle and therefore resembling a spindle used for spinning thread. Spindle turning was a popular treatment for balustrades, chair backs and bed posts, particularly between 1830 and 1890.

Stile: vertical member used in the frames of panels and case furniture, and in the doors of storage furniture, or adding support to the structure of seating furniture.

Stretcher: lower rails of a table or chair, joined to the legs to solidify them. The rails may be joined together to form an X or an H, and they may be either straight or serpentine. The X-shaped stretchers of the Louis XIV and Victorian eras often had flame finials at their central junction.

Swing-frame mirror: mirror suspended between two uprights by horizontal pins that allow it to be tipped at various angles.

Tenon: see Mortise-and-tenon.

Tester: a frame suspended over a bed. It is covered in fabric and supports the canopy and curtains that hang around the bed.

Torchère: tall floor lamp that provides indirect light.

Torus moulding: moulding with a large convex profile.

Trefoil: decorative motif consisting of three arcs of a circle joined at their extremities to form a three-petalled shape.

Tripod: table support consisting of three equidistant curved legs converging on a pedestal.

Trophy: decorative motif consisting of an arrangement of weapons or, by extension, any arrangement of objects symbolizing an art, craft or field of interest.

Turning: result of shaping a piece of wood, metal or other material by turning it around its axis while holding it against a template that cuts it into even shapes. This technique, which dates back to antiquity, is applied to chair and table legs, bed posts, balusters and chair stiles and rails. Styles throughout the history of furniture can be identified with one or another of the various patterns obtained by turning and the way that these patterns are combined. Split balusters are made by fixing two pieces of wood together lengthwise, turning them as if they were one piece of wood, and then taking them apart again. In Québec, the wide vase-like shapes of baluster turning were especially popular in the French-speaking community.

Twist turning: turning with a convex spiral shape that gives the effect of a cable.

Varnish: transparent coating used to finish wood and protect it from moisture. Varnish is applied as a liquid consisting of a resinous substance like shellac dissolved in a solvent such as alcohol or turpentine, which evaporates to leave a hard glossy surface.

Veneer: very thin layer of material, especially decorative or exotic wood, fixed to the surface of something made of more ordinary material. A wood veneer is chosen for its grain, figure or color.

Vitruvian scroll: decorative motif consisting of a row of identical inward-turning spirals in the shape of a wave and therefore also called a wave scroll. The motif was first used in antiquity.

Volute: decorative motif in the form of an elongated scroll.

Wing chair: armchair with extensions on either side of the upper back, intended to provide extra support for a person's head. Rustic armchairs made in Québec sometimes have wings made of wood. The upholstered wing chairs used by the bourgeoisie were first made popular by Madame de Maintenon at Versailles, under the reign of Louis XV.

Bibliography

A large number of different sources, many more than are listed here, were consulted to provide the historical background to this study of Québec furniture. The following bibliography contains only the books that have a direct bearing on the subject and excludes trade directories, periodicals and all the notarial records that have supported my research over many decades, as well as the hundreds of catalogues produced by manufacturers, wholesalers and retailers of furnishing items. I have also excluded from the bibliography books on etiquette and the domestic arts, various commercial publications, literary texts, personal journals, travel writing, pattern books, dictionaires, reference works, general articles and surveys, and records of furnishing work carried out in historic buildings by professional advisors working for various government agencies.

American Manufactured Furniture: A Complete Guide to Furniture Produced in the 1920's. Atglen: Schiffer, 1996, 407 p.

AMES, K. L. "Designed in France: Notes on the Transmission of the French Style to America." *Winterthur Portfolio* 12. Charlottesville: University Press of Virginia, 1977: 103-114.

AMES, K. L. "Grand Rapids Furniture at the Centennial." *Winterthur Portfolio* 10. Charlottesville: University Press of Virginia, 1975: 23-50.

AMES, K. L. "The Rocking Chair in the Nineteenth Century America." *Antiques* vol. 103 no. 2 (February 1973): 322-327.

ARONSON, Joseph. *The Encyclopedia of Furniture*, 3rd edition. New York: Crown Publishers, 1965.

AUSSEL, A. *Études des styles du mobilier*. Paris: Dunod, 1996, 173 p.

BAIRD, Henry Casey. *Victorian Gothic and Renaissance Revival Furniture: Two Victorian Pattern Books*. Reprint of 1868 edition. Philadelphia: Athenaeum Library of Nineteenth Century America, 1977.

BATES, Christina. "Le mobilier de la villa Bellevue." *Research Bulletin* no. 175, Parks Canada (August 1982).

BEACHER, Catherine and Harriet BEACHER STOWE, *The American Woman's Home or Principles of Domestic Science*. Reprint of 1869 edition. Hartford: Stowe-Day Foundation, 1975, 500 p.

BEAUREGARD, Gilles. "La ferronnerie d'ameublement." *Technique* vol. II no. 2 (February 1936): 293-295.

BECKERDITE, Luke (ed.). *American Furniture*. Hanover and London: Chipstone Foundation, University of New England, 1998, 293 p. (A remarkable bilbiography summarizing the current state of knowledge in this area in the United States.)

BEDEL, Jean. *Le grand guide des styles*. Paris: Hachette, 1997, 224 p.

BIRD, Michael. *Canadian Country Furniture: 1675-1950*. Toronto: Stoddart, 1994, 403 p.

BISHOP, Robert. *Centuries and Styles of the American Chair, 1640-1970*. New York: Dutton, 1972.

BLACKIE & Son. *The Victorian Cabinet Maker's Assistant (1853)*. New York: Dover Publications, 1970.

BOUCHARD, Gérard and Yvan LAMONDE. *Québécois et Américains. La culture québécoise aux XIXe et XXe siècles*. Montréal: Fides, 1995, 418 p.

BUTLER, Joseph T. and Katleen EAGEN JOHNSON. *Field Guide to American Furniture*. New York: Henry Holt & Co., 1985, 399 p.

CATHEART, Ruth. *Jacques & Hay: 19th Century Furniture Makers*. Erin: The Boston Mill Press, 1986.

CHIPPENDALE, Thomas. *The Gentleman Cabinet Maker's Director (1762)*. New York: Dover Publications, 1966.

CHOUINARD, Louise. "L'École du meuble de Montréal (1935-1958): son histoire et sa production." Master's thesis, Université Laval, 1988.

COLLARD, Elisabeth. "Montreal Cabinet Makers and Chairmakers 1800-1850: A Checklist." *Antiques* vol. 105 no. 5 (May 1974): 1132-1146.

COOK, Clarence. *The House Beautiful*. New York: Charles Scribner's and Sons, 1887, 336 p. (Dover Publications, 1995.)

COOK SALOMONSKY, Verna. *Masterpieces of Furniture in Photographs and Measured Drawings*. New York: Dover Publications, 1974.

DARLING, Sharon. *Chicago Furniture Art, Craft & Industry*. Chicago and New York: The Chicago Historical Society and W. W. Norton & Co., 1984, 416 p.

DAVIS, Felice. "Victorian Cabinetmakers in America." *Antiques* vol. 44 no. 3 (September 1943): 111-115.

DEAN, Ben H. and Walter J. PETERSON. *Modern American Period Furniture*. Grand Rapids: n.p., 1917, 324 p.

DE SÈVE, Andrée-Anne. *Hommage à Jean-Marie Gauvreau*. Montréal: Conseil des métiers d'art, 1995, 36 p.

DESMEULES, Claire. "Le vocabulaire du meuble." *Continuité* no. 38 (winter 1988): 32-33.

DROUIN, Daniel. "Les meubliers du Québec aux expositions provinciales, internationales et universelles, 1850 à 1900." Master's thesis, Université Laval, 1992, 155 p.

DUBÉ, Richard (dir.) and Paul TRÉPANIER (co-ord.). *Objets de civilisation*. Québec City: Musée de la civilisation/Broquet, 1990, 153 p.

DUBÉ, Richard. *Trésors de société, les collections du Musée de la civilisation*. Québec City: Musée de la civilisation/Fides, 1998, 256 p.

DUBROW, Eileen and Richard DUBROW. *Styles of American Furniture, 1860-1960*. Atglen: Schiffer, 1977, 208 p.

EARL, Polly Anne. "Craftmen and Machines: The Nineteenth-Century Furniture Industry, Technological Innovation and Decoration Arts." *Winterthur Conference Report (1973)*. Charlottesville: University Press of Virginia, 1974, 307-329.

ETTEMA, Michael J. "Technological Innovation and Design Economics in Furniture Manufacture." *Winterthur Portfolio* 16. Charlottesville: University Press of Virginia, 1974, 197-225.

FLEMMING, John A. *The Painted Furniture of French Canada, 1700-1840*. Camden East and Hull: Camden House and Canadian Museum of Civilization, 1994.

FORREST, Tim. *Les meubles anciens. Un guide illustré pour reconnaître et évaluer vos meubles de style*. Paris: Célin, 1997, 160 p.

FOURNIER-VALLIÈRE, Suzanne, *Philippe Vallière, 1832-1919, ébéniste et manufacturier de meubles à Québec et sa généalogie*. Lévis, 1992, 154 p. and 86 pl. (unpublished)

FOSS, Charles H. *Cabinetmakers of the Eastern Seaboard, A Study of Early Canadian Furniture*. Toronto: M. F. Feheley Publishers, 1977, 156 p.

Furniture for the Victorian Home Comprising the Abridged Furniture from A. J. Downing's Country Houses of 1850 and J. C. Louden's Encyclopedia of 1833. New York: Watkins Glen, The American Life Foundation, 1968, 217 p.

GAIRAUD, Yves and Françoise DE PERTHUIS. *Guide des meubles anciens*. Paris: Hervas, 1992, 375 p.

GAUTHIER, Joseph. *Graphique d'histoire de l'art*. Paris: Plon, 1911, 272 p.

GAUVREAU, Jean-Marie. *Artisans du Québec*. Trois-Rivières: Les éditions du Bien Public, 1940, 224 p.

GAUVREAU, Jean-Marie. "Bois du Québec et décoration intérieure." *Technique* no. 16 (1941): 331-333.

GAUVREAU, Jean-Marie. "Décorateurs d'hier et d'aujourd'hui." *Revue trimestrielle canadienne* vol. 15 no. 59 (1929): 286-311.

GAUVREAU, Jean-Marie. "Évolution et tradition des meubles canadiens." *Proceedings and Transactions of the Royal Society of Canada, Ottawa* vol. 38 (May 1944): 121-128.

GAUVREAU, Jean-Marie. "Fabrication d'un fauteuil moderne." *Technique* no. 7 (1932): 45-48.

GAUVREAU, Jean-Marie. "L'ameublement rustique." *Technique* no. 6 (1931): 1-4.

GAUVREAU, Jean-Marie. "La petite industrie à Chicoutimi." *Technique* no. 11 (1936): 285-289.

GAUVREAU, Jean-Marie. "La romance du bois." *Technique* no. 8 (1933): 351-354.

GAUVREAU, Jean-Marie. "L'École du meuble." *Technique* no. 18 (1943): 268-278.

GAUVREAU, Jean-Marie. "L'École du meuble; son esprit, son but." *Mémoires de la Société royale du Canada, Ottawa* (1950): 19-26.

GAUVREAU, Jean-Marie. "Le meuble moderne." *Opinions* no. 4 (1931): 20-25.

GAUVREAU, Jean-Marie. *L'enseignement de l'ébénisterie à l'École Technique de Montréal*. Montréal: Imprimerie de l'École Technique, 1931, s. p.

GAUVREAU, Jean-Marie. "Le premier Salon du meuble." *Technique* no. 11 (1936): 330-334.

GAUVREAU, Jean-Marie. "Le quatrième Salon de l'École du Meuble." *Technique* no. 14 (1939): 473-476.

GAUVREAU, Jean-Marie. "Les arts appliqués." *Vie des arts* no. 8 (1963): 31-38.

GAUVREAU, Jean-Marie. "Nos bois, richesse nationale." *Technique* no. 6 (1931): 8-12.

GAUVREAU, Jean-Marie. *Nos intérieurs de demain*. Montréal: Les Éditions de l'Action catholique française, 1931, 92 p.

GAUVREAU, Jean-Marie. "Québec, visage français d'Amérique." *Technique* no. 12 (1937): 52.

GAUVREAU, Jean-Marie. "Qu'est-ce qu'un plan de meuble?." *Technique* no. 7 (1935): 7-10.

GAUVREAU, Jean-Marie. *Secrets et ressources des bois du Québec*. Montréal: Fides, 1945, 225 p.

GAUVREAU, Jean-Marie. "Utilisons nos bois de la Province de Québec." *Technique* no. 8 (1933): 116-119.

GENEST, Bernard and Yves BERGERON. *Guide d'inventaire des objets mobiliers*. Québec City: ministère de la Culture et des Communications, 1994, 247 p.

GENEST, Louise, Louise DÉCARIE-AUDET and Luce VERMETTE. *Les objets familiers de nos ancêtres*. Montréal: Les Éditions de l'Homme, 1974, 304 p.

GOSSELIN, Bernard. *Le discours de l'armoire*. Montréal: Office national du film du Canada, 1978 (videocassette, 56 min 41s).

GREENE, Bowman. *American Arts and Crafts, Virtue in Design*. Los Angeles: Los Angeles County Museum Associates, 1990, 255 p.

HIESINGER, Kathryn B. and George H. MARCUS. *Petit lexique des arts décoratifs de la Renaissance à l'Art déco*. Paris: Éditions Abbeville, 1997, 213 p.

JEANNEAU, Guillaume and Jacques FRÉAL. *Le meuble populaire français*. Paris: Serge et Jacques Fréal, 1977, 2 vol., 319 p. and 287 p.

KIMBERLAY, W. L. *How to Know Period Style in Furniture*. Grand Rapids: Periodical Publishing Company, 1912, 147 p.

KING, Thomas. *Neo-classical Furniture Design: a Reprint of Thomas King's Modern Style of Cabinet Work Exemplified, 1829*. New York: Dover Publications, 1995.

KOLTUN, L. A. *The Cabinetmaker's Art in Ontario 1850-1900*. Mercury Series Paper No. 26. Ottawa: National Museum of Man, 1979.

KOVEL, Ralph and Terry KOVEL. *American Country Furniture 1789-1875*. New York: Crown Trade Paperbacks, 1987, 248 p.

LABIAU, Jean-Pierre."Le mobilier des XIXe et XXe siècles." *Objets de civilisation*, Québec City, Musée de la civilisation, Éditions Broquet (1990): 51-60.

LAMONTAGNE, J. G. "L'école des arts et métiers de Chicoutimi." *Technique* no. 12 (1937): 458-459.

LECLERC, Denise. "Musée du Québec: regard sur le mobilier victorien." *Bulletin d'histoire de la culture matérielle* no. 122 (spring 1981).

Le meuble régional en France. Paris: Réunion des musées nationaux, 1990, 189 p.

Le meuble des grands ébénistes et des designers. Milan: Arnoldi Mondadori Editore, 1984. Paris: Célin, 1990, 419 p.

LÉONIDOFF, George P. and Jean-Pierre LABIAU. "Un mobilier sous influence." *Continuité* no. 38 (winter 1988): 26-29.

LÉPINE, Johanne. "Historique et étude du design au Québec." Master's thesis, Université de Montréal, 1987.

LESSARD, Michel. *Antiquités du Québec: Objets anciens. Vie sociale et culturelle*. Montréal: Les Éditions de l'Homme, 1995, 384 p.

LESSARD, Michel. *Aux sources du peuple québécois et de l'Amérique française, L'île d'Orléans*. Montréal: Les Éditions de l'Homme, 1998, 415 p.

LESSARD, Michel. "De l'utilité des catalogues commerciaux en ethnohistoire du Québec." *Cahier des Dix* vol. 49 (1994): 213-251.

LESSARD, Michel. *Encyclopédie des antiquités du Québec*. Montréal: Les Éditions de l'Homme, 1971, 526 p.

LESSARD, Michel. *Objets anciens du Québec. La vie domestique*. Montréal: Les Éditions de l'Homme, 1994, 335 p.

LESSER, Gloria. "Jean-Marie Gauvreau et l'art déco." *Vie des arts* no. 110 (March-May 1983): 37-39.

LESSER, Gloria. *L'École du meuble: 1930-1950. La décoration intérieure et les arts décoratifs à Montréal*. Montréal: Musée des arts décoratifs de Montréal, 1989, 119 p.

LESSER, Gloria. "Le design au Canada de 1940 à 1980." *Cahier des arts visuels au Québec* no. 6 (1984): 6-16.

MACKINNON, Joan. *A Checklist of Toronto Cabinet and Chair Makers 1800-1867*. Mercury Series Paper No. 11. Ottawa: National Museum of Man, 1974.

MACKINNON, Joan. *Kingston Cabinet Makers 1800-1867*. Mercury Series Paper No. 14. Ottawa: National Museum of Man, 1976.

MARTIN, Paul-Louis. *À la façon du temps présent. Trois siècles d'architecture populaire au Québec*. Québec City: Les Presses de l'Université Laval, 1999, 378 p.

MARTIN, Paul-Louis. *La berçante québécoise*. Montréal: Boréal Express, 1973, 173 p.

MARTIN, Paul-Louis. *Le mobilier de mariage au Québec*. National Film Board of Canada, 1974, slides.

MINHINNICK, Jeanne and Philip SHACKLETON. "Early Furniture of Canada: the English and American Influence: 1760-1840." *Canadian Antiques Collector* (January-February 1974): 25-29.

MONTENEGRO, Ricardo. *Les arts décoratifs de la Renaissance à nos jours*. Paris: Les Éditions de la Martinière, 1997, 288 p.

MOUSSETTE, Marcel. "Sens et contresens: l'étude de la culture matérielle au Québec." *Canadian Folklore canadien* vol. 4 no 1-2 (1984): 7-26.

OLIVIER, Lucille. *Mobilier québécois*. Paris: Charles Massin, 1979.

PAIN, Howard. *The Heritage of Upper Canadian Furniture: A Study on the Survival of Formal, Vernacular Styles from Britain, America and Europe, 1780-1900*. Toronto: Van Nostrand Reinhold, 1978.

PALARDY, Jean. *Les meubles anciens du Canada français*. Paris: Arts et Métiers Graphiques, 1963, 401 p.

PARISIEN, Steven. *Regency Style*. London: Phaidon Press Limited, 1992, 240 p.

PHILIP, Peter, Gilligan WALKING and John BLY. *Field Guide to Antique Furniture*. Boston: Houghton Mifflin, 1992, 336 p.

PIVA, Dominico (ed.). *Mobilier. Le monde fascinant des antiquaires*. Milan: R.C.S. Libri & Grandi Opere, 1996, 477 p.

POISSON, Esther. "Étude du vocabulaire du mobilier d'habitation de la région des Bois-Francs d'après les journaux publiés depuis 1866." Master's thesis, Université Laval, October 1982.

Popular Furniture of the 1920s and 1930s. From Traditional to Early Modern. Atglen: Schiffer, 1977, 224 p.

PORTER, John R. "L'avènement de l'industrie et la persistance des pratiques artisanales à l'époque victorienne au Québec: quelques notes exploratoires touchant le cas des meubliers." *Les cahiers du CÉLAT*, Québec City, Université Laval no. 1 (1989): 91-96.

PORTER, John R. (ed.). "Les meubliers Pierre Drouin et Honoré Roy et l'industrie du meuble à l'époque victorienne." *Les cahiers du CÉLAT*, Québec City, Université Laval no. 10 (1989), 197 p.

PORTER, John R. (ed.). *Un art de vivre. Le meuble de goût à l'époque victorienne au Québec*. Montréal: Musée des beaux-arts de Montréal, 1993, 527 p.

PORTER, John R. and Micheline HUARD. "La création québécoise." *Continuité* no. 38 (winter 1988): 18-21.

ROMPRÉ, Danielle. *Un rêve art déco: la collection Bélanger-Blatter*. Québec City: Musée de la civilisation, 1994, 58 p.

ROUSSEAU, Francis. *Le grand livre des meubles. Reconnaître les styles du XVIe au XXe siècle*. Paris: Sélection du Reader's Digest, 1998, 224 p.

ROUSSEAU, Gabriel. "Le développement des Écoles d'Arts et Métiers." *Technique* no. 14 (1939): 85-91.

ROY, Antoine. "Le coût et le goût des meubles au Canada sous le Régime français." *Les Cahiers des Dix*. no. 18 Montréal (1953): 228-239.

RYDER, Huia Gwendoline. *Antique Furniture by New-Brunswick Craftmen*. Toronto: Ryerson Press, 1965.

SALLÉ, Alix. *Le mobilier de jardin d'hier à aujourd'hui*. Paris: Bibliothèque Fornay, 1998, 14 p.

SANTORE, Charles. *The Windsor Style in America, 1730-1830*. Philadelphia: Running Press, 1981, 215 p.

SCHWARZ, M. D. and T. HERBERT. "La commode bombée de la Nouvelle-France." *Vie des arts* vol. 21 (Christmas 1960): 30-37.

STRANGE, Thomas Arthur. *English Furniture Decoration Woodwork and Allied Arts*. London: Studio Edition, 1986, 368 p.

SURPRENANT, Jean-Pierre. *L'industrie du meuble et des articles d'ameublement*. Québec City: Bureau de la statistique, 1987, 43 p.

TRÉPANIER, Paul. *Le patrimoine de ma famille. Comment le reconnaître et bien le conserver*. Québec City: Musée de la civilisation, 1998, 64 p.

VALLIÈRE, Suzanne. "Philippe Vallière, ébéniste et manufacturier de meubles." *Cap-aux-Diamants* vol. 2 (spring 1986): 25-28.

VALLIÈRE, Suzanne. "Philippe Vallière 1832-1919, ébéniste et manufacturier de meubles à Québec." Lévis, 1998, 154f, ill.

VERMETTE, Luce. "Ébéniste à meublier: l'ébénisterie au Québec au milieu du XIXe siècle." *Canadian Collector* (May 1985): 45-50.

VON VERGESACK, Alexander. *Thonet, Classic Furniture in Bent Wood and Tubular Steel*. New York: Rizzoli, 1996, 160 p.

WEBSTER, Donald Blake. *Canadian Georgian Furniture*. Toronto: Royal Ontario Museum, 1981, 32 p.

WEBSTER, Donald Blake. *English Canadian Furniture of the Georgian Period*. Toronto: McGraw-Hill Ryerson, 1979, 232 p.

WEBSTER, Donald Blake. *The Book of Canadian Antiques*. Toronto: McGraw-Hill Ryerson, 1974, 352 p.

WEBSTER, Donald Blake. "The Identification of English-Canadian Furniture, 1780-1840." *Antiques* vol. 115 no. 1 (January 1979): 164-179, 38 ill.

WILSON, Anne Elisabeth. "A History of Canadian Furniture: Some Distinguished Canadian Craftmen Contemporary with Duncan Phyfe." *Canadian Homes and Gardens* vol. 5 no. 5 (1928): 40-52.

WINCHESTER, Alice. "French Canadian Furniture." *Antiques* vol. 45 no. 5 (May 1944): 238-241.

WINCHESTER, Alice. "The Armoires of French Canada." *Antiques* vol. 45 no. 6 (June 1944): 302-305.

Index

Figures in Roman type refer to page number, while figures in italics refer to illustration number.

Aalto, Alvar, 79, 531
Abbott, William, 94
Adam (brothers), 16, 21
Adam, George, 69, 284
Adam, Robert, 69
Adhemar (notary), 204
Aesthetic movement, 79, 434, *753, 773, 775*
Ailleboust, Madame D', 106, *176, 248*
Albert, Patrick, 108, *337*
Armstrong, George, *336*
Art Deco, *35, 36, 38, 40, 41, 42, 45, 54,* 79, 93, 474, 483, 486, 490, 492, 501, 508, 510, 531, *810-812, 816-820, 840, 851-854, 859, 861, 863-866, 869, 885, 887*
Art Furniture Movement, 75, 79, 334, 428, 434, 446, *753*
Art Nouveau, 29, 37, 62, 75, 76, 91, 407, 434, 444, 446, 458, 493, 531, *724, 776-781, 786, 816, 820*
Arts & Crafts, 26, 62, 75, 76, 401, 403, 407, 410, 411, 412, 434, 498, *721, 724*
Ashbee, C. R., 410
Aubert de Gaspé, Philippe, *3*
Audet, Bernard, 89, 152, 204
Auger, Lorenzo, 96
Baillargé, François, 69
Barbeau, Charles Marius, 84, 85, 96, *96-98, 760*
Baroque, 68, 152, 186, *237, 248,* 334, 340, *341, 347, 440-445, 444, 466*
Baroque Revival, *399,* 531, *639-646*
Bazin, Neuville, *569*
Beaulac, Henri, 486, 492, 506, *870*
Beaulieu, Elzéar, *747*
Beaulieu, Jacques, 506
Beaulieu, Louis (see also Louis Jaque), 492, *837, 838*
Behrens, Peter, 79
Belanger, Adolphe, *336*
Bélanger, Henri, *37,* 490
Bélanger, Jeannot, 108, 111
Bell, David, *107*
Belzile, Jean-Marc, 108, 111
Berczy, William, *10,* 61, 84
Bériau, Oscar, 500
Bertrand (family), 391
Bertrand, Louis, *11, 20,* 390, 391, 392, *705*
Bieler, André, 85
Bilodeau, Raynald, *89-92,* 108
Blain, Jeannette, *34*
Blais, Anick ("Dyonis" table), *907*

Blatter, Robert, *35, 36, 37, 41,* 79, 486, 487, 490, *839, 841-846, 851-854*
Bonne, Pierre Amable de, *10*
Borduas, Paul-Émile, 498
Bosworth, Newton, 237
Bouchard (family), 414
Bouchard, Georges, *26*
Bouchard, Joseph, 414, *721, 741-746*
Boucher, Pierre, 59
Bouchette, R. S. M., *60*
Boudreault, Étienne (notary), 243
Boulle, André Charles, 62
Bowman, Lesslie Green, 410
Brassard, Sylvio, 88, 96, *217, 220,* 284, *419-423*
Breuer, Marcel L., 79, 458, 508, 523, *841*
Briand, Jean Olivier, Monseigneur, *232, 326*
Bruneau, Arthur Aimé, 95, 96
Bruyère, Boucher de la, 96
Burgess, Cecil, 96
Caldwel, Henry, 390
Cantin, Pierre, *58*
Carleton, Guy, Lord Dorchester, 238
Carlu, Jacques, 486
Cartier, George-Étienne, *326*
Cartier, Jacques, 13, *558, 559*
Casgrain (family), 498
Chabot, Ronald, 54, 55
Champlain, Samuel de, 13, *333*
Chapais, Jean-Charles, 21, *565-568*
Chateaubriand, François René de, 96
Chaussegros de Léry (family), *38*
Chippendale, Thomas, 69, *428*
Chouinard, Louise, 100, 497, 498, 501
Classicism, 13, *19, 28, 29, 53,* 68, 140, 143, 152, 186, 334, 340, 391
Clavet, Étienne, 243
Clendinneng, William, 387
Coles, May, 96
Collard, Elisabeth, 91, 242
Connell, J. E., 320
Cormier, Ernest, 486
Côté, Benoît, 521-523
Côté, Jean-Baptiste, *582-585, 597-599*
Cousin, Victor, 74
Coverdale, William, 96
Craig, A. I., *336*
Darwin, Charles, 29
Davies (family), *427*

Dawson, Nora, 96
Demers, Jérôme (Father), 69
Denault, Salomon *dit* Luneau, 119
Denoncourt, Maurice, 506
Desgagnés, Alain, ("Charlotte" stool), *908*
Désilets, Alphonse, 153
Desjardins (studio), *34*
Desmeules, Claire, 323, 334
Dion, Donald, 108
Dionne, Georgina, *25, 565-568*
Drouin, Daniel, 91, 98, 327
Drouin, Pierre, 89, 98, 327, 336, *546, 560, 564, 656*
Drum, William, 325, 336
Dubé, Richard, 529, 532
Dubuc, J. E. A., *630-634*
Ducharme, Robert, *911*
Dufresne, Maurice, 79
Dugal, Jean-François, *904*
Duncan, John, 237
Du Sault, Jean-Marie, 66
Eastlake, Charles Locke, *28, 32, 37,* 75, 330, 334, 406, 434, 446, 531
Eastlake, George, 403
Ellice, Katherine Jane, *66*
Émond, Pierre, 232
Fabre-Surveillé (family), 428
Faucher, Rosario, 807
Faucher, Sylvain, 521, 525, 526
Fauteux, Aegédius, 96
Feure, George de, *779-781*
Fillion, Philéas (Father), *535-540 b*
Fitzgibbon, James, 243
Fleming, John A., 235, 242
Follot, Paul, 79
Fontaine, Léo, *858*
Forget, Sir Rodolphe, *27, 45,* 88
Fournier Vallière, Suzanne, 331
Fréal, Jacques, 68
Functionalism, 45, 75, 140, 246, 401, 486
Gadoury, Ginette, 521
Gagné, J. D., 474
Gagnon, Albéric, *858*
Gagnon, Clarence, 84, 86, 392
Gagnon, Joseph, 320, *534*
Gagnon, Maurice, 498
Gagnon, P., 243, *534*
Gale, Robert, 466
Gallé, Émile, 75, 403, 406
Gariépy, Edgar, *212, 545*
Garneau (family), *589*
Garneau, François-Xavier, 96
Gauldrée-Boileau, Charles-Henri-Philippe, 95
Gaumond, Michel, 243

Gauvreau, Charles Herménégilde (notary), 243
Gauvreau, Jean-Marie, *35, 36,* 45, 55, 57, 62, 79, 93, 100, 153, 410, 483, 487, 497, 498, 500, 501, 506, 531, 532, *840, 858, 860, 861, 866-868*
Gignac, Joseph Narcisse, *535-540 f*
Gingras, Philippe, 807
Girard, Firmin, *59*
Godwin, William, *28,* 75, 76, 330, 334, 403, 406, 428, 434, 446, 531
Gosselin, Amédée-Edmond (Father), 320, *535-540 a*
Gosselin, Bernard, 100
Gothic, 334, 340
Gothic Revival, 340, 555, *556a, b, c*
Gouin, Paul, 96
Gourdeau, François, 330, 336, *582-585*
Greene, Charles and Henry (brothers), 75, 412
Grenon, Joseph, *621-626*
Gropius, Walter, 79, 486
Guérin, Kino, *910*
Guillet, Joseph, *dit* Tourangeau, *530, 531*
Guilmard, Désiré, 327, 330
Guimard, Hector, 75, 406, 411, 444
Hague, George, 696
Hamel, Théophile, *18*
Hébert, Pierre (Father), *534, 535-540*
Hepplewhite, George, 67, 69, 248, 284
Herbst, René 490, 492
Hilton, John, 336
Hodge, E. B., *576*
Hoffman, Josef, 410, 458
Holgate, Edwin H., 86
Horta, Victor, 75, 403, 406, 411, 444
House (see also manor, residence)
  Adjutor-Pelletier, 406, 488
  Alphonse Desjardins, *753, 772, 775*
  Amable Morin, 50, 391
  Bédard, *419-423*
  Bourdon, *35*
  bourgeois, 310, 372, *506-516*
  Chapais, 54, 391, *402, 570*
  Estèbe, *250*
  Garneau, *56*
  George-Étienne Cartier, Sir, *55,* 94, 95, 100, *587, 588*

Gurd, *51*
Imbault, *193*
Jean-Baptiste-Pâquet, *19*
Joseph Elzéar Cyril Pelletier, *12*
Jourdan-Fiset, *333, 553*
Létourneau, *352, 764*
Louis-Bertrand, *11, 20,* 100, *390, 391, 395, 397, 399, 697-705*
Pelletier, *349, 351*
Québec, *392, 593*
rural, 124, 140, *264, 325*
Saint-Roch des Aulnaies, 99, 102
Sifroy-Guéret *dit* Dumont, *174, 391, 413*
Sifroy-Roy, *49*
Villeneuve, *217, 220,* 284
Hubbard, Elbert, 412
Huot, Charles, 85
Jackson, Alexander Y., 86
Jaque, Louis (pseudonym of Louis Beaulieu), 494, *837, 838*
Jacques, Jean-François ("Baby-Face"chair), *906*
Jacobson, Arne ("Egg" chair), *897*
Jacques & Hay, *617, 618, 649-654*
Japonisme, 434
Jeanneau, Guillaume, 68
Jeanneret, Pierre, *dit* Le Corbusier, 79, 486, 490, 492, 523, 531, *835*
Juneau, Émile, 506
Kalm, Pehr, 143
Kelly, John Hall (family), 385
Kieffer, Henri, *36, 40*
Kilgour (family and company), *73,* 458, 512, 886
Knox, John, 55
Kohn, Joseph, 458
Krieghoff, Cornélius, 84, 392
Labelle, H. P., 336
Laberge, A., 490
Labiau, Jean-Pierre, 327
Lacasse, Yves, *582-585*
Laferté (family), *342*
Lambert, Adolphe, *28*
Lamonde, Yvan, 78
Laperrière, Céline, *895*
Lasnier, Raymond, 506
Laurier, Sir Wilfrid, *30, 713*
Laval, Monseigneur de, 320
Lavigne, Azarie, 336
Leahy, Georges, 242
Lebrun, Jean-Cyrille and Hugues (brothers and workshop), 506, *879, 880, 882, 884*

540

Leclerc, Eugène, 55
Le Corbusier, 79, 486, 490, 492, 523, 531, *835*
Legaré, Pierre-Théophile, 92, 93
Legay, Alexis, 204
Leleu, Jules, 490
Lemieux, Émile, 493
Lemieux, Jean-Paul, 497, *858*
Lessard, Joseph, 474
Lessard, Michel, 9, 57, 116
Lessard, Rénald, 327
Lesser, Gloria, 100, 490
Létourneau, Roland, *99*, 100, *219*
Levasseur, Roland, *881*
Limbert, Charles, 412
Livernois, Jules, *176*
Livernois, J.-Ernest, *589*
Livernois (studio), 88
Loos, Adolf, 458
Mackintosh, Charles Rennie, 75, 79, 410
Magne, H. M., *172 a, b, c, 175 a, b*
Mailhot, Marguerite Alexis, *2*
Majorelle, Louis, 62, 75, 444
Maisonneuve, Paul de, 237
Malchelosse, Gérard, 96
Malepart, François de Beaucourt, *2*
Mallet-Stevens, Robert, 490, 492
Manor (see also house, residence)
  Aubert de Gaspé, *3*
  Beauharnois, *66*
  Charleville, *53, 58*
  Dionne, *553, 563, 569*
  Louis-Bertrand, *11, 20,* 100, 390, 391, *395, 397, 399, 697-705*
  Louis-Joseph-Papineau, *67,* 96, 100, *102, 212,* 376, *399, 545, 655, 679, 687*
  McPherson, *396*
  Mauvide-Genest, *26,* 100, *392- a, b, 404,* 490, *648, 725-730, 752*
Marceau, Georges (Father), 320
Marcoux, Louise Élysabeth, *10*
Mare, André, 79, 490
Martel, Joseph, 204
Martel, J.-B., *46*
Martin, Charles, 506
Martin, Paul-Louis, 91, 96, 100, 124, *132-148,* 150, 151, 242, 249
Massicotte, Edmond J., *65,* 84
Massicotte, E. Z., 96
Maurault, Olivier, 96
McGarvey, Owen, 336, 458, 474, *761, 762*
Mercier, Honoré, 54
Mérimée, Prosper, 96
Meunier-Biéler, Jeannette, 493, *847, 850*
Michaud, Charles-Eugène, 391
Michaud (family), 399
Michaud, Pierre and Robert (Fathers) 100, 391, 399
Mies Van der Rohe, Ludwig, 79, 458
Mission, 406, 434
Modernism, 45, 63, 490

Modernity, 45, *34,* 56, 140, 330, 403, 434, 474, 490, 505, 508
Molière, *195 a, b*
Montesquieu, *10*
Morewood (family), *15*
Morin, François-Xavier, 506, *878, 883*
Morin, Victor, 96
Morisset, Gérard, 96
Morris, William, *28, 31,* 37, 56, 62, 75, 76, 330, 334, 403, 406, 407, 410-412, 414, 428
Moussette, Marcel, 98
Murison, Alexander, 243
Nelligan, Émile, 401
Neoclassicism, *10-13, 17,* 21, *47, 53,* 60, 62, 67, 69, 140, 237, 310, 320, *333,* 347, 399, 406, 440-445, 459-466, 490, 532, 639-644, *679,* 765
Nesbett, Thomas, *17*
Nielson, Albert, 506
Nobbs, Percy, 96
Norton, Charles, 411
Notman (studio), *70,* 86, 88, *615, 616, 683, 693*
Nutting, Wallace, 78
Olbrich, Joseph Maria, 410
Palardy, Jean, 54, 57, 78, 96, 84-88, 98, 186, 242, *303, 311-317,* 523
Palladio, Andréa, 21, 237
Panet, Jean-Antoine, 238
Papineau, Julie, 89
Papineau, Louis-Joseph, 54, 89, 391
Pâquet, Jean-Baptiste, *19*
Paquet, Zéphirin, 69, 406
Paradis, Jacques, 204
Paré, Alfred (Father), *535-540 d*
Parent, Omer, 486
Parent, Pierre, 243
Pariseau, Charles E., 336
Parizeau, Marcel, *35,* 490, 492, 498
Parks, J. G., *67, 655, 679, 687*
Pelletier, Adjutor, 100
Pelletier (notary), *11, 349-351*
Perriand, Charlotte, 79
Pétrin, Léa, 494
Phyfe, Duncan, 248, 284
Pineau, Nicolas, 306
Poisson, Esther, 98
Porter, John, 54, 89, 98, 325, 327, 434, *582-585*
Post-Modernism, 485, 531
Pouliot (Judge), *26, 392 a, b*
Pouliot, Louis-Joseph (Jesuit), 490
Pratte, Noël, 336
Pre-Modernism *26, 27, 28,* 37, *47, 52,* 54, *74, 78,* 93, 140, 330, 403, 458, *712-715, 716, 765*
Price, William, 390
Pugin, Augustus, 62
Quéry, William and Adélard (brothers), *27, 45,* 88, 406, *716*
Rémillard, France, 117
Renaissance, 21, 29, 74, 76, 78, 152, 334, 340, 397
Renaissance Revival, *19,* 337, 342, 399, 639-644

Residence
  bourgeoise, *274-276, 690*
  family, 699
  Gil'Mont, *27,* 88
  Rodolphe Forget, 406, *716, 723*
  W. R. Miller, *52*
Revival-era, *21,* 28, 29, *37,* 47, *51,* 54, 62, 63, 68, 74-76, *102,* 140, 326, 330, 337, 340, *347,* 376, 399, 403, 406, 407, *545, 614, 635-638, 873*
Rickaby, D. S., 434, 458
Rietveld, Gerrit Thomas, 79, 531
Rimbaud, Arthur, 7, 204
Riopel, *556 a, b, c*
Rivet, Alain, 410
Rocaille, 235
Rococo, 334, 340, 341, 444
Roisin, Maxime, 490
Rompré, Danielle, 490
Roquebrune, Robert de, 323
Rose, Sir John, *617, 618*
Roubo, A.-J., *195, a, b,* 211, *236,* 252
Rousseau, E. Antoine, *41, 851-854*
Rousseau, Jacques, 486
Routhier, Joseph, *548*
Roux, Alexandre, 330
Roy, Honoré *dit* Belleau, 89, 98, 327, 330, 336, *546, 548, 560, 564, 656, 684*
Roy, Pierre-Georges, 96
Ruhlman, Jacques Émile, 79, 490, 531
Ruskin, John, 62, 75, 407, 410, 411
Saindon, Appoline, 390
Saint-Amand, Onésime, 337
Saint-Jacques, Alphonse, 36, 40, 483, 496, 497, 503, *855, 856, 858, 859, 861*
Saint-Martin, Madame (nun), *328*
Saint-Vallier, Jean-Baptiste de la Croix de Chevrières de, *8, 216*
Scott, M. H. Baillie, 410
Second Empire, 62, 74
Séguin, Robert-Lionel, 89, 96, 143, 152, 204
Sève, Andrée-Anne de, 497
Sheraton, Thomas, 67, 69, 248, 284
Sifroy-Guéret *dit* Dumont, *174, 369, 413*
Simard, Henri (Father), *53, 540e*
Sottsass, Ettore, 531
Spénard, Jean-Jacques, 506
Stickley, Gustav, *28,* 75, 403, 406, 411, 412, 428
Stratton, William, *12*
Style (and synonyms: type, movement, manner), 44, 47, *53,* 56, 61-63, 67-69, 74-76, 78, 79, 88, 96, *93,* 106, 124, 138, 140, 152, 153, 164, 192, 232, 242, 246, 249, 260, 264, 272, 284, 310, *311-317,* 326, 327, 340, 358, *361-368,* 403, 446, 467, 474, 491, 492, 492, 648, *810-812*
  Art Deco, 93, 492, 500, 506, 508, *843, 861, 863-869, 885, 887*

  Art Nouveau, *793-795*
  Arts & Crafts, *27,* 75, 93, 94, 414, 446, 508, 531, *716, 718, 721, 723, 724, 725-730, 792-795*
  Baroque, 29, 146, *201,* 334, 340, *356, 358,* 358
  Baroque Revival, 334, 382, *571-575, 627-629, 639-646, 681*
  classical, 278, 334
  Confederative, 29, 74, 323, 326, 335, 372, 382, *594-596, 600-610, 682, 687*
  Constitutional, 21, 69, *212,* 235, 348, 375, 682, 687
  Directoire, 63, 69, 78, 238, 248, 531
  Eastlake, *67, 73,* 74, 94, *165,* 268, 397, 434, *753-765, 768-773, 775*
  Empire, 10, 17, 21, 63, 69, 238, 248, 380, 387, *502-505,* 531
  Federal, 21, 62, 69, 238
  Georgian, 21, 44, 54, 64, 238, 246, 531
  Gothic, 62, 74, 326, 334, 340
  Gothic Revival, 62, 334, 391, *555, 556 a, b, c*
  Hepplewhite, 106, *330,* 334, *335, 341, 342,* 344, 348, 357, 658
  Late Georgian, 21, *63, 67,* 69, 237, 239, 242, 248, 399
  Louis XIII, *47,* 68, 146, 152, 153, 156, 164, *176, 195,* 250, 264, 387, 531
  Louis XIV, 68, 146, 152, *250,* 529
  Louis XV, *5, 9,* 21, 47, 62, 67, 68, 74, 78, 146, 152, 153, 164, *235,* 250, 264, 306, 326, 382, 387, 468, 523, 531, *779-781*
  Louis XVI, 69, 74, 78, 248
  Louis-Philippe, 238, 248, 326, *370-373, 502-505,* 523
  Medieval, 53, 340, 414
  Mission, 56, 75, 76, 93, 94, 403, 406, 412, 414, 446, 508, 531, *714, 716, 717, 719, 721-722, 725-730, 792-795, 810-812, 816-820*
  Modern, 54, 78, 486
  Neoclassical, *10, 16,* 21, *50, 67,* 69, 84, 96, 106, 164, *174, 235,* 239, 242, 243, 246, 248, 249, 264, 294, 310, 318, *330,* 334, 337, 349, *352-358,* 370, *375, 376-380, 385,* 386, 391, 392, 399, *389-391, 393-397, 399, 402-404, 414-418,* 452, 486, 487, *491-505, 563,* 639-646, 680
  New France, 2, 13, 69, *167, 170,* 143, 186, 192, *195 a, b*
  Pre-Moderne, *165,* 406, *550*
  Queen Anne, 74, 434, 523
  Régence, *5, 9,* 68, 146, 152, 164, *235, 250, 252,* 353

  Regency, 21, 54, 63, 69, 237, 238, 242, 246, 248, 326, *330, 353, 355, 370-373, 385, 399, 529-531,* 531
  Renaissance 74, 326, 334, 358, 370
  Renaissance Revival, 22, 23, 67, 74, 94, *165,* 337, *541-544, 582-585, 637-644, 659-678, 758, 759*
  Restoration, 63, 69, 78, 238
  Rocaille, 62, 776
  Rococo, 29, 146, 306, 326, 334
  Rococo Revival, 21, 25, 44, 94, 334, 337, 382, 386, *541-544, 582-585, 683-686, 693*
  Second Empire, 19, 326, 330
  Sheraton, 106, 330, 344, 354, 357, 399, 489, 648
  Victorian, 20, 21, 67, 96, 323, 326, 330, 554
  Waterfall, 486, 508
Süe, Louis, 79, 490
Tardieu, Suzanne, 84
Taschereau (family), *41,* 347
Taschereau, Elzéar-Alexandre, *558, 559*
Taylor, Henry, 94
Tempest, Willy, *694*
Tessier, Grégoire (Father), 506
Têtu, Cyrice (family), *18*
Thibault, 523, *900-903*
Thonet (brothers), 63, 458, *841*
Thonet, Michael, 76, 406, 434, 458, *779*
Tourangeau (family), 491, 492
Traquair, Ramsay, 55, 59, *82, 83,* 88, 96, *171,* 232, *251, 271, 272, 285,* 326, *451,* 500
Trépanier, Esther, 78
Trottier, Eustache Ignace *dit* Desrivières, *2*
Trudel, Marcel, 145
Vaillancourt, Gilles, 524, 526
Vallée (studio), 88
Vallière, Philippe, *25,* 325, 326, 331, 336, 474, *547, 549-552, 558, 559, 565-569, 571-576, 578-581, 589, 706-707, 774*
Velde, Henry Van de, 75
Vermette, Luce, 91
Viau, Jacques and Guy (brothers), 492
Villas, *900-903*
Villiard, Germain, 150
Wagner, Otto, 458
Walker, John Henry, *73*
Webster, Donald Blake, 54, 96, *235,* 242
Wegner, 531
Woolsey (family), 84, *61*
Wright, Frank Lloyd, 75, 412, 486, 531, *792*
Zotique, Édouard, 84

Credits

In keeping with the wishes of most of the private collectors who made their collections accessible but wished to remain anonymous, all the photographs of privately owned items are identified as belonging to a "private collection." Anyone wishing to gain more specific knowledge of the provenance of such items should first contact the publisher. If the owner gives assent, the author will gladly forward any requests for information. All the collectors who provided assistance for the purposes of this book are named in the acknowledgements. The credits for the double-page descriptions of stylistic periods which open each chapter are given at the end of my two previous books on old objects, from which the illustrations are taken.

PHOTOGRAPHERS

Except where page numbers are given, each number corresponds to the number of the illustration in the book.

Altman, Patrick: 2, 10, 18, 59, 839, 841-846
Barbeau, Marius: 96-98
Brassard, Sylvio (attr.): 217, 221, 284, 419
Couture, Guy: 6, 8, 12, 13, 32, 37-41, 48, 53, 57, 58, 63, 107, 108, page 114, 109, page 118, 119, 113, 128, 132-135, 149, 150, 153, 154, 156, 163, 164, 166, 184-192, 216, 219, 221-225, 253, 255, 268, 277, 293, 295, 302, 329-332, 336, 338, 341-347, 349-358, 360-363, 376-379, 381-390, 393, 394, 397, 398, 401, 404, 408, 423, 425-430, 449, 450, 453, 458, 468-472, 476-478, 485-488, 491-506, 516, 518-526, 530-533, 534, 553, 558, 559, 563, 565-568, 627-629, 645-651, 653, 654, 657, 672-678, 663-666, 718, 719, 721, 722, 724, 763, 765, 766, 768-771, 777, 778, 791-804, 809, 851-854, 863-865, 869, 872-890, 897, 904, 912 (unnumbered)
Dufour, Claire: 36, 63, 250, 328
Elie, Michel: 110, pages 118 and 119, 635,
Gariépy, Edgar: 212, 545
Guest, Christine (MMFA): 23, 556, 561, 562, 582-585, 613, 614, 617-620, 760, 762
Lessard, Michel: 99, 111, 193, 406
Létourneau, Michel: 9, page 115, 178, 359, 410
Notman (Studio): 51, 52, 70, 615, 616, 683, 693, 696, 809
Ostiguy, Brigitte: 21, 28-31, 56, 105, pages 120-123, 114-118, 120-122, 144-148, 152, 162, 179-183, 213, 218, 300, 301, 317, 327, 370-373, 391, 392, 409, 447, 456, 529, 571-576, 578-581, 590-593, 594-599, 609, 610, 635-637, 659-666, 679, 684-686, 688, 689, 695, 725-730, 736-739, 741-746, 748-753, 767, 774, 775, 780-782, 784-790, 792, 793, 795, 810-812, 814-820
Parks Canada: 55, 94, 95, pages 112 and 113, 587, 588, 693
Parks, J. G.: 67, 102
Quéry Frères: 27, 46, 716, 723
Rajotte, Normand: 14, 16, 20, 33, 42, 54, 100, 101, 155, 159, 174, 197-199, 226-231, 256-261, 265, 266, 269, 270, 286, 288, 299, 303, 319, 325, 334, 337, 340, 348, 356, 358, 369, 374, 396, 400, 402, 405, 407, 412, 413, 446, 458, 459-467, 484, 517, 528, 570, 612, 621-626, 630-634, 658, 682, 690, 697, -711, 764, 773, 794, 796, 798-802, 821, 832
Roy, Anselme-Romuald: 19
Soulard, Pierre (Musée de la civilisation): 15, 20, 47, 89-92, 123-131, 136-144, 151, 152, 173, 175, 176, 200, 250, 262, 263, 267, 308, 309
Traquair, Ramsay (attr.): 251, 271, 326, 451,
Unknown: 3, 7, 11, 26, 35, 43, 46, 49, 50, 64, 68, 69, 84-88, 103, 104, 106, 153, 160, 161, 193, 194, 196, 201-204, 214, 215, 235, 237, 249, 254, 273-276, 278, 279-283, 289-292, 294, 296-298, 304, 305, 307, 310, 318, 333, 346, 364-368, 375, 380, 399, 403, 431-445, 452, 455, 473-475, 479-483, 527, 535-540, 552, 554, 638, 652, 687, 720, 747, 783, 797, 803, 805, 806, 837, 838, 840, 847-850, 855-857, 859-862, 867, 868, 870, 871, 886, 895, 898, 906-911
Vézina, Alain: 17, 62,

COLLECTIONS

Archevêché de Québec: 32, 558, 559, 680, 765
Archives nationales du Québec in Québec City: 3, 35, 67, 69. 102, 375, 399, 490, 545, 569, 655, 679, 687, 783
Bibliothèque centrale de la Ville de Montréal: 27, 46, 716, 723
Canadian Museum of Civilization: 760
Collège de Lévis: 29, 659-662, 785, 792, 793
Collège Sainte-Anne de la Pocatière: 590-592, 609, 610, 795
Dismo International: 895, 905-908
Fonds Jean-Marie Gauvreau, Cegep du Vieux-Montréal: 837, 857, 858, 866, 867
Louisbourg, Fortress (Parks Canada): 4, 193, 201, 214, 215, 249, 310, 318,
Maison Alphonse-Desjardins: 753, 772, 775
Maison Chapais, Saint-Denis, Kamouraska: 682
Maison Louis-Bertrand, L'Isle-Verte: 11, 20, 42, 697-711
McCord Museum: 380, 527, 696
Montreal Museum of Fine Arts: 7, 64, 106, 202-204, 273-276, 346, 652, 840, 868, 870, 871, 898
Musée d'art de Saint-Laurent: 16, 155, 400,
Musée de la civilisation: 5, 15, 17, 20, 37-40, 48, 62, 120-131, 136-148, 152, 153, 165, 179-183, 196, 197, 200, 235, 237, 254, 262, 263, 267, 278, 279-283, 289-292, 294, 297, 298, 300, 301, 307-309, 333, 364-368, 370-373, 385, 416, 420-422, 452, 454, 455, 473-475, 479-483, 519, 553, 565, 568, 635, 645, 646, 872-877, 887, 889, 890
Musée de Lac-à-la-Croix: 33
Musée du Québec: 2, 10, 18, 59, 550, 839, 841-846.
Musée du Saguenay–Lac-Saint-Jean: 303, 457, 459-466, 612, 621-626, 630-634, 794
Musée François-Pilote: 796
Musées des Augustines hospitalières de Québec: 8, 21, 30, 162, 175-177, 205-210, 213, 216, 304, 305, 311-317, 594-599, 667-671, 685, 686, 689, 767, 814
National Gallery of Canada: 66
Parks Canada: 94, 95, 546, 548, 587, 588, 693
Private collection: 6, 9, 12, 13, 19, 22, 23, 26, 31, 34, 41, 43, 46, 49, 51-53, 57, 58, 63, 65, 68, 70-81, 96-98, 103-105, 108, 112-118, 132-135, 154, 156, 157, 160, 161, 163, 164, 166, 171, 173, 178, 184-192, 212, 218-231, 251, 253, 255, 256-261, 264-266, 271, 278, 288, 293, 295, 302, 319-324, 336, 338, 349-352, 353-360, 369, 385-388, 391, 392, 393-397, 401, 408-411, 414, 415, 417, 418, 423, 425-430, 446-450, 453, 456, 458, 467-472, 476-478, 484, 485, 487, 488, 491-516, 530-533, 552, 561, 562, 571, 576-586, 589, 613-617, 627-629, 639-644, 647, 648, 683, 684, 693, 695, 718, 719, 721, 722, 724, 725-739, 741-746, 748-752, 754-757, 761-764, 767-771, 774, 777, 778, 781, 782, 784, 786-791, 803-811, 815-820, 847-850, 851-856, 885, 886, 888, 897, 904, 910, 912 (unnumbered)
Séminaire de Québec: 24, 158, 159, 198, 199, 286, 299, 325, 334, 337, 348, 374, 389, 390, 517, 534-540, 649-651, 653, 654, 657, 658, 663-666, 672-678, 690, 773, 798-802, 821-832, 909
Séminaire de Trois-Rivières, Musée Pierre-Boucher: 547-549, 863-865, 869, 878-883
Société historique de la Côte-du-Sud: 50

Acknowledgements

The publication of this book was made possible thanks to the assistance received from a team of publishing professionals, and reflects seven years of continuous collaboration. Countless collectors, researchers and museum curators the length and breadth of the country also made a contribution. Although I cannot name them all here, I will doubtless have an opportunity to salute their work publicly in other places.

First, I must acknowledge all the time and energy devoted to this project by the production team at Les Éditions de l'Homme, and especially by graphic artist Josée Amyotte. Our work together over a number of years has always been enjoyable, intense and productive and has culminated in this daring, large-scale project. Josée Amyotte is sensitive, inventive and methodical, and her eye for detail provided a constant creative inspiration that has influenced the finished product.

My thanks go also to Mélanie Sabourin for her often miraculous digitization and the polychromatic adjustment of literally hundreds of snapshots, engravings, photographs and early works of art and to other members of the team that worked on this exceptional project: Martine Lavoie, who was in charge of co-ordinating the computer layout, Christiane Houle, who designed the cover, Renée Bédard, Céline Bouchard, Linda Nantel, Nicole Raymond and Sylvie Tremblay for proof-reading, Rachel Fontaine and Fabienne Boucher for editorial co-ordination, and Claude Lapierre, who created special plates for each theme.

I thank all the professionals working in museums, interpretation centres and national and regional archives who provided support for the project from its inception, including the Musée de la civilisation and the Musée du Québec in Québec City, the Montreal Museum of Fine Arts, the Musée des arts et des traditions populaires and the Musée Pierre-Boucher in Trois-Rivières, the curators of the McCord Museum, of the Musée du Séminaire de Québec, and of the museums set up by various religious communities, especially the Augustinian Hospitallers of l'Hôtel-Dieu and the Hôpital Général in Québec City, and many different regional museums, from Gaspé and Sainte-Anne-de-la-Pocatière to Knowlton and Stanstead in the Eastern Townships, not to mention the Musée du Saguenay–Lac Saint-Jean in Chicoutimi and the Musée de Lac-à-la-Croix in Sagamie. I would especially like to mention Linda Corcoran, Nathalie Thibault, Nicole Vallières, Conrad Graham, Father Loïc Bernard, Christian Denis, Thérèse Latour, Serge Desaulniers, Paul-André Leclerc, Guy Toupin, Gaétan Giguère, Sister Nicole Perron, Sister Alvine Bouillé, Jacques Saint-Arnaud, Sister Rita Caron, and Sister Yvonne Saint-Pierre. Special thanks to Heather Gillis at the photographic archives at the Fortress of Louisbourg for dealing so efficiently with requests and for her open-minded approach to the project. I am indebted to my friend Richard Dubé, previously in charge of collections at the Musée de la civilisation and to René Villeneuve at the National Gallery of Canada in Ottawa. Thanks to the entire Parks Canada team in Québec City, to Diane Lebrun and Yvan Fortier, who also lent assistance as collectors, and to Jeannot Bélanger and Raynald Bilodeau of the restoration and reproduction services of this federal agency in Québec City. Thanks to Patrick Albert, Bernard Vallée and France Rémillard at the Centre de Conservation du Québec (CCQ) for their scientific explanations of furniture restoration, varnish and colour.

My thanks go to to all the photographers who helped illustrate the book, both those who received payment for their services such as Guy Couture, Brigitte Ostiguy, assisted by Donald Dion, and Normand Rajotte, and those whose prints were supplied by the institutions that commissioned them: Michel Élie, Pierre Soulard, Jean Jolin and Christine Guest, respectively from the CCQ, the Musée de la civilisation, Parks Canada and the Montreal Museum of Fine Arts, and photographer Michel Létourneau in Saint-Constant. I must also thank all the people who kindly agreed to lend photographs by unkown photographers.

I am grateful to all the outstanding professionals working in the ethno-historical field who generously contributed to the research: Professor Paul-Louis Martin of the Université du Québec à Trois-Rivières, owner with his partner Marie of the famous Maison de la Prune in Saint-André de Kamouraska; Bernard Genest, of the Ministère de la Culture et des Communications; Claire Desmeules, art historian and specialist in historic interior design; and geographer and archaeologist Michel Gaumond, a generous and passionate expert in the field of Québec heritage. I also benefited from the skills of many antique dealers: Gérard Bourguet, Marcel Bolduc and Louis Bolduc in Québec City, Jean and Suzanne Lafrance in Drummondville, Jean-Marie Du Sault in Deschambault and many others. I am deeply grateful to the remarkable experts who guided me in selecting artifacts and discussing them, including Jean-Marc Belzile, his partner Danielle and his daughter Annick. Mr. Belzile of Lachute, with over 40 years' experience based on detailed observations of furniture, wood and colours, was able to comment on hundreds of pieces. I also received help from outstanding collectors such as Monique and André Larivière in Sorel, Michel Sauvé and Sylvie in Grenville, environmentalist Gaston Cadrin in Lévis, Clermont Bourget in Saint-Michel de Bellechasse, Christian Richer and Sylvie Pomerleau in Rivière-du-Loup, Mme Suzanne Pratte and her son, architect Georges Leahy, whose passionate and cultivated interest in history opened my eyes to the wonders of Neoclassical furniture, and Alain Rivest, a collector of Mission furniture.

I would like to thank all the research assistants who worked on specific aspects of this study, mainly as paid student assistants: Judith Pinsonnault, Raymond Idoux, Andrée-Anne de Sève, Élisabeth Naud and Serge Gauthier of the Société historique de Charlevoix. Several archivists and librarians also provided assistance: Daniel Olivier from the Salle Gagnon in the Bibliothèque centrale de la ville de Montréal, Jean-Marie Dion, curator of the archives of the École du meuble at the Cégep du Vieux-Montréal, Father Armand Gagné at the Archdiocese of Québec City, Louis Campeau and Benoit Thériault at the Canadian Museum of Civilization in Hull, Nora Hague at the Notman Archives in Montréal, Jacques Morin and Antoine Pelletier at the Archives nationales du Québec in Québec City, Sister Juliette Cloutier at the Augustinian Hospitallers of l'Hôpital Général in Québec City, the entire team working at the Archives des collections of the Canadian Museum of Civilisation, especially Danielle Aubin and Madeleine Faucher, François Taillon at the Archives de la Société historique de la Côte-du-Sud, and many others. Special thanks go to my friend Ronald Chabot in Lévis, a tireless collector of early sales catalogues, to whom I owe much of the information contained in this book, and to Donald Dion, a specialist of old hardware and a history and heritage enthusiast, whose assessments are always gratefully received. I also thank the dozens of experts and collectors to agreed to give interviews on various subjects, especially the painter and decorator Benoit Côté in Saint-Pierre on Île d'Orléans, Gilles Vaillancourt at the Galerie du meuble in Québec City, Alphonse Saint-Jacques of the École du meuble de Montréal and historian Donald Guay in Lévis.

Finally, I would like to thank various private collectors and curators of public collections: Father Jacques Lemieux, superior of the Grand Séminaire de Québec, who opened the doors of his three-century-old institution in Québec City and displayed its treasures, Annie Bonhomme and Pierre Cantin in Boischatel, Fathers Robert and Pierre Michaud at the superb Louis-Bertrand house at L'Isle-Verte, my friend Pierre Moussard and Luc Emond de Calixa-Lavallée, clock enthusiast Father Georges Marceau at the Séminaire de Québec, Roland and Cécile Létourneau in Saint-Roch-des-Aulnaies, Rosaire Saint-Pierre in Beaumont, Jacques Portelance and his partner in Berthier-sur-Mer, M. and Mme Robert Carrier in Beaumont, Réal Perrault in Lévis for his catalogues, Anne Carrier and Robert Boily in Québec City, Paul-Henri and Madeleine Guimont in Québec City, notary Reynald Lagueux in Lévis, Ernest Thériault in Montréal, Adjutor Pelletier in Beaumont, filmmaker Philippe Baylaucq, and the many, many other people who entrusted me with one or two objects. Thanks to the guides at the Manoir Dionne in Saint-Roch-des-Aulnaies, the Maison Chapais in Saint-Denis de Kamouraska and the Maison Alphonse-Desjardins in Lévis. I also wish to thank all those whom I have, with the best will in the world, overlooked.

Lastly, my infinite and affectionate thanks go to my dearest France Rémillard, for her companionship, long-suffering patience and critical collaboration.

Lithographically printed on 200M Supreme gloss paper

in Canada in october 2001

on the printing presses of Interglobe inc.